CW01210994

Performing China

Performing China

Virtue, Commerce, and Orientalism
in Eighteenth-Century England, 1660–1760

CHI-MING YANG

The Johns Hopkins University Press
Baltimore

© 2011 The Johns Hopkins University Press
All rights reserved. Published 2011
Printed in the United States of America on acid-free paper
2 4 6 8 9 7 5 3 1

The Johns Hopkins University Press
2715 North Charles Street
Baltimore, Maryland 21218-4363
www.press.jhu.edu

Library of Congress Cataloging-in-Publication Data

Yang, Jiming
Performing China : virtue, commerce, and orientalism in eighteenth-century England, 1660–1760 / Chi-ming Yang.
    p. cm.
Includes bibliographical references and index.
ISBN-13: 978-1-4214-0216-1 (hardcover : alk. paper)
ISBN-10: 1-4214-0216-5 (hardcover : alk. paper)
 1. China—Foreign public opinion, British—History—18th century.
2. China—Civilization—History. 3. European literature—18th century. I. Title.
DS754.25.Y364 2011
303.48'24205109033—dc22   2011004101

A catalog record for this book is available from the British Library.

Special discounts are available for bulk purchases of this book. For more information, please contact Special Sales at 410-516-6936 or special sales@press.jhu.edu.

The Johns Hopkins University Press uses environmentally friendly book materials, including recycled text paper that is composed of at least 30 percent post-consumer waste, whenever possible.

CONTENTS

Acknowledgments *vii*

Introduction   China as Exemplar: Eastern Spectacle
and Western Discourses of Virtue   1

1   Heroic Effeminacy and the Conquest of China   32

2   Sincerity and Authenticity: George Psalmanazar's Experiments
in Conversion   75

3   Transmigration, Fabulous Pedagogy, and the Morals of the Orient   114

4   Luxury, Moral Sentiment, and *The Orphan of China*   148

Epilogue   Orientalism, Globalization, and the New Business
of Spectacle   184

Notes   *199*
Bibliography   *237*
Index   *261*

ACKNOWLEDGMENTS

This book would not have been possible without the generosity of numerous individuals and institutions along the way. It was completed with the assistance of a junior faculty research leave from the University of Pennsylvania School of Arts and Sciences, and key research for this project in its early stages was conducted in the United States and in England thanks to a Sicca Fellowship for International Research from Cornell University, a Mellon Postdoctoral Fellowship at Barnard College, and a Faculty Research Grant from Fordham University. Of the library archives I have visited, I would especially like to thank Xiaoxin Wu, Mark Mir, and the staff at the Ricci Institute for Chinese-Western Cultural History at the University of San Francisco and John Pollack and Daniel Traister of the University of Pennsylvania Rare Book and Manuscript Library. Their service, breadth of knowledge, and camaraderie are exceptional.

Since arriving to the University of Pennsylvania, I have had multiple opportunities to present my work on campus, including at the McNeil Center for Early American Studies and at the History of Material Texts, Latitudes, Race and Empire, and Eighteenth-century Group workshops. My thinking has benefited from the feedback I received from these groups and from sundry conversations with my terrific English Department colleagues Toni Bowers, Stuart Curran, David Eng, Jed Esty, Michael Gamer, Tsitsi Jaji, Amy Kaplan, Suvir Kaul, David Kazanjian, Ania Loomba, and John Richetti. I am especially grateful to my fellow junior faculty cohort members Zack Lesser and Melissa Sanchez for their company, solidarity, and good spirits. Previously, at Fordham University, I was also lucky to have wonderful colleagues in eighteenth-century and early modern studies—Stuart Sherman, Susan Greenfield, Michael Suarez, Frank Boyle, Kim Hall, Katie Little, and Nina Rowe.

At Cornell University, my graduate community of friends and allies provided jollity that sustained me through the winters and inspired me to pursue the links between eighteenth-century and postcolonial studies, academics, and activism: Akin Adesokan, David Agruss, Rhodante Ahlers, Mona Barghout, Joseph Campana, Zahid Chaudhury, Iftikhar Dadi, Javier Lezaun, Sheetal Majithia, Yoshiaki Mihara, Aaron Moore, Anna Parkinson, Saadia Toor, Adelheid Voskuhl, Meg Wesling, and Anna Zalik. I must also include in this group of extraordinary people members of the Cornell faculty, Brett de Bary, Laura Brown, Biodun Jeyifo, Barry Maxwell, Natalie Melas, and Shelley Wong.

More recently, my work has benefited from lively discussions and colloquia with scholarly interlocutors across the academic disciplines of British and East Asian studies, including Rey Chow, Lydia Liu, Jeng-Guo Chen, Isabelle Duceux, Minghui Hu, Eng-Beng Lim, Robert Markley, David Porter, Benjamin Elman, Victor Mair, Peter Perdue, and Eun Kyung Min. I would like to thank Eun Kyung Min for inviting me to share my research in Korea at Seoul National University as well as at an extremely productive interdisciplinary gathering, "China and the Making of Global Modernity," at the Harvard-Radcliffe Seminar for Advanced Study in 2007. I have been touched by the openness of historians of Asia, especially those of earlier generations, to those of us studying the European reception of China from literary, revisionist, cultural studies, and Asian American standpoints. The dialogue between English Literature and Area Studies is one I am increasingly committed to fostering, and I have greatly appreciated the invitations to present my work overseas at Academia Sinica in Taipei, at Shanghai International Studies University, and at East Asia programs at Princeton University and the University of San Francisco.

I am thankful to everyone who has read and commented on my manuscript at various stages, including Srinivas Aravamudan, Toni Bowers, Michael Gamer, Ania Loomba, Natalie Melas, Peter Dear, Brett de Bary, Cecilia Cancellaro, Frank Palmeri, Neil Saccamano, Stuart Sherman, Chris Cynn, Lisa Estreich, Maja Horn, Hiram Perez, and, especially, Javier Lezaun. I am indebted to my doctoral dissertation adviser Laura Brown, who continues to be a source of inspiration and a vital sounding board. I received useful suggestions for revision from the anonymous readers of the Johns Hopkins University Press and the University of Pennsylvania Press. It has been my fortune to work with Matt McAdam at the Johns Hopkins University Press, whose advocacy of my project, along with the help of Julie McCarthy, Courtney Bond, Dennis Marshall, and Tom Broughton-Willett, has made the publication process both straightforward and pleasant. My heartfelt thanks go also to the intrepid Alyssa Connell, Dave Alff, and Daniel DeWispelare, who took time out of their University of Pennsylvania graduate studies to help with the preparation of the manuscript and the images.

At a crucial stage while I was writing, acquaintances old and new offered me moral support and spaces of refuge: Rick Osburn, Frank James, Jiasong Yuen, Rena Ziegler, Susan Gold, and the coffee shops of Bellingham, San Francisco, and Philadelphia. I am most grateful to dear friends who without hesitation lent their time, scrutiny, and care to my work in progress: David Agruss, Joon Oluchi Lee, Amanda Swarr, and Sanjay Krishnan. To Suvir Kaul and Meg Wesling, whose comments and advice have been both charitable and incisive, I can't express enough gratitude and affection.

Several sections of this book incorporate research previously published in different forms, including "Virtue's Vogues: Eastern Authenticity and the Commodification of Chinese-ness on the Eighteenth-Century Stage," *Comparative Literature Studies* 39, no. 4 (2002): 326–46; "Gross Metempsychosis and Eastern Soul," in *Humans and Other Animals in Eighteenth-Century British Culture: Representation, Hybridity, Ethics,* ed. Frank Palmeri (Burlington, Vt.: Ashgate, 2006), 13–30; "Asia Out of Place: The Aesthetics of Incorruptibility in Behn's *Oroonoko,*" *Eighteenth-Century Studies* 42, no. 1 (2008): 235–53; and "Chinosierie and the Figure of the Asian Convert," *Horizons: Seoul Journal of Humanities* 1, no. 2 (2010): 119–34.

This book is dedicated to the Yang family—Chi-hui, Chi-wang, Ho-chin, and Ellen—whose love, intellect, and support have meant the world.

Performing China

INTRODUCTION

China as Exemplar

Eastern Spectacle and Western Discourses of Virtue

To early modern Europe, China emerged as an exemplary and controversial model of empire, by turns enlightened and despotic. Representations of virtue in British cultural production were significantly shaped by the intensified trade with the East Indies and by a new environment that combined consumerism with didacticism. In such a climate, the public reception of China and places associated with China enabled the process of imagining and consolidating a number of ideas of virtue in literature, theater, and material culture. China's empire, more than any other, appeared to superimpose conflicting systems of value, moral and monetary, with radical consequences for English traditions of honor, patriotism, piety, sentimentality, and temperance.[1] As the increasing commercialization of British life upended traditional ideals of the private and public spheres, these contestations in notable instances coalesced with controversial and contradictory attitudes toward Chinese culture and commodities. How did the presence of the foreign "good" help to resolve moral crises and to articulate key forms of virtue whose efficacy and meanings were highly disputed in the changing economic milieu? As modern values were reconceptualized for a new era of overseas commerce, ideas of "China" exemplified fundamental contradictions of British consumer society by testing the changing boundaries between virtue and vice.

A crucial vector linking virtue to vice was the fascination with spectacle: indeed, the sheer scope of Chinese civilization has continued to enthrall and unsettle Western audiences, and performance is a principal site of this persistent ambivalence. To illustrate the phenomenon of "performing China," I begin by presenting three quite different instances of Chinese spectacle.

The opening ceremony of the 2008 Beijing Summer Olympics was an unprecedented televised event. Tens of thousands of live performers, including military personnel, helped enact consecutive scenes that showcased Chinese history and culture over the centuries. At one point, the world's largest LED screen stretched across the stadium floor in the shape of an ancient scroll as the choreographed movements of the dancers painted upon it supersized calligraphy and classical landscapes. Prime-time television commentators in the United States repeatedly found the pairing of the "most modern" and "most ancient" technologies a paradox with some cause for concern: it was an evening of extremes "both awe-inspiring and perhaps a little intimidating."[2] Other reports deemed such tactical exhibitionism a long-standing rather than novel occurrence. According to one British article, "From the nation which brought you the 8,000 buried terracotta warriors of Xian in 210 BC and the 7,500-mile Long March in 1934, you would anticipate nothing less than a spectacle."[3] Indeed, the increased frequency of China's state-sponsored displays of military and economic might in the few short years since the Beijing Olympics has made a familiar media event of enumerating the nation's monumentality.[4] In attempting to capture the sheer scale of these performances, the rhetoric of numerical hyperbole ("8,000" warriors, "7,500" miles) links in one transhistorical sweep an ancient with a modern theater of war. Taken together, the media commentaries suggest a temporal contradiction at the heart of the spectacle: China exhibits at once a progressive coming of age, a cycle of empire reincarnated ("you would anticipate nothing less"), and a marvelous coincidence of being always ancient yet hypermodern.

The second instance of Eastern spectacle is found in a textual scene rather than a live event. The Western media's discernible ambivalence over the 2008 Olympics ceremony is far from novel, and in fact reiterates a much earlier, protocapitalist moment when the vision of China's epic history also held a special relevance to the changing global order. Evidence of this particular fascination with Chinese antiquity can be found, for example, in the *Dialogues des Morts* by the seventeenth-century polemicist François Fénelon, in which the author includes a staged confrontation between Socrates and Confucius. As the Greek sage observes, "Your nation appears to me to be a grand and beautiful spectacle from afar, but a highly dubious and equivocal one."[5] Indeed, what begins as a discussion of philosophical and pedagogical differences quickly turns into a diatribe against the reputed merits of Chinese civilization. When Confucius defends the singularity of his country's manners, governance, and achievements in the arts and sciences, Socrates points to similar accomplishments by the Greeks, and he further claims that much of the ingenuity attributed to Chinese invention, from printing and gunpowder to laws and lacquering, in fact derives from ancient Egypt and Babylonia. Additionally, the Chinese have inherited from those fellow Easterners false superstition and the unfortunate tendency to mix fable with truth for self-aggrandizing ends. According to Socrates, "The Chinese are the most vain, superstitious, unjust, self-interested, and deceitful people in all the world."[6] Fénelon in turn concludes that the widespread perception of China as an unrivaled example of imperial grandeur is a fiction perpetuated by biased Chinese historians and the Jesuit missionaries whose accounts were wholly colored by their own Sinophilia.

In this invented conversation between ancient philosophers, an authoritative perspective from classical Greece calls into question the legitimacy, indeed authenticity, of China's "grand spectacle." What appears to be a foundational civilization is, in this view, derivative ("highly dubious and equivocal"). Moreover, the necessary corollary to China's technological spectacle is its moral deficiency, as evident in the list of cultural vices ("vain, superstitious, unjust, self-interested, and deceitful"). Such accusations continue to resonate in contemporary visions of China, as demonstrated in the media coverage of the Beijing Olympics, meaning that this is not the first, or last, time China has been or will be accused of putting on too good a show. The Olympics ceremony, for instance, generated both awe and controversy over the conditions of its production, not only in the implied exploitation of the thousands of citizen-performers, but in charges that the live fireworks, singing, and acrobatics were in fact digitally enhanced, and hence morally suspect. Here, too, accusations of artifice and fakery indicate the intense interest in assessing China's *performance* of antiquity, while modeling its civilization, philosophy, and commodities for Western consumption.

If Chinese spectacle turns on questions of paradoxical temporality and cultural legitimacy, these properties also manifest themselves in a third instance, in which China is made a moral example in commodified form—that is, in descriptions of the artifacts and consumer objects manufactured there and imported to the West. To consider the cultural impact of "China" upon eighteenth-century British society is also to invoke its peculiar, dual identity as "china," a prized, and arguably spectacular, object named by the same five letters. In his famous description of a country estate filled to the brim with costly porcelain on the verge of a collective collapse, Daniel Defoe issued a clear warning of the dangers of "china":

> The queen brought in the custom . . . of furnishing houses with china-ware, which increased to a strange degree afterwards, piling their china upon the tops of cabinets, scrutores, and every chymney-piece, to the tops of the ceilings, and even setting up shelves for their china-ware, where they wanted such places, till it became a grievance in the experience of it, and even injurious to their families and estates.[7]

Imagined as a predictor of financial ruin, *china* conveyed the precariousness of a system of Western wealth based on importing novel, Eastern goods. In this instance it also evinces a peculiar temporality. Its appearance suggests imminent fall and shattering, a negative futurity associated with its physical properties of translucence and fragility. Competing against this image of the breakable, fallible surface and its materialization of modern ills was its feature of extreme durability. The original Jesuit reports that porcelain resulted from a centuries-long gestation period underground were eventually disproved, but its ancient origins and ability to preserve shape and luster under exceptionally high oven temperatures made it a technological wonder to European manufacturers obsessed throughout the eighteenth century with producing a substance of comparable quality.[8] China's linguistic double register—empire/commodity, subject to falling and yet ultimately resilient—thus yokes together contiguous yet distinct orders of meaning and value: political, material, and moral.

I begin with these three diverse instances of the imagined spectacle of "China"— technological, philosophical, commercial—because they embody the contradictions associated with a civilization of exemplary and often duplicitous extremes. They speak to the desirability of China's export products, both then and now, as well as to questions of imagining and containing the scale of Chinese empire. The dubious morality and strange temporality attributed to the effects of antiquity in a modern frame suggest that China seems to be time out of place. To be a spectacle, after all, is to be a warning of sorts, a lesson in the ethics of exhibitionism alongside the irresistible appeal of an Eastern civilization that is at once backward and forward-looking. In literature of the period from 1660 to 1760, China was not only charged with duplicity but also hailed for its global might. In 1691, Sir William Temple declared China "the greatest, richest, and most populous kingdom now known in the world."[9] A proliferation of travel accounts in the later seventeenth century supplied details of a Confucian governance system stretching back for thousands of years and of the immense imperial wealth that so captured the imaginations of European merchants, rulers, and writers. Evidence of China's empire arrived in England indirectly, most often through translations and popularized excerpts from Jesuit missionaries' descriptions, on the one hand, and the physical presence of novel commodities like tea and porcelain, on the other. Because the China vogue was to a large extent a Continental import, Europe also figures prominently into this discussion of the reception of China in England. Just as the ongoing rivalries and shifting alliances within European states defined the emergence of a consolidated British national identity over the course of the eighteenth century, it was through multiple routes, translations, and mediations—a back-and-forth channeling of texts, commodities, and ideas—that China emerged as nothing less than an ethical, economic, and political spectacle to audiences and consumers on both sides of the English Channel.

For England in the mid-seventeenth century, access to China signaled hopes for national prosperity through advancing an East Indies trade formerly dominated by the Portuguese and Dutch trading empires; China was a means to attain a global standing that would rival its European contemporaries. The East-West circuits of commerce, after all, spurred the advent of what we now call globalization as far back as centuries ago. By the late seventeenth century, the growing imports of tea, chintz, calico, lacquerware, and porcelain from China, Japan, and India had ignited the zeal of European collectors as well as efforts to imitate the novelty and superior quality of Eastern objects and designs. This new wave of commodities, following an earlier trade in spices, perfumes, and groceries, signaled not only an intensification of British consumerism but also the strength of Asia in the world economy. During the Restoration period, the first orders of Chinese tea were placed by the East India Company, and although the trade did not take off until the early 1700s, tea drinking was already fashionable by 1663, as noted by Edmund Waller in his poem to Queen Catherine:

> The best of Queens, and best of herbs, we owe
> To that bold nation which the way did show
> To the fair region where the sun does rise,
> Whose rich productions we so justly prize.[10]

The marriage of Charles II to Portugal's Catherine of Braganza brought a dowry that included control of two key ports, Tangier and Bombay, thus transferring a piece of the Portuguese Empire's past century of mercantile dominance in the East Indies. So, too, would the influence of the Dutch East India Company trade enter England along with William and Mary in several decades' time, in particular the vogue for Asian porcelain whose shipments beginning in the 1630s would reach the level of "fatal excesses" that Daniel Defoe so vividly described.[11]

Although for Defoe and other critics *china* conveyed the precariousness of a system of Western wealth based on importing foreign novelties, the reality was that by the mid-eighteenth century, the climate of manufacturing that had developed and would continue to fuel the British Empire at its height was in large part a response to a new century of imitating Asia in the manner of "import-substituting industries."[12] In the past decade or so, the work of economic historians such as Kenneth Pomeranz, Andre Gunder Frank, R. Bin Wong, K. N. Chaudhuri, and Giovanni Arrighi have confirmed what was already recognized in the seventeenth and eighteenth centuries, that China was the predominant force of the early modern global economy. Before the so-called rise of the West, it already possessed what are generally considered the conditions of modernity: a developed state formation, advanced market system, government bureaucracy, and high standards of living relative to other parts of the world.[13] With its vast tribute trade, market economy, and desirable exports, China held up to one-third of the world's silver supply from the sixteenth to the eighteenth centuries. Given its prosperity, referred to as the "Chinese miracle" of the eighteenth century, it has been deemed an "exemplar" of the market and a "model" for European political economy.[14]

Inasmuch as China was a model for Europe, it was a model both economic and moral. The dual register of china and China suggests not only the importance of commodity culture to the fantasies of a nascent British Empire, but also the extent to which cultural imports formed, and in some cases even preserved, ideas of eighteenth-century virtue. At the turn of the century, the travel writer John Ovington, for one, lobbied for importing Chinese tea for its "admirable Effects, either out of *Curiosity*, because of its *Novelty*; or out of *Pleasure* of gratifying the *Palate*; or because of some *Medicinal Vertues*, with which it is pregnant." Described as a "modern Liquor" with remarkable "Virtues" of improving digestion, enhancing one's powers of rationality, and promoting temperance, Asian tea is deemed particularly beneficial when contrasted with the insalubrious effects of French wine and American sugar.[15]

In this example, as in many others, the commodity, through its material and discursive effects, exhibits a certain "thingliness," or that which remains "physically or metaphysically irreducible to objects," to borrow from the cultural theorist Bill Brown. In this view, "things" exceed their concrete, bounded object forms through their ability to not only inhabit but to construct an environment. Rarely do we stop to ponder our relationship to the things that thoroughly pervade our worldly existence and structure our most basic perceptions. As Brown writes, "The story of objects asserting themselves as things, then, is the story of a changed relation to the human subject and thus the story of how the thing really names less an object than a particular subject-object relation."[16] *China*, the word that names an empire as well as an object, epitomizes this theory of relation-formation at the level of changing patterns of individual consumption as well as through establishing imagined links and hierarchies between and among disparate parts of the globe. As evident in Ovington's estimation, tea, like porcelain, became an acquired taste and a gauge of national character: its thingliness articulated Englishness in relation to Chineseness. Moreover, his ranking of commodities according to their cultural, moral, and scientific effects upon the consumer (whose "virtue" thrives under Chinese rather than French or American influence) speaks to the increasing globalization of British life and the mutual imbrication of virtue and commerce.

In what follows, I examine a number of discrete circumstances under which the contemplation of Eastern values—in the shape of spectacle—helped determine the bounds of British morality. The strong ambivalence toward the Asiatic other, and China in particular, drove the cross-cultural comparisons through which new forms of virtue were, and continue to be, negotiated. In myriad forms, spectacle foregrounds the highly mediated acts of looking that structure the fraught relationships between virtue and commerce, objects and things, East and West. Consider the multiple comparisons at work in the frontispiece to *La Balance Chinoise, ou Lettres d'un Chinois*, a mid-eighteenth-century novel that in a fashion typical of epistolary satire features a foreigner's reflections upon European progress and modernity. Dominating the foreground are two halves of a scale, from which are suspended the equally balanced spheres of Europe and the Empire of China. The figure of a Chinese mandarin is positioned behind and between these weights, and as the writer of fictionalized letters that compare the two education systems, he is presented as an exemplar of rational inquiry. In that the half-drawn curtain frames the entire scene as a proscenium, we are asked to contemplate the Chinese figure as the measurer of the comparison between self and other, as well as the object being measured. It is this striking doubling of "China" as subject and object that signals the value of theatricalized Eastern perspectives to Western visions of selfhood. Through relations of imitation, admiration, and competition, as well as denigration, such examples of Eastern spectacle provided ways of imagining and thus shaping the tensions between new and old models of civilization and progress.

Virtue and Commerce

Material things were not the only imported goods of the East: virtue, too, entered the market as an object of consumption. When the Anglo-Irish playwright and novelist Oliver Goldsmith referred to China as the "home of superior morality and government *and* the source of agreeable luxuries," he identified a combination that proved to be particularly compelling to British audiences.[17] In this instance, the example of China successfully and surprisingly combines two presumably antithetical entities: virtue and commerce. Bernard Mandeville, in his 1714 *The Fable of the Bees; or, Private Vices, Publick Benefits*, famously claimed that virtue was a mere "performance" created by political elites to make their subjects

Frontispiece to *La Balance Chinoise, ou Lettres d'un Chinois*, ca. 1763. Courtesy of Columbia University Library, Columbia University, City of New York.

governable and by self-interested individuals who needed a way to rationalize their pursuit of profit. Despite his indictment of social hypocrisy, however, Mandeville believed that private vices in the form of "strangers and superfluities" ultimately benefited the public; he simply sought to expose the disjuncture between truth and appearance.[18] To extrapolate from Mandeville's theory, the truth was that with the growth of England's mercantile and credit economy came not only new forms of wealth but also a need for new modes of conceptualizing the relationship between consumption, exchange, and morality.

The moral ambiguities posed by the example of China and the critique of performance can to an extent be mapped onto the clashing value systems and contested meanings of *virtue*, an all-encompassing catchword of the eighteenth century, in the context of marked economic, social, and epistemological change. New profits from foreign trade and increased commodity consumerism challenged the established ideals of aristocratic honor and civic ideals by introducing the competing bourgeois virtues of exchange and sociability. Whereas a classical model of virtue put public good over personal profit, the ethic of the modern entrepreneur was self-interest and the fulfillment of appetite. Of primary importance was the shift from inherited, land-based wealth and the paragon of the autonomous citizen-patriot to the unstable, mobile wealth of a commercial society. According to the historian J. G. A. Pocock, the turbulent 1670s saw a revival of the republican ideals of the freeholder put forward by political theorists like Niccolò Machiavelli and James Harrington. Tradition in the form of arms or property was thought to shield the individual from forces of corruption. Before, the citizen, unlike the merchant with his specialized vocation, could perform all functions for the polis; he was not tied to relations of dependence and the desires of others, nor to the vicissitudes of public debt, investment capital, and mercantilist warfare.[19] Now, instead of owning property, which had heretofore provided the material assurance of a stable self, the modern individual who engaged in exchange and "symbolic" property faced the real threat of losing his civic bearings. While the world of credit and speculation was oriented toward the future, and agrarian wealth toward the past, the eighteenth-century individual searched for a vocabulary and for tropes to bridge the change and manage the uncertainty. Even the eighteenth-century virtues of frugality and moderation—which combated the vice of luxury and contributed to the public good—could be seen as attempts to transfer the civic virtues of the landed man to the modern individual.[20]

Pocock's work focalizes historical change as internal to the workings of British society; by his account, the modern crisis in conceptualizing virtue is seen largely as a temporal problem of translating the paradigms of a classicized past for use in the present. While ideas of Greek and Roman antiquity did continue to shape the public perceptions of so-called Augustan eighteenth-century life, so, too, were more distant, external parties made to perform the pitfalls and potentials of a new economic structure based on commercial wealth. As indicated by the fictional encounter between Socrates and Confucius, the idea of classical antiquity was itself being reshaped by the news of China's historical timeline entering European consciousness. The exemplarity of Eastern empires—at once ancient, prosperous, heathen, and civilized—thus disrupted received traditions of moral authority. In an era of moral uncertainty, a figure such as Confucius could be deemed an exemplar of moderation and virtuous antiquity potentially at odds with China's equally miraculous manufacture of precious commodities.

A contested symbol of both imperial excess and Confucian moderation, China received extreme praise and censure throughout the eighteenth century; by turns a threat to and an expression of British overseas commerce, China's Eastern empire encapsulated the widespread ambivalence toward social change.[21] And in straddling the line between virtue and vice it exposed the constructedness of the boundary so scrutinized by Mandeville and others.

Performances of China

In highlighting the phenomenon of performing virtue in conjunction with performing China, my aim is neither to classify in an exhaustive manner the meanings of virtue of the period nor to catalog eighteenth-century representations of China, but rather to identify exemplary instances where the construction of spectacle reveals the performativity, or constructedness, of British ideas of virtue. Among the types of performance to be explored here, the first is the theater, for its conspicuous display of imported, Eastern fashions. Restoration and eighteenth-century drama plotted Eastern histories in translation and featured elaborate costumes, stage designs, ornamentation, and commodities that in various ways signaled a world of emerging bourgeois consumerism. Even the most domestically oriented play might integrate some form of Chinese spectacle into its depiction of daily English life. In one famous scene from William Wycherley's *The Country Wife* (1675), Lady Fidget pays a visit to the "China-House," not to shop for chinaware, her collecting passion, but to conduct her amorous affair with the knave Jack Horner ("for we women of quality never think we have *China* enough.")[22] Exhibiting an equally exaggerated taste for "China," the eccentric Sir Timothy Tallapoy of Nicholas Rowe's *The Biter* (1705) dresses, eats, and speaks in the "Chinese manner." Having made his fortune from the East India trade, he fancies himself a patriarchal mandarin whose daughter shall "engender a Male Offspring, who shall drink nothing but the Divine Liquor Tea, and eat nothing but Oriental Rice, and be brought up after the Institutions of the most excellent *Confucius*."[23] In these plays, China becomes pun and proxy for the insatiable appetites of the merchant classes, whose tastes, morals, and gendered identities are performed in tandem with the performance of China. Whether considered a reforming or corrupting influence, the stage was a locus of debates over the secularizing influences of modern economic transactions, in particular the dangers of modeling sexual and commercial excess for new middle-class theatergoers. Indeed, the theater, a site of staged virtue and glittering wealth, was a natural simulacrum of sociability and commerce, much to the disapproval of eighteenth-century moralists for whom performance was primarily the transmission of vice.[24]

Through interactions of text, source material, mise-en-scène, and the framing commentaries of their epilogues and prologues, the drama of the period tied the interests of a consuming public to the "strangers and superfluities" of the East India trade. Domestic comedies such as *The Country Wife* and *The Biter* may appear to be far removed from the staging of honor, empire, and the "grand spectacle" of Chinese history and dynastic change in tragedies like Elkanah Settle's *The Conquest of China* (1676) or Arthur Murphy's *The Orphan of China* (1759) (works examined in chapters 1 and 4 of this book). And yet, the disjointed temporality of staging past empires according to the modern-day vogue in Eastern designs also captures the contradiction of ancient and modern that undergirds Chinese spectacle. Although they might not directly reference the contemporary China trade or the integration of foreign commerce into everyday English life, plays chronicling the rise and fall of Eastern empires proliferated during the expansion of the East India Company in the years 1669–77. As keenly surveyed by Bridget Orr in her study of theater and empire, the commercial interests of the English, Dutch, French, and Portuguese vying for access to Asian markets were matched by the interest in Asia and the Levant taken by the Restoration stage and by the travel literature that provided playwrights with theatrical source material.[25] Set in locales ranging from the Near to the Far East, dramas of heroic conquests were produced during key disputes over England's naval campaigns and trade voyages to strategic sites like Morocco and China.[26] The theater, a space of "interculturalism," to borrow from Mita Choudhury's study of the London stage, offered perspectives on empire as varied as domestic scenes that showcased the contemporary China trade and epic histories of the distant origins of such Chineseness.[27]

The differing perspectives on the effects of Chinese empire, as represented by the distinct genres of comedy and tragedy, nonetheless shared a guiding principle that China was uniquely suited to theatrical interpretation. In other words, China appeared in performance and *as* a performance. This second sense of performance refers to the idea that costume, ornamentation, and fashion were defining features of Chinese moral character. Writings on China by travelers such as the Jesuit Louis Le Comte, whose influential *Nouveaux mémoires sur l'état présent de la Chine* (1696) underwent multiple translations and editions, contributed to the widespread impressions of China's performance-oriented culture. In one discussion of China's "peculiar character" and manners, Le Comte's praise of "Politeness and Civility . . . Grandeur and Magnificence" turns into an extensive catalog of women's and men's fashions that ranges from hats and boots of silk, sable, and other fabrics and designs to styles of haircut and footbinding. The lesson to be gained from these multiple pages of description is that China is an innately ornamental civilization in the grand scheme of world culture. Le Comte pronounces: "A man must be a Barbarian with Barbarians, Polite with Men of Paris, Austere and Rigid to Excess among the *Indian* Penitents, handsomely Drest in *China*, and half Naked in the Wilderness of *Medura*."[28]

The idea of being, as a matter of course, "handsomely Drest in *China*" continues to resonate in later discussions of the empire; it is in the language of fashion that another influential Jesuit text on China, by Jean-Baptiste Du Halde, offers an assessment of China's impressive ability to preserve a stable system of rituals, laws, and monarchal order over centuries:

> As for what is here called the Fashion, it has nothing at all in it like what we call so in *Europe*, where the manner of Dress is subject to many Changes. It is not so in *China*, which is a Sign of good Order, and the Uniformity of the Government, even in the most trifling Matters; for which reason the Fashion of Dress has been always the same from the Infancy of the Empire to the Conquest of it by the *Tartars*, who without changing the Form of the ancient *Chinese* Government have only obliged them to dress in their Manner.[29]

Structured through differences in fashion, the comparison between Europe and China attributes to the latter a cultural authority based in an enduring antiquity. For Du Halde, dress bespeaks the centrality of the ceremonial rituals of a well-governed state to Chinese society, as also evidenced by the multiple plates of elaborately illustrated processions included in his text. Whether a wedding, funeral, or courtly parade, the practices of pagan excess signal the affinity of Chinese culture with European state and religious pageantry, on the one hand, and the fascination with exotic Chinese technologies—fireworks, acrobatics, and the sublime display of subjects-as-performers, long before the Beijing Olympics—on the other.[30] As Du Halde's comments suggest, the "uniformity" of Chinese customs and manners over time offers a continuing supply of novel styles to the ever-changing tastes of the European consuming public. It is no wonder that performances of China on the British stage might appear to be a natural consequence of its perceived culture of spectacle.

Rather than suggest a façade that belies an underlying authenticity, performance thus designates the ongoing construction of China's empire within the British imaginary and, in turn, the construction of the British subject as specta-

The 2008 Beijing Olympics Opening Ceremony. Courtesy of Zhang Rukui.

tor. At the same time, spectatorship rarely delimits a one-way gaze. As evidenced in the earlier passages from Du Halde and Le Comte, the act of looking upon China as a fashion show also enables a scrutiny of European manners. Modeling Chinese dress leads to adopting an imagined Chinese perspective, and, in this sense, performing China signals a mode of domestic social critique. As Le Comte imagines his readers' objections to Chinese manners and appearances, he introduces a hypothetical scenario in which the cultured Chinese viewer deems European fashion fit for the stage, rather than the streets:

> Notwithstanding I am perswaded these ways would not please all our *French* People; nay, and the Modes, of which we are so fond, do not appear so handsome to the *Chinese* as we imagine; but above all, the Periwig does strangely run in their Mind; and they look upon us as a sort of People, who, for want of a Beard, would get an Artificial one clapt to the Chin, that should reach to the Knees. This Phantastical Head-dress, say they, and that prodigious heap of curled Hair, are proper upon the Stage for a Man that would represent the Devil; But has one the shape of a Man when he is thus disguised? Insomuch that the *Chinese* Politeness will go near upon this Article alone to arraign us of Barbarity.[31]

CONVOI FUNEBRE d'un GRAND de la CHINE.

"A Chinese funeral procession," 1729. Etching by Bernard Picart. Reproduced by permission from The Getty Research Institute, Los Angeles (1387-555).

Such an exercise in cultural relativism forms the basis of the contemporary genre of foreign-observer fiction, including the aforementioned *Balance Chinoise*, which staged Eastern perspectives on European manners and mores. Giovanni Marana's *Letters Writ by a Turkish Spy* (1687), Montesquieu's *Persian Letters* (1722), and Oliver Goldsmith's *The Citizen of the World* (1762), to name a few prominent titles, feature Oriental visitors who write letters commenting on the strengths and weaknesses of Western society. The making public of private observations through epistolary exchange is one mode of theatricality, among others, that signaled the pervasiveness of the idea of spectatorship in eighteenth-century print culture. The social historian Jean-Christophe Agnew has argued that the widespread usage of the metaphor of the world-as-a-stage in this period was crucial to the development of the modern individual and his or her moral sense of self. Under new market conditions that positioned commodity relations at the center of human relations, the "commercialization of virtue" made a public spectacle of private feeling; attitudes such as sympathy can thus be seen as the "ultimate commodity: a universal equivalent into which all other goods could be converted."[32] The language of economic-moral transaction resonates with the figure of the foreign commentator, whose effectiveness as a narrator lies less in his cultural authenticity than in his enactment of imagined distance between East and West; and it is this relation that produces new perspectives and identifications, and hence the virtuous effects of spectatorship.

In the Restoration and eighteenth-century contexts, theatrical acts can thus be seen in varying degrees of remove from the physical stage, ranging from the civic pageantry that featured the commercial activities of the East India Company to the fabricated social commentaries of a letter-writing mandarin. If we understand performance to include "theatrical acts" in addition to "theater" per se, then cultural translation, ritual, live arts, and textual practices of public culture are included in our purview.[33] Performance studies scholar Richard Schechner has stressed the importance of off-stage processes to the study of performances, which "exist only as actions, interactions, and relationships."[34] By this measure, texts that foreground cross-cultural encounter and translation also perform China in relation to Europe. By considering the performativity of an Oriental tale, for example, we attend to its self-conscious commentary on framing Eastern antiquity according to modern commercial interests and to its imitation of Eastern manners to impart lessons of moderation and excess to a consuming public.

The seventeenth- and eighteenth-century European writings that examine China through the lens of performance emphasize the interactions between West and East even as they create a space for imagining other geographic units of comparison. Indeed, performance foregrounds the highly mediated conditions of relations that exceed a straightforward, self-other model of cross-cultural encounter. The suspicions of fraud and duplicity built into the discourses of spectacle discussed above are central to ideas of performance in and beyond the theater. Eighteenth-century acts of adopting Chinese "dress," for instance, include cases of Europeans impersonating Asians, actors modeling new fashions in exotic costumes, and fictional figures whose foreign perspectives cast a knowing eye on England's changing moral and economic climate. China is more often than not a placeholder for British historical concerns and cultural anxieties, and that which is called or presumed to be Chinese is designed to achieve a specific, didactic end. As suggested by the rubric of performance, this is and is not a book *about* China. Rather, it considers China to be a cultural intermediary that links together a greater Orient whose pagan empires were by turns idealized and denigrated for their alternatives to Western virtue—for China's effectiveness as an early modern exemplar of fashion and morality derived from its unique cultural character as well as its strategic ties to other times, places, and civilizations of the East and the West.

The Example of China

Before continuing with a discussion of the moral geography signified by *China* in the eighteenth century, let me clarify that this book is an inquiry not only into examples of China but also into the logic of its exemplarity. To make an example of something, whether positive or negative, is less an act of representation than one of performance. One employs an example with both an audience in mind and a didactic end in mind. Its usefulness lies in its concretization of the abstract, or what the Restoration poet John Dryden praised thus: "There is nothing of the tyrant in example; but it gently slides into us, is easy and pleasant in its passage, and in one word reduces into practice our speculative notions. Therefore, the more powerful the examples are, they are the more useful also, and by being more known they are more powerful."[35] To consider the heuristic force of an example is therefore also to consider its subtle negotiation of particular and universal: we value examples for their specificity and novelty, even as they must be severed from their original context and rendered generic in order to fulfill their communicative end. They are etymologically correlated with the idea of the sample, from the Latin *essample*, a specimen that is exempted from the rest and hence excluded from its membership in the group that constituted its original identity. The philosopher Giorgio Agamben, for one, has identified a similar structure of exception, or "inclusive exclusion," as crucial to the founding of Western political sovereignty and the reach of juridical authority. In Agamben's discussion, "The example is truly a *paradigm* in the etymological sense: it is what is 'shown beside,' and a class can contain everything except its own paradigm."[36] On a fundamental level, then, the example must be at once exceptional and typical, discrete yet paradigmatic. It belongs to a set until singled out for scrutiny; all the while, what makes it instructive is its ability to be representative.

There have been numerous attempts, past and present, to theorize the productive contradictions of the example (in Dryden's account, deemed "gentle" and "pleasant" yet "powerful" and "useful") in political and literary context. The structure of inclusive exclusion is one way of accounting for the elusive quality of China's appearances in eighteenth-century literature and for its capacity, as a cultural proxy, to stand in for, typify, universalize, or even contradict the mores of European modernity. More than a stable referent or fixed object of representation, "China," through its myriad usages and evocations of moral ambivalence, is best understood as a critical node of intercultural relations. In his work on exemplarity, literary theorist Alexander Gelley argues that the example confirms or tests an existing norm precisely because it is "never merely an instance; it is an instance plus its vector of reception." It has "no autonomous standing" but rather is part of a "nexus of converging articulations."[37] This emphasis on the contingency of example-making has been developed more recently with respect to China by Eric Hayot, whose book *The Hypothetical Mandarin* offers an elegant approach toward understanding the relationship between China and the West.[38] Hayot's study is concerned largely with Sinophobic representations of Chinese pain and suffering in nineteenth- and twentieth-century U.S. travel and medical writing. Western perspectives on the Chinese body, he argues, have shaped the modern emergence of sympathy as a culturally specific humanistic ideal that nonetheless continues to undergird contemporary discourses of universal human rights. Hayot suggests that, as early as the eighteenth century, anecdotes about Chinese cruelty functioned as thought experiments for writers testing the boundaries of European ethical consciousness. In the capacity of an example, "China" occupied a marginalized yet absolutely central position across a range of texts. In appearing to be extraneous to the subject at hand, the invocations of China are "anecdotal," or precisely not representative of a larger whole. In such a way, they produce an "example-effect" that provides us with heightened insight into the Eurocentric biases of post-Enlightenment thought.

My reading of Chinese exemplarity extends and historicizes one of the central questions raised by Hayot: if the example is a performed utterance defined only in relation to what it is meant to illustrate, then what difference does it make that "China" is the thing named? To put it another way, aren't references to China in eighteenth-century literature simply Englishness in Chinese dress? Of course, not all examples function in the same way. They can be representative to varying degrees with respect to the set within which they are situated, and my analyses of performance will attend to the multiple sets to which China belonged in the early modern period. Its status as an ancient yet modern civilization made it in some instances the best, in others the worst, paradigm for empires of the Orient as well as the Occident. With respect to the former, the early-eighteenth-century idealization of China is a marked departure from the predominant mode of denigrating the East by modern expressions of Orientalism as well as early modern attitudes toward the Ottoman Empire and the Islamic Orient. There is in fact a great deal to be learned from the example of China.

For one, the ambivalence toward the idea of Chinese empire stemmed also from its affiliation and continuities with classical antiquity, and hence its role as cultural mediator between civilized and uncivilized regions of the world. To understand this state of being in-between, we must first understand that eighteenth-century theories of exemplarity were deeply concerned with the lessons of antiquity to the present and future states of modern empires. Would Augustan England follow the rise, and hence fall, of ancient Rome? The example qua example was conceived of within a didactic tradition that drew prophetic moral lessons from historical reflection. An example creates similitude out of difference by the act of comparison; in this case it imports a past instance into the present context and establishes a relevance between new and old, foreign and familiar, in order to predict the future. This future could often be ruinous, as illustrated by the following entry from Ephraim Chambers's *Cyclopaedia, Or, An Universal Dictionary of Arts and Sciences* (1728):

> EXAMPLE, in Rhetoric &c. is defined an imperfect Kind of Induction, or Argumentation; whereby it is proved that a Thing which has happen'd on some other Occasion, will happen again on the present one; from the Similitude of the Cases.
>
> As, the Wars of the *Thebans*, against their Neighbours the *Phocians*, was ruinous; consequently, that of the *Athenians* against their Neighbours, will likewise be ruinous.

What makes the example "imperfect" is the potential for false predictions, or the interpretive risks in subscribing to reiterative or cyclical history. Such a process, though, explicitly foregrounds the comparisons at work in the yoking together of disparate spaces and histories, and its pedagogical work translates past into present, and future, relevance.

Moreover, the example, whether positive or negative, was defined by its moral effects. According to Samuel Johnson, the exemplary figure has a duality built into its definition as "a Model, or Original, to be imitated, or copied" and "such as may deserve to be proposed to imitation," yet, at the same time, "such as may give warning to others."[39] Together, the rival entries capture well the mixed praise of China's society of spectacle and embodiment of contradictions like civilization and barbarism, enlightenment and despotism. Eighteenth-century definitions of moral exemplarity such as Johnson's developed out of an early modern tradition of modeling ethical ideals through the transmission of classical examples. Renaissance didactic literature narrated the ancient deeds of those like Socrates and Cato, whose lives were meant to be imitated as if they were a "coherent moral statement" with transhistorical, universal appeal.[40] In the humanistic and rhetorical tradition of illustrative, moral anecdotes like the exemplum, aristocratic virtues were textually disseminated as part of a culture of mimesis that borrowed from medieval religious iconography to teach public virtue by exemplifying individual actions. Singling out past lives for present emulation called for a complex negotiation of historical continuity and discontinuity. At work is a tension between allegorizing the distant past, thus minimizing the difference history makes, and historicizing or differentiating the particularity and contingency of the past with respect to the present moment. Such model-making involves the reification of past moments to momentary universality, or the transformation of temporal difference into a relation of identity. Numerous studies of Renaissance exemplarity have considered how historical models for virtuous behavior are made relevant to the present context through establishing a system of resemblances; at the same time, the example's distinction from the present or from other instances in the past constitutes its original merit, and thus its force of injunction. It is this exceptionalism that also threatens to disrupt the tradition of values that the exemplar ostensibly imparts.[41]

The traditional process of exemplifying prominent individuals becomes even more unruly when the cultural alterity of an ancient yet non-Western figure is factored into the pedagogical structure. Along with its exemplary fashion, China's philosopher-icon Confucius was considered a sign of a virtuous antiquity that, although long past, was held to be a defining force of its contemporary empire. The distinctly moral character assigned to China through multiple generations of Jesuit translations of Chinese classical writings (the Five Classics and Four Books of the Analects, Great Learning, Doctrine of the Mean, and work of Mencius) made available a Confucian ethics of filial piety to European audiences searching for new ways of articulating changing socioeconomic, and hence domestic, hierarchies. The publication of the collection *Confucius Sinarum Philosophus* in 1687 developed a cult of Confucius that was furthered by its abridgement and translation into English in 1691 as the *Morals of Confucius*. The idealization of the philosopher's pagan moderation, humility, selflessness, and secular ethics—that is, a manufacturing of Confucianism[42]—extended the work of the Renaissance exemplum by integrating Eastern with Western chronologies and thus expanding the conventional canon of philosophical antiquity.

Efforts of Jesuit missionaries to reconcile the two chronologies into a "Confucian-Christian synthesis" led to the Chinese Rites Controversy of the 1630s onward; arguments for the compatibility of Chinese ancestor rituals and Confucian philosophy with Christian precepts had since the time of Matteo Ricci divided Jesuits and non-Jesuits alike. The theological debates would extend to successive generations of Enlightenment philosophers, from Spinozists like the

Englishman Anthony Collins to Deists such as Voltaire, who sought models of rational moral systems independent from church authority. Others such as the Jesuit Figurist Joachim Bouvet and Jean-François Foucquet, along with the German philosopher Gottfried Wilhelm Leibniz, argued that divine revelations of Christianity were prefigured in Chinese classics such as the *I Ching* and that China's legendary founder Fu Xi (or Fo-hi) was in fact a descendant of Noah.[43] Newly published Jesuit records of Chinese history give the date 2952 BC as the beginning of the empire, which conflicted with the biblical timeline for the great flood (2349 BC) that was supposed to have annihilated the entire earth. Despite the disagreements over the exact age of China's empire, its moral status as an unparalleled ancient was established by late-seventeenth-century scholars and adopted by later Enlightenment philosophers looking eastward for an alternative to the perceived state of Western religious corruption.[44]

In the general division of history into ancient and modern, the Chinese were aligned with a core group of ancient Greek philosophers, including Plato and Aristotle, whose revered wisdom was disputed only by their paganism. The basis of their moral authority in antiquity produced controversy insofar as it marked them non-Christian, or, to use the early modern term, "ethnic" philosophers. Although Confucius was thought to transcend Christian and pagan sects alike in the sheer rationality of his teachings, his alignment with the ancients fueled debates in "ethnic theology" over the Mosaic origin of humankind and postdiluvian peopling of the globe across Asia and the Americas. Jesuit accommodationists compared him with the Oracle at Delphi or mythologized him as the Ethnicus Philosophus par excellence to reinforce sapient paganism as a class of ancient virtue that could partially escape contemporary religious censure because of its pre-Christian origins. To the extent that Confucius was deemed an "ethnic philosopher" akin to and in dialogue with Socrates, his pagan morality seems far less disruptive to Christianity than other vilified pagan figures from Hindu, Buddhist, and Muslim traditions. It is precisely for this reason that Chinese paganism, fashionably ancient, could be held as both the epitome of enlightened philosophy and a heathen instrument of delineating the boundary between civilization and barbarism.

Postcolonial Enlightenment, Early Modern Orientalism

Throughout the eighteenth century, empires of the East would continue to be drawn into comparison with Europe in relations of similitude and proximity that contrasted with depictions of Africa or the Americas. Despite the tendency to write the history of racism in black and white, attitudes toward Asia were not exempt from the imagining of racial hierarchies tied to the transatlantic slave trade and European colonization efforts around the globe; rather, they played a crucial role in mediating the religious and racialized logics of Enlightenment universalism. Immanuel Kant, in his writings on national character, paired East and West according to Asia's resemblances to Europe: while Arabs were the "Spaniards of the Orient," Persians could be considered the "French of Asia." In one episode of the *Observations on the Feeling of the Beautiful and Sublime* (1764), Arabs are classified as noble, followed by poetic Persians, Japanese who appear English but lack fine feeling, Indians deemed idolatrous and hence grotesque, and finally Chinese, whose exemplary antiquity is to blame for their own brand of grotesquery: "They also have venerable grotesqueries because they are of very ancient custom, and no nation in the world has more of these than this one."[45] To further emphasize the excessiveness of the Chinese, Kant includes a footnote detailing a ceremony used to ward off dragons in the event of an eclipse. Immediately following this, a paragraph begins, "The Negroes of Africa have by nature no feeling that rises above trifling."[46] Whereas an identity-based reading of this passage might focus on the representations of a given people, an exemplarity-based approach helps us to see that China, an embodiment of moral contradictions, is positioned at a transitional point in the passage—actually in lieu of a transition—in the abrupt shift between descriptions of Europe, Asia, and Africa. If read as a catalog of "inclusive exclusions," to recall Agamben's discussion of the example, the ordering of non-European races juxtaposes China's surfeit of customs with Africa's lack thereof; the one in effect reinforces the other.

In his study of the rhetorical tradition of exemplarity, Gelley tracks the shift from the medieval and classical exemplum, used as an instructional guide to behavior, to its eighteenth-century function to imagine and enact moral judgment within Enlightenment systems of morality. Whereas Kantian universal ethics cannot be derived from empirical proof, the example, through its embodiment of practical wisdom, is an instrumental activation of moral judgment; its rhetorical force bridges the gap between worldly experience and a priori truth and hence enables the transformation of particular instances into universal tenets.[47] The illustrative role of the example in Enlightenment moral and aesthetic theory has been further theorized by postcolonial critics who argue that references to culturally and racially marked others were crucial components in European subject formation. David Lloyd, for one, has shown how the hierarchical and developmental schema of Kant's aesthetics performs a cultural logic of racism by encoding epidermal blackness with metaphorical significance and temporal backwardness.⁴⁸ In her deconstructive reading of the *Critique of Judgment,* Gayatri Spivak tracks the interruptive force of the aboriginal, or "raw man," whose position as a subject proper is foreclosed within the text's representational structure. Borrowing from the language of anthropology, Spivak identifies the cultural other as a native informant, a "not-quite-example," whose presence crucially supplements the philosophical system, and "whose lack of access to the position of narrator is the condition of possibility of the consolidation of Kant's position."⁴⁹

Enlightenment universalist aesthetics and ethics were made possible, we must remember, through the massive influx of new knowledge about far-flung places of the globe. The Enlightenment was an era of turning this knowledge of foreign places into lessons of human diversity and universal history. As the growing body of travel literature was disseminated, excerpted, and reproduced across eighteenth-century print culture, European writers grafted the civilizations and customs of the East onto traditional ideas of Western virtue to produce universal models of virtue and vice. A nation's moral exemplarity became crucial to the expanding vocabulary of cultural and racial difference and to the structure of ambivalence that assigned China a special place in the shifting landscape of eighteenth-century British virtue. It was the encounter of disparate worlds through the East and West Indies trade that produced anthropology as a field of inquiry and introduced alternate histories and temporalities of peoples that appeared to be situated between ancient and modern notions of ethnicity.

While studies of race and the Enlightenment analyze Western subject formation via the structural, discursive status of the marginalized example, assessing empire from the peripheries of the philosophical or literary text also implicitly locates in such historical representation moments of resistance to colonial ideology that can be developed through the process of reading and interpretation. The attention to racially marked figures in postcolonial literary studies of the 1990s exercised the limits of dominant Europe-centered narratives and began to expose the highly mediated relations between history and text that enabled such representation. This mapping of postcolonial theory onto earlier historical periods—a "catachrestic gesture"⁵⁰—opened up questions of colonial resistance embedded within European metropolitan discourses and cross-cultural relations in historical contact zones. In his mapping of a "postcolonial" eighteenth century, Srinivas Aravamudan introduced the spatialized figure of the tropicopolitan, which troubles the dichotomy of colonizer/colonized through its dual register as an "object of representation *and* agent of resistance."⁵¹ This attempt to think beyond the either-or, self-other strictures of colonial identity also takes up a cautionary point made by Spivak about the limitations of a type of colonial analytical frame:

"Colonial Discourse studies, when they concentrate only on the representation of the colonized or the matter of the colonies, can sometimes serve the production of current neocolonial knowledge by placing colonialism/imperialism securely in the past, and/or by suggesting a continuous line from that past to our present."[52]

The relevance of postcolonial studies to eighteenth-century histories of imperial expansion continues to be an area of critical inquiry that challenges our practices of reading European interpretations of history and reading history through literary representations.[53] In their recent collection, *The Postcolonial Enlightenment*, Lynn Festa and Daniel Cary make a case for the ongoing need to interrogate the legacy of eighteenth-century example-making, noting that "The Enlightenment made plural has remained curiously parochial, bound to its European origins and contained within these texts."[54] Following these calls to think beyond representations of Europe or the Other, the example of China in this study extends the spatial and temporal parameters of colonial discourse. A self-other model of cultural difference fails to account for the routes, mediations, and shifting hierarchies of race and racism that were emerging in the period of colonial expansion.[55] My intention is not to fetishize China as the new exception to European colonialism, but, rather, to examine its role as a cultural broker. In other words, it mediates and performs—rather than represents, per se—the global encounters of virtue and commerce that comprised the ideological and epistemological contradictions of modern British values. To this end, the tools and methods of postcolonial and colonial discourse studies are valuable not only for exposing and exploring European ideologies of empire, but also for highlighting the politicization of cultural difference and cultural exemplarity, however complex and mediated, as they were articulated in the early modern period.[56]

In recent years, China has become something of a test case for eighteenth-century as well as postcolonial studies, in part because it appears to fall outside traditional considerations of Orientalism, subalternity, and the mapping of European imperialism. China, the argument goes, was never colonized and hence cannot be made to fit into the type of ideological East-West dynamic uncovered by Edward Said's seminal study of nineteenth-century Orientalism.[57] Combined with the questioning of the applicability of postcolonial theory is, at times, a countervailing tendency to dismiss postcolonial studies while celebrating East Asian empire as an unrivaled exception to European rule. Robert Markley, in *The Far East and the English Imagination, 1600–1730*, makes such a case by placing a dominant China at the center of his argument that the "Far East" has been too long omitted from Marxist theories of international relations and the purview of postcolonial studies. For Markley, China becomes an exemplary exception to a reductive colonizer/colonized paradigm that overstates European dominance. While I agree with the assessment that England was far from a hegemonic force in the early eighteenth century, Markley's critique of postcolonial studies' Eurocentrism also risks its own Sinocentrism and reminds us of the need for ongoing scrutiny of the terms by which China has been and continues to be exemplified across a number of disciplines and area studies.

The example of China has only recently become the focus of literary studies of the British Empire and British colonialism despite, as Markley and others are right to point out, China's dominance within the world economy up through the mid-eighteenth century. Earlier generations of scholarship on Europe-Asia relations have approached the topic from the fields of Asian history or art history, as per the invaluable work of Donald Lach, Edwin Van Kley, Jonathan Spence, David Mungello, Michael Sullivan, and Hugh Honour. Only in the past decade have literary critics in eighteenth-century British studies begun to examine China within the legacy of Orientalism, on the one hand, and global culture, on the other. Among the scholars working in this new field, we could include Ros Ballaster, Robert Batchelor, Yu Liu, Robert Markley, Eun Kyung Min, David Porter, George Starr, James Watt, and Eugenia Zuroski.[58] Such revisionist work has begun to put into critical focus earlier generations of "China and the West" studies that surveyed the European fascination with China with little theorization of or engagement with the literary or the terms of the comparison.[59] Most instrumental in putting China on the recent map of British literary studies is David Porter's *Ideographia: The Chinese Cipher in Early Modern Europe*, which brings together traditional Sinological and linguistic concerns regarding Jesuit missionary activities with questions of material culture and Chinese artistic influences on European tastes, in particular the often dismissed phenomenon of chinoiserie. He offers a valuable study of British strategies for deciphering China across the distinct areas of linguistics, religion, commerce, and aesthetics. At the same time, this approach continues to isolate the example of China from the broader Orient with which it was associated during the eighteenth century and that a critical engagement with Orientalism and postcolonial studies brings to the fore.

Most accounts of contacts between China and Europe, including Porter's, follow a particular historical narrative; namely, the shift from the idealization of China in the early Enlightenment period to its denigration in the late eighteenth century. In essence they track the progressive weakening of the Chinese state and concurrent rise of British control in the region epitomized by the colonization of India and the takeover of the tea and opium trade. While such a linear trajectory of de-idealization can be drawn, the march toward modern history can too easily gloss over the strong ambivalence toward the East at work throughout the eighteenth century. Even the Jesuits' praise for China was, it should be pointed out, by no means uniform. My focus on exemplarity, the culture of virtue and performance, and the mediating role of China attempts to account for the interplay of positive and negative assessments of the "grand spectacle" of China in the years of England's colonial expansion in the West and East Indies, where considerations of the English Restoration and British eighteenth century meet those of its contemporary, the early Qing dynasty (1644–1911). Organized around comparisons between China and key sites of the Orient, I offer a theory of exemplarity that, from a literary and cultural studies approach, asserts the complexity of premodern racial categories while factoring in the specific formation of early modern orientalism.[60] The coupling of virtue and commerce offers a theoretical framework for the phenomenon of early modern orientalism explored in this book.

Far from being a stable, systematic, or scientific construction of the East, what I am calling early modern orientalism was a structure of ambivalence resulting from the desire for East Indies markets and the encounter with their superior moral *and* economic example. The British demand for Eastern goods and ideas took place in a culture of imitating and performing the virtues and vices of the East. In the case of China, the ambivalence constitutive of early modern orientalism stemmed from a built-in contradiction between two temporalities that would appear to be at odds: modern commodity culture and ancient civilization. Early modern orientalism bestowed commercial value upon an idealization of Asiatic antiquity as manifested in print and material culture, particularly as seen in the modern objects and the decorative sensibility of chinoiserie.[61] China was imagined to contain the secrets of maintaining past glory in a commercialized present. Although Confucius was long dead, the spirit of his laws lived on in Enlightenment idealizations of Chinese governance, and even in the form and utility of chinoiserie. This element of idealization differentiates early modern orientalism from Said's description of Orientalism, which emphasizes a nineteenth-century discourse of backwardness, sensuality, despotism, effeminacy, and other largely negative attributes generated primarily by Western representations of the Islamic Middle East. Of course, Said acknowledges that idealizations of the East's classical past were folded into the widespread denouncements of its backwardness; in the case of eighteenth-century and Enlightenment literature, however, the controversies over China's moral exemplarity constituted a different sort of structural ambivalence, one far less anchored by the institutions and attitudes of cultural superiority characteristic of the later British Empire.

The relationship of early modern orientalism to Orientalism has been explored by a number of Renaissance scholars who extend Said's geographic frame of reference to Western representations of the Ottoman Empire, South Asia, and, to a certain extent, East Asia, in the period from the fifteenth century to the seventeenth. These studies refer to "proto-orientalism" or an era "before Orientalism" to articulate the complex circuits of trade and diplomatic encounters between England and the superior forces of the Islamic Orient, and the "Turks" in particular.[62] Gerald MacLean has characterized this early era as one of "imperial envy" evidenced by the popularity of Ottoman goods, textiles, and dress with English royalty and aristocracy, who made a fashion of "performing East." MacLean's idea of performance, unlike mine, is derived from English travelers' construction of national identity away from home. As he argues, it was through adopting foreign dress and customs, or "turning Turk," in North Africa that the English subject bodily enacted an English identity, or in some cases a disavowal of Englishness, with an agency and theatricality that exceeds Said's analytical framework of an Orient primarily of metaphorical performance and European literary representation.[63]

In the eighteenth century, China's secular civilization, unlike the Islamic Orient of the Renaissance period, presented less a political threat or a possibility of a strategic regional alliance but, rather, a far more hypothetical model of virtuous paganism for England's new mercantile empire. This allowed for a greater plasticity of representation, and my approach recognizes the many uses to which China was put. Thus, individual sections of this book deploy different modes of analysis to demonstrate the richness of China as a phenomenon of meaning-making. Similarly each chapter is structured around key geographical comparisons so that while China is an organizing figure, it is far from the sole object of inquiry. Throughout, I underscore the importance of geographical and temporal comparison both to the understanding of "China" in the eighteenth century and to the cross-cultural formation of Western virtue and epistemology. In fact, in discussions of commerce and of public virtue, "China" is approached as a question of mistaken identity, a limit case, and an instance of the interplay between general and particular in its connection to other parts of the Orient.

The Chinese *Hethnic*

To return to the fictional dialogue between Socrates and Confucius, let us recall the idea of "ethnic" philosophy that China shared with ancient Greece. Derived from the Greek *ethnos*, nation or people, and the Hebrew *goy*, gentile, the designation of ethnic over the course of the eighteenth century applied to those non-Christians and non-Jews deemed heathen and irreligious. The word *heathen* was in fact an etymological variant of *ethnic (hethnic or heathenic)*, thus attesting to the intimacy between nation, religion, and antiquity in the pre-ethnological imagining of the non-West. The trace of the heathen in the ethnic establishes a derogatory religious precedent to modern understandings of race and ethnicity. Unlike *heathenic*, the term *hethnic* was not widely used, but for the purposes of this study, the idea of the pre-Christian or proto-Christian hethnic calls attention to the fluctuating boundary between heathen and ethnic and to the early modern efforts to fit a virtuous pagan such as Confucius into a template of Western antiquity. Confucius, in the capacity of a model hethnic, evokes the complexity and contradictions of an increasingly incoherent Christian universal history in a global context. Not-quite-heathen, the Chinese hethnic occupied a challenging liminality. China's indisputably ancient civilization might have saved it from the brand of barbarism, and in theory signaled a predisposition for Christian virtue; and yet, the same temporal alterity that characterized its exemplary "ethnicity" also potentially disrupted any such integration of its morality within a Christian frame. Above all, the hethnic demanded a reevaluation of Western chronology and cultural primacy and a new role for the foreign exemplar.

Each chapter of this book examines the coarticulation of morality and cultural difference by pairing a debate over a particular virtue with an exemplary trope or hethnic figure that embodies key contradictions of modernity and translates Eastern ideas and values to Western audiences. Often, what appears to British audiences to be a vice can acquire virtuous properties, or the other way around, through its connection to China. Indeed, the thin line between virtue and vice is exposed through the eighteenth-century positing of Eastern examples. Confucius, a touchstone for the book, is a virtuous pagan who illustrates the debates over heroic and moral virtue in a climate of commercialism. He acts in the capacity of a hethnic to bridge ancient and modern and to embody the tensions between virtue and commerce. He is, like the other hethnic figures I identify—the Amazon heroine, the converted heathen, the preacher of transmigration, and the sentimental patriarch—a border figure and a cultural broker who performs an idea of China and the contested meanings of particular virtues. These hethnics are nominally Chinese figures, perhaps more accurately dubbed impostures or fakes, who together illustrate how virtue was itself shaped by practices of cross-cultural exchange. The texts that they populate also exemplify the ideas of translation, adaptation, and performance. Far from a survey of the British reception of China or Asia, this book isolates key texts and cases where the ambivalences of the moral exemplar come to the fore. These are moments where generic innovation is tied to the imitation and incorporation of foreign imports and where performances of conventional virtues are transformed by the foreign example.

A number of the texts featured in this book were significant conveyors of ideas about China even though they have largely been neglected in studies of eighteenth-century literature. It is my hope that the focused attention to plays like Arthur Murphy's *The Orphan of China* (1759) will contribute in some small way to expanding the British literary canon of our classrooms and curricula. As for some of the other examples included here, it is no coincidence that the trio of Murphy's *Orphan of China*, Elkanah Settle's *The Conquest of China* (1676), and Giacomo Puccini's *Turandot* (1926), discussed in the conclusion and epilogue, are all staged performances concerned with the situation of Chinese empire under siege by neighboring nations; for the Western fascination with the political spectacle of a nation able to preserve intact its ancient yet modern civilization continues to shape East-West moral discourse into our current day, and in ever-changing Orientalist forms. Even when China is the titular object of inquiry, it often stands in for other places and times. As discussed above, China was imagined to be part of a larger Orient, and for this reason I include a number of other "Oriental" sites in my consideration of Oriental exemplary and the performance of China.

The first chapter examines the contested Restoration aristocratic ideal of heroic virtue through a comparison of two unlikely heroes of English empire, Confucius and the character of a Chinese Amazon. The 1644 conquest of the Ming dynasty by the northern Manchus, or Tartars, was a world news event documented in numerous Jesuit historical sources and fictionalized by an English play by Elkanah Settle, *The Conquest of China, By the Tartars* (1676). The play featured a warrior woman in its translation of Chinese historical records into Restoration stage spectacle; these combined performances of gender and cultural exoticism in turn challenged the generic constraints of heroic virtue. In Western literary and historical accounts, China's ancient empire was more commonly exemplified by the moral figure of Confucius; yet both the woman warrior and the philosopher-king, in their respective characterizations, embodied the gendered quality of effeminacy traditionally associated with the downfall of exemplary empires such as ancient Rome. In the late-seventeenth-century climate of political turbulence, however, effeminacy, when routed through China, becomes aligned with a new type of heroism, one based not simply upon valor or conquest but on the ethos of perpetual peace and commercial dominance. Thus, Confucius and the Amazon not only test the limits of moral and heroic virtue by introducing Chineseness to the canon of Western classical examples; they expose the importance of gender ambiguity and the nexus of cross-cultural comparisons at work in constructing China as a model empire.

The production of a different sort of spectacle is analyzed in my chapter 2. The subject is a performance of Asian identity by the eighteenth-century impostor George Psalmanazar, a fair-skinned Frenchman who arrived in London in 1703 and for a number of years passed as a native of Formosa. Through his public debates with Royal Society scientists and his publications about the island, he fashioned an elaborate world of pagan rituals, government, and language founded upon European missionary and mercantile observations of China and Japan. This chapter focuses on Psalmanazar's claims to being a converted heathen; it explores his hethnic performances of "sincere conversion" in light of the history of Chinese converts in Europe, the politics of Protestant-Catholic tensions, and the contemporaneous vogue in "china" ware and "japan" ware. Above all, Psalmanazar's case offers a theory of conversion as a performative activity operating across multiple cultures of knowledge production. His fraud, in all its self-reflexivity, conflating Formosa, Japan, and China, tested the limits of demonstrable knowledge in the mutually informing discourses of science, religion, and commerce.

My third chapter continues the inquiry into religious and cultural conversions. It examines the uses of Eastern "superstition" in didactic fiction of the first half or so of the eighteenth century. The idea of attaining immortality through transspecies reincarnation, or the transmigration of the souls, was a commonly cited example of Eastern idolatry stretching from Egypt to China. At the heart of Jesuit missionary efforts in China was the effort to synthesize Christianity and Confucianism while expelling the syncretic blending of Confucianism, Taoism, and Buddhism—beliefs considered idolatrous and conflated with the Pythagoreanism and Hinduism of other parts of the so-called Orient. The early eighteenth century also saw a transvaluation of Eastern excess into Western moderation, evidenced by the proliferation of Oriental-tale fiction following the 1704 translation of the *Arabian Nights*. My chapter focuses most explicitly on the popular and influential *Spectator* papers as texts that rewrote the Oriental tales to serve as a form of what I call "fabulous pedagogy." With Joseph Addison and Richard Steele, the writings of John Dryden, John Toland, and Thomas Gueullette espoused the virtues of moderation by taming "Oriental extravagance" into entertaining yet instructive fables. Even in satirized form, transmigration radically blurred distinctions between species, calling into question the uniqueness of Western human rationality. The ability of reincarnated memory to span vast distances in time and space also offered radical possibilities of transferring the ancient history of past empires into the present, a *translatio imperii* routed through the empires of "Eastern nations," rather than Greece or Rome.

While these theories of transmigration deliberately moderated the excesses of Eastern superstition, the century also saw a reconceptualization of material excess, the idea of luxury, into a new form of virtue. Arthur Murphy's tragedy *The Orphan of China* (1759) was one of several European adaptations of an actual thirteenth-century Yuan dynasty play, *Zhaoshi Guer*. Through the play's exotic costumes, set designs, and the hethnic figure of the virtuous Confucian family, China becomes both a model for British sensibility and fashion and a chastised source of luxury and unhealthy consumerism. Unlike Settle's *Conquest of China*, this work, which I discuss in chapter 4, staged midcentury theories of commerce and sentimentality and debates between Montesquieu's ideas of Chinese despotism, Voltaire's theories of Chinese enlightenment, and the philosophies of Adam Smith, who in his *Theory of Moral Sentiments* (1759) relied on key metaphors of China, theater, and foreign spectatorship to articulate British moral subjectivity. An exemplary China functions in these instances as a secular alternative to theistic moral authority and an example and counterexample of England's moral conscience.

The exemplary cases of Chineseness examined in these chapters cover a period of Western knowledge in the making, when what passed for Eastern must be understood through the politics of virtue and commerce and the ideological reception of an imported Asia. Asia was largely defined by the marketability of its difference, even though often what passed for Eastern had less to do with cultural authenticity per se than with the strategic commercialization and moralization of the increasing distinction between East and West. In the book's epilogue I argue that the performance of Oriental exemplarity persists, although in a globalized economy of new East-West rivalries and transnational configurations. We can trace the continuing cycle of cultural translation—from Western imitations of Eastern sources to Eastern copies (of Western copies) of Eastern originals—in present-day visual culture. The ubiquitous marketing of cultural authenticity and Chineseness today originated in eighteenth-century ambivalence toward and exemplifications of Asia in the areas of virtue and commerce. Drawing upon this lineage, we can study the continuing production of Chinese spectacle in the work of filmmaker Zhang Yimou, and the epilogue focuses on his 1998 staging of Puccini's opera *Turandot* in Beijing's Forbidden City. The multimillion-dollar phenomenon of performing an exotic opera in its "original" site is a type of made-in-China chinoiserie. The spread of *Turandot* throughout East Asia attests to the continuing reinvention and marketing of early modern orientalism in the modern context of global tourism.

For a nascent British Empire of the eighteenth century, China provided an instructive set of paradoxes. Then, as perhaps now, China's reception as an exemplary culture in the formation of Western morality turned on the paradox of its being an ancient yet modern, and far from defunct, empire. Eighteenth-century British ideas of virtue were comparative in scope; such ideas were constitutively engaged with the project of looking to the East for answers as well as modes of grappling with social and historical change. Importantly, then, the force of China's example lay in its dual character as both warning and as object to be imitated. This book theorizes the two dimensions of the referent *China,* whose doubled and duplicitous status as a preeminent empire and import commodity formed a dialectic of particular relevance to the mercantile culture of eighteenth-century England. Virtue was shot through with commercial concerns and the translation of foreign excesses—of wealth, government, manners—into novel objects for consumption. The ambivalence toward China provided an imaginative slate, or hethnic potential, onto which to write new standards of morality and the ideal form of historical progress.

CHAPTER ONE

Heroic Effeminacy and the Conquest of China

Buried in the annals of English theater history is an obscure play by Elkanah Settle, *The Conquest of China, By the Tartars* (1676), perhaps most notable for its resounding failure with Restoration audiences. As an eighteenth-century critic remarked, the play was terribly acted and "the plot is (with exception of the historical part) romantic, and the dialogue badly written."[1] One "romantic" element was the character of a provincial Chinese warrior queen who, disguised as a male, fought valiantly to save her otherwise powerless country from the onslaught of Tartar enemies from the north as well as domestic bandits intent on usurping the throne of China's effeminate "King." Along with several other love intrigues, the play features her doomed romance with a virtuous Tartar prince who is unaware of her double life as a soldier. When they fight each other on behalf of their respective countries, she is killed, only to magically revive once the king of China accedes defeat. In the end, the Tartar is welcomed to the throne and she assumes the place of his wife. Despite the aesthetic shortcomings of the play, the female masculinity of this Chinese Amazon named Amavanga offers a surprisingly multifaceted and gendered interpretation of a recent world historical event: the cataclysmic fall of China's Ming dynasty (1368–1644).

I will return later to the formal and ideological import of the play's many shortcomings; for now, I want to highlight the unusual and productive placement of this female warrior. Amazons as such are not usually associated with China, and yet this hybrid heroine, far from a mere instance of exotic histrionics, indicates a particular discursive lineage of translating Chinese history for English audiences. Settle's play is thus consequential, not for its poetic sophistication or popularity but for its manipulation of historical sources into stage spectacle. China's history of regime change was scripted into the heroic ideals of European history-writing and Restoration English literature, at the same time that the example of China subtly reconfigured Western traditions of heroism, and in particular its representations of gender and effeminacy. The Amazon, an embodiment of alternative masculinity, exemplifies a much larger process of interpreting the pitfalls and potentials of warring empires according to their perceived sexual and cultural mores. Continually reinvented as figures of cultural translation and ethnographic voyeurism, Amazons perform the ideological work of representing ethnic differences and establishing universal standards of moral and commercial virtue. As such, they register the early modern ambivalence toward a Chinese empire of seemingly spectacular contradictions: ancient and modern, feminine and masculine, despotic and heroic.

In mid-seventeenth-century England, China was a contradictory example of a powerful empire, in part because of its much-admired antiquity. The idealized image of a continuous, Asiatic monarchy of extraordinary size and duration was challenged—although, interestingly enough, not disproved—by the fall of the Ming dynasty. News of the conquest of China traveled westward through diplomatic and religious channels in the decades that followed, and detailed histories of China proliferated in mid-seventeenth-century Europe on an unprecedented scale.[2] These works presented an ancient empire with a remarkable ability to preserve its customs and manners despite being attacked and even conquered repeatedly by "Tartar" nations from the north. Two landmark invasions came to symbolize China's resiliency: one by the Mongols in the thirteenth century; the other, the conquest of "Peking" in 1644 by the Manchus, founders of the new Qing dynasty. Though twice defeated, the Chinese were seen to have maintained their cultural infrastructure, to the degree that they became a much-cited paradox of conquered conquerors, ostensibly absorbing and even civilizing their Tartar invaders.[3] Of the irrepressible spirit of the Chinese, the philosopher Baruch Spinoza wrote, "[They] are a Famous Example, who . . . have thereby preserved themselves so many thousand Years, that their Antiquity exceeds all other Nations, they have heretofore recovered their lost Empire, and without doubt will do so again, when the Courage of the Tartars, hath lain a while longer buried in Wealth, Luxury and Sloth."[4] Such an image of political stability had special appeal to a Europe plagued by frequent crises of royal succession, internecine wars, and, as a result, massive expenditures and monetary deficits.[5] In England alone, the second half of the seventeenth century saw a staggering number of plots and revolutions that threatened its foundations of hereditary rule.[6]

Beginning in the Commonwealth of the 1650s, the "imperial moment of the English Republic," state interests in empire building had invoked the ideology of Roman imperialism and Elizabethan adventurism to formulate new understandings of England's wealth and conquest in the terms of maritime trade.[7] The fashioning of English national identity through literary explorations of Greece and Rome has been well documented.[8] With the Restoration of the Stuart monarchy, and in the context of marked political and economic transition, comparisons to Augustan Rome continued to be made as a part of ongoing efforts to reconcile the legacy of an inherited *translatio imperii* with the changing economic realities of a globalized, and China-centered, long-distance trade. An alternative to the customary examples of Greece and Rome, China's ancient yet modern civilization, and its recent dynastic upheaval, offered new incentives and ways of conceptualizing the forms and social consequences of empire. Although the Ming dynasty may have fallen, the Chinese Empire was far from obsolete. One only had to look to the intense competition between European powers over accessing Asian markets to realize China's far-reaching influence. Along with the increasing importance of the East and West Indies trade to English maritime ambitions, a new form of global empire was emerging, one based primarily on economic dominance rather than territorial conquest.[9] China held a special place in the canon of exemplary antiquity used to model the virtues and values of this new empire; the force of historical continuity and cultural preservation attached to the "Famous Example" of Chinese civilization also shaped English notions of honor and heroism.

China was all the more fascinating and contradictory an example of the "greatest kingdom now known in the world"[10] because not only had it been conquered and yet prevailed, but it also appeared to lack the heroic virtue expected of a global power—the heroism that Spinoza and other European writers instead associated with the "Courage of the Tartars." The warring character of the Tartars had long signaled moral danger in the Western imagination. In the early modern period, *Tartars*, a possible corruption of *Tatars*, the word used for the Eastern neighbors of the Mongols, broadly referred to nomadic nations of northern and central Asia; they were often conflated with Saracens, Moors, or Turks, all neighboring threats to Western Christendom, and tied mythically to northern Scythia as well as to the lost Ten Tribes of the Jews. In histories of China, they signified a formidable race of Mongols who united various Scythian nations and whose conquests, spanning Europe and Asia, made legends of Tamerlane, his successors, and his competitors; these khans, or "Chams," could be traced up to the current Manchu emperor of China.[11] Throughout the eighteenth century, the Tartars (very broadly defined) were thus viewed with a mixture of ambivalence and admiration. Edward Gibbon, in *The History of the Decline and Fall of the Roman Empire*, considered them to be insolent barbarians, compared with the "civilized nations of the globe ... the manners and opinions of a European or a Chinese"; yet even he acknowledged, along with the likes of Spinoza, the Tartars' "invincible courage and rapid conquests."[12] Neither Tartars, considered barbarians in essence, nor Chinese, civilized yet corrupt, were in the 1640s obvious models of heroism. Yet the language of heroic virtue was used to frame their relationship as a contrast between two types of national character, masculine hero and feminine victim, even as these divisions were themselves subject to change.

Well before Gibbon's chronicle of Rome, the examples of Chinese civilization and Tartar barbarism were, as an interrelated unit, incorporated into lessons of classical antiquity and the fate of empires' rise and decline. The idealization of China, despite its recent defeat, posed numerous contradictions to Western tenets of heroic virtue. Among these was the expression of its effeminacy. The trope of the masculine Tartar was commonly paired opposite that of the soft, or effeminate, Chinese; and yet, since the Chinese were understood to assimilate their conquerors, the ambiguity surrounding the true winners and losers of this epic conflict generated less an opposition than a complex negotiation of the uncertain boundaries between civilization and barbarism, effeminacy and masculinity. More often than not, Tartars were seen to have liberated China from the tyranny of its effeminate mandarins and eunuchs. In the comparisons with Greece and Rome that ran throughout seventeenth-century histories of China's conquest, Tartars typically incarnated the martial virtues of Western antiquity. According to the Dutch writer Johann Nieuhof, Tartars "for Antiquity go beyond all other people in Asia."[13] The bishop Juan de Palafox y Mendoza's history of the Tartar conquest claimed that "The *Tartars* are like the men in ancient times, according to the notion we have of them, as plain, blunt persons, averse to all Luxury and Pride." The "prince" of the Tartars performed "Heroick Actions" that recalled a number of past conquerors: "*Alexander,* the two *Caesars, Julius,* and *Augustus* ... young Xunchi; who for his Valour may justly be parallell'd with all these *Hero's,* and like them seems to have been born only for Victory and Triumph."[14] In his *History of the Two Tartar Conquerors of China*, the Jesuit Pierre-Joseph d'Orléans argued that the Chinese rarely ever exhibited "that constancy which we admire in the ancient Romans"; he praised one Chinese rebel, an exception to the rule, for "resolution [as] more akin to the firmness of ancient Rome than to the effeminacy of the Chinese."[15] Comparisons with Rome made Asiatic history legible, even as these associations could, of course, be made in a number of ways. A fallen China was at once seen to be following the path of Roman decadence; at the same time, the continuation of the Chinese Empire, under Tartar-Manchu rule, resembled the greatness of the Roman Empire; and the extensive conquests of Tartars, stretching from Persia to Muscovia and the eastern European states, paralleled Roman territorial ambitions and acquisitions.[16]

In chronicles of conquest and empire, opposing sides are traditionally assigned to the forces of heroic virtue and civilized effeminacy, a duality seen to drive the cycles of empires' rise and fall. Martial prowess founds and extends the reach of civilizations; in turn, ruinous overindulgence in material comforts necessitates dynastic change, or the destined end of one reign and start of another. The familiar pattern of demise makes effeminacy a negative structuring force in narratives of conquest as well as in discourses of Orientalism. In the early modern period, "effeminacy" primarily signified a gendered form of moral decay: for example, the weakness or "softness" of male sovereignty corrupted by luxury, and hence neglectful of martial discipline and the vigilant defense of territory. Along these lines, the empires of Rome and Turkey were each thought to have collapsed due to their rulers' excessive sensuality. Moral decay offered a powerful, if often inaccurate or insufficient, explanation of large-scale change; both cause and symptom, effeminacy embodied cultural degeneracy, with particular reference to Eastern civilizations. Critiques of Asiatic luxury and the foreign contagion of the East date back to the Roman writings of Sallust, Livy, and Pliny.[17] In the long history of Orientalism laid out by Edward Said, the construction of an innately feminine and enervating East can already be seen in ancient Greek characterizations of Persia. Following Said, other scholars have made the case for an explicitly Orientalist interpretation of effeminacy with respect to nineteenth-century colonial encounters between East and West. Whereas Vinay Lal identifies "the trope of effeminacy, the first element of an Orientalist grammar of India," Revathi Krishnaswamy describes effeminacy as a "critical and contentious idiom through which the racial and sexual ideologies of empire are mediated." Such an "idiosyncratic and contradictory construct," she argues, was used to explain India's loss of independence and to consolidate racial and linguistic stereotypes, as well as subvert these same concepts. By this token, the figure of the "effeminate Bengali" was not the opposite of Victorian manliness, but rather a mimicry of that ideal—"at once resemblance and menace," to borrow the postcolonial critic Homi Bhabha's phrase.[18] As these studies suggest, effeminacy and masculinity have historically been products of intercultural encounters at the imperial frontier; in these physical and conceptual border zones, gender forms and racial identities are deeply entangled in ways that smack of Orientalism and yet defy a simple East-West or feminine-masculine binary.[19]

The example of China reveals two facets of effeminacy that distinctively shaped the orientalism of the early modern period: female effeminacy (gendering of women) and cultural effeminacy (gendering of empire). Both were ambiguous rather than purely negative traits. Invocations of effeminacy in the seventeenth century did look back to a bygone era of heroic virtue and of ancient civilizations to gauge the progress of empire and morality in the current day.[20] The fateful combination of eroticism and violence which constituted the effeminacy of dissolute rulers was a long-standing trope of early modern orientalism that would carry over into the nineteenth century.[21] The key features of oriental effeminacy—harems, seraglios, eunuchs, despots in drag, extravagant courts, extreme scenes of mass death, and male and female suicide rooted in the distant past—were also major components of theatrical spectacle and the dramatization of empires' rise and fall in Restoration England.[22] And yet effeminacy in its early modern form was also a more fluid concept and part of a different discursive field than its nineteenth-century counterpart in that masculinity was not yet strictly opposed to femininity; nor was effeminacy limited to its later associations with homosexuality or male same-sex desire. While the verb *effeminate* designated the act of "making into a woman," *an effeminate* could refer to a sodomite as well as an epicure. The two were linked through a spectrum of attributes (lascivious, covetous, fornicating, sinful, lustful) often appearing in conjunction as vices in religious tracts of the period.[23] The broader range of moral decay included military emasculation, excessive consumption, and immoderate heterosexual passion. The female body thus played an important role in signaling effeminacy; effeminate sensuality could be expressed either through consorting with women or by imitating them through adopting traditionally feminine modes of dress or appearance. Although largely used to describe men, *effeminacy*, interestingly enough, could also apply to women who did not live up to an accepted standard of femininity. Given its range of meanings, *effeminacy*, by the mid-eighteenth century, acted as "civilization's barometer," to borrow literary scholar Felicity Nussbaum's apt phrase.[24] An Amazon is most obviously a figure of masculinity. The performativity of masculinity along the vectors of gender and culture, however, allows us to reconsider the Amazon in terms of female effeminacy. This unlikely identification of masculine female with feminine male is, I contend, one of the surprising effects of performing China in early modern England.

In the Restoration period, the vocabulary of oriental effeminacy was used to interpret the "grand spectacle" of Chinese history and the heroism of the Chinese in relation to the Tartars in a number of ways. The sensational histories of China's fall and their theatricalization by Elkanah Settle's *The Conquest of China*, both examined in this chapter, illustrate these two modes of the gendering of imperial conflict. Eastern customs and manners helped shape conceptualizations of heroic virtue in the mutually informing genres of theater, history, and travel writing. Together these genres produced a translation event out of a contemporary world news event, the defeat of the Ming dynasty.[25] This chapter is as much an interpretation of how Chinese history was theatrically staged according to conventions of heroic virtue as it is an interpretation of how historical sources themselves incorporated spectacle into their translations of Chinese empire. The accuracy of the translations is not of primary concern here; rather, what is important to examine is the Chineseness that emerges from literary and theatrical technologies of performing China. China's resilience was a feature of empire that implied a new type of heroism, one that entailed a subtle rewriting of conventions of masculinity through blending competing binaries and constructions of East and West, male and female, Tartar and Chinese, ancient and modern.

In examining this performance of Chineseness, I focus on how effeminacy appears to be an alternative to rather than an opposite of heroic virtue in the cases of the two quite different hethnic figures examined here: first, the fighting Amazon, and second, the sage Confucius. Both are unlikely heroes that exemplify the resiliency of the Chinese Empire and address the questions posed by seventeenth-century historians: How can an ancient empire be preserved in the modern era, and what role does effeminacy play in its downfall? The appeal of the contradictory power of warrior women, who invert gender roles but embody the valor that their men seem to lack, along with Chinese philosopher-kings, effeminate yet able to Sinicize conquering Tartars, reflects the crisis of heroism in the commercializing culture of Restoration England. Foreign empires, and the exemplar of China, captured the ideals of a heroic past and the possibility of a living, breathing antiquity. In turn, the shifting values and generic features of English heroic drama were intimately tied to performances of cultural difference, the East, and China in particular.

Translating the Amazon

The female masculinity of Amazons, whose warring actions flout decorum and accepted standards of femininity, has long been used to map the shifting borders of empires; women warriors signal resilience in the face of defeat and as such make tragic heroes of the losers of epic battle.[26] Located in the border zones and liminal spaces of imperial frontiers, they are also a product of intercultural encounter and, hence, translation. The term *Amazon* itself mediates racial and sexual ideologies of empire. By Roman accounts, the word signified, from the Greek, *a* (without) + *mazos* (breasts), reflecting the widespread myth of one-breasted fighters. Such a vision of misshapen femininity has since been disproved by archaeologists and historians who have tracked the etymological origins of the term to the Old Persian *hamazan* (warrior) or *Amazigh*, what Libyans called themselves before being renamed Berbers by the Greeks.[27] When on the losing side of history, what one calls oneself can be lost as well. What once meant warrior comes to signify an anomaly of gender or civilization; and as the multiple translations of the term reveal, the clashes of cultures in the conquest encounter are inscribed within the Amazon's sexual and cultural ambiguity.[28] Therein lies her continuing appeal: embedded histories of epic loss are presented in the figure of the Amazon as singular examples of resilience, resistance, and transgression within bounds. The English literary and dramatic tradition of the fighting Amazon was built on her appearances in ancient Greek histories and early modern romances alike.[29] In the exempla of Elizabethan sexual politics, she evoked a virtue/virago ambivalence that was mobilized positively and negatively throughout the eighteenth century. A trope of actual and idealized female power, the Amazon signaled above all the culturally unknown, referencing remote regions of the world, from Scythia to South America, to enact the anxieties, dangers, eroticism, and virtues of the female as foreigner. In their respective studies of foreignness and female sexuality in Renaissance literature, Kim Hall and Ania Loomba have powerfully shown the affiliation of unruly women with foreign geographies.[30] Furthermore, Renaissance scholar Kathryn Schwarz calls the colonizing reach of the Amazonian imaginary "a fantasy pursued by its own potential literalization; using Amazons metaphorically or referring to them historically coincides with looking for them in Africa or Asia or America or Northern Europe."[31] In other words, the Amazon's association with a given geographic locale maps it as a place of mythic, and likely futile, resistance against all odds.

Heroes are made in the ideological vicissitudes of translation. Indeed, the existence of actual fighting women in various parts of the globe only augments the heroic mystique of the figural Amazon. I suggest that these exceptional women, situated between myth and history, are effeminate in two senses of the term: their surfeit of courage makes them anomalous women at the same time that it compensates for the lack thereof in their male counterparts; their anomalous gender reinforces the effeminacy of the men, as well as a nation in need of strong leadership.

Significantly, although Amazons were not typically associated with China, they were used to interpret a historical tradition of Chinese women warriors, including legends like that of the third-century sergeant's daughter Hua Mu Lan, who fought alongside their military husbands or male family members in defense of regional or dynastic terrain, sometimes earning respected positions of military leadership.[32] Western accounts of China's conquest made special mention of a female general of Sichuan Province who defended the Ming reign against the Tartar-Manchu invaders and who was a likely historical source for the lead female character of Elkanah Settle's *Conquest of China*.[33] In his *History of the Two Tartar Conquerors of China*, for example, d'Orléans tells of a "Queen" akin to "the most renowned of Amazons" reigning in the mountains of "Suchuen" who fought on behalf of her son, too young to bear arms.[34] This history and numerous others followed the lead of Martino Martini's influential *De bello tartarico*, a description of the events surrounding the 1644 Manchu overthrow based on his own missionary experiences in China. The publication went through seven editions in Latin and translations into nine other European languages, totaling at least twenty-five editions and translations by the end of the seventeenth century.[35] In a section on the history of "Tartar" incursions entitled "The valiant Amazon of China," Martini describes an extraordinary female effort to defend the Ming regime:

> Amongst other Commanders which came with succours to their Prince, there was one *Heroick* Lady, whom we may well call the *Amazon* or *Penthesilean* of *China*. She brought along with her three thousand, from the remote Province of *Suchuen* [Sichuan], *carrying all*, not only Masculine minds, but mens habits also, and assuming Titles more becoming men than women. This noble and generous Lady gave many rare proofs of her courage and valour, not only against these *Tartars*, but also against the Rebells which afterwards [rose] against their Lord and Emperour.[36]

The language of heroic romance ("heroick lady," "princess," "valiant Amazon," "Penthesilea of China") juxtaposes a Western, mythic, literary past with recent Chinese history, making it at once exotic and familiar.[37] At the same time, the admiration for "Masculine" female valor and the momentary appearance of three thousand cross-dressed women in the text renders China's male leadership negligible, despite the ongoing need to protect the country against enemies domestic and foreign. In this instance, the invocation of female masculinity, through Western tropes of virtue and the Amazon, reflects ambivalently upon the idea of Chinese heroism and national character. In the broader representational scheme of the conquest of China, these Amazons are emblems of female effeminacy—exceptional women and exceptional heroes—that inadvertently reinforce the strength of the Tartars over the Chinese.

With a few exceptions, Chinese heroism is absent from Martini's account. Instead, we read of the heroic virtue of the Tartars, which in turn depends not on its opposition to or exclusion of Chinese weakness, but rather on incorporating the Chinese into an idea of successful conquest. The Tartars, given the outcome of the conflict, more apparently embody the noble qualities befitting conquerors. Notably, the most prominent Tartar in Jesuit histories of the conquest is neither the founder of the Manchu state nor his successors, the emperors of the Qing dynasty, but rather an "uncle" and "tutor" to the sovereign named Amavan or Amavangus.[38] The translation history of his name across multiple languages—Manchu, Chinese, Latin, and English—links him etymologically, associatively, and ideologically to the Chinese warrior woman named Amavanga featured in Elkanah Settle's play. His place in the dense genealogy and transliterated names of Manchu ruling succession thus frames the conquest as mutually beneficial to Tartar and Chinese. As roughly outlined by Martini, northern tribes had for decades made repeated incursions into China from the frontier zones, further taxing a Ming central government already rife with corruption and internal conflicts over its bureaucracy of eunuchs and scholarly mandarin officials. Having developed a military governing system organized under eight banners across tribal and ethnic divides, the Jurchen tribal ruler and self-titled khan, Nurhaci, founded the Manchu state in 1616 and claimed the Chinese reign title of Tianming (Thienmingus), or Heavenly Mandate.[39] His grievances against the Ming court included the murder of his father and grandfather and the instigation of border wars that continued under his successor Abahai, or Hung Taiji, who was also known by two reign titles—first, Tiancong (Thienzungus) and, later, Chongde (Zungteus)—to mark his initiation of the Qing dynasty in 1635–36. Upon Abahai's death in 1643, a year before the conquest of China, his six-year-old son Fulin, or Shunzhi (Xunchi), was declared the first emperor of the Qing empire. Mentored for several years by Abahai's brother Dorgon (Amavangus), Shunzhi reigned from 1644 to 1661.[40] Although the process of quelling Ming loyalists in the south continued after Shunzhi's death into the reign of the next emperor, Kangxi (K'ang-hsi), by the early 1700s Taiwan and Tibet were taken, and a century of Qing imperial expansion would also claim inner and central Asia.[41]

Martini not only presents these key events and historical figures in Latinized form, as per custom, but he gives particular preference to Dorgon, or Amavangus, for his combination of military prowess over and humane treatment of the Chinese. The Tartar is heroic because he appeals to both Tartar and Chinese, and he embodies both sides in Western histories of the conquest.[42] A prince and warrior in his own right, Dorgon/Amavangus is credited with implementing the new Qing government and welcoming foreigners into the court, while continuing the old Ming institutions. His greatness as a Tartar leader, and his embodiment of the masculine traits of heroic virtue, are memorialized by Martini in the following:

> He was a Man to whom the *Tartars* owe their Empire in *China*, and such an one as whom both *Tartars* and *Chineses* loved and feared, for his prudence, Justice, humanity, and skill in Martial affairs. . . . But I cannot doubt, but the death of *Amavangus*, must needs endanger the *Tartarian* Empire, and bring all their affairs into great disturbance; for they will hardly find a Man so beloved, feared, and expert in all Military Discipline and Government as he in effect shewed himself to be.[43]

In his masculine roles of "uncle, tutor, father," Amavangus wields a long list of heroic attributes, including counsel, prudence, fortitude, fidelity, reason, justice, humanity, and martial skills. His efforts to fight rebels, quell the lingering Ming resistance, and solidify the Manchu reign are lauded in a number of other Jesuit writings as well.[44] It would appear that China's loss is tempered by its gain of a humane ruler whose fighting prowess is balanced by his benevolence.

To return, then, to the question of translating the Amazon, the blending of Tartar and Chinese into a harmonious entity of the Qing empire takes place at the level of discourse, through multiple translations of the trope of the Amazon. According to Martini, the Tartar word *Amahan* and its Chinese equivalent *Amavang* signify "Father-King." From a linguistic point of view, *ama* does mean father in Manchu, while *han* has no clear meaning. However, *vang*, the seventeenth-century Latin spelling for *wang*, denotes "king" in Chinese, allowing for the possibility of a hybrid, Manchu-Chinese name that underscores the fusion of the two peoples into a heroic ideal.[45] In his foundational study of European news sources for China's conquest, Edwin Van Kley points out that the English playwright Elkanah Settle borrows his characters' Latinized Chinese names (Theinmingus, Zungteus, Amavanga) from Martini's account and a number of texts that followed its lead.[46] As we see, then, Settle re-genders the historical *Amavangus* into the character of the woman warrior *Amavanga*, a regional queen of China disguised as a man to defend the ailing empire. Drawing on the Western literary tradition and foreign-sounding name of the *Amazon*, Chinese legends of warring femininity, and Jesuit idealizations of Tartar masculinity, Settle creates in Amavanga a heroine who historically embodies both sides of the conflict, Chinese and Tartar, as well as both sexes.

The manipulation of these names and details in Western accounts was meant to justify the Tartar invasion by establishing China's effeminacy and a gendered division between Tartar and Chinese. At the same time, histories of the conquest

Ming Dynasty female warrior Shen Yunying, portrait by Ren Xiong included in *Ren Weichang Yuyue xianxian xiang*, ca. 1856. Courtesy of the Ricci Institute for Chinese-Western Cultural History, University of San Francisco.

tended to emphasize the continuity between the Ming and Qing dynasties and the enduring spirit of the Chinese under foreign rule. It would seem that one way of imagining the longevity and extended antiquity of China's empire was to balance its defeat by masculine northerners with its ability to Sinicize its enemies.[47] The translations of the Amazon across the genres of history and romance, stage and text, culture, traditions, and genders form a palimpsest of overlapping significations. At its heart is the mythic invocation of female difference and cultural resilience.

Tartar warriors and the conquest of China. Engraving included in Juan de Palafox y Mendoza, *Historia de la Conquista de la China por el Tartaro*, 1670. Reproduced by permission, © The British Library Board.

Structures of Effeminacy in *The Conquest of China*

Elkanah Settle's *The Conquest of China*, in borrowing and manipulating the events of the 1644 Manchu invasion, reinvents the language of effeminacy to make heroes of the Tartars, and even of the Chinese. With notable exceptions, the Chinese characters convey the excessive passions of oriental effeminacy. They are moral degenerates and stock Restoration types: a weak king who cannot protect the empire, his tyrannical daughter, the princess Orunda, who is in love with a

Chinese general Quitazo; he is in turn caught between court politics and his love for the virtuous Alcinda. While Orunda must choose a husband to become the future ruler of China, the royal plan is thwarted by a horrifically violent usurper to the throne named Lycungus. On one hand, China's internal corruption makes heroes of the Tartars, who had long connoted nomadic freedom and premodern courage—warring masculinity at the edges of civilization. The plot of the play is in fact premised upon the presumed binary between masculine Tartars and effeminate Chinese, such that the eventual marriage between its two heroes, the Chinese warrior queen Amavanga and the Tartar prince Zungteus, consolidates the empires and hence meets a theatrical as well as ideological denouement. On the other hand, although the play ultimately foregrounds the heroic masculinity of Zungteus—whose name, as discussed above, refers to the Qing founder Abahai—the process of his ascension to power reveals the enduring virtues of a female-gendered China.[48]

The consolidation of male virtue in the play is dependent upon the spectacle of Amazonian female masculinity; as such, female effeminacy is crucial to the play's performance and plot. To begin with, Settle's China lacks a male successor to the throne, which creates an opening for the virtuous outsider Zungteus. Secretly raised in China and enamored with a regional Chinese queen named Amavanga, he is already torn between two allegiances. Unbeknownst to him, Amavanga leads a double life in the guise of a man, defending China in place of its effeminate and ineffectual "King." The text identifies her as a "Queen of a Province in China, in the Disguise of a Soldier," and in this capacity she emerges as the most heroic, and arguably masculine, presence in the play. She is also an Amazonian exemplar in a number of ways. As discussed above, her name alone offers an historical and ideological palimpsest; moreover, her female masculinity is ambivalently heroic—it highlights the effeminacy of China's male rulers and injects a dose of romance into the conquest plot.[49] Initially, though, Amavanga, not Zungteus, embodies dominant masculinity. She makes the first epic entrance, and her legendary feats of conquest are recounted thus by Zungteus:[50]

[I]n a Masc'line shape
She from her Father's Court made an Escape.
Amongst the thickest dangers still she flew;
And Honours reap'd where they were great, and new.
Her own disguise could not her Glory's shroud:
Fighting, she spoke in Thunder from her Cloud.

And.when the Conquering *Chanquincungus* stood
On her dead Brothers Neck, his yet warm blood
She at one stroke Reveng'd; and at one blow,
A Rebel, and his Army, did overthrow.[51]

Performances of heroic virtue on the Restoration stage regaled audiences with marvelous feats of combat and chivalry by a tormented hero who attempted to protect simultaneously his conflicting loyalties to romantic love, honorable friendship, and the fate of the nation. And yet, female characters, through their embodiment of passion and morality, whether noble or ignoble, tested men to enable them to rise to their true greatness, and thus enabled the development of the hero's morality.[52] Here, Amavanga's masked femaleness appears not to detract from her extraordinary courage. A Chinese Amazon in drag, she fits within a Western literary tradition of exemplary female fighters who embody both love and martial glory—what literary critic Dianne Dugaw in her work on women warriors has called a "hermaphroditic ideal." The hermaphroditic hero poses only a limited disruption of the patriarchal system that ultimately dictates the terms of battle; her transvestism allows her to be masculine without being unwomanly, such that the "putting on of manliness" adds novelty to virtue without threatening the socially accepted stability of the actual woman underneath. She does not necessarily desire to be a man, but, more typically, aspires to the masculinized ideal of honor.[53]

The performance context underscores the importance of the female body to ideas of effeminacy that linked gender and cultural character, and female with cultural effeminacy. It also makes evident that understandings of China were built upon more than discursive representations; foreign histories were performed on the Restoration stage through innovations that included costume, music, and set designs, on the one hand, and the novelty of female actresses, on the other. Women's novel presence on stage powerfully reinforced the novelty of Chinese history. If Chineseness on the page was a question of female effeminacy and gender experimentation, on stage it was also a matter of displaying the new technology of the female body. Restoration conquest plays, which codified cultures according to masculine and feminine virtue, used Eastern exoticism as an excuse to indulge in the new performance styles. In the case of Settle's *Conquest of China*, Amavanga's transvestism, when enacted on the Restoration stage, relied upon the audience's recognition of the "authentic" sex beneath the male costume. The first legal appearance of actresses on stage marked a shift from cross-dressed boys playing women's parts to women representing women—ironically, often in the form of the cross-dressed woman. So-called breeches roles were designed to show off the female body through the baring of legs and breasts and the eventual uncovering of disguised identities.[54] The competition between theaters led to what historian Judith Milhous has called "escalating spectacles of feminine sexualities"; or, as Restoration theater scholar Elizabeth Howe puts it, "With real women and elaborate scenery at its disposal, the restoration theatre could attach visual detail to a suggestive description."[55]

Recognizing the crossed-dressed woman as such entails a voyeuristic investment in the "true" woman behind the performance. In the epilogue to *The Conquest of China*, for example, Mary Lee, a popular "breeches role" actress who played Amavanga in the 1675 performance (a year before the play's publication), chided the audience for not appreciating female actors' use of their sex appeal to reform the homoerotic gaze of the pre-Restoration theater audience:[56]

> Did not the Boys Act Women's parts Last Age?
> Till We in pity to the Barren Stage
> Came to Reform your Eyes that went astray,
> And taught you Passion the true English Way.

In the play, when Amavanga begs to be disqualified from a duel against her lover Zungteus, her adviser Vangona argues that a woman should all the more pursue great deeds because "from a woman [they are] more rare, and new" (3.1.25). The newness of which she speaks augments her heroism and infers the presence of the female actor on stage. In the epilogue, amid her flirtatious complaints about being hectored by male audience members, Lee's use of sexual innuendo—"[I] took all shapes, and used most means to Please"—highlights the combined novelties of gender, sexuality, and cultural difference on the English stage. While breeches reveal the "real" woman underneath, the identity of this lesser sex is also coded Chinese in the world of Settle's *Conquest of China*. Ultimately, making a spectacle of Chinese history entails the gendering of Tartar/Chinese cultural difference as much as performing the distinction between the male and female sex.

The play, as it works to unveil its heroine as a woman beneath the disguise, underscores the paradox of female effeminacy: if to effeminate is to "turn woman," the cross-dressed woman turns woman through her eventual transformation from warrior to wife. In that she simultaneously turns woman and becomes representative of China, the process of layering sexual upon cultural difference makes a spectacle of Chinese effeminacy. The plot of Settle's play portrays China as an effeminate culture through a progressive disavowal of female masculinity.

It is the Amazonian heroine who makes visible the overlapping performances of gender and heroic virtue. By praising Amavanga's heroism, Zungteus borrows her glory—courage, masculinity, furious eloquence, fidelity, and vengeance—to reflect his own. The performative power of recognition confers authority upon him who speaks it, and the Restoration hero's "linguistic energy," to borrow literary scholar Eugene Waith's phrase, holds a privileged place in a discursive world where words speak as loud as actions.[57] Zungteus's father, Theinmingus, king of the Tartars, thus initially approves of his son's complimentary rhetoric:

> Praising a Foe in such a stile as this,
> You prove your glory in describing his.
> Heroe's from Heroe's tongues, no Fame e're lost:
> They give praise frankest who deserve it most. (3.1.23)

If recognition carries with it the power of heroic virtue, then misrecognition diminishes one's virility. Although Zungteus acknowledges Amavanga's past history of conquests, he remains ignorant of her current guise and her dual identity as his foe and lover. Zungteus's own heroic status is assumed only at the moment of Amavanga's apparent death, when he publicly denies the greatness in her that he previously acknowledged.

The moment of sexual crisis comes when Amavanga is chosen to represent China to end the Chinese-Tartar war by fighting Zungteus one-on-one. Upon being fatally wounded in the duel, Amavanga reveals her identity in her dying breaths to Zungteus, and he proceeds to gain the weak king of China's esteem by denying the legitimacy of the duel. His immediate call for a rematch reveals more than his loss of a lover or his impropriety over having killed a woman; his indignation masks an anxiety that he has admired a false man, or inauthentic hero. "I scorne to wear a Crown so cheaply bought," he declares; "Choose out a Manly Hand to Guard your Throne" (4.1.40). The king of China, impressed by such a display of chivalric honor, refuses the challenge, citing the Tartar's "Vertue so Sublime" and "mind so God-like, great" (4.1.40). Ultimately China's desperate need for male authority only makes Amavanga's performance of masculinity futile and inadequate, for she will never be a man. In turn, Zungteus achieves virtuous masculinity only by differentiating himself through a process of recognizing and then disavowing her female masculinity. Tartar and Chinese assume sexually representative identities in the course of Amavanga's demise and Zungteus's rise to fame. As the Tartar king Theinmingus insists, Tartars embody warlike masculinity, and China, effeminacy. When Theinmingus overhears Zungteus praising his dead love and contemplating suicide to atone for the murder, he reprimands his son in the name of masculinity:

> Traytor! Is this a Language for my Son?
> Wher's all the martial *Tartar's* Greatness gone?
> Such an Effeminate design will shame
> Thy sleeping Ancestors untainted Fame.
> This Action, thy more Masc'line mothers Ghost
> Will Blush at, and disturb her Crumbling Dust. (4.1.43)

Theinmingus reinvokes "revenge," "duty," "honour," "nature's laws," and the call to filial duty into the scheme of Zungteus's lovelorn vocabulary. Zungteus, as he adopts his new heroic status, decides to follow "nature's laws" and side with his father and his "new Mistress, Victory; / Ruine and Blood shall all soft thoughts remove, / I'le be as great in Vengeance as in Love" (4.1.44). By taking on a new "mistress," Zungteus both accepts Amavanga's death and refuses to recognize their past relationship as one between peer warriors. To assume "the martial Tartar's Greatness" and conquer China is to consolidate the division of cultural stereotypes, Tartar and Chinese, along the lines of male and female, conqueror and conquered.

In the end, the Tartar achieves eminent heroism through the civilizing force of the warrior woman. Amavanga miraculously returns from the dead. She attributes her revival to "God that smil'd on Love" and memorializes her fighting days in terms of love's conquest: "I have your Love and Honour try'd: / And without blushing own their Conquering Pow'rs: / Accept a Heart by Fate and Justice your's" (5.2.67). Her final stance falls short of the fighting spirit she displayed at the start of the play and the terms of honor by which she dies; her progressive effeminization thus serves not only to consolidate empire, but also to masculinize Zungteus's previously undetermined heroism. Heroic virtue is thus understood as a process of delimiting cultural and sexual character. No matter how masculine her performance, Amavanga is always-already a woman, and a "Chinese" woman at that. After all, as stated in the play, "China's crown has . . . been worn / By lazy kings, with Female spirits born" (5.2.62). The Amazonian heroine pays for an agency that is structurally denied her: if she wins, her love dies; if she loses, her love also dies. And either way, the hermaphroditic balance of man-woman will be upset. Interestingly enough, if we were to follow the historical sources of their names, the marriage of Zungteus and Amavanga would actually be one between kin, as both Abahai and Dorgon were sons of the Manchu progenitor Nurhaci by different mothers, and both were Tartars to begin with. As such, their union incorporates Chinese into Tartar history to a degree that Settle would likely not have planned, but that nonetheless fits the ideological framework of the play.

When in the end Zungteus magnanimously offers to share his throne, his comments are directed ambiguously toward either the Chinese general Quitazo or Amavanga, or possibly both of them:

> Your milder presence will auspicious be
> And civilize my Rougher Tartary
> And whilst the Chinans pay Allegeance here
> I'le teach their softer Natures Arms and war. (5.2.67)

The ambiguity of the address ("Your") creates a moment of productive confusion; in theory, both man and woman could be considered the effeminate party by virtue of their Chinese identity—"soft" and "civilizing," a force of "Nature."[58] The ideological resolution is the injection of Tartar rule of law and masculinity into China through a Tartar who marries his warring nature with China's effeminate civilization by taking a Chinese queen as his wife and offering to share his crown with the Chinese. The mutual submission of Tartar and Chinese to a harmonized unit of husband and wife, respectively, stages a fantasy of legitimate dynastic succession and a reassuring lesson of monarchical stability for an English audience all too aware of its own turbulent political climate. The complementary union is noted by a number of Jesuit accounts, where the balance between Chinese and Tartar is achieved through invoking a harmony of soft and rough and concurrent praise for Tartar militarism and Chinese arts and sciences.[59]

As a Chinese Amazon in drag, Amavanga thus embodies a number of contradictions. By passing for a man, she reveals Zungteus's anxious masculinity; by coming to China's rescue, she highlights the Chinese king's emasculation; by finally giving up warrior status for that of wife, she stands in for an empire that is, to begin with, effeminate and therefore lost. Yet the female masculinity of Amavanga remains heroic despite her submission to the male hero of the play. Becoming a properly feminine female, she assumes the place of Chinese wife to a new Tartar king. The masculine-feminine, Tartar-Chinese divide is meant to uphold the tenets of heroic virtue; and yet, the hybrid forms of female masculinity and the merged Tartar-Chinese lineage of her Amazonian identity—at once sources of novelty and spectacle that drive the play—make an unlikely virtue of Chinese effeminacy. An effeminate China may have been rescued by the Tartars, but at the same time it has virtues of its own to offer. For the quality of "softness" or effeminacy is ultimately also aligned with a virtuous, civilizing force, a force

that is, as I will come back to discuss, also exemplified by another antiwarrior, the ancient philosopher figure of Confucius. Here, civilization and barbarism can be mutually beneficial, and in such a dynamic, heroic effeminacy becomes a necessary condition for aiding Tartar rule and constructing its benevolent imperialism.

Effeminacy, Violence, and the Uses of History

Before turning to the question of Confucius's enlightened effeminacy, we must understand further the despotic dimensions of effeminacy as they were used to characterize Chinese empire. How did ideologically charged translations of China's history of regime change contribute to the production of gendered spectacle in English print and performance culture? In its portrayal of the demise of the Ming regime, Settle's play, as well as its source materials, featured a heroically transgressive warrior woman who appeared in a time of crisis to redress the horrific consequences of her country's ineffectual, morally corrupt, and excessively passionate male leaders. This version of history is perhaps what one seventeenth-century theater commentator had in mind when he summed up *The Conquest of China* in a sentence: "This is also wrote in Heroick Verse, and founded on History."[60] In fact, the play ironically comments on its fidelity to historical truth. In the epilogue, Settle addresses the perception of the play's wild "improbabilities" by referring to the "history and truth" behind their representation:

> Well, a Romantick, and a Slaught'ring Lass,
> With th'Hectours of the Pit, will never pass.
> I said as much; but the Insipit Ass
> Would needs rite on; and told me that his Muse
> Had *History and Truth* for her Excuse. (Epilogue; my emphasis)

However ironically, the poet blames the truth of Chinese history itself for the play's fantastic plotting of gender trouble; namely, the inverted roles of "a Romantick, and a Slaught'ring Lass," a militarily emasculated man and an unfeminine woman. On one hand, that these figures could be attributed to the "history and truth" of Chinese effeminacy underscores the importance of translated histories to English performances of gender and spectacle. On the other, the processes of staging and justifying the plots and techniques of the play according to its Chineseness reveal the extent to which performance technologies also produced, rather than simply reflected, a discourse of orientalism.

As discussed earlier, cross-dressed women on stage were instruments of new stage technologies that created an excuse for heightened effects of horror. The use of cultural alterity as an excuse to put sex and violence on graphic display is most evident in Settle's signature bloody ending, which features the mass suicide of the Chinese king's harem:

> The Scene opens, and is discovered a Number of Murdred Women, some with Daggers in their Breasts, some thrust through with Swords, some strangled, and others Poyson'd; with several other forms of Death. (5.2.60)

The final gruesome display epitomizes the various suicidal tendencies of the Chinese in both the play and in the historical source texts. In fact, the history of China's conquest offers the perfect excuse for excessive violence and the representation of China qua female. This twinned depiction of a passive, feminized Asia awaiting conquest and a violently effeminate Asia inflicting conquest is an orientalist trope of the seventeenth-century dramatic tradition that extends to modern representations of China as an "empire of cruelties."[61] That the climax of the performance is a scene of dead Chinese female bodies shows the abject depths to which the empire has fallen. Its self-inflicted and excessive violence is a sign of China's moral degeneracy: ruthless villains, a weak and suicidal ruler, women who set the example for the men. For, after the king has already ordered his wives to die with him, he cannot bring himself to enact the plan. Only after the women's "honorable" acts of obedience does he follow suit and attempt to be "Manly" (5.2.61). The female members of the court, portrayed as an Oriental harem, accentuate male emasculation, on the one hand, and excessive brutality, on the other; together with the figure of the Chinese Amazon, their femaleness embodies the empire's cultural effeminacy. Each female action forms a turning point in the conquest plot: first, when Amavanga dies; next, when the harem and the king die; and finally, when Amavanga comes back to life.[62] Indeed women's bodies become the physical symbols of national character as well as the effeminacy that denotes the martial weakness of male leaders. As an instrument of stage spectacle, the female body in performance also adds an important, extratextual layer to the images and representation of Chinese effeminacy on the page.

Demonstrations of virtue and constancy by the female characters of heroic tragedies set in the Orient—suicidal wives and suffering women warriors—relied in part on details from travel accounts of Asian women to convey the poet and playwright John Dryden's idea that "women emasculate a monarch's reign" to a particular, orientalized, and sensational extreme.[63] However convenient a means of staging dramatic action, the excesses of oriental effeminacy posed a problem for the refined aesthetics of heroic tragedy. Heroism was thus often a product of translating foreign histories, even as such extreme instances as discussed above threatened to devolve into mere spectacle. Significantly, heroic virtue was a much debated topic in a mid-seventeenth-century England whose turbulent political climate offered little in the way of heroism.[64] Performances of the heroic ideal in Restoration tragedy repeatedly relied on the histories of distant empires—Persia, Morocco, Granada, Mexico, Turkey, China—translated and molded into neoclassical plots and romances imported from France and Spain. From William Davenant's *Siege of Rhodes* (1663) to John Dryden's *Aureng-Zebe* (1675), these epic-themed tragedies marked the return of the Stuart monarchy and the reopening of the theaters by staging themes of conquest and courtly intrigue. The genre featured the magnanimous actions of protagonists who live by the aristocratic codes of love and honor amid the turbulence of revolutions and the uncertain fate of absolute monarchy. With providence on their side, they battle the conniving despots, villains, and villainesses who threatened to undermine the security of the state and its attendant institutions of marriage, hereditary succession, and social hierarchy. The distant locales of Asiatic empires provided a fitting backdrop for the performance of heroic virtue, which, after all, was defined by otherworldly actions: "a habit of mind not attain'd by humane industry, but inspir'd from above, to undergo great actions with an irresistible violence, and a most happy success, which other mortals were not able to perform."[65]

From an ideological perspective, Restoration heroic tragedies unfolded in distant times and places as a means of dramatizing England's court politics and concerns with political succession in a safely disguised form. The exalted themes of epic poetry further manifested English imperial ambitions by recounting the glory and ruin of strategic parts of the globe. As literary scholar Bridget Orr has shown in her important study of theater and empire, Asia was typically depicted in various states of decay, despite the robustness of the East Indies trade in the early modern global economy. Furthermore, the staging of Asiatic themes often mirrored the practices of English court politics: representations of despotism, polygamy, and fraternal strife, for example, resonated with the problems of maternity and succession faced by the Stuart court.[66] More importantly, Orr calls attention to the "double-jointedness" of the plays, which represented growing concerns with overseas trade and international relations as much as they were allegories for English domestic politics. Given this context, the China or the India of a given play was more than merely Englishness in foreign dress; the settings themselves had material substance and import. The vacillation between admiration and repulsion toward these differences comprised a doubled discourse that familiarized the East through conventions of romance and heroism, while differentiating the East through specific customary differences and mercantile interests on the part of playwrights and the English public.[67]

By the same token, China's history cannot be studied in isolation from the context of early modern orientalist representation. My reading of *The Conquest of China* is premised upon recognizing and further exploring multiple vectors of signification, beyond one-to-one comparisons of either China and the West or Occident and Orient. General ideas of oriental effeminacy were constantly being juxtaposed with particular customs and manners of China, just as Chineseness was always a question of both historical discourse and new performance technologies of the Restoration theater. China was not only drawn in comparison with England, but also as part of and yet distinct from the Orient. It was a typical and yet exceptional example of the Orient, and this doubled reference reflects the ambivalence of constructing Eastern morality. As literary critic Robert Markley has argued, it is not that the East was inferior in the orientalist discourse of this period, but that the English attitudes of ambivalence indicated a widespread recognition of China's exemplary empire.[68] Certainly, the plays of the period took enormous creative license in adapting foreign histories for the stage; their fidelity to the source material could easily be dismissed, along with any pretensions to cultural authenticity. And yet, in all its artifice, the theater made explicit the rendering of conquest into a translation-event that layered generic conventions and styles of performance upon cultural particularities to produce an exemplar of China's ancient yet modern history. The figure of Amavanga, for example, complicates a straightforward interpretation of the text as either English political allegory or representation of China. Her double-jointed, cultural hermaphroditism captures the tensions between foreign and familiar that not only characterized Restoration exoticism but were also subject to intense debate and scrutiny. Incorporating other cultures' customary differences into the theater was understandably controversial; when foreign cultures become the models for innovations of the stage and of representations of heroic virtue, they threaten to overpower their subordinate function as examples qua examples.

Although a certain degree of spectacle was built into the idea of heightened chivalric actions, this was by no means intended to justify the type of plebian sensationalism that as a result threatened to contaminate the purity of the poetic ideals of aristocratic, heroic virtue sponsored by the Stuart court. In his larger body of work, Settle had developed to a violent and indelicate degree the principle of the extraordinary upon which heroic drama was originally premised.[69] Three of his heroic plays set in the Orient—*Cambyses, King of Persia* (1671); *The*

Empress of Morocco (1673); and *The Conquest of China*—combined horror with stage spectacle. According to one commentator, "Though Settle was one of the worst poets, he was one of the best planners of spectacles and pomps."[70] Where Settle lacked poetic sophistication, he exploited images of alterity, terror, and oriental effeminacy, in particular the combination of violence and eroticism. The *Empress of Morocco*, which included a Moorish masque with black dancers, a palm tree, and a torture chamber in which the villain Crimalhaz was flayed, established Settle's reputation for working with machinery and initiating early modern versions of the blockbuster and horror genres.[71] While he would go on to gain notoriety for his antipapist writings, staging of drolls and pageants, and vocation as the last City Poet of London, a number of Settle's later works built on his earlier experiments with horror in continuing to feature the fiery demise of ancient empires.[72]

It is no surprise, then, that a series of published attacks by John Dryden and his peers against *The Empress of Morocco* accused Settle of abandoning the high seriousness of poetic form and character development for mere stage acrobatics.[73] Dryden had, of course, been the first to popularize the use of rhymed heroic couplets in dramatic speech to elevate the aristocratic ideal of honor; although considered unnatural and constrained compared to blank verse, the form was thought to require greater compositional skill and, according to Dryden, to stimulate the imagination while reining in excessive flights of fancy.[74] One consequence of the call for heroic plays to "heighten Nature" and rise "above the ordinary proportion of the stage" was the pairing of poetic eloquence with controversial new stage effects.[75] In addition to using the form to convey heroic ideals, contemporary playwrights set the action in locations where the struggles for idealized love and immortality could be spectacularly played out with the rise and decline of ancient empires. As evidenced in literary debates of the period, adapting "forreign stories" into stage spectacle runs the risks of borrowing too little or borrowing too much.[76] The controversies around proper execution of the heroic and the tensions between realistic and fanciful representation turned on the moderation of foreignness in performance. Costumes and ethnographic details of customs and manners appropriated from histories of conquest became a material basis for Restoration spectacle even as they threatened to supercede the very morals these plays sought to communicate.

The much-noted aesthetic failings of *The Conquest of China* were thus not merely incidental to its representation of Chinese history; for its borrowing of Chinese spectacle came at a moment of the demise of a genre of heroic tragedy that had been popular for nearly two decades. It was no coincidence that Settle, a playwright known for horror, would borrow from Chinese history to deliver the latest spectacle of the rise and fall of an Eastern empire. In histories of the conquest, violence and effeminacy were similarly used to explain and justify the conquest of China. While Martini's *De bello tartarico* is considered the primary, legitimate source of Settle's play, the florid account of Juan de Palafox y Mendoza's *The History of the Conquest of China by the Tartars* (1644–49; trans. 1671), considered far less authoritative, even unreliable, nonetheless exemplifies the intersection of spectacle, effeminacy, and violence at work in the theatrical construction of "Chinese" history. Reading these two accounts together and in dialogue with Settle's play reveals how a discourse of China's conquest was compiled through multiple senses of effeminacy; in particular, through theatricalized violence. For both Martini and Palafox, Chinese effeminacy is a matter of "history and truth" that becomes an "excuse" for the intertwined spectacles of violence and gender transgressions that flout decorum and the aristocratic propriety of elevated heroic ideals. As such, these source histories of China's conquest can be seen as literary constructions of ethnographic voyeurism integral to the transformation of foreignness into the stage spectacle for which Elkanah Settle was known.

Written from Puebla, Mexico, and based on news of China received from the Philippines, the work of Palafox attests to the global significance of the fall of the Ming dynasty.[77] Palafox y Mendoza, a Roman Catholic bishop and colonial administrator from Spain, known for his reforming agenda while stationed in New Spain in the 1640s, antagonized viceroys and Jesuit, Dominican, Franciscan, and Augustinian representatives alike—Jesuits, in particular—for his defense of Indian parishes against Spanish colonial interests. His criticism of Jesuit policy extended to their control of the China mission. It was no wonder that he distrusted their idealization of China and constructed a sympathetic account of Tartars as reformers of state corruption: even Spain could learn from their revolutionary actions in dealing with its Ottoman neighbors.[78] His history of China was published only after his death in 1659, whereupon it prompted the Jesuit Pierre-Joseph d'Orléans, a fellow chronicler of China and an ally of Martini, to declare, "I have taken nothing from Palafox. A man who wrote the 'History of China' in Mexico on information sent to him from the Philippines, could not be a good guide to follow."[79] It is not the factual accuracy of Palafox's text that interests me here, however, but rather its negotiation of orientalism and Chineseness. Palafox portrays a Chinese government that had deteriorated due to civil strife in the days leading up to the capture of the capital by the Tartars and culminating in the suicide of the emperor, Chongzhen (Ch'ung-chen), on the imperial palace grounds. In describing "the most Tragical manner that ever Histories related" and "the Tragical *Catastrophe* of this unfortunate Monarch," his text includes a detailed quotation of the suicide note, which incriminated the mandarins as traitors and pronounced the fated end of the royal line.[80] The emperor, who had already beheaded his daughter, untied his hair, covered his face, and hanged himself. Palafox casts the "Scene of Sorrow" in the template of an oriental-tale romance in that the emperor is known as "The Chaste Prince" who never visits his "Seralio" and abstains from drinking wine, with the exception of a draught before his suicide (35). Not only does the luxurious setting of the court mimic conventions of heroic romance, but the love of the empress for her prince is recorded in the idealized language of the genre: "not being able to express the passion of her Soul otherwise than with her Eyes" (34).

What is presented by Palafox as generically oriental gains ideological specificity, though, in the depiction of the Tartar-Chinese dynamic of conquest. A "soft" China has indeed already foreseen its own submission to "rough" Tartar rule: "The Chinese themselves . . . say it was decreed from above, that the Empire of China should be subdued by the Tartars" (54–55). In fact, the Tartar invasion is justified by Chinese effeminacy:

> As for the Chinese in the Southern Provinces, which are more remoate [*sic*] from Tartary, they are soft and effeminate, beyond all the inhabitants of Asia, and that which did produce this effeminacy in them and was a great cause of the ruin and destruction of their Empire, and ever will be to all other states, was the profound peace and security in which those provinces had been so long involved. (157)

The author's preference for the Tartars provides them an explicit rationale for entering the palace; they are saving an oppressed state, and what follows is a markedly legitimate transfer of power: "[T]hough Conquest could never rightly entitle a Rebel to the Soveraignty, yet it might a second time confer the just and lawful possession of *China* upon the *Tartars*" (50). As historian Edwin J. Van Kley has argued, the emperor's suicide note and will presents the Tartar conquest as a fantasy of legitimate succession.[81] Indeed, Palafox makes an even stronger case than other sources for the authorized succession from Chinese to Tartar rule. One of the consequences of his ideological bias is thus the production of Tartar heroism.

In a section entitled "The Virtuous Freedom of the Tartarian Women," Palafox makes further heroes of the Tartars through the signifying bodies of Tartar women who are, interestingly enough, linked to Amazons through their traditional, regional association with Scythia, and hence, Tartary broadly defined. The familiar invocation of Chinese effeminacy and Tartar masculinity illustrates once

The Emperor Chongzhen kills his daughter. Engraving included in Martino Martini, *De bello tartarico*, 1655. Courtesy of the Mandeville Special Collections Library, University of San Diego.

again the importance of the figure of the Amazon and the female body to the textual as well as theatrical performances of China's conquest. For Palafox, Chinese women remain passive and confined, "immured up in prisons, and caves all their lives" (583). Moreover, the practice of polygamy effeminates Chinese men:

> But to speak of the virtues and vices of the Tartars, it must be acknowledged, that they are not so effeminate and sensual as the Chinese. They are not allowed to have so many wives, and do detest and abhor those infamous and abominable vices which are not fit to be named, and yet were frequently committed by the Chinese. (212)

The more wives, the higher the degree of male effeminacy. Conversely, the warring Tartar female signals an innately masculine culture and noble, martial spirit. In other words, Tartar masculinity is in effect demonstrated by the toughness of its women, who shoot, ride, and accompany their husbands in war. Instead of being an exception, the Tartar female is the fighting norm:

> The women there do both spring from, and are made of a warlike bloud and spirit, and from their very cradles they both recreate themselves by the practise of those qualities with which nature hath endued them, and in which they have made themselves by habit, and custom, so expert. (586)

Even European women, according to Palafox, could take a lesson from Tartarian women by actively riding horses instead of being transported by coaches and sedans (584). At the same time, manly Tartar women exhibit a recognizable femininity: "though they affect to ride on horse-back and go to the War, yet are very chast and virtuous" (565). Their comparison to "Amazons" renders them exemplary and heroic by both male and female standards. In an extensive digression on fashion, we read of vests, buskins, shoes, bows, and arrows, "like so many of the ancient *Tyrrhian* Nymphs, *or the Amazonian Scythians*," in explicit contrast with the accoutrements of the oppressed Chinese women (583). It turns out that Tartars treat their women and Chinese women with equal magnanimity by allowing them freedom to choose their own dress.

We can see in the catalogs of clothing the production of a marketable spectacle for Western tastes. Men's and women's bonnets differ by the season; lest men be mocked for wearing bonnets, the reader is told to keep in mind that fashion is relative, and just as mercurial in the West. Fashion, like the treatment of women, is used to gauge the virtue of a culture and nation and to deliver a universal critique of European restrictions on femininity. Yet, lest Tartar "habit and custom" be thought to be superior to Europe's, Palafox turns Tartar exemplarity into a lesson in cultural relativism. Ultimately, what virtuously holds in the heathen East need not apply in the West:

> And therefore, either they are not very blameable to follow those exercises which are not so usual for women in other Countries; or if herein they commit a fault, it ought to be esteemed a very pardonable one.... And as we cannot excuse men, who in effeminacy, and a sollicitous care to trick and trim up themselves, exceed even women: So neither can we approve, that women should surpass men in those Exercises which are more proper for the masculine than feminine Sex, But *usage and custome* may render those things *excusable*, which in themselves are neither contrary to religion or honesty. (584; my emphases)

What is typical in one country might not only be improbable and morally reprehensible in a Western context, but *excusable* when confined to the non-West.

Cultural difference is highlighted, as is the adherence to an implicit universal moral standard ("those things . . . which in themselves are neither contrary to religion or honest"). In short, fighting Tartar women should, in their capacity as Amazonian exemplars, be admired, but not imitated. The ambivalence toward foreign women's freedom illustrates the dialectic between cultural relativism and Christian universalism at work in assessing European values according to an Asian standard. In ethnographic descriptions of Asiatic customs, manners, and fashions, the exemplary masculinity of one culture is evidenced by the fighting spirit of women, much as the observed treatment of women, either enlightened or despotic, is used to define the nature of the government.

In that Chinese effeminacy becomes an explanation for the repeated implosions of the Chinese empire, it also occasions the extreme violence that accompanies the internal demise of the Ming dynasty in multiple historical accounts, including those of Palafox and Martini. The uses of Chinese history for the purposes of horror and theatricalized violence make female bodies the expression of Eastern excess. Such excess, a corollary to China's imperial effeminacy, is most graphically evoked through the violent exploits of the notorious Chinese rebels Li Zicheng (Li Tzu-ch'eng) and Zhang Xianzhong (Chang Hsien-ch'ung), whose roles in usurping the throne contribute to the bloody dramatization of the event. Martini, like Palafox, dramatizes the actions of the bandits, named Ly and Cham, alongside a diagnosis of the illness of the Chinese state when he recounts the mass murder of usurpers "Licungzus" and "Changhienchungus." He spares no detail in describing the "Theater of all . . . Brutalities" and "bloody Tragedy," though he justifies the graphic nature of his first-hand account in terms of bearing witness. On the invasion of "Suchuen" by Changhienchungus, the usurper assumes the character of a "monster" and epic force of nature (300). The narrator-as-witness goes on to give a report of the destruction of cities, rape of women, and general slaughter to an "excess of all inhumanity." A four-day "horrible butchery" of 140,000 soldiers in Sichuan in 1645 concludes with the slaughter of 18,000 students who are lured to the city with the promise of honors for their examination results. Martini provides dialogue for heightened dramatic effect: "*Kill, kill*, saith he, *and cut off all these Rebels*, upon which words, they were all massacred in one day out of the City Wals, in the presence of this bloody monster" (302).

We should keep in mind that it is this violence that necessitates the sudden appearance in the text of three thousand warrior women who accompany the Amazonian "Queen of Suchuen." The vilification of the Chinese bandits, which underscores the empire's effeminacy, provides ready material for Settle's *Con-*

quest of China. In one episode from the play, Lycungus kills "an entire school of 16,000 law students" by setting them on fire, and then proclaims: "And this was all he for that Deed could say, / Learning should light the World, and so did they" (5.2.58). The degree of violence is matched by the badly punned verse: Dryden put it most concisely, "This Elkanah is a very Bloody Poet."[82] *The Conquest of China* indulges in such "bloody poetry" in scenes like the emperor-king's suicide. Faced with the demise of his throne, the king of China writes a will in his own blood that cedes the crown to the prince of Tartary. Moreover, he orders his wives to join him in "authoring" their own deaths (5.2.59). As discussed earlier, the women show their obedience by offering themselves first. Again, their rhyme is as crude as their deed is horrific: "Here take a Flood, / Great Prince, of thy own Dearest Royal Blood" (5.2.61). The spectacular violence of the Restoration stage, while not unique to representations of China, nonetheless enlists details from theatricalized accounts of the Ming conquest to make China at once a typical case of orientalized effeminacy and an exceptional example and counterexample of a fallen empire. Effeminacy is at once the "cause" of the "Ruin and Destruction of [its] Empire" and the reason for its remarkably preserved Confucian antiquity so admired by Jesuits such as Alvarez Semedo and Louis Le Comte.

China was, on one hand, part of an early modern Orient depicted by its despotism; on the other hand, it was an exception to this norm by virtue of its enlightened empire. The comparisons used to render China and Tartary intelligible to Europe cast the East as violent, idolatrous, and improper and at the same time courageous and liberated, such that the foreign exemplar becomes an unstable figure, at once a model to be imitated and avoided. When legends like the Chinese resistance fighter Qin Liangyu are interpreted as "Penthesilean" or "Amazonian," they become hybrid tropes of Greek and Roman antiquity blended with women warriors rooted in the history and truth of other civilizations. In the context of the Restoration stage and the staging of Chinese history, female figures, abject and heroic, are instruments of cultural translation that across the spectrum of Chinese effeminacy capture the contradictions and controversies of representing heroic ideals through new modes of spectacle, excess, and theatrical representations of cultural alterity.

Commerce, Effeminacy, and Heroic Virtue in the Case of Confucius

There is an unlikely counterpart to the Amazon, who straddles borders, blending history with romance, classical virtues with Christian ones, and performing dual standards of gender propriety—the legendary figure of Confucius. For Confucius, too, can be read as a critical node of gendered comparisons between East and West and an exemplar of cultural effeminacy tied to China's novel embodiment of heroic virtue. Heroic virtue was charted by far-flung spatial coordinates, on the one hand, and the performative roles of masculinity, femininity, and effeminacy, on the other. From this structural nexus emerge our two rather anomalous heroes: the philosopher-king and the Amazon, both products of cultural translation whose Chineseness further inflects and shifts the discourse of conventional, classical heroism by testing its limits as well as possibilities. The philosopher, like the female hero, disrupts the conventions of male-dominated epic even as he is meant to affirm the principles of empire. I will show that both figures exemplify a milder, gentler face of empire and provide a heroic, albeit effeminate, alternative to masculine heroic virtue. And both, in their capacity as hethnic exemplars, embody the historical and literary Sinicization of the Tartars to exemplify China's resilience despite its defeat, and its paradoxical status of being a conquered conqueror.

In the Restoration period, the ideals of heroic virtue were imagined as chivalric and aristocratic, rooted in the past, and far from commercial, despite the widespread involvement of aristocrats and landowners in overseas trading, stockholding, and colonizing enterprises.[83] Even Sir William Temple, a famous critic of modern commerce, noted in his writing on heroic virtue that China was the "greatest, richest, and most populous kingdom now known in the world."[84] The commercial interests of the European East India trading companies vying for access to Asian markets were reflected in the world of the theater; between 1660 and 1714, no fewer than forty plays were set in the East.[85] As theater scholar J. Douglas Canfield puts it, "[E]ven as Restoration heroic romance represents a late feudal swan song for aristocratic ideology, in its ubiquitous exotic settings it reveals a subtext of Western Europe's struggle for cultural and economic hegemony."[86] At the same time, importantly, themes of trade were not featured, but rather, as Bridget Orr has pointed out, strategically "effaced" in these plays.[87] While commerce was not explicitly part of the elevated world of heroic tragedy, the goods of the East offered both material and conceptual resources for imagining, and enacting, the future of English empire in contemporary writings on political theory and economic policy equally invested in presenting China's effeminacy as a new model of heroism.

China exemplified an empire of trade for proponents of commerce interested in representing England's island nation and its lack of resources as a strength, rather than a weakness. It was becoming increasingly apparent that the future of the English empire lay in being a powerful middleman. According to the seventeenth-century author and diarist John Evelyn, "That a Spirit of Commerce, and strength at Sea to protect it, are the most certain marks of the Greatness of Empire. . . . That whoever Commands the Ocean, Commands the Trade of the World, and whoever Commands the Trade of the World, Commands the Riches of the World, and whoever is Master of That, Commands the World it self." A relative newcomer to the East Indies trade, England's promise lay in its ability to feed China's appetite for silver: "We, and other Nations have driven the Trade of the *East-Indies*, with his Treasure of the *West*, and, uniting, as it were, Extreams, made the *Poles* to kiss."[88] According to Evelyn, the Romans fell from power once they replaced their maritime pursuits with territorial ambitions. Far from a force of luxury or effeminacy, trade and the early sea voyages of Osiris, Hercules, Cadmus, and Ulysses, he argues, constituted a "Heroic Age." Moreover, it is the East that models this maritime and commercial heroism:

> The *AEthiopians, Persians, Indians* and *Chinezes* (for those of *Tartary,* present, or ancient *Scyths*, come hardly into this Account) may be reckon'd among the nations of Traffic; Especially, the last nam'd, as who are by some thought to have had knowledge of the *Magnet* before the *European*: nay, so addicted were they to *Sailing*, that they invented *Veliferous Chariots* and to Sail upon the Land: It was long since that they had intercourse with those of *Madagascar,* and came sometimes as far as the *Red Sea* with their Wares; and for *Vessels* have to this day about *Nankin, Jonks* of such prodigious size, as seem like *Cities*, rather than *Ships*, built full of Houses, and replenish'd with whole Families: In short, There is hardly a Nation so [made], but, who in some degree, Cultivate *Navigation*, and are Charm'd with the Advantages of *Commerce*.[89]

According to Evelyn, the Tartars are incidental to Chinese maritime greatness: the Chinese were the first to develop ocean navigation. Although the feats of Ming oceanfaring were no longer a priority for the Qing empire as it entered the eighteenth century, the former glory is here invoked to represent a Tartar-Chinese ideal and model of maritime *translatio imperii*.

In addition to modeling an early empire of trade, China exemplified an empire of morality. As with the stage performances of cultural difference, writings on English empire injected new life into the ideals of classical antiquity; they also established a heightened moral and commercial basis for spectacle—a nexus exemplified by China's history. Representations of China's conquest distilled the encounter between Chinese and Tartars as an encounter of two types of virtue, moral and heroic. Tartars had to be rescued from barbarism, and China from effeminacy. And yet, the lack of militarism signaled by effeminacy corresponded with emerging idealizations of commerce and of political stability. In that the Chinese example contested the geographical and gendered parameters of heroic virtue, its hethnic virtues provided a new script for classical antiquity and Christian history, indeed for conjuring the spectacles of the conquest of empires.

Of the numerous categories of "virtue" operative in seventeenth-century England, one in particular—moral virtue—was closely identified with China and garnered it the most acclaim, and most controversy. In his *History of the Great and Renowned Monarchy of China*, the Jesuit Alvarez Semedo wrote of the "many morall vertues, thou wilt find them so far to transcend us therein, that they may be proposed as an excellent patterne, (as also they are a shame) to Christian states."[90] Along a similar vein, Louis Le Comte remarked, "China for two thousand years had the knowledge of the true God, and [has] practis'd the most pure Morality, while Europe and almost all the World wallow'd in Error and Corruption."[91] It is no wonder that this proposition, along with other sections of his *Nouveaux mémoires sur l'état présent de la Chine*, was formally impeached by Sorbonne theological authorities in 1700.[92] In part, such radical accolades reflect the strategic approach of European Jesuits seeking continued support for their overseas missionary policies; they indicate as well the extent to which access to China had become an object of inter-European rivalry and an index, even, of Western progress. Le Comte's English translator grudgingly acknowledges the "indefatigable Industry" of the Roman Catholic Church in China and admires the French missions to the East Indies recently authorized by Louis XIV.[93] At the same time, the discussion of foreign missionary activity in China rouses his patriotic sentiment: "We in England ought not to despair but that Heroic Arthur, who justly vies with the Grand Monarch in the fame of War, will also contend with him for the Glory and Empire of Learning, and dispute every Art and Science."[94] There are several points worth emphasizing here: first, that an "Empire of Learning" is a desirable target of and occasion for invoking expressly English, heroic action ("Heroic Arthur"). The ancient, pre-Saxon King Arthur was in this period considered a new type of Christian hero and icon of English nationalism, here used to counter the figure of the grand monarch of France.[95] As further suggested by Le Comte's translator, the two nations at war, England and France, are nonetheless both Christian forces committed while abroad to civilizing the pagans of India and China and to developing the arts and sciences, as per the Jesuits: the skills of astronomy, geography, and natural history. The East thus provides opportunities for research and civilizational progress as well as what is forewarned as a "fatal Stop" to prosperity given that "the Treasure of Christendom flows daily to the *Banians* and *Genteés*."⁹⁶ The "Empire of Learning" heroically sought after by European nations thus encompasses the riches and knowledge of a pagan East.

Given the highly divergent and contested as well as mediated views on China's superior morality, making an example of Chinese morality required a delicate negotiation of Christian authority. On one hand, the invocation of an "excellent patterne" of Chinese moral virtue transcended and replaced the traditional exemplarity of Christian icons, presenting natural religion as a model for Christianity. It is important to realize that "morality" was considered not only a subset of virtue but also a potential menace to its religious authority and its foundations in Christian scripture. In seventeenth-century discourse, morality could simply be the means or praxis of attaining virtue, as practiced by the ethical teachings of lay people or ancient moral philosophers guided by natural reason. Morality could also be a separate and distinct domain of customs, manners, or teachings outside the realm of religion. A commonly cited example from classical antiquity was Socrates, described in one instance as "the great Author of moral Philosophy, [who] proposed to himself as its end the correcting and regulating of Manners." Such ancient "Heathen Moralists" who "acted under the conduct of meer Reason" were nonetheless faulted for lacking the requisite spiritual devotion to qualify as properly virtuous.⁹⁷ This, of course, raised the conundrum and contradiction of pagan virtue, and with respect to China of a hethnic figure such as Confucius. The terms *ethnic* and *heathnic* were used interchangeably in the early modern period to refer to pagans—non-Christians and non-Jews. Only in the nineteenth century did the idea of ethnicity become secularized to signify, primarily, ethnological, racial, or national—and later, minoritarian—identity groups.⁹⁸ The English word *heathen*, deriving from *heathenic* or *hethnic*, is linked etymologically to Greek, Septuagint translations of the Hebrew *goyim*, or nations of non-Israelites, and through a process of intercultural translation, *heathen* and *ethnic* came to mean non-Christian. By applying the obsolete term *hethnic* to Chinese exemplarity, I highlight the hybridity of religious exclusions used to interpret the alternative model of virtue presented by Confucianism. The Chinese *hethnic* presents a paradox of civilized paganism. *Hethnicity* captures the ambivalence surrounding Chinese morality, which both evoked ancient Greek philosophy and unsettled Christian universalism. With reference to the modern category of ethnicity, it also implicates the emerging hierarchies of civilizational, ethnic, and racial difference in eighteenth-century structures of empire.⁹⁹

The popularization of Confucius in England depended on the Christianization of Chinese antiquity and the exemplification of its empire as one of moral, rather than martial, prowess. The 1691 translation of *The Morals of Confucius*, from the French, included excerpts from *Confucius Sinarum Philosophus*, a Latin compilation and adaptation of Chinese classical writings published by the Jesuits Philippe Couplet, Prospero Intorcetta, Christian Herdtrich, and François Rougemont in Paris in 1687.[100] In the English version, truncated selections of three of the *Four Books*—*The Great Learning*, the *Doctrine of the Mean*, and the *Analects of Confucius*—were accompanied by a life of Confucius and the printing of eighty maxims on practicing personal, familial, and social virtue. Throughout, Confucius is presented as a philosopher-king deserving of continued veneration for his universal wisdom: "This great Man instructed, as well by his Manners and Example, as by his Precepts" (preface). His moral exemplarity turns on his challenge and yet conformity to Christian foundations of virtue. Having been born 551 years before Christ, Confucius is deemed at once more practical than Christ in his teachings of "Natural Reason" and yet part of an emphatically postdiluvian Chinese civilization descended from Shem, a son of Noah. From their earliest days, the Chinese were hence aware of and subject to the Old Testament God; moreover, Confucian morality paralleled and refined Christian virtue in its focus on reason, self-improvement, and moderation. The text echoes the approach of Jesuit accommodationists who favored the integration of Chinese customs with Christian teachings by asserting that classical Confucians, unlike their materialist, neo-Confucian predecessors, believed in the fundamental precepts of an all-powerful creator god, heaven and hell, and the immorality of the soul.[101]

The praise of Confucian rites and tradition that had begun with the missionary work of Matteo Ricci provoked fierce critics within the Jesuit order, such as Niccolo Longobardi, as well as from competing schools of Jansenists, Dominicans, and Franciscans. The issues of the Chinese Rites Controversy, moreover, extended beyond the politics of these theological circles to Enlightenment debates over the possibility of secular ethics represented by China's superior morality. What appealed to Enlightenment philosophers as different as Pierre Bayle, Anthony Collins, Gottfried Wilhelm Leibniz, and Leibniz's student Christian Wolff was the rationality of an ethical system based not exclusively in Christian revelation but in nature or primitive religion. Whereas Bayle, an ardent proponent of the radical thinker Spinoza, might interpret Confucianism as sophisticated atheism, Leibniz, along with the Jesuit Figurists Joachim Bouvet and Jean-François Foucquet, and even earlier, Athanasius Kircher, held that Christian mysteries and spirituality had existed in Chinese antiquity; although assigned different names, the founding figures of these Chinese classics and those of ancient Egypt and Greece were held to be one and the same. The comparisons of Confucius with figures as diverse as Plato, Strato, and Spinoza emphasized his practice of virtue for virtue's sake; and tributes continued to be written into the 1730s and 1740s, most notably by deists like Voltaire, who penned secularized versions of the Jesuits' earlier arguments to promote Chinese morality as the highest form of natural religion.[102] As historian Jonathan Israel has remarked, "Prior to 1750, for several decades, all strands of the Enlightenment (except perhaps the Thomasians) had agreed that classical Chinese society was a model society adhering to an ethical system and awareness of the law of nations equaled by no other. . . . [I]t seemed there was no need of the Gospels, or any revelation, to achieve an orderly, secure society based on wisdom, justice, virtue, and 'le bien public.'"[103]

Even as China in the theatrical performances of the Restoration stage could appear a despotic land of effeminacy, its Confucianism made it an empire of exemplary tradition and good governance. In the English text of *The Morals of Confucius*, Chinese sovereigns are advised to promote virtue by "Example" and by adherence to universal rules of patriarchal familial relations; indeed, Confucius was able to spread his influence such that virtue alone became the defining structure of China's exemplary empire: "For in fine, Virtue is the Basis and Foundation of an Empire, and the Source from whence flows whatever may render it flourishing" (*Morals of Confucius*, 61). What is most striking, though, is the ability of the hethnic, a Christianized heathen, to revise and broaden the discourse of virtue by commingling the domains of the moral and the heroic; the result is the promotion of an "empire of learning" over the traditionally masculine ideals of conquest. If great men like "Alexander, &c. Caesar" had only focused on improving their inner character instead of the self-aggrandizing "Ambitious Designs" of battle, they might have achieved true valor (A2, A3). Indeed, valor is found not in great actions but in tempering violence and submitting the passions to "Right Reason" (73). The "Heroick Generosity" that is posited yokes together different orders of virtue and subjects the terms of conquest to those of charity and self-improvement, as do maxims that restage battle in terms of moral struggle: "That it is necessary to conquer thy self," and to "Combat Night and Day against thy Vices; and if by thy Cares and Vigilance, thou gainst the Victory over thy self, courageously attack the Vices of others" (110, 132, 134–35). Although China is lamented to have long since failed to uphold the standards of virtue established by Confucius, his legacy, the "Doctrine of the Ancients," nonetheless makes China a universal exemplar of idealized antiquity and ideological utility.

Crucially, in its promotion of the Chinese classics, *The Morals of Confucius* incorporates the example of China into contemporary debates in England that pitted ancient virtue against the corrupting forces of modernity. Most notably, Sir William Temple, known for his staunch defense of ancient learning and interest in Eastern civilizations, ranging from Chinese gardening to histories of conquest, promoted China's primordial civilization to deliver a scathing critique of European modernity. The Sinophilia of Temple and his acquaintances Isaac Vossius and Charles de Saint-Évremond was based on their sense that Chinese society approximated a Platonic republic ruled by philosophers.[104] In his *Essay Upon the Ancient and Modern Learning* and *Of Heroic Virtue* (1688–90), Temple asserted a theory of "native genius" in which Eastern government, arts, and sciences outshone Western modernity's derivative claims, in particular the Royal Society science that he alleged had spread pedantry, superciliousness, and the production of false knowledge. Given their lack of ingenuity, contemporary thinkers could only rely on their forefathers and "make the best copies they could, after those [Eastern] originals."[105] The civilizations of China and India, Temple argued, predated Christian as well as Greek cultural achievements—a proposition that challenged accepted biblical chronologies and enflamed his famous quarrel with William Wotton, whose *Reflections Upon Ancient and Modern Learning* (1694) contested the legitimacy of China's antiquity. In the context of early modern historiography, China was, as literary scholar Eun Kyung Min has argued, a "product of the quarrel between the ancients and moderns" at the same time that European modernity was "the product of a quarrel with China."[106] Although these debates have been framed as a clash of temporalities—ancients against moderns—the arguments for China's superiority relied equally on a spatialized logic of comparison that produced alternative geographies of morality, which in turn suggested alternatives to conventionally masculine heroism. How was China's moral virtue, coded as "effeminate," recoded as "heroic" in conflicting accounts of its conquest and continuing resilience?

China's geographic location contributed to its heroism in a number of key ways. First, Temple's essays attempted to de-center the exclusively Western locus of great men and establish a new heroism based not on conquest or military might but on the ethos of philosophy, ethics, and good government as practiced outside the conventional parameters of Greek and Roman antiquity.[107] It was China's global position at the furthest east that ultimately reoriented heroism and assigned moral virtue, as exemplified by Confucius, heroic status. Temple's organization of the globe according to innate, geo-moral state formations situates heroic virtue outside the West:

> Yet the stage of all these empires, and revolutions of all these heroic actions and these famous constitutions [Greece and Rome] . . . is but *a limited compass of earth that leaves out many vast regions of the world* . . . [that have] exceeded all the others

in the wisdom of their constitutions, the extent of their conquests, and the duration of their empires or states. (*Of Heroic Virtue*, 322, my emphasis)

Indeed, compared with the "limited compass" of the Greeks and Romans, Confucius discourses on virtue "with great compass of knowledge" (334). Temple finds the true examples of heroic virtue at the world's furthest extremes: China in the East, Peru in the West, Tartary in the North, and Arabia in the South. The more remote an observed culture may initially appear, the greater its heroic potential.[108] Their overlooked, ancient histories combined with their remote locations offer a new curriculum of virtue that is global and comparative in scope; as interrelated sites of cultural difference, they combine into a ringed periphery of moral exemplarity that opposes the corrupt center of late seventeenth-century England. By establishing structural similarities between one non-European culture and its global counterpart, Temple bridges distances with effortless intellectual leaps while at the same time tracing universal standards of morality across exotic distances. In particular, China and Peru, deemed cultures with impressive political structures, a strong presence of Christianity, and no history of military encroachment upon Europe, are held up as more virtuous than warring Tartary or an idolatrous Arabia overridden with an "enthusiasm" for Mahomet. As Temple writes, "[T]he furthest East and West may be found to agree in notions of divinity, as well as in excellence of civil or politic constitutions, by passing at one leap from these of China to those of Peru" (*Of Heroic Virtue*, 345).

Second, China's amenable climate produces a "naturally greater force of wit and genius, of invention and penetration" embodied in the philosopher-hero Confucius. Geographical place, as well as the virtues of ancient civilization, determines moral character. Such arguments followed the climate theory of the Renaissance writer Jean Bodin, who revised the ancient theories of Galen and Ptolemy by dividing the earth into zones of latitude, longitude, geological formation, and climate; these zones could in turn be mapped onto humans' physical and moral constitution. For Bodin, the East was a temperate zone that nurtured "operations of the practical intellect, such as law and jurisprudence," the union of intelligence and skill, and men of physical and moral strength governed by reason rather than a warring mentality.[109] All great empires were considered to be temperate, in contrast with the cold, northern climes, which produced vigorous peoples who lacked the intelligence and perseverance to sustain empires, and the warmer torrid zones, which were populated by natives prone to languor and licentiousness.[110] Accordingly, the temperate zone of the so-called Middle Kingdom endowed China with every type of natural resource as well as an exemplary balance of virtues.[111] The German Jesuit scholar and orientalist Athanasius Kircher, one of Temple's sources, thus remarked that "the whole Tartar-Chinese empire is so large from south to north that it contains both the tropics and the cold and frozen northern zones" (159). Kircher also commented that "The Chinese Empire is the richest and most powerful of all. . . . Also, nature has separated it from the rest of the world and it seems different from anywhere else" (159). Johann Nieuhof further linked the "most Opulent, Potent, and Populous" empire of China to its situation as an enhanced temperate climate and universe unto itself: "not content with the proper Munificences of the Temperate Zone, it hath moreover subjected both the Torrid and Frigid unto its Jurisdiction. . . . What Monarch ever had the happiness every Day to have his Table furnish'd with the seasonable and proper Fruits of the *Indies* brought from the Burning Zone, and to be delighted with the variety and abundance of all Fruits peculiar to the Temperate Zone." The variety of fruit trees, he noted, "answer to all the Products of that nature in every Climate of the World, whether in the *Torrid, Temperate* or *Frozen Zones*" (403, 411). For Nieuhof, the temperate character of the Chinese elevated them above the Tartars:

> The *Chinese* is of an affable and peaceable Disposition, addicted to Husbandry, and loving all good Arts and Sciences: But the *Tartar*, on the other Hand, delights in nothing so much as Hunting, being very cunning and deceitful, lusting after War, and of a very loose and uncivil Comportment. It is true, both endeavor to shun Idleness, but with Intentions very incoherent; the one to live temperately and honestly; but the other only to range abroad in a wild and beastial Barbarism.

The temperate zone thus signaled moral fortitude as well as geographical diversity. If, in the Renaissance tradition, climatically determined moral character produced a relativist world view, an emphasis on geography allowed Temple to make a universal exemplar of China, indeed to extend the idea of *translatio studii*—that learning had progressed through a movement from east to west through a series of conquests and empires—to the more eastern origins of India and China.[112] Because China's ancient history troubled the Christian chronology it was in part meant to exemplify, Temple's use of spatial metaphors also shifted the focus away from the controversies of contested biblical time to the constitution of universal heroism across vast distances, from China to Peru.

For Temple, China's location at a virtuous Eastern extreme reoriented the traditional canon of heroic exemplars. *Of Heroic Virtue* begins in the classical style of praising individual men, indeed by cataloguing the "common examples of virtue and honour"; but it offers a radical departure by concluding that those who provide the "usual instructions of Princes and Statesmen"—Romulus, Cyrus, Alexander, and Caesar—lack the true spirit of heroism (321). A more compelling ancient hero can be found in China's "Prince of philosophers, the great and renowned Confucius," whose "moral virtues" continue to permeate a society that prioritizes the perfection of the mind and an ethics of living and governing well (332). Rather than the heroism of a conqueror, Confucius embodied China's climactically determined "native genius" through his many assets: "[he] appears to have been of a very extraordinary genius, of mighty learning, admirable virtue, excellent nature, a true patriot of his country, and lover of mankind" (321, 334). Temple's work followed Jesuit writings on Confucius that commented on how he lived "by example as well as precept exciting to virtue."[113] By privileging Confucius over an Alexander or a Caesar, Temple constructs a new ideal of virtue, the philosopher over the warrior, and the empire of learning over that of conquest.[114] In the grand scheme of moral exemplarity, valor takes second place to civility, and hence histories of conquest should, according to Temple, pay more attention to the achievements of sustainable governments rather than the spectacular, martial acts that found empires. In fact, Temple interprets conquest as an extension of civilization rather than as the basis of heroic virtue: "After all that has been said of conquerors or conquests, this must be confessed to hold but the second rank in the pretensions to heroic virtue, and that the first has been allowed to the wise institution of just orders and laws" (405). For this reason, Tartars play a relatively minor role in Temple's telling account of the fall of China's Ming dynasty. While he concedes that Tartars are "the boldest and the fiercest people in the world, and the most enterprising," they are most notable for their political union with the "effeminate," albeit dominant "excellence of the Chinese wit and government" (343). The fall of China twice to Tartars is recounted as a process of civilizing the barbarians, whereby China's laws and stalwart constitution withstood, indeed absorbed, the conquerors' intrusion and rendered Tartar rule merely nominal: "So great a respect, or rather veneration, is paid to this wise and admirable constitution, even by its enemies and invaders, that both civil usurpers and foreign conquerors vie with emulation, who shall make greatest court and give most support to it" (344). By this account, China remained victorious in defeat through its exemplification of customs and manners, of moral virtue, and even "effeminacy."

However subtle, the favorable impression of Chinese effeminacy in Temple's essay once again highlights the ambiguity of female-gendered empire. For Temple, effeminacy signals civilizational progress and a newer, gentler heroism in contrast with that of ancient Greece and Rome. Following the climate theorists

CONFUCIUS
The celebrated Chinese Philosopher.

Portrait of Confucius, "The celebrated Chinese Philosopher." Engraving included in Jean-Baptiste Du Halde, *The General History of China*, 1741. Courtesy of the Rare Book and Manuscript Library, University of Pennsylvania.

who argued that the hardy constitutions of northern peoples like Goths and Tartars explained their histories of conquering lands further south, Temple also praised the vigor and ferocity of the Tartars, or Scythians, in his writing on heroic virtue. He chose, however, to elaborate upon the artistic merits of the Western Scythians and the cultural rather than military feats of their Goth leader, Odin. In advocating the ideal of heroic effeminacy, Temple focused on the period after the Goths invaded western Europe, when the civilizing influence of Christianity subdued Tartar restlessness and perpetual warring. A new phase of poetic and artistic production was thus initiated along with a Christianized empire of learning worthy of the label "heroic virtue." Temple's praise for the Tartars thus depends on their conversion from war heroes to civilized exemplars under the aegis of a morally advanced empire. Here, the archetypal China-Tartar dynamic— the conquered conqueror civilizes the barbarian—has an added relevance to English historiography. In linking the Western Scythians to the Saxon ancestors of modern England, Temple identifies the Tartar warring spirit as the pagan precursor and foundation for English constitutional freedom and virtuous national character (*Of Heroic Virtue*, 138). One of the best attributes of English empire, it appears, derives from its hethnic, Tartar roots, and hence its ties to the East. Parallels between China and England are made through their shared vulnerability to Tartar invasions; they are both civilized cultures that have faced a common northern menace and emerged stronger and improved. Rather than binaristic oppositions, East and West thus contain mutually developing empires with shared fates. The same Tartar threat that rendered England's situation similar and proximate to China's also demonstrates the superior force of China's pagan civilization in the current day. In civilizing the Manchu Tartars, it has performed a world-historical moral act comparable to the Christianization of the Goths, thus ushering in a new empire of learning whose hethnic Confucian morality is paradoxically deemed effeminate yet heroic—pagan yet Christian—in contrast with the outmoded heroes of ancient Greece and Rome. Implicit in the "excellent patterne" of China's civilized effeminacy is the reshaping of the masculine ideal of heroic virtue imagined at the frontiers of empires.

The narratives of comparative history and of China's conquest explored in this chapter turn on spectacles of heroism and effeminacy ranging from discursive examples of Confucian morality to material bodies on the Restoration stage. The fascination with Chinese history was expressed through its links to other Oriental empires and its distinctive morality that exercised the force of learning, reason, natural religion, and even virtuous effeminacy. The ambivalence toward the fall of the Ming dynasty in historical and literary accounts exemplifies the controversies of representing heroic ideals in a commercializing age of inter-European rivalry over access to China and the riches of Eastern empires. Even as the representation of Tartar heroism was a product of European religious and commercial interests intent on appeasing the newly installed Manchu-Qing regime, Chinese antiquity was monumentalized in histories and performances that foregrounded China's status as a more perfectly preserved, yet newer, Greece or Rome; its fall, however, marked not the end of a cycle of greatness but the possibility of a new "empire of learning" that combined moral with heroic, and commercial, virtue. Examples of Chinese effeminacy raised the possibility of codes of valor more appropriate to the new, kinder, gentler conceptions of commercial exchange rather than territorial conquest. Confucius and the Amazon are heroes less for representing China than for mediating between cultures, reconciling extremes, and merging civilizational types. They are, so to speak, hethnic brokers that exemplify the negotiation of Tartar and Chinese models of empire. The morals of Confucius and the genealogies of Chinese and Manchu rule undergo processes of cultural translation to make Chinese history speak European values. They became test cases for imperial ideologies and new technologies of representation in the Restoration period, which together comprised the performance, and performativity, of Chinese empire. A palimpsest such as Amavanga contains in its transliterated name a spectrum of ideological formations of heroic virtue that reference Tartar men and women, Chinese women, and Westernized Amazons. The ideological stakes in performing foreign histories on the Restoration stage consist not only in political allegories of consolidating English monarchy but also in the production of Chineseness through a constellation of borrowed names—Tartar, Amazon—whose etymologies and uses attest to the layered encounters of sexual and cultural alterities across East and West, ancient and modern. Even the negative examples of China that made heroes of the Tartars acknowledge the enduring civility of Chinese antiquity. Because neither Tartars nor Chinese were straightforward heroes, they were in the discourses of China's conquest merged into a synthesis of heroic effeminacy, a paradox that illustrates the uneven and ambivalent reception of Chinese empire in the English Restoration period. Insofar as China was imagined to be effeminate in relation to its Tartar conquerors, it tested alternatives to Western classical exempla. Effeminacy was not just a cause of an empire's downfall or a straightforward vice. In the context of early modern orientalism, it was a mediating idiom and a barometer of gender propriety and civilizational character.

CHAPTER TWO

Sincerity and Authenticity
George Psalmanazar's Experiments in Conversion

The staging, in England, of Chinese history was as much an exercise of spectacle as it was an experiment with the conventions and limits of heroic virtue. The unruly example of China's conquest, imagined in relation to a number of gendered places and times—Tartary, Greece, Rome—produced a constellation of conflicting attitudes about empire and cultural effeminacy. This ambivalence toward China, rendered alternately triumphant and abject in the Jesuit annals of the Ming-Qing period, was exemplified by the idealized figures of Confucius and the Amazon. When viewed as heroes of a queer sort, their performances of gender and nation disrupt the received tradition of *translatio imperii* and signal the possibility of looking East for new models of commercial empire. As hethnic figures, they negotiate overlapping controversies over the merits of Chinese civilization and the sensationalism of English theatrical spectacle and push the boundaries of generic conventions to show that binaries like masculine/feminine and East/West are not sufficient to explain the complex mapping of China in the Restoration period. The hethnic figure to be explored in this chapter is not a virtuous pagan like Confucius, who presents a challenge, alternative, or corollary to Christian virtue, but rather, the example of a pagan convert to Christianity. I continue the examination of the virtues and vices of the Eastern heathen, but framed as a performance of identity rather than an enactment of theater.

Heathen conversion is a particular type of performance, one that posits a journey from barbarism to civilization; the convert, though technically no longer a pagan, is a hethnic figure in having to continually differentiate past from present self. Having crossed from other to self, he bears the burden of proof and the negotiation of the binaries of East and West. Added to the performative nature of conversion is that of cultural fraud in the case of a European impersonation of an Asian convert. This is not then an instance of staging China for theater audiences, but rather of mimicking Jesuit accounts of China to fabricate a cultural proxy off stage and in the flesh. What are the commercial, religious, political, and scientific stakes of impersonating the "Far East" in England? There are two types of performance, then, to be discussed: performing piety, and performing culture. Conversion entails a disavowal of paganism and an engagement with the politics of Protestant piety, while fraud exploits the commercial as well as religious channels of circulation by which news of the East entered English public consciousness. Just as the effeminate heroes Confucius and the Amazon expose the gendered and racialized constructions of cultural character at work in the staging of empire, the fake native convert conjoins these two modes of self-display to reveal the performativity of cultural conversion.

Well-constructed frauds can long outlive even their authors' intentions. Repeated as good anecdotes, they typically lionize the cunning of an individual against a society deemed gullible enough to be tricked by its own standards of possibility. The imported travel literature and commodities that inspired theatrical spectacles and imitations of "Chinese" fashions also spawned a number of cultural impersonators who attempted to pass as exotic Asians.[1] One of the most memorable cases of the eighteenth century was George Psalmanazar, a fair-skinned Frenchman whose elaborate impersonation of a heathen from Formosa enthralled British readers and confounded Royal Society scientists. From the beginning, his public self-fashioning combined techniques of theatrical performance and print testimony to enact an exemplary native of both East and West. In addition to making public appearances as an eater of twigs and raw meat, Psalmanazar published a number of writings on Formosa, including the false ethnography *An Historical and Geographical Description of Formosa, an Island Subject to the Emperor of Japan*, first published in 1704.[2]

A comprehensive and fabricated first-hand account of native customs and culture, complete with maps, engravings, and a chart of an entirely invented alphabet, Psalmanazar's *Description of Formosa* improvised upon actual travel narratives of China, Japan, and Formosa and continued until the early nineteenth century to be an object of historical and linguistic debate. Such was his influence that, even in his lifetime, Psalmanazar's fraud had already taken on a satiric life of its own. Jonathan Swift's *A Modest Proposal* cited the "famous *Sallmanaazor*, a native of the island of Formosa," as a bona fide consultant and inspiration for its Irish cannibalism scheme. It was this Asiatic visitor who offered expert advice on the edibility of human carcasses and thus encouraged Swift's narrator to propose eating children as a solution to the country's food shortage. Nearly two decades earlier, when a delegation of Mohawk Iroquois chiefs paid a diplomatic visit to England, their foreign appearance caused a sensation in the streets of

London and generated multiple accounts of the "Four Indian Kings"; one of the more skeptical pamphlets, published in 1710, described "four unknown Persons, *Psalmanaazar's* I suppose, from the *West-Indies*, under the notion of Kings and Emperors."[3] Within years of Psalmanazar's arrival in England, *Psalmanazar* had become a catchphrase for the spectacle of a fake East, broadly applied to sites of colonial conflict stretching from Ireland to North America.

Not from Formosa but from France, George Psalmanazar arrived to London in 1703 accompanied by a Scottish chaplain, the Reverend Alexander Innes. Together they launched the hoax that has become one of the most notable forgeries of the period: Psalmanazar purported to be a native of Formosa, an island he claimed was Japanese territory. According to his story, he had been kidnapped by Jesuit missionaries and taken to France; there he escaped the clutches of Roman Catholicism and eventually converted to Protestantism with the aid of his religious mentor, Innes. This account was published in his *Description of Formosa*, which included not only fabricated details of the island of Formosa but also a history of Christians in Japan and exhaustive proofs of his own conversion to Christianity. From his later memoirs, we learn that Psalmanazar had in actuality begun his imposture in France as a disillusioned university student who left his studies and took to the road; impoverished, he begged for alms in the guise of first an Irishman and eventually a Japanese convert to Christianity. As he traveled through Germany and the Netherlands spending time with various military regiments, he also posed as a Japanese heathen, in part by inventing a language based on his knowledge of Hebrew and by adopting the name Salmanazar, after Shalmaneser, the ancient Assyrian king of the Old Testament. His encounter with Alexander Innes in a Scottish regiment at Sluys formalized the fraud, as Innes saw an opportunity to advance his own career through exhibiting an Asian convert. After baptizing Psalmanazar, Innes secured him an invitation to London from Bishop Henry Compton. Psalmanazar was to begin his career spreading the word of Formosa as a pupil at Oxford University. Like other impostors of the period, he displayed a genius for ancient languages and cultures with the hopes of gaining patronage, profits from publications, and fame.[4] Although he was from the beginning suspected of fraud by a number of London's scholarly and social elite, he did for a number of years pass as a Formosan. Even after he was widely revealed to be a fake, his actual name remained unknown and his background unverified except by his own accounts, in particular, his penitent, posthumous *Memoirs of *****. *Commonly known by the Name of George Psalmanazar; A Reputed Native of Formosa* (1764). By the 1740s and 1750s, he had undergone an actual religious conversion and become active in London's publishing industry, contributing to a number of history and printing projects and earning the especial admiration of Samuel Johnson, who remarked: "George Psalmanazar's piety, penitence and virtue exceeded almost what we read as wonderful even in the lives of the saints."[5]

Beyond describing Psalmanazar's fraud, his spectacular impersonation of an exemplary Asian, and his notoriety, more specifically I want to explore a set of epistemological crises revealed at the heart of his performance. One such crisis concerned the performance of virtue as a means of indexing commercial relations between Europe and Asia; another involved the conditions of establishing verifiable truths in the culture of eighteenth-century science. Virtue and commerce were mutually implicated in the construction of a hypothetical Asian who was not-quite-other and who posited the heathen civilizations of the East as immanently convertible. Such relations proved the limits of moral and scientific knowledge and elicited the question: What does it take to prove the existence of a vastly distant place, whether located on the other side of the world or deep within the soul? In one sense, performing virtue was central to the identity that Psalmanazar had forged: a native Formosan who was above all a pious convert to Christianity. His efforts at denying worldly artifice while indulging in public spectacle expose his performative work of conversion. The relative dearth of information about Formosa, and its association with the empire of China, made it an appealing site of abstraction for Psalmanazar's epistemological experiment. Now called Taiwan, Ilha Formosa, or "beautiful island," was thus designated by the Portuguese in the late 1500s. While nominally Chinese in the early 1700s, in its proximity to the mainland the island was then, as now, a contested offshore zone with respect to China's borders. The heathen convert's moral authority, though, was tied less to his purported origins than to being in "in-between" places. As I will demonstrate, his particular form of exemplarity, that of a hypothetical heathen, involved the constant conversion of the geographical place into a theoretical space for testing competing political and religious ideologies while borrowing from their techniques of legitimization to create a typical yet exceptional native.

The early years of his imposture in particular reveal a multifaceted performance of Asian identity. Formosa at the beginning of the eighteenth century was contested territory. It had been partially occupied by the Dutch between 1624 and 1661, then for several decades by Han Chinese resistance forces fleeing the Manchus, and next by China's Qing government, which formally annexed the island in 1683. Psalmanazar, though, chose to make Formosa an island of Japan, given Japan's inaccessibility to foreigners following its closed-door policy of the mid-seventeenth century.[6] Long fought over by European and Asian nations working out the boundaries of power and regional trade, Formosa, referred to by one scholar as "China's island frontier" in this period, became a strategic site of contested meanings for Psalmanazar as well.[7] In this light, it is not the accuracy of his representation or misrepresentation of Formosa that concerns us, but rather the construction of East Asia as a model composite of civilized heathenism and lucrative markets, of appropriable virtue and commerce. Psalmanazar's attempts to prove his Formosan identity focused heavily, for a number of reasons, on proving his religious conversion. Given his lack of empirical evidence about the island, he used piety to legitimize his truth claims. Through his elaborate defenses of his identity as a converted heathen, he put religious and scientific authority into dialogue, in particular showcasing the persuasiveness of moral certainty over absolute truth. Thus, Psalmanazar's biography and the question of whether or not he was believed is ultimately not the primary inquiry of this chapter.[8] Rather, how did key aspects of his fraud, especially in the early years of his feigned conversion, test the limits of demonstrable knowledge? While we may focus on his strategies of passing as a native of Formosa, his fraud is but a symptom of a larger question: the mutual construction of morality and cultural difference.

This chapter, then, is primarily about the experimental nature of conversion: cultural impersonation offers a theory of conversion as epistemology. The importance of conversion to Psalmanazar's cultural and racial passing has largely been overlooked in favor of the literary or ethnographic elements of his fraud.[9] Along with Gauri Viswanathan, I approach conversion as an epistemological phenomenon, a "knowledge-producing activity" rather than mere "spiritual self-transformation."[10] Experimental knowledge as practiced by seventeenth- and eighteenth-century natural philosophers entailed collecting physical evidence and eyewitness testimony, concrete pieces of experience, from exotic places and protocolonies. Linking abstract ideas and fantasies of a convertible East to these material things was key to Psalmanazar's embodiment of heathen self-improvement. Conversion can thus be seen as a contact zone of competing moral claims and a negotiation of visible and invisible truth—an experiment in truth-telling at the intersection of religion, politics, commerce, and science.

Significantly, converts are exemplars of self-improvement and self-transformation because they have willingly chosen to give up a previous life in exchange for a new one. Their piety is exemplary because they operate not out of ignorance but from the experience of being part of two worlds. Conversion presumes the division of the world into a dichotomy of false and true, a distinction that needs to be maintained to assert the righteousness of the chosen religion. Being a convert is an ongoing process of proving oneself, of demonstrating the certainty of one's faith through the labor of distinguishing between self and other. However, a contradiction is built into the virtue of such a converted heathen: he is exemplary because of having moved from one extreme to another, from error to truth, and from East to West; he must convincingly demonstrate the movement from one state into another, as well as confirm the opposition between civilization and barbarism. His heathenism needs to have been thoroughly expelled to constitute his virtue, and yet it is this past—this foreignness—that makes his piety so remarkable. The identity of "convert" forever calls attention to his foreignness, making him the constant object of suspicion and skepticism. In his ambivalence, he is a perfect exemplar: a model of piety and imitation, and a warning about the dangers of the foreigner within domestic borders. The converted heathen is an exception to the rule; yet he is also meant to be a representative or typical native. He is an example of the ongoing process of ascertaining the general character of the East.

The composite identity, heathen and convert, required Psalmanazar to pose as a paradigmatic specimen of the East in the West. In that he was a typical yet exceptional native of Formosa, his fraud demonstrates the "inclusive exclusion" at the heart of the *example* as theorized by Giorgio Agamben: to make an example of something is to single it out from the mass and imbue it with an instructive purpose that belies its exclusion from the very norm it is meant to represent.[11] A public persona whose career spanned the first half of the eighteenth century, Psalmanazar was also an instructive *exemplar* of virtue in both senses of the exemplary as defined by Samuel Johnson: "such as may deserve to be proposed to imitation," and "such as may give warning to others."[12] The ambivalence articulated by these theories indicates the heathen qua exemplar's suspension between systems of value: rather than simply oppose the Christian worldview, the heathen represented a state of potential, the possibility of being converted.

At the same time, Psalmanazar's performance reveals much at stake in the material relations, as well as the imaginative ones, between Asia and Europe. His fraud illuminates the extent to which the converted heathen embodies a fantasy of colonial acquisition, the promise of access to and appropriation of the desirable markets and commodities of the East, and thus, the further contradiction of material gain tied up with demonstrable virtue. Psalmanazar is an example of how performance is at the heart of religious attempts to keep conversion separate from the corrupting world of commerce. Yet missionary work was intimately tied to the territorial claims and commercial transactions of the long-distance trade that was so highly profitable for Europeans fighting over access to Chinese tea, porcelain, and silk. Converts were also commodities in and of themselves, circulated along with the goods of the East as embodiments of virtue to be exchanged for profits and patronage. In both instances, the distance traveled added value to the sincerity of the conversion or the authenticity of the manufacture. The converted heathen is a figure of ambivalence and contradiction: he represents the purity of religious truth and verification of the "other" in all his alterity; he is at once removed from commercial concerns in his lack of worldly self-interest, and yet is a hybrid or composite figure exhibited as a commodity circulating in an East-West market. Conversion, broadly understood, is the continual circulation and transformation of one order into another. Like conversion's false and true binaries, East and West were fictional oppositions constantly being posited to uphold a fantasy of certain knowledge. Through his fraud, Psalmanazar performs a theory of religious conversion and the undoing of such binaries, testing the limits of an either/or worldview, in the context of moral and commercial investment in East Asia.

Given the China-centered global economy of the early eighteenth century and the proliferation of knowledge about China circulating throughout Europe, the Formosa of Psalmanazar's construction was constantly presented in contradistinction to China. However tactical or disingenuous, his refusal of a homogenous East Asia and his continual efforts to distinguish between China, Formosa, and Japan illustrated the performance of China as a set of relations beyond "China and the West." Ultimately, his fraud shows that East and West were, in the first decade of the eighteenth century, less fixed oppositions than nodes of an ongoing process of differentiation. Psalmanazar's exemplification of Formosa relied on an accretion of textual evidence more than any physical markers of alterity. One of his obituaries referred to a man "well known for many ingenius performances in different parts of literature."[13] One of the key methodological obstacles to studying his forgery is the inevitable reliance upon his own writings as the main source of information about his background. I take his works, fake and true, to be performances, and I work here not to distill them according to their relative veracity or falsity, but to uncover within them the constitutive contradictions at the heart of the convert-as-exemplar. By mimicking the mechanisms of authority in several knowledge regimes—science, religion, and commerce—he exposed the conditions of epistemological proof; indeed, the mutual demonstrations of piety and of cultural alterity. We can examine closely Psalmanazar's argumentative strategies across several of his key writings: *A Description of Formosa* (1704, 1705), *A Dialogue Between a Japonese and a Formosan, About Some Point of Religion* (1707), and *An Enquiry into the Objections against George Psalmanaazaar* of *Formosa* (1710). In particular, below I bring together two areas of his fraud often mentioned anecdotally but underexamined, especially in relation to each other: his religious conversion and his efforts to market himself as a type of chinoiserie object. Each constituted "proof" of his Formosan identity in the respective areas of virtue and commerce. In practice and in theory, his performance of cultural self-transformation tested the limits of hethnic virtue in material and immaterial form.

Proofs of Sincerity

Psalmanazar's impersonation has become a pithy anecdote in the annals of literary forgery, as well as the focus of a number of notable studies on exoticism, plagiarism, authorship, translation, and anthropology—an example par excellence.[14] However, for me, the endless reproducibility of this case derives from its self-reflexive conceptualization of demonstrable knowledge at the heart of conversion. Its driving force is, in fact, an epistemology of example-making. An example operates through indirect proof; it makes the abstruse graspable and, to borrow from John Dryden, "in one word reduces into practice our speculative notions."[15] Psalmanazar's concretization of an abstract Formosa asks us to consider the nature of native expertise—how ethnographic facts were produced and ascertained amid eighteenth-century scientific and religious culture. For matters of fact and faith were of equal relevance to the construction of a converted heathen; the sincerity of the native's eyewitness account worked in tandem with the convert's authoritative claim to the first-hand experience of revelation. Both entailed proving the unseen through performed experiments, and both aspired to moral certainty rather than absolute truth.

In a climate of Protestant patriotism, making a public display of one's faith was a matter of political as well as spiritual exigency. Too recent fears of a popish threat to the Church of England were inflamed by the government's concessions to dissenting sects and legislation such as the Toleration Act of 1689.[16] Just as tallying the number of converts could build partisan and nationalist might, rooting out cases of occasional conformity or nominal conversions was meant to crush the enemy within. In fact, religious fraud was an ever-present threat, as addressed in the preface to one "true" conversion narrative:

> The World has been so often deceived in many pretended Converts, who make a Trade of changing their Religion, that it is no wonder if Men are not easily perswaded of the sincerity of those who come over from one Religion to another.[17]

Against the charge of duplicity, the convert must distinguish himself or herself from these ubiquitous impostors. The task of joining the fold, after all, requires the denial of one's erroneous past and any possibility of reversion. The question remains, however: how does one ascertain the "sincerity" of a convert given the all too frequent trade in religious identities?[18] Christian writings on sincerity characterized an inner "State of Soul," simple and unadorned, immune from the taint of the commercial and in direct opposition to worldly artifice: "Sincerity is a Uniform thing, always steady, and one and the same for ever; but Hypocrisie and Dissimulation is Changeable and Various, and goes always under a disguise."[19] Just as we are supposed to know a hypocrite when we see one, the "Sincere Christian" should be self-evident.[20] Indeed, sincerity is described as a vehicle for rendering visible the elusive idea of virtue itself: "For certainly, if ever Virtue could be made Visible to Mortal Eyes, it must be by this Excellent Frame and Temper of Mind which we term *Sincerity*."[21]

The challenge of verifying an internal state of the soul, a matter of depth rather than appearance, was also in Psalmanazar's case a question of materializing unseen places, spiritual and geographical. He would later refer to his various actions as cumulative "proofs of [his] sincerity."[22] Contemporary assessments of his story prioritized the sincerity of his conversion as a matter of public debate. According to one report, "others who have convers'd with him believe that he is a sincere Convert to the Christian Faith, *and* a real Native of the Island from whence he pretends to come."[23] Mentions of Psalmanazar consistently linked the two parts of his performance with this tell-tale "and"; the theoretical implications of the conjunction, I argue, are key to understanding his exemplarity. While his strategies of passing for a Formosan were far from consistent, they did repeatedly draw on the idea of sincerity to construct the figure of a real, or authentic, native. Although sincerity and authenticity both infer trustworthiness and integrity, they also differ in emphasis. Sincerity entails a communication or "making Visible" of genuine affect—what Lionel Trilling in *Sincerity and Authenticity* called the "congruence between avowal and actual feeling."[24] We might consider this a type of "people-knowledge," in contrast with authenticity's "thing-knowledge"—that which tends toward empirical verification, historicity, and traceability to a fixed origin.[25] A focus on sincerity shifts the test of identity from evidence of one's origins to exemplification of social relations in the world at hand. The figure of the convert, after all, provides an index of the existing antagonisms and ongoing processes of differentiation between competing ideologies of self and other, Protestant and Catholic, native and foreign, true and false. In practice, of course, religious communities are constituted by a much more complex mesh of multiple and overlapping identifications, what Gauri Viswanathan has called the "indeterminacy of conversion."²⁶ Nonetheless, the conflict generated around such polarized positions can be understood as the formal expression of conversion's before-and-after narrative.

Significantly, the concept of a "convert," or its linguistic variant "converse," derives from the Latin *conversus*: one that has been turned, something that is opposite to, or that which involves conversation. Michael Questier has studied the importance of verbal retaliation in the seventeenth-century climate of religious factionalism, as evidenced by public "manuals of controversies" meant to arm individual debaters with a stock of arguments and a "systematic answering machine to deal with their opponents' tracts."²⁷ Such methods of disputation were the training ground for Psalmanazar's forgery. His account of traveling with the Dutch army before arriving to England describes "Papists and Protestants . . . so intermingled, their guides are better stored with arguments against each other, than against the common enemies of the Christian faith" (*Description*, 172). In acting the part of a pagan outsider, he learned to play one system of knowledge against its own inconsistencies and competing Western factions against each other. In his words, "I refused all other means to be converted, but the right one, which was *arguing*."²⁸

For Psalmanazar, to be convincingly Formosan, or Japanese—and *not* Chinese—was largely a tactic of playing to the anti-Catholic sympathies of his Anglican audience. Fluency in church doctrine was a primary means of exhibiting this strategic affiliation. Arguing one's true conversion also meant discrediting the Papists who represented the opposite of everything sincere—hypocrisy, dissimulation, disguise. These qualities in fact described Psalmanazar's own situation; instead of shirking the topic of fraud, he made it central to his assertions of truth. In particular, he targeted Jesuit missionary work in Asia. Japan, even more than China, had long evoked in the English imagination a site of resistance to Western missionizing efforts. Seventeenth-century European histories of Japan emphasized the persecution of Jesuits and Japanese Christians by the Tokugawa regime beginning in 1613–14 and leading up to the 1638 Shimabara Massacre, after which all European traders were banished except for the Dutch, who were confined to the small island of Deshima in Nagasaki harbor.²⁹ In light of these reports, the *Description of Formosa*, Psalmanazar's first and most influential publication, is framed by a scathing critique of the Jesuit mission. Its title page mentions his "Conferences with the Jesuits" and refutation of "a Jesuit lately come from China." The preface, dedicated to Bishop Henry Compton, establishes Japan and Formosa as the antithesis of the "lies" spread by the Jesuits:

> The Europeans have such obscure and various Notions of Japan, and especially of our Island Formosa, that they can believe nothing for Truth that has been said of it. But the prevailing Reason for this my Undertaking was, because the Jesuits I found had impos'd so many Stories, and such gross Fallacies upon the Public, that . . . I told the Reasons why this wicked Society, and at last all that profess'd Christianity, were, with them, expell'd [from] that Country.

Following the example of Anglican apologists, Psalmanazar essentially displaced his forgery onto the Jesuits, themselves accused of being "impostors" guilty of conspiring with Spain to infiltrate and conquer Japan, promising spiritual deliverance through the use of "pious Frauds," and even going so far as to pass as Asian "natives." He drew from accounts of missionary practices in China to narrate his firsthand experience of their "*Insincerity and cheating Tricks*, by their counterfeiting themselves to be Heathens."[30] He tells of being seduced to leave Formosa with one Father Alexander de Rode, who entered the country disguised as a "Japanner." Once in France, the young Psalmanazar was forced to convert and subjected to public display; he repeatedly refused to accept the tenets of Roman Catholicism until threatened with inquisition, at which point he managed to escape.[31] Along with this narrative of kidnapping and resistance, we learn of Japan's detailed history of banishing Catholics from its borders, such that the island nation in effect becomes a site of missed opportunities for proper conversion and a virtual placeholder for Anglicanism.

As if to foreground the related but distinct projects of sincerity and authenticity so crucial to Psalmanazar's self-presentation, the *Description of Formosa* is itself divided into two parts. Juxtaposing conversion and ethnography, sincerity and authenticity, the structure of the book establishes the halves as mutually dependent; for it aims to make self-evident the concurrent truth of two unseen entities, God and Formosa. The ethnography of the island, which contains many marvelous facts accompanied by engravings of pagan ceremonies, coinage, and an alphabetic writing system, appears in the second half; only in the second edition of 1705 was the order reversed.[32] In the first section, the formal proofs of Psalmanazar's conversion by "mathematical Method" are presented as an exhaustive, step-by-step demonstration of the fundamental attributes of God and the legitimacy of the Church of England. The passage has been summed up by biographer Frederic J. Foley as "over a hundred pages of dry theological discussion."[33] Indeed, despite its predominance in the text, this episode has been all but ignored by most commentators. What it reveals, though, is a remarkable performance of moral authority. In rehearsing axiomatic truths, Psalmanazar weds the privileged perspective of the divine with his own heathen exceptionalism; the effect, however intentional, is a transference of truth claims across experiential divides. He begins by reprinting the scheme of "Definitions, Axioms, Postulata, and Propositions" presented to him by the chaplain Innes and next reiterates these claims in the first person, playing the dual roles of his pre- and postconversion self to "answer the principal Objections which I made while a Heathen, against the truth and certainty of the Christian Religion" (48). The exposition is meant to be at once a literal representation of official doctrine and a performative reenactment of his conversion in the order—and rational manner—of its occurrence. Indeed, his displays of rationality make him an extraordinary heathen whose very conditions of existence also seem curiously to mirror those of the God he seeks to prove. Without God, he reasons, the world would be self-fabricated and self-reproducing, which is out of the question given that "there cannot be an infinite succession of Causes producing one another" and that "nothing can produce nothing; but every thing that has a Being, must be produc'd by something" (50, 51). And as for the possibility of conflicting or multiple realities, "Since God is a most perfect Being, 'tis certain that he cannot contradict himself, and establish two contrary Religions . . . only one of these Religions is true, and of Divine Authority, and that the rest are Human Inventions, Frauds, and Forgeries" (68).

In these and other instances, one could easily substitute *Psalmanazar*, or his Formosan identity, for *God*. Self-reflexivity, after all, is an integral feature of Psalmanazar's writings, especially given the public questioning of his legitimacy leading up to as well as immediately following the publication of the *Description of Formosa*.[34] His insistence that God's miracles are grounded in empirical truth gives vicarious credence to his own situation; instead of proving his Formosanness through authenticating the island, in this section he presents himself as the incontrovertible voice of universal truth and moral certainty. True miracles, unlike the "absurdities" of other religions, pagan or Christian, can be ascertained through experience, eyewitness testimony, and an appeal to reason. In that they are performed publicly and made "apparent to the Senses," they offer material "evidence" in contrast with the "monstrous Doctrines of Transubstantiation, Consubstantiation and absolute Predestination" of Catholicism, Lutheranism, and Calvinism, respectively.[35] To discredit transubstantiation, Psalmanazar argues that "the same Body cannot, at the same time, be in two distant places" (18). Of eucharistic bread, which symbolizes as well as embodies Christ, he writes, "[I]t is impossible that the same thing should be both the Sign and the Thing signified, or that any thing should be a sign of itself" (30). Ironically, making the case against these tenets highlights Psalmanazar's own condition of being in two places at once, of being a living contradiction of both sign and signified—and a Formosan in theory and in the flesh.

The ultimate irony of a divinely authored universe mirroring Psalmanazar's self-produced and self-reproducing fictions comes in the second half of the book, when we learn that Formosa's legendary prophet was also named Psalmanaazaar (this version with double *a*).[36] This is a figure that demands the yearly sacrifice of twenty thousand children along with hundreds of livestock to the island's pagan God. The namesake is in a sense the false double to Psalmanazar, the Christian convert and Anglican apologist represented in the book's first half. If the sincerity of Psalmanazar's conversion is meant to authenticate his identity as an exemplary native, the enumerations of the island's pagan rituals equally prove the validity of his conversion to Anglicanism. He goes as far as to note, "Some perhaps may think that I have done too much Honour to the Pagan Religion as it is profess'd in Formosa, by giving such a long and particular Explication of it . . . nay, I am fully persuaded that [it is] false" (324). The descriptions of corrupt priests, elaborate funeral rites, ceremonies, and festival days, child sacrifice, and the consumption of human flesh more than once insinuate not only the rituals of the Roman Church but also the Confucian rites and customs so infamously tolerated by Jesuit missionaries in China. The equation of Roman Catholicism with Asian paganism is made explicitly when Psalmanazar recalls his challenge to the priests who formerly attempted to convert him: "Since you condemn our Pagan Religion, because our Religious Worship consist only in Externals, how can you alledge your external Ceremonies in Confirmation of your Religion" (129). The priests reply that without the true gauge of "internal Virtue," external rituals alone are insufficient (130).

Of course, it is inner virtue that Psalmanazar seeks to make visible through his rehearsal of Anglican doctrine in the book's first half—his proofs of sincerity—and through his condemnation of "externals" in the form of Formosan and Catholic ritual. The authenticity of Formosa, in other words, is premised upon its religious falsity, which in turn relies on the demonstration of spiritual truth. The different components of the text can thus be seen as iterations of conversion and performances of a dialectic of sincerity and authenticity. In attaching his Formosan translations of the Lord's Prayer, the Apostles' Creed, and the Ten Commandments, Psalmanazar imparts yet another textual performance, which crucially hinges on the question of language. The polyglot appearance of the words on the page manifests the merging and hybridizing of worlds. In that the translations exhibit his native knowledge, they are signs of authenticity; but as linguistic conversions, they signal his continual efforts at proving the sincer-

> *the Isle* Formosa. 271
>
> *The Lord's Prayer.*
>
> Koriakia Vomera.
>
> OUR *Father who in Heaven art,* Hal-
> Amy Pornio dan chin Ornio viey, Gnay-
> *lowed be thy Name, Come thy King-*
> jorhe sai Lory, Eyfodere sai Ba-
> *dom, Be done thy Will as in Heaven,*
> galin, Jorhe sai domion apo chin Ornio,
> *also in Earth so, Our bread dai-*
> kay chin Badi eyen, Amy khatsada nadak-
> *ly give us to day, and forgive us*
> chion toye ant nadayi, kay Radonaye ant
> *our trespasses, as we forgive our trespas-*
> amy Sochin, apo ant radonem amy Sochia-
> *sers, do lead us not into temptation, but*
> khin, bagne ant kau chin malaboski, ali
> *deliver us from Evil, for thine is the*
> abinaye ant tuen Broskaey, kens sai vie
> *Kingdom, and Glory, and Omnipotence to*
> Bagalin, kay Fary, kay Barhaniaan chi-
> *all ages. Amen.*
> nania sendabey. Amien.
>
> *The*

Psalmanazar's "Formosan" translation of the Lord's Prayer, from George Psalmanazar, *An Historical and Geographical Description of Formosa*, 1704. Courtesy of the Singer-Mendenhall Collection, Rare Book and Manuscript Library, University of Pennsylvania.

ity of his Christianization and self-improvement—at giving external form to the "internal Virtue."

Psalmanazar's construction of a Formosan language is perhaps the most sensational and commented upon aspect of his impersonation.[37] His exercises in translation enabled "Formosan" prayers and catechisms to be reproduced and circulated independently from its author, lending his physical imposture a degree of textual uniformity. As a testament to the longevity of Psalmanazar's religious-linguistic fraud, his faux Formosan Lord's Prayer continued to be included alongside actual transliterations of Formosan dialects in nineteenth-century linguists' accounts. To the untrained eye, his version bears a decent resemblance to actual

Portrait of George Psalmanazar, frontispiece from *Memoirs of *****, *commonly known by the name of George Psalmanazar*, 1765. Courtesy of the Rare Book and Manuscript Library, University of Pennsylvania.

transliterations of the Lord's Prayer into the Formosan language. Michael Keevak has argued that the qualities of consistency and uniformity demonstrated by his fake translations of the Lord's Prayer were matched by his stalwart adherence to his stories of Formosa in the face of contradictory accounts, as well as by his genuine and "regular" displays of piety later on in life. Keevak writes, "Regularity, in fact, is also what binds together Psalmanazar the impostor and Psalmanazar the convert."[38] At the same time, it is the indeterminacy of translation, and the impossibility of matching exactly words and concepts, that makes the performance of conversion, linguistic and religious, an ongoing and incomplete negotiation of inconsistency and irregularity. As Lydia Liu points out in her work on translation, Psalmanazar, through his forgery of the Formosan alphabet, mimicked the work of the missionaries and linguists who romanized indigenous languages to create a universal idiom that might standardize the project of colonialism and its system of uneven exchanges. Despite these efforts, there is always the trace of the foreign that remains in excess of the equivalences drawn.[39]

The performance of language acquisition, insofar as it signals the movement between East and West, reveals the tensions of demonstrable virtue. Asian converts, Protestant and Catholic, were meant to demonstrate their piety through reciting prayers and church doctrines. The depth of their conversion could always be called into question by critics of the missions; in fact, exemplary performances could just as well signal insincerity. Such a paradox manifests in the challenges to Psalmanazar's too-perfect mastery of language highlighted in the second edition of his *Description of Formosa*, which adds a detailed preface documenting and responding to the objections to his facts and figures. As Psalmanazar reported one challenge to his knowledge of theology:

> How came this young Pagan by such valid Arguments against Transubstantiation, Consubstantiation, and absolute Predestination? . . . Is it not reasonable to think that he copy'd them from some of our best Casuists and polemical Divines?

To which he brazenly answered:

> This Objection . . . proceeds from the too mean opinion you have of the Intellects of us Indians . . . if you will but allow the natural Faculties of Indians and Europeans to be equal, you must allow them equally able to draw natural conclusions.[40]

In supplying systematic responses, the diligent convert is accused of merely rehearsing arguments without sincerity, of being a fake or "copy." Against the imputation of religious fraud, Psalmanazar invokes a different order of truth—Formosan virtue. He holds the "natural Faculties of Indians" to be at once exceptional and typical, original and derivative. It is the hethnic potential of an antipodal yet equal Formosa that supplies the proof of sincerity when other arguments fail. Psalmanazar's linguistic conversions of a known script into its Formosan equivalent attempted to make visible an unseen place, and, moreover, the vastness of movement between places. The translations concretize the abstract, and as "proofs of sincerity" signify outwardly an internal conversion from one spiritual state into another. Language acquisition, a form of learned virtue, signals the universal force of a religion capable of converting a heathen who is at the same time idealized as innately virtuous.

While his reception in England may not have been based on widespread knowledge of actual Formosans, Psalmanazar's performance responded to the production of Indian converts of the East and West who, through discipline and training, could be held up as a models of learned virtue. Dutch Protestant missionary activity in Formosa generated an enviable quota of conversions in the mid-seventeenth century.[41] Of the successful baptisms, all could repeat multiple prayers and articles of faith in addition to answering questions concerning Christian doctrine. Indeed, those accepted into the mission seminary of the "Church of Tayouan" should possess "a good character, good memories, and quickness of apprehension" and "know by heart the Prayers and the Catechism, be very adept in learning the Dutch language, and well acquainted with reading and writing, having already proved themselves to be among the most willing to receive this training."[42] Consider the praise for the constancy of the converted heathen, whose entire being is defined by the turn from paganism:

> Moreover, many of them are so able, in such fervencie of spirit, to poure out their prayers before God, Morning and Evening, and before and after taking of Meat, and in other Necessities; and that with such comeliness and fitnesse of speech, and with such moderation and decencie of gesture; that may provoke tears to such as heare and behold them. And there are some of them, that being called to pray about any matter of business, are able to perform it in *conceived* prayer, *ex tempore*, so readily, in such fit expressions, and with such arguments and pithinesse, as if they had been spending some houres for the contriving and so framing of them.[43]

The natives perform their virtue through their imitation of rituals, internalized to the point of *seeming* "as if" they had contrived them or in fact, having done so themselves. Of course, the seemingly natural piety of the convert has been learned. When charged with being a mere copy, the sincere convert must claim originality of intention, yet also embrace his status of being a virtuous copy rather than a mere fake. In other words, a civilized heathen must maintain a natural, or inner, sense of true religion even though he has mechanistically learned its tenets through repetition and regurgitation.

In order for the Formosan's piety to carry the authority of a heathen convert, his learning must be seen as the externalization of inner virtue that is at once foreign and local—"native," in multiple senses of the term. Raymond Williams has noted the dual significance of the term *native*, which can refer either positively to one's own nation and place of birth or, alternatively, signify not the self but those non-European others subjected to political conquest and assigned inferior status.[44] Although everyone is a native of some place, the biases embedded within the term nonetheless assign Native 1 and Native 2, so to speak, to their respective places in the colonial hierarchy. Once converted, though, the colonial subject affirms the religious ideology and expansionist agenda of the English subject by being brought into the fold. The Native 2, whose virtue replicates that of a Native 1, becomes an exemplary imitation. There is merit, even genius, in the skillful reproduction that not only duplicates but potentially improves upon the original. By his own account, Psalmanazar's "proofs of sincerity" employed a strategy of "passing" counter to the modern sense of blending in; rather, he practiced maximum visibility through exploiting the ideal of a converted and civilized heathen whose authenticity was accompanied by a necessary show of sincerity and moral virtue.[45] Such acquired erudition and gentility, or people-knowledge, won Psalmanazar credibility in London polite society. As one socialite Elizabeth Thomas reported of his exceptional learning and manners:

> If he be real (and as *Musidora* says, there is an Air of Sincerity accompanies all he says, as well as what he writes) who knows the Design of Providence; for, setting aside Inspiration, the Apostles were more unlikely to convert Nations than this Man. He is allowed by all to have good Parts, both natural and acquired; he is master of six Languages, has an acute Apprehension, tenacious Memory, and considering how he was educated in Pagan-Superstition, it is methinks little less than a Miracle to hear him already Discourse with such Clearness and Strength of Argument on the sublimest Articles of our Faith, as might shame Christians, who tho' baptized into this Church in their Infancy, and have all their Lives professed its Doctrine, are yet, nevertheless, more ignorant of the Fundamentals than this poor Pagan, who was so lately admitted a Member of it.[46]

The foreigner's "Air of Sincerity" is both persuasive and difficult to quantify precisely because it is a performative category that exceeds questions of translational accuracy or cultural authenticity. In Thomas's passage above, his good intentions are manifested in his mastery of languages and "Discourse" insofar as they give him the tools to "convert Nations" better than the "Apostles" themselves. The writer Corinna admires not only the novelty of Psalmanazar's tobacco smoking and stories of the snake-eating habits of Formosans, but also his willingness to suffer for religion and, indeed, to save his countrymen from their pagan state of error. What appeals to the good Christian and at the same time puts her to shame is the exemplary native convert whose faith and fluency exceeds her own, native understanding. The Formosan possesses an administrative potential to reproduce the ideal English subject in heathens and Londoners alike, making him both converter and convert, Native 1 and Native 2. Beyond a mere sign of Formosan authenticity, his linguistic prowess and skills of translation are a form of cultural capital that endow him with not only heathen, but gentlemanly credibility.

Testimony, Credibility, and the Virtues of Inconsistency

Despite religious commonsense, sincerity was far from a transparent matter of innate or even individual character. Methods for evaluating truth-telling and personal testimony were at the center of modern scientific inquiry and the institutional practices of the Royal Society, whose members took an avid interest in the news and specimens brought back from the East Indies. In a culture of experimental knowledge, both conventional knowledge and personal accounts, however strange, were subjected to moderate amounts of skepticism rather than outright dismissal. A number of criteria were developed for determining the credibility of witness testimony, as outlined by Shapin and Schaffer in their study of scientific experiment: plausibility (conformity to common knowledge); multiple testimony (more than one eyewitness); consistency between sources; immediacy and reliability of sources (original over copies); knowledge and skill level of sources (learned experts rather than uneducated lay people); confident style (not impassioned or fancy rhetoric); and sources of acknowledged integrity. These factors not only at times overlapped but also potentially contradicted each other, depending on the claim at hand.[47]

Beyond the reach of formal reasoning, though, was also the question of a class-based system of honor that bound together English civil society and enabled the circulation of credible knowledge. The gentleman-scientist, given his reputable status, was able to legitimize the knowledge claims of a nascent field of scientific inquiry in part by transferring his perceived honesty—or sincerity—across social spheres. Through the figure of Robert Boyle, chemist, director of the East India Company, and member of the Royal Society, Shapin also describes the concurrent "making of a personal identity and the making of items of public knowledge."[48] Boyle exemplified the "Christian virtuoso"—philosopher, worshipper, and gentleman—who argued for the importance of experimental science as well as for the compatibility of faith and science; both were, Boyle argued, rigorously invested in methodical epistemological inquiry and in establishing the role of experience, witnessing, and testimony in determining standards of truth. In advocating the science of religion, Boyle called for an "Experimental Knowledge of God's Works."[49]

Psalmanazar's demonstrations of sincerity, in positing two types of abstract truth, God and Formosa, mimicked the expertise of the Christian virtuoso to test the limits of credibility and moral certainty. His performances of conversion, gentility, and erudition not only granted him access to London's social elite but also to a community of Royal Society experts, whose records indicate that he was met with skepticism at the outset. Of the various criteria for evaluating witness testimony, the Royal Society accused Psalmanazar above all of presenting information inconsistent with other accounts of Formosa by travelers to and from Asia, with China as a primary point of reference. The society had in its possession, for example, a "very exact Chart of China & Formosa, drawn in the year 1667; which is altogether incompatible with the Account of Formosa lately published by George Psalmanaasaar." Members also had books in Chinese as well as "in the Language of Formosa."[50] Despite their suspicions or even conclusive rejections of Psalmanazar's details, however, textual incompatibilities of geography or language alone could not prove him inconsistent enough to be declared false. Such conundrums proved the limits of scientific knowledge and the epistemological crises exploited in Psalmanazar's fraud and at the heart of European constructions of the Asian other.

By holding the society accountable to its own nascent rules of probability and skeptical inquiry, Psalmanazar found holes in their own credibility and manipulated in particular the criteria of consistency regarding knowledge about Formosa as reported by his rival witnesses, merchants, travel writers, and missionaries. He drew from the entire repertoire of argumentative strategies outlined above; moreover, by embracing the contradictions between different ways of knowing—reason and revelation—he used Formosa to experiment with the abstract conditions of truth-telling. His strategies were far from systematic; rather they drew on variations of being a credible "native" witness in the areas of science and religion. The onus for the challengers was to prove Psalmanazar wrong with absolute certainty; the beauty of his approach of embracing inconsistency is that all things will be right some of the time.

Partly, Psalmanazar benefited from the general skepticism over the reliability of travelers' reports. Increasing numbers of new discoveries and the emerging field of natural history created what Michael McKeon has identified as a dialectical split between "naïve empiricists," who embraced the factual accuracy of the newly reported phenomena, and "extreme skeptics," who rejected the validity of such accounts. Two sides of a common development in empiricist epistemology, both naïve empiricism and extreme skepticism, contested "romance idealism," or the "dependence on received authorities and a priori traditions."[51] Psalmanazar joined the campaign against romantic travel writing first in the preface to his *Description of Formosa*, where he proposed to correct the "fabulous Reports,"

"Misrepresentations," and "so many Romantic Stories of all those remote Eastern Countries." Later, he would denounce his former forgery as itself "scandalous romance."[52] He also repudiated the "fabulous" account of George Candidius, the Dutch minister whose *A Short Account of the Island of Formosa in the Indies, situated near the Coast of China* was in fact one of the various sources for his own descriptions of the island. By grouping the "forgeries of Candidius" with the accounts of fallible merchants and biased Jesuits, Psalmanazar challenged the very possibility of verifying the characteristics of an unseen place through textual proof alone.[53] It should count in his favor, Psalmanazar argued, that his narrative was in fact *inconsistent* with these others.

Given the questionable authority of written travel accounts, the Royal Society sought to discredit Psalmanazar's consistency by inviting eyewitnesses to contest his descriptions of Formosa. An exchange of letters from Mr. Henry Newman of the Royal Society to Mr. Sam Griffiths queried the validity of "the Situation, Products, Government, Religion, Languages, and Customs of that Country" as described in Psalmanazar's recently published book:

> This Gentleman Psalmanaazar is now in Town and is Suspected by many to be an Impostor because of the *Inconsistencies* of his Relation to others that have been given of that countrey. But I have not been able to find out any person in London that has been there, or nearer to it there than Tyowan and therefore I hope you will Excuse the trouble of the Enquiries above.[54] (my emphasis)

As Newman goes on to say in his next letter:

> You will easily perceive that I have askt most of these and the former Questions from what Psalmanaazaar has asserted in his Book which Supposing it Romantick may Seem an Impertinency not to be forgiven, but the Gentleman I made bold to Communicate your Letter to being very well Satisfied of the *Sincerity of your Relation* urged me to give you this further trouble, that we may be able to Charge Psalma. with all his *Inconsistencies* at once, and if you can furnish us with any Remarkable Test to prove him by it may Contribute to facilitate detecting him.[55] (my emphasis)

One might compare this solicitation of a "sincere relation" with the earlier testimony of the French Jesuit Jean de Fontaney, recently returned from China, a friend of the Royal Society who met in person with Psalmanazar and argued that Formosa was Chinese territory. His expertise was discounted by Psalmanazar on account of his never actually having been to Formosa proper. The Royal Society thus turned to Griffiths (someone "in London that has been there, or nearer to it than Tyowan") instead to provide more direct access.[56]

That the Royal Society prioritized Griffiths's report over the other textual accounts of the island certainly speaks to the assumed legitimacy of an accepted gentleman's word over an otherwise impervious outsider; but it also reveals the dearth of material witnesses who could counter Psalmanazar's "native" authority. Ultimately, though, Psalmanazar needed the testimony of others to supplement his credibility. In response to the Royal Society's search for countertestimony, he appropriated the power of "people knowledge," producing his own witnesses to expose the biases of gentlemanly society. Importantly, he disputed not only the facts presented by the Royal Society but also their standards of exclusivity and sincerity.[57] In one defense of revelation, addressed to a deist rationalist, he wrote, "I am confident a great part of your Gentlemen, as well as your self, can believe Things upon the Authority of another man."[58] He also supplied his own defendants in a pseudonymously authored pamphlet, *An Enquiry into the Objections Against George Psalmanaazaar of Formosa. In Which the Accounts of the People, and Language of Formosa by Candidius, and the other European Authors, and the Letters from Geneva, and from Suffolk, about Psalmanaazaar, are proved not to contradict his Accounts* (1710). As the title suggests, the work was a compilation of interrogations and counterinterrogations that, through its documentation of public controversy, constituted a case study of Formosa as truth-claim. The *Enquiry* was in name authored by other members of the community, impartial third parties who came to Psalmanazar's defense against the naysayers. One, "John Albert Lubomirski," a purported missionary for forty years in China and three years in Formosa, confirmed Psalmanazar's claims of child sacrifice, his fair appearance, and his Formosan language with the "credibility of witness," though Lubomirski's actual existence has never been verified.[59]

In the *Enquiry*, Psalmanazar outlined his critics' three major objections to his purported Formosan identity: (1) difference from other accounts of Formosa, (2) irreconcilable particulars between his facts and these accounts, and (3) his European appearance. In each case, he answered the charges of inconsistency not only by claiming to be consistent within a feigned community but by foregoing the criterion of consistency altogether through a combination of deferral and supplementarity, or the constant expansion of the terms under consideration. Consider, for one, Psalmanazar's claim that in 1630 Formosa was not a Chinese territory (historically accurate) but was a part of Japan. Citing a "confusion of names," he distinguished between Formosa proper, otherwise known to its natives as Paccando, and "Tyowan," the smaller Dutch settlement on the island.[60] Amid the colonial confusion, he argued, the Dutch could be faulted with misnaming "Tayavan" as Formosa. Furthermore, merchants and missionaries, confined to "Tyavan" and the coasts of Formosa (where the "Coasters" resided), mistook a part for the whole of the island. To further his point about local knowledge, Psalmanazar pointed to another terra incognita, the small island of "Tugin," situated between China and Formosa and unclaimed by either China or Holland. Unlike the Coasters, these natives of Tugin were supposed to be the principal Formosans and therefore unconverted by the Dutch (*Enquiry*, 8–9). According to the *Enquiry*—and specifically its pseudonymous authors—there was thus the "Formosa of Candidius, and of all us Europeans," and the true, inaccessible Formosa that Psalmanazar represented (17).

In the manner of a deconstructionist, Psalmanazar continuously substituted one meaning for another to compensate for the lack of his actual origins: there could always be a third term in excess of a given signifier.[61] In response to the investigation into his fabricated Jesuit kidnapper Alexander de Rode, he retorted, "The Reader will please to note, They speak but of Two of this Name, but does not exclude a *Third*, who may be the Man we want."[62] This is an instance of endless supplementarity and self-reflexive fiction, of preventing closure rather than resolving a particular problem, and of establishing moral rather than absolute certainty. When pressed on an issue, he could claim ignorance based on cultural difference, youth or lack of expertise, cultural incompatibilities of language and standards for measurements, and bad translations—displacing blame and error onto anyone and everything other than himself. In fact, not only did Psalmanazar supplement his own inconsistencies, but he displaced the quality of inconsistency onto the East itself. When accused of contriving a false language, he pointed to the existence of various dialects instead of any single language in China and Japan. Moreover, the tense political relations between Japan and China, he explained, resulted in his lack of access to China and hence his ignorance of the Chinese language. Formosa also differed from both China and Japan, and resembled Europe, in several key respects, including its standards of beauty. Whereas the Asian empires prefer artificially blackening their teeth, the Formosans "preserve theirs white."[63] By branding the Eastern object of inquiry internally inconsistent, Psalmanazar wielded the disruptive force of the local, Native 1 knowledge against the universal standards that the Royal Society sought to put into practice.

Given that existing accounts of Formosa described the inhabitants as having a dark or olive complexion, how did what would appear to be Psalmanazar's most damning inconsistency—his skin color—become an asset to his impersonation?[64] As noted in the Royal Society minutes, "George Psalmaanasaar was permitted to be present. He said he was a Native of Formosa, and that he is about printing an account of that Island: He look'd like a young Dutch-man."[65] In the *Enquiry*, Psalmanazar explains his whiteness as an aberration that falls within the realities of natural variance in color. Although Formosans should be black-haired and olive, yellow, or tawny-skinned, he argues, there are always some exceptions to the norm in any given country, especially given his time spent out of the sun as a member of the sheltered nobility. Not only did the association of Formosa with whiteness align it with Europe in the case of teeth color; Psalmanazar also posited white Formsanness as a sign of universal gentility in remarking elsewhere that "the Formosans are also white and very fair, but chiefly the Women; and if we may believe the Proverb, Turkey and Japan breed the fairest Women in the World."[66] In the eighteenth century, as Roxann Wheeler has demonstrated, racial complexion was a lesser indication of cultural alterity than the markers of religion, language, and dress.[67] Among the numerous theories of racial difference, the idea that climate determined race matched Psalmanazar's added pitch that the change of climate in the journey from East to West was apt to turn a person white.[68] Two types of explanations, one based on the fact of lived inconsistencies, the other on the effect of distance traveled, perpetuated the contradictions of his identity as an exceptional yet typical native. In these instances, Psalmanazar again appealed to the idea of conversion, not religious or linguistic, but racial, to posit cultural difference as a highly mediated and unstable category.

Argumentation and an overengagement with rather than retreat from opposition helped compensate for Psalmanazar's lack of visible Formosanness. Audience reactions supplied him with a cause to defend, preconceptions to correct, principles to supplement and revise, and an idea of Formosa that supplemented existing knowledge of China and Japan. More effective than any individual riposte was the accumulation of responses into the staging of public dialogue. Throughout his career, he rendered his contradictions transparent, *as if* there were nothing to hide. The *Enquiry*, after all, is a compilation of all the objections to his conversion and native authority, including the Royal Society correspondence with Newman. From the start, he publicized his debates in the preface to the *Description of Formosa* by listing his meetings with foreign ministers and officials, theologians, travelers, Royal Society members, and even an encounter in a coffee house with "several Noblemen present."[69] He solicited public inquiry, moreover, by inviting readers to contact his bookseller with their reactions: "But whosoever is not entirely satisfy'd with what I have said, may come to me . . . [or] send me his scruples in a Letter." In the *Enquiry*, he reprinted these objections, which consisted largely of Roman Catholic contestations of his Protestantism, and responded to each point. His fraud, and his performance of virtue in the public sphere, thus relied on conversion as *conversus*, or prolonged conversation, as much as on the idea of a simple opposition of true and false, West and East.

Matters of Fact and Faith

While Psalmanazar's performances demonstrated the limits of and connections between sincerity and authenticity as modes of authoritative knowledge, they also illuminated the epistemological bases of faith and fact. In his case, we see that self-promotion in the name of transparency mirrored both the scientific method of securing one's credibility through public experiment and the religious criteria for determining the true God. What makes God's miracles valid, Psalmanazar argued in the *Description of Formosa*, is their public nature. They must, as he put it, be "performed everywhere":

> They were plain Objects of our senses, every Body present could see them; they were not done in a Corner, or in a particular secret Place, but publickly, before the Face of the Sun, so that it can never be said that these Demonstrations of Omnipotency were subtle Deceits and Impostures. (72)

Whereas an impostor, Jesuit or otherwise, might hide from public light, Psalmanazar exposed himself to it. Although he did not explicitly claim godly omnipotence, he did model his authority after divine infallibility. Religion and science run together in Psalmanazar's assertions of authority regarding matters of uncertain faith and fact; and in his defense of his Christian virtuosity, he was at once a true convert and a genuine Formosan.

In the late seventeenth and early eighteenth centuries, what was commonly referred to as "matter of fact" or "moral certainty" by definition could not be proved by empirical demonstration.[70] Defenders of scriptural truth and divine or churchly authority, in particular, used spiritual matters of fact against the deists and skeptics who argued for rational alternatives to received wisdom. To accommodate his split personality, Psalmanazar put both skepticism and revelation to work by attempting to establish his credibility as a divine witness as well as a native eyewitness of Formosa. Sincerity plays a key role in this dual demonstration. In his thinly veiled pseudonymous work *A Dialogue Between A Japonese and a Formosan, About Some Points of The Religion of the Time* (1707), Psalmanazar dramatized his conversion through a mock discourse between two Easterners, a Japanese skeptic and a Formosan church conformist, who debated the nature of religious authority and the limits to human reason. In the preface, Psalmanazar asserted the "Sincerity of [his] Narrative" by disavowing his authorship of the text. After these prefatory remarks, he absents himself from the purportedly overheard conversation between the two friends; in a gesture typical of eighteenth-century authorial self-effacement, he claims a disinterested perspective on the views expressed, "the whole Matter being justly and impartially laid before you." That is to say, he in effect creates a script for another hypothetical Formosan to perform the role of virtuous church citizen. Once again, he generates his own, fictive double, as if to show that the falsity of this Formosan only affirms his own truthful existence. In the preface Psalmanazar identifies himself as a credible witness to a discussion that takes place in Formosa on the topic of, appropriately enough, reliable witnesses to God's word. At the level of both form and content, then, is the question of how individual experience, ever fallible even when firsthand, can rival the certainty of divine authority.

Through his Formosan character's apology for scriptural and institutional authority, Psalmanazar enacted his own political alignment with high church ideology. The *Dialogue*'s Formosan advocates the power of revealed religion and a line of direct access to God himself. Through a series of point-by-point questions and responses, he trumps the Japanese deist and skeptic, for whom the mere existence of false prophets and corrupt lawgivers proves the human and priestly tendency to abuse power. As a critic of traditionally inherited authority and a believer in the ubiquity of human error, the Japanese figure demands a rigorous process of weeding out any false claims to authority to maintain perfect consistency among all pieces of textual evidence. The Formosan, however, argues that so-called inconsistencies fit within a God-centered paradigm that is in fact characterized by contradictions, or precisely those phenomena that cannot be explained by reason. Religious doctrine must be accepted wholly, because to excerpt only the "reasonable" parts would threaten the sanctity of the original. Against the deist's assertions of doubt and reasoned probabilities, the Formosan claims revelation to be, paradoxically, a matter of fact.

Such a declaration of certainty takes us back to the complicity between virtue and commerce, for this is a question of establishing the fact of Japan, here a spiritual rather than physical place, as a knowledge claim—an abstract or invisible truth—that cannot be accessed commercially or demonstrated empirically. The assertion of truths contrary to reason uses the imagined space of Formosa as a testing ground for knowledge claims and matters of fact, where Formosa, and Psalmanazar's fraud more broadly, becomes a hypothetical space of truth, much like other exotic sites of the period became experiments in perspective. In a time of mercantile expansion, mapping of "new worlds," travel narratives, and the uncertain relationship between "fact" and "fiction," out-of-sight geographies provided useful examples for demonstrating the epistemological limits and possibilities shared by religious and scientific investments in distinguishing certain from uncertain knowledge. Unvisited, antipodal places of desirable resources and commodities provided ready testing grounds for knowledge claims. One such theoretical commonplace in the late seventeenth century was the story of a hot climate where water could not freeze. John Locke, the influential deist whose positions were targeted through the Japanese figure of Psalmanazar's *Dialogue*, established an important precedent for the discussion of matters of fact in his *Essay Concerning Human Understanding*. The place in question is in this case not Formosa but Siam, another integral part of China's tributary trade network. Locke argues that one should be skeptical of second-hand information about foreign places:

> And as it happened to a *Dutch* Ambassador, who entertaining the King of *Siam* with the particularities of *Holland*, which he was inquisitive after, amongst other things told him, that the Water in his Country, would sometimes, in cold weather, be so hard, that Men walked upon it, and that it would bear an Elephant, if he were there. To which the King replied, *Hitherto I have believed the strange Things you have told me, because I look upon you as a sober fair man, but now I am sure you lye.*[71]

Told from the perspective of the king of Siam, the frozen-water anecdote is also an exercise in imagining the grounds of reliable testimony through imagining cultural difference antipodally. Locke argues that when given a choice between personally experienced "matter of fact" and another's testimony, however reliable, one tends, like the king, to be skeptical of the second-hand account. Moreover, such "Siamese skepticism" is warranted, considering the likelihood of witness fallibility.[72]

Of course, the Dutchman's report on cold weather turning water hard happens to be true. What Locke's readers take for granted as fact, the foreigner presumes to be impossible. A tropical Siam conveniently fits within an antipodal framework whereby it neatly contradicts the West: true is false, and false is true. A familiar law of nature does not apply; and instead, one must proceed according to the rules of reason and doubt. At issue is not why water turns hard, nor how the Dutchman might persuade the Siamese king of this fact—neither scientific experimentation nor sincerity has much place in this particular scenario—but rather, what constitutes a reasonably skeptical outlook and the subjective conditions of proof.[73] In the *Dialogue Between a Japonese and a Formosan*, Psalmanazar again stages the frozen-water exchange, although this later version is to support the Formosan's trust in religious authority over the Japanese voice of skepticism—to create a space for the seemingly impossible. As the Formosan argues:

> For when to my knowledge, you have been told by several Men, that in very Cold Countries they had seen the Water grow so hard, that a Cart went over it: You have believ'd it upon the Honesty, of these Relators; tho' I don't know how you'll make this and Reason agree. (30)

Turning the Lockean example of Siamese skepticism on its head, Psalmanazar teaches a lesson about sincerity. The honesty of the native Westerners is meant to mirror the word of religious lawgivers who, like those with firsthand knowledge of their own climate, should be believed on account of their experience of revelation and access to certainty of knowledge. It is thus both the authorities' personal experience of God and their trustworthiness that confirm the facts of existence, often against reason. As the Formosan remarks, "How many Things are there which have appeared contrary to Reason, impossible, &c. which either by a more mature Consideration, or by experience, have been made as clear as the Sun!" (38).

As an indication of his theoretical investment in bridging sincerity and authenticity, in the *Description of Formosa* Psalmanazar also rehearses a variation of the frozen-water argument:

> Suppose a Man born in a very cold Climate, should go into a hot country, where the Natives never saw Snow or Ice, and should tell them, That where he was born, the Water, at a certain Season of the Year, was so hard that a Horse can run over it; these People would say, It is against Reason, and contrary to the Nature of Water to grow hard; and therefore because neither Reason nor Experience taught them otherwise, they would conclude the Traveller had a mind to impose upon them: But if these Inhabitants were persuaded he was a *faithful honest Man*, and said he saw it with his own eyes ... then certainly they would believe it upon his testimony, tho' they could not conceive how such a thing should be. (141; my emphasis)

In both documents, Psalmanazar employs the anecdote to argue for verifying the man's "faithful honesty" as well as the natural phenomena that contradict reason. If applied to his own performance of native authority, the lesson would be that his firsthand experience of an unseen place should trump the rational arguments of other travelers: one does and should accept the fact of water freezing, however counter to reason, on the condition of being "persuaded" of the native's sincerity.

In both the context of his Royal Society engagements and his theological writing, Psalmanazar relied on the idea of moral certainty to combat the expert testimony of challenges to his claims of fact and faith. Formosa, a supplement to China, becomes an abstract place of truth used to prove the virtue of revealed religion, even as its existence must also be proved, without the aid of concrete empirical evidence, through networks of witness testimony. These are experiments in visualizing sincerity in the absence of physical proof. The hard water of the unseen West, or the hot climate of the unseen East or South, rings true because it seems to contradict the visible laws of nature. So, too, does Psalmanazar embody contradiction. He alleges, after all, his "Soul, the principal Part of him, if that may be said to be a part, which has in it self no parts," to be "Japonese" even if his skin and features do not appear to be authentic (*Enquiry*, 48). The move inward essentially discounts the category of the body altogether. He performs a theory of conversion that emphasizes the lack of epistemological closure rather than absolute proof, or proofs of sincerity rather than authenticity, per se. What determines Psalmanazar's persuasive honesty, or sincerity, exceeds the mere accumulation of argumentation, postulata, ethnographic detail, or, for that matter, the sphere of gentlemanly influence. Instead, he impersonates Formosa by converting the theoretical and improbable antipodes into a concrete example.

Converts as Commodities

The discourse of conversion's before-and-after dichotomy emphasizes a movement between extremes that in Psalmanazar's case strategically positioned West and East at opposite ends of the earth. He had traveled "from Paganism to the most pure and Primitive part of the Church, from the farthest Eastern to the farthest Western Isles of the world" (*Enquiry*, 52–53). The commercial value attached to this long-distance passage is perhaps best expressed by the pseudonymous authors of the *Enquiry into the Objections*, who defended Psalmanazar's "sincere" conversion in terms of England's worldly gain:

> [Psalmanazar is a] great Addition both to the Glory of our Church, and to the Numbers of its Members, by the Conversion of the great and populous, the Rich, and the potent Empire of *Japan*, of which *Formosa* is a very considerable dependant, and the only door by which our Religion can enter as things now are. . . . [W]e can only add our hearty Prayers that God would move the Hearts of all sincere Christians to promote the Conversion of *Japan*, and in order thereto incourage and assist the noble Intentions of this Convert, the First Fruits of the *East Indias*. (53)

It was not merely Psalmanazar's soul at stake but the economic conversion of Japan's empire, praised in terms generally reserved for China, "great and populous ... Rich, and Potent." Japan is here fantasized as a gateway to the entire East Indies trade and as a site of yet unattained markets and immeasurable profits.

The appeal of the converted heathen lay in his embodiment of a doubled potential—the potential convertibility of Eastern manufactures, as well as morals, into a Western market. Psalmanazar was part of a continuum of foreign visitors who were over the years displayed for their exemplary virtue and commercial prospects. Two instances in particular resonate with Psalmanazar's creation of public spectacle at the intersection of scientific, religious, and commercial culture. The one-month visit of four American Indians to London in 1710 was a remarkable instance of native performance and politicized exoticism.[74] The foreignness of their dress, features, and demeanor made these visitors a spectacular presence in the city's streets and public spaces, memorialized in a range of publications. While attending the theater, the so-called Indian Kings were on display, as audience members, for their reactions of "native sensibility" and for appearing as live versions of Restoration tragedy's exotic kings and queens.[75] Less visible were the religious and political reasons behind their trip. The Mohawk delegation had been selected by New York colonial administrators to make the transatlantic voyage as part of a push for increased British support in the ongoing war against France over North American territories. This visit was meant to improve Anglo-Indian relations and win reinforcements for the colonial cause, which included strengthening the foothold of Protestantism abroad.

As participants in the politics of conversion, the Americans also visited the Society for the Propagation of the Gospel in Foreign Parts (SPGFP). They were there—in the capacity of converted heathens—to request additional missionaries for native churches. Formed in 1701, the SPGFP responded to the perceived "growth of vice and immorality" and the crisis of the Anglican Church of the 1690s. Amid the upsurge of voluntary religious societies across the country calling for "a general reformation of the lives and manners of all our subjects," this particular group advocated gentle rather than coercive measures to spread Christianity at home and abroad, but especially in the colonies. It was no coincidence, then, that the church proponents of the SPGFP, Bishops Tenison, Compton, Sharp, and Burnet, were the same authorities who had previously welcomed the Reverend Alexander Innes and his gifted convert, the newly baptized George Psalmanazar, to England. In this climate of missionary activity, a time of "moral renewal," "'internalised' faith," and the "vitality of Anglicanism," the Indian Kings were part of a tradition of exotic indigenes whose Christianized virtue exemplified the universal power of reform alongside access to the abundant material resources of the New World.

Print matter announcing the arrival of the Indian Kings made explicit the connections between missionary and mercantile interests, namely through the comparison to Psalmanazar. Referring to them as "*Psalmanaazar's*... from the West-Indies," one pamphleteer protested that the idealization of the Indian Kings had "no other reasonable Design but that of lessening the Honour due to the Majesty of Kings."[76] By invoking the fake Formosan, he transferred the taint of illegitimate nobility to these most recent visitors. For *Psalmanazar* evoked a genealogy of far-flung peoples, hethnics whose Christianized paganism illustrated the limits and possibilities of universal Protestantism. The activities of missionaries to the West and East Indies in the early modern period have been well documented; however, travel in the reverse directions was less frequent, and religious visitors to Europe from East Asia were rare, though not unprecedented. In the tradition of Jesuit "propaganda tours," a retinue of Japanese "Christian kings" arrived in the late 1500s, followed sporadically by individual Chinese youths brought to pursue Jesuit orders and assist with scholarship on China.[77] One such pairing was the French missionary Alexandre de Rhodes and his ward, Cheng Wei-hsin, also known as Emmanuel de Siqueira; the two left Macao in 1645 and traveled overland to Rome, where Siqueira undertook a Jesuit education and eventually became ordained the first Chinese Jesuit priest in Coimbra, Portugal around 1664.[78] Their story, widely known in Avignon as well as Rome, was a likely source for Psalmanazar, who had been exposed to the Jesuit news circuit through his education while in France. It is an unlikely coincidence that he chose the name Alexander de Rodes for the priest who had brought him from Formosa.[79]

Another prominent Chinese Christian in Europe, and the first to visit England, laid the groundwork for Psalmanazar, preceding him by a little more than a decade. Shen Fuzong (Fu-Tsung), also known as Michael Alphonsus, arrived to Holland in 1683 with the Belgian Jesuit Philippe Couplet to lobby for the Chinese mission abroad.[80] Representations of Shen from his time in England and France present divergent interpretations of the "Chinese convert" as a model of virtue, on the one hand, and of commerce, on the other. The first, a painting entitled "The Chinese Convert" by royal portraitist Sir Godfrey Kneller, portrays a pious figure in Jesuit dress, a fantasy of sincerity made visible. It is all the more remarkable in that it was commissioned in 1687 by James II, who hung it next to his bedchamber as a source of inspiration for his own conversion to Roman Catholicism less than a year later.[81] The portrait is a testimony to the effectiveness of the mission, and it also addresses and dispels the concerns within the Roman

Sir Godfrey Kneller, *Michael Alphonsus Shen Futsung, "The Chinese Convert,"* 1687. Reproduced by permission of The Royal Collection © 2010 Her Majesty Queen Elizabeth II.

Catholic Church over what constituted genuine conversion: to what degree local customs must be considered idolatrous and exorcised, despite their tendency to persist. The title *Chinese Convert*, like the moniker Indian King, suggests a paradox of hethnic virtue by yoking together identities that are meant to be mutually exclusive in the colonial order of Native 1 and Native 2.[82]

Neither the English portrait of Shen Fuzong done by Sir Godfrey Kneller nor a French engraving made during his time in Paris could be considered authentically Chinese, though for contrary reasons. While both display the convert as a figure of alterity, indeed as a spectacle of the East in the West, the second image accentuates the commercial fruits of the incipient French mission in China. The

Costume plate engraving of "Chin Fo Cum," c. 1684. Reproduced by permission of the Österreichische Nationalbibliothek, ÖNB/Wien, PORT_00018960_01.

caption of this fashion plate, engraved by Nicolas Langlois in 1690, refers to the Chinese convert by his Latinized name, Chin Fo Cum, and describes his presentation at Versailles. In the capacity of a converted heathen, Shen's appearances before Louis XIV demonstrated his doubled value as a model of learned piety and new consumer object, of immaterial and material wealth. As proof of his Native 1 and Native 2 authority, he was asked to recite the Pater Noster, Ave Maria, and the Credo in Chinese, as well as to demonstrate how to use chopsticks.[83] Indeed, the convert, a specimen of cultural exchange, was presented alongside the Jesuits' cargo of Chinese paintings and vestments.[84] Unlike the Jesuitical robes of Kneller's portrait, this costume flattens Shen's figure into a pattern of decorative, chinoiserie surface with no hint of spiritual depth. And yet, both the engraving and the oil portrait draw attention to the cultural and religious syncretisim at work in representing and circulating the convert as a model of Chineseness in the West. The convert occupies a state of unrealized potential. His foreignness offers virtue to be imitated in the spheres of religion as well as commerce. The images of the Chinese convert address the question of the relation between inner self and outer appearance, sincerity and authenticity, and the performance of not only a place but the movement from one place to another—the commercialization of virtue across this distance traveled.

The representational space occupied by the Chinese convert-turned-art-object is a type of cultural liminal zone. Though the distinction between present and past, self and other, is itself key to understanding the virtue of the converted heathen, he is also someone neither of one world nor the other, but somewhere between the two. In the circuits of East-West commodity culture, the idea of true Chinese is elusive and easily appropriated by phenomena such as chinoiserie, which made an art of faking Asian designs. But, as Psalmanazar's case illustrates, fakes compel us to reexamine our faculties of discernment and our criteria for telling the original from the copy. The vogue for Asian designs and decorative objects that arose along with the East Indies trade in the mid- to late seventeenth century spurred a culture of chinoiserie imitations far more imaginative than accurate. Motifs ranging from free-floating pagodas to tropical botanical specimen and Asiatic human figures were arranged in whimsical scenes of unnatural proportions following the rococo break with neoclassical order. They appeared on all manner of surfaces, including wallpaper, textiles, porcelain, furniture, and architecture.[85] By the mid-eighteenth century, chinoiserie was dismissed for its grotesquery, excess, and lack of taste. Critics since have also distinguished it as fake Chinese along the lines of "Orientalist" misrepresentation of China.[86] It has been branded illegible, inauthentic, irrational. In his analysis of chinoiserie as an "aesthetics of illegitimacy," David Porter notes a shift "from the scholarly to the aesthetic" in the reception of Chinese culture over the course of the eighteenth century; he contrasts an earlier period of Jesuit scholarship on Chinese culture and semiotics with the "aesthetic deflation of the cultural authority of the Chinese."[87] Porter's analysis of chinoiserie offers an important and productive intervention into the field of early modern China-Europe relations. I will, though, steer the discussion away from the progressive delegitimization of Chinese authority and the representational inaccuracies of chinoiserie to enable us to consider the epistemological utility of fakeness, and faking China, in the mutually operative realms of virtue and commerce. When viewed not as a mere European or "Orientalist" construction of Asia but as ground of experimentation, chinoiserie offers a theoretical deconstruction of the idea of authenticity.

Like the mixed form of chinoiserie, Psalmanazar's fraud is useful to think with because it refuses Orientalism's self-other dichotomy. It demonstrates, more than simply the difference between a real and a fake Asia, how cross-cultural exchanges produce a visible syncretism and hybridity at work in knowledge-production across a number of interrelated spheres. Even in Psalmanazar's theological and scientific debates, truth was a matter of approximating rather than authenticating his Japanese origins. His efforts to transfer his religious fraud into the commercial realm included a notable instance of marketing his imitation of the East. While Psalmanazar's self-presentation lacked the visual exoticism of the Indian Kings and their display of New World wealth, the "grand spectacle" of East Indies commodities was never far from his rendition of the exemplary native. The circulation of Psalmanazar's identity as a fake had commercial value, at least in theory, given his promotion of a new lacquer paint called Japanese white. In his *Memoirs*, he claims to have schemed with one Edward Pattenden to make a "white sort of Japan" that would "yield a kind of convincing *proof* to the fabulous account I had given of myself. We accordingly advertised it under the name of White Formosan Work; and it was viewed and greatly admired by the curious for its fine whiteness, smoothness, and hardness, and for the beauty of the other colours painted upon it" (*Memoirs*, 235).

In fact, an advertisement printed in the December 1708 issue of *The British Apollo* read:

> The fine white Enamell'd Work, as it is improved according to the right Japan way, by Geo. Psalmonaazaar . . . is of as fine, smooth and shining a white as any Chinaware, and the Paintings upon it done with the best of Colours, and according to the Indian manner. . . . It never looses its Colour, by either dampness of Air, Dirt, Smoak, or any other accident of the like nature. In a word, it is as good in every respect as any that comes from Japan.

The advertisement itself blends together a number of techniques, materials, and place-names in the manner of Psalmanazar's continual juxtapositions of different sites of Asia. Enamelwork, a paint coloring made from ground glass, was used as a protective base for other layers of painted decorations as well as to "give the Lustre and Polish to their Works"; it was thus closely related to japanwork, or japanning, "the Art of varnishing . . . after the same manner as the Workmen do who are Natives of *Japan*, a famous Island not far from the Coast of *China*."[88] Unlike the common monikers japanwork, chinawork, and indiawork, all used to describe the origins, at least in theory, of imported goods, no such thing as "Formosa work" existed. In concert with his efforts to associate Formosa with Japan and not China, Psalmanazar marketed a product that was specifically *not* chinaware, or porcelain, but rather a type of Japanese varnish, or lacquer.[89] And yet, chinoiserie blended together, as did Psalmanazar's advertisement, references to India, China, and Japan in European form. Here, the question of authenticity is less important than the quality of the imitation (*it is as good . . . as any that comes from Japan*). In fact, the real Japan becomes irrelevant to the "right Japan way," a technique that can ostensibly be applied to an array of objects, regardless of origins.

Just as the place-name China circulated in the commoditized form of china, Japan held double meaning in English consumer culture as a desirable Eastern manufacture, replicated in the West. The lacquerwork of Japan and China had been imported to England in the shape of screens, cabinets, boxes, chests, and luxury accessories beginning in the 1600s; chemical experiments to formulate a recipe to rival the resin of *Rhus vernicifera* would eventually produce a domestic industry of varnishing called japanning. Technically defined as "a varnish of exceptional hardness, which originally came from Japan" japanwork invoked the "Orient" in general and could refer to engraved or embroidered designs, entire objects or pieces of furniture, the varnish itself, or the people and practices of Asia.[90] In its domestic capacity, japanning, as distinct from lacquerwork, was a type of chinoiserie, or the European imitation of Asian arts. It embodied a fantasy of the resilient surface, the smooth, ideally preserved, and eminently transportable commodity. Unlike an object such as china, japanning was valued not for its fragility but its durability as a protective patina added onto an existing thing. Seventeenth- and eighteenth-century discourses of japanning, for example, idealized its powers of preservation:

> Japanning has taught us a method, no way inferior to it, for the splendor and preservation of our Furniture and Houses. These Buildings, like our Bodies, continually tending to ruin and dissolution, are still in want of fresh supplies and reparations . . . the Art of Japanning has made them almost impregnable against both [time and weather]. . . . True, genuine Japan, like the Salamander, lives in the flames, and stands unalterable.[91]

Japanning was thus a fantasy not of virtuous depths but in fact marvelous surfaces and the value of the East in improving upon the West. Psalmanazar, in his continuing experimentation with the form and appearances of an Asiatic convert, attempted to render the material virtues of the East into a marketable Western imitation. His tarnished virtue, too, entered the market as an object of consumption; his fraudulent status was in fact meant to add value to the product—the value not of authenticity but of approximation. In this light, the sincerity of the convert becomes a fiction of transparency put to commercial ends. Rather than contradict his efforts at proving the truth of his sincere conversion, his incorporation of chinoiserie into his hoax can be read as part of the experiment in converting a Formosan native. The gesture deconstructs the fetishization of absolute truth; it further defers the idea of an original Formosa and instead dwells in-between East and West in the realm of the hypothetical and ever convertible East.

Conversion Between Worlds

The name Psalmanazar, like the phenomenon of chinoiserie, was an experiment in sincerity and fakery. Formosa, a copy of Japan, which was a copy of China, was a floating signifier that in its circulation became an example of knowledges in the making and, above all else, the potential of converting the East's morals and wealth into Western virtue. Even his name connected hethnic natives of the distant East and West, deriving from Salmanazar or Shalmaneser, an ancient Assyrian king known for conquering the nation of Israel and exiling its peoples to remote parts of the world. The diaspora of these Ten Lost Tribes, as they were called, founded nations ranging from Scythians, or Tartars, to Native Americans, those "*Psalmanaazar's* from the *West-Indies*" included. Psalmanazar's case is a fascinating study of cultural alterity in its combination of bodily impersonation and textual forgery, on the one hand, and the utter lack of material evidence, on the other. He stood alone before the London public, without the traveler's telltale, authenticating mementos—feathers, coins, utensils, plants. The Royal Society had been for years developing its anthropological impetus to collect evidence, if rather indiscriminately, from the world over.[92] At one meeting, Royal Society members examined an assortment of things *alongside* Psalmanazar: an air-pump experiment, news of a person who pretended to live without food, dissections of the male opossum, the presentation of bones, an ovary, the foot of a body from the Canary Islands, and a log of wood from the East Indies.[93] These things out of place comprise a curiosity cabinet of free-floating signifiers awaiting attachment to a narrative or an argument that would assign them the representative status of an example.

In this case, Psalmanazar was the primary object in search of a narrative. He argued that his lack of cultural adornment supported the transparency of his account: after all, he was kidnapped from Formosa and had no time to bring any evidence of the island with him. Of course, his book supplied ethnographic descriptions and engravings of sites and objects in place of what he did not carry. And, as part of his live performance, his diet of raw meat and his threadbare habit functioned as material, and theatrical, accessories to his respective cannibalism and piety. By and large his proof, however, did not rely on "thing knowledge." He presented himself as an example of Formosa, and this self was constantly compensating for and contesting the sufficiency of empirical proof. Unlike the spectacle of the American Indian converts in the streets of London or the Chinese convert in the courts and university halls of Europe, Psalmanazar's Formosan engaged a different kind of visualization of foreignness: beyond the display of customs or dress, the demonstration of the movement between heathen and Christian. Ultimately, Psalmanazar founded his Eastern identity upon two truth claims about being "native," each of which he went to great lengths to prove: that he was a convert to the Anglican Church; and that he was from the island of Formosa. In each of his works, the two halves were exercised in tandem. The concluding sentence of the *Dialogue Between a Japonese and a Formosan* encapsulates the conjunction of his two-pronged identity: *That P———r is the Man he pretends to be, and that the History of* Formosa, *and of his Travels, is true, and his conversion to our Faith sincere and unfeigned* (*Enquiry*, 53). Situated somewhere between self and other, neither simply native nor convert, but a hybrid of the two, Psalmanazar relied on religious discourses of conversion to prove the moral certainty of his native status. A native convert should be a model of devotion who exemplifies the promise of self-improvement, of colonial conquest not by force but by assimilation. The convert's inner transformation, demonstrated through public debates, acts of piety, and the politics of sincerity, is often visualized as a journey, or the distance traveled from other to self, Native 2 to Native 1. All along, Psalmanazar emphasized the immaterial truth of his conversion and depth of piety over visible, authenticating signs of his cultural difference. Of course, one's inner character can only be read through outward signs, and it is this tension between reading the surface as a sign of underlying virtue and as an indication of sheer superficiality that fueled his performance of conversion.

Psalmanazar's "proofs of Sincerity" evidence the tension of materializing the true Formosan via the inner virtue of the soul. In the spirit of display, he concerned himself with the mere expression of virtue, "so that as long as the character or shadow of moral virtue procured me so much regard and esteem, I never troubled myself about the want of the real substance" (*Memoir*, 177). He deferred the question of "real substance" in favor of external appearances, and in so doing exposed the criteria of demonstrable knowledge itself. Theological disputation bolstered his claims to an origin that was not self-fabricated, but instead a testament to God's authority; linguistic mastery presented an exceptional native whose authority drew from religious partisan politics. Far from systematic, his repertoire of strategies tested different modes of being "native." Psalmanazar's exemplarity consisted of being a model for imitation (the native convert), then warning (the fraudulent Formosan), and finally, a combination of warning and imitation—exemplarity's double turn—through being a true convert who confessed and warned against his false past. In fact, his "native" authority, that which he established as a supplementary rather than authentic truth, once put in motion, could not be fully brought to closure. His mature confessions would seem to complete the turn toward absolute truth—a closed, uniform, consistent state that has conveniently rid itself of the problem of inconsistency or contradiction. Psalmanazar, the name and identity that remains in circulation, however, marks the contradictions of idealizing the East's hethnic potential. By claiming to be a native of an unseen place, he performed an epistemology of the East that made Formosa, not quite China and not quite Japan, a stage for working out the conditions and parameters of visualizing virtue.

The performance of Formosan virtue, a mimicry of theological and ethnographic authority, took place in the courts, coffee houses, universities, sitting rooms, and print media of an early-eighteenth-century public sphere. More than a novel anecdote of literary forgery, Psalmanazar's experiments covered questions of colonial discourse, institutional politics, gentlemanly science, and the social history of truth. His self-fashioning entailed a nexus of identity claims that together created a spectacle of piety at the intersection of virtue and commerce. He drew on religious and scientific discourse to convert theory to life and arguments into an identity that itself questioned the fixedness of identity. In this context, the convert proves to be a hybrid subject and object of East-West exchange, one who moves between and destabilizes fixed perspectives, even as Eastern convertibility becomes exemplary of Western virtue.

CHAPTER THREE

Transmigration, Fabulous Pedagogy, and the Morals of the Orient

We can explore the spectacle of heathen conversion not only through a cultural forgery such as Psalmanazar's but through the literary and philosophical fashioning of Eastern religions into consumable objects of moral pedagogy. "Virtue," as we have seen, is an ever-shifting ground of competing ideologies. Morals are reinvented at the intersection of discursive and material encounters between East and West; and China, though positioned at the eastern endpoint of such an imagined moral geography, at the same time powerfully captured the contradictions of such constructions of the Orient's religious exemplarity. As the Orientalist scholar Antoine Galland wrote, the eighteenth-century Orient encompassed "tous les peuples de l'Asie jusqu'à la Chine, mahométans ou païens et idolâtres."[1] Confucianism may have distinguished Chinese civilization from others, even while affiliating it with the ethnic philosophers of ancient Greece; but Buddhism and Taoism also tied China to India and other parts of a heathen Orient made up of "Mahometans or pagans and idolaters," to borrow Galland's phrase. This conflation of places and religions was nowhere more apparent, or popularized, than in the Oriental tale tradition, a European literary phenomenon that featured marvelous stories, far-flung regions of Asia, and idolatrous excess.

The publication of the first volumes of *Les Mille et une nuits* (*Thousand and One Nights*) in 1704 and their appearance in English in 1706 as the *Arabian Nights Entertainments* launched the popularity of the Oriental tale in English print culture. The tales also introduced to the English public a diverse Arab world far more enchanting than the long-held perceptions of Islam's religious and military threats to Western Christendom.[2] Translated and adapted by Galland, the corpus of the *Nights* included a wide assortment of folktales derived from Arabic, as well as Persian, Indian, and Turkish sources.[3] The stories' fantastical journeys, sorcery, and schemes and misfortunes of humble folk as well as sultans evoked a spectrum of places, customs, and times that, while entertaining, nonetheless represented an integrated cosmos of "Mahometan" idolatry that included but was not limited to Islam. Alternately denounced and romanticized for its assortment of beliefs in the supernatural, the Orient was imagined as a hethnic space of potential conversions, both religious and economic, and thus offered new didactic possibilities to English moralists of the early eighteenth century.[4] They constructed a broader Orient with which China was affiliated, and "China" came to designate not only a specific geographic empire but also a shared set of ambivalences toward an early modern Orient defined by religious excess.

Among the most controversial and satirized examples of Eastern religion was metempsychosis, or the transmigration of the souls. Identified both as a praiseworthy tenet of ancient Greek philosophy and as a vulgar, modern practice of Eastern civilizations, transmigration appeared to blend supernatural elements of Islamic "Mahometanism" with theories of spirit life and reincarnation linked to Egypt, India, and China, and with belief systems as different as Hinduism, Buddhism, Taoism, and Zoroastrianism. Often thought to have spread from the fifth-century teachings of Pythagoras eastward to Asia, the doctrine of transmigration generally held that the soul was immortal and could be transferred from the human body, after death, into that of successive animals. By some accounts, one's personal identity or consciousness would remain intact and eventually return to human form, enabling a person such as Pythagoras to tell of his multiple lives and legendary travels over thousands of years.[5] The idea that the body's animating force could travel between species and even between earthly and heavenly stations along the Great Chain of Being was deemed blasphemous by the defenders of a divinely ordered Cartesian cosmography as well as by those committed to the Aristotelian rationalism of classical antiquity. In early eighteenth-century discourse, the East is invariably cited as a source of both blame and inspiration for the hypothetical disruption of the human-animal hierarchy and the overactive imaginations that entertained such interspecies intimacy. For the fluidity implied by the transmigrations of old souls into new bodies also conjured possibilities of illicit forms of contact, whether erotic or even cannibalistic, between oneself and another whose identity might not match their outward appearance.

Paradoxically, the vices of Eastern idolatry are reinterpreted as virtues by English fable writers who combine the principles of transmigration with the Oriental tale tradition to forward new ideologies of consumption and, ironically enough, the moderation of excessive passions. The idea that the soul thwarts death by passing into other bodies conveniently allows reincarnated animals to reason and for experiences to be recollected across time and space. The philosopher Walter Benjamin once attributed the epic storytelling of the Orient to its "virtues of a comprehensive memory."⁶ This purported capacity for historic preservation has long been considered a part of the Orient's ancient yet modern character. Like transmigration, Oriental tales, after all, are touted for their inexhaustible reproduction of stories, travels, and self-transformation—for the performance of marvelous memory. Transmigration offered complex didactic as well as narrative possibilities for stories of infinite memory and multiple lives punished and rewarded. The literary conversions of the Orient from a place of heathenism into one of edification drew upon the translations of the *Arabian Nights* (1704–17) and a number of other French collections, most notably François Pétis de la Croix's *Turkish Tales* (1708) and *The Thousand and One Days: Persian Tales* (1714–15), hereafter cited as *Persian Tales*.⁷ The extension of the form to increasingly faraway settings can be seen in parodic variations such as Thomas-Simon Gueullette's *Chinese Tales* (1725) and *Mogul Tales* (1736) and, later in the period, *Tartarian Tales: or, a thousand and one Quarters of Hours* (1759) and *Peruvian Tales* (1764). These writings were referenced and reinvented in English print culture through a range of journalistic publications, including the *Tatler, Guardian, Freeholder, Rambler, Adventurer*, and perhaps most influentially, Joseph Addison and Richard Steele's *Spectator* papers (1711–12). But this chapter, unlike the rich body of scholarship on Oriental tales, focuses on the subgenre of the Oriental fable, and a selection of *Spectator* essays in particular.⁸ The *Spectator* essays, through their deliberate and self-reflexive appropriations of Eastern thought, perform the cultural and political work of making examples of its religious alterity. In attempting to make the Oriental tales morally intelligible, the essays also comment upon the pedagogical utility of the fable form as a matter of proper perspective: one must see through the guise of a talking animal, or an instance of Eastern superstition, in order to derive the moral and aesthetic pleasures of allegory. By correcting Oriental "error" while drawing on its capacious trove of imagination, the essays develop their epistemological authority. They collect the knowledge of the globe into a space of cultural synthesis and English self-edification.

In fictional and heuristic form, then, the idea of transmigration negotiates a number of crucial boundaries: those between human and animal, immortal soul and mortal body, feminine vice and masculine virtue, Eastern superstition and Western science. In so doing, it functions as a type of cultural fable, to borrow from Laura Brown's illuminating study of eighteenth-century discourses of modernity.⁹ Whereas Brown approaches the fable as a broad, organizing rubric, this chapter focuses more narrowly on an inventive theory of moral pedagogy that emerges from the encounter of the traditional Aesopian beast fable with developments in natural philosophy and early modern orientalism. I build upon

Ros Ballaster's important book *Fabulous Orients: Fictions of the East in England, 1662–1785*.[10] Ballaster offers an informative account of four sequences of Oriental-tale fiction spanning the course of the eighteenth century. Transmigration functions as a powerful trope of literary transmission in her survey of narratives according to specific customs and geographical regions of Asia, and her valuable insights help me to highlight the ideological and moral impact of what I think of as "fabulous pedagogy"—that is, a pedagogy of seduction and astonishment that utilizes the fable as truth in Oriental disguise. Standing out as particularly crucial to the period of English-Chinese contact in the early eighteenth century, the "fabulous" has a purported ability to convey, to convince, instruct, or even convert. Its transformative force stems from its capacity to imitate the East while asserting a method of proper borrowing, or moderating, its idolatrous excesses.

The study of transmigration also brings up the topic of the preservation of cultural memory, which has important consequences for England's expanding empire. The idea of the movement of souls, in connecting bodies across vast distances, implies multiple states of preservation: the extension of an individual's life and memory, the presence of the human in nonhuman entities, and the transference of the legacies, customs, and fables from ancient to modern civilizations. Transmigration, and the didactic fables that asserted its possibility, channeled the comprehensive antiquity of the East into an imagined global perspective crucial to the modern construction of individual and collective English identity. Transmigrational fables are thus at the center of an imperial consciousness and mode of collecting, borrowing, and preserving the resources of far-flung places of the globe. In its dual purpose of entertaining and moralizing, of denying and embracing the riches of the East, Oriental fable discourse also exposes the demands and contradictions of a new system of commodification that took its lead from China in particular.

China exemplifies in this period two temporalities that would appear to be at odds: modern commodity culture and ancient civilization. However, its coveted manufactures showcased superior technologies of design and durability at the same time that they conveyed a romanticized idea of antiquity, and hence an imagined escape from the ills of modern consumerism. Imported objects like porcelain or lacquer, referred to respectively as chinawork and japanwork, were as yet inimitable by English artisans. In preserving the secrets of Eastern antiquity in contemporary commercial form, they represented a fantasy of the resilient surface that both protected the commodity and made it eminently transportable. The powers of self-improvement espoused by fabulous pedagogy, reliant as it was upon Oriental ornamentation, thus have a counterpart in the material practices of imitating Eastern decorative techniques for English domestic consumption.[11] Oriental fables and japanning, religious and commercial examples of "China," can alike be seen as chinoiserie techniques of idealizing everlasting life and combining the locales and legends of the East into didactic cultural hybrids. Reading these practices together invites us to consider how a discourse of Eastern immortality informed that of British progress in the early eighteenth century.

Oriental Idolatry, Universal Kinship, and the Defense of Pythagoras

The problem with superstition is its perceived promiscuity, both in the sense of its indiscriminate mixing—of fact with fiction—and in its powers of contamination. The English essayist Sir William Temple, for one, cited China as an exception to the "contagion" of the "Mahometan," or Islamic, religion that had stretched from Arabia into Egypt, Syria, and Tartary.[12] In this account, Confucianism offered an antidote to the perceived superstitions of other Oriental empires; indeed, it was Confucius that modeled for Temple a new ideal of heroic virtue. An integral part of the conversion strategies of Jesuit missionaries in China, Confucianism, the official doctrine of the Ming imperial court, had in fact been instrumentally synthesized with Christian doctrines of self-improvement and theism. Though it was argued to be a civil rather than religious belief system, by the beginning of the eighteenth century, the culture of Confucius had become a matter of increasingly heated debate within the Roman Catholic Church. In 1704, the same year the *Arabian Nights* was published, Pope Clement XI issued a declaration censoring "the sacrifices or oblations that are regularly offered to Confucius and the deceased ancestors." While Jesuit missionaries had for centuries practiced a policy of accommodating Chinese rites, their jurisdiction was finally being brought to an end, and over the following decades Rome would grow increasingly intolerant of the religious contradictions posed by Confucius, by turns a secular sage and a falsely worshipped deity.[13]

Far less disputed was the idolatrous status of Chinese Buddhism, which had been particularly disparaged from the beginning of the Jesuit mission in China.[14] Buddhist sects were generally conflated into a common set of beliefs in transmigration known to have arrived to China from India in AD 63 or 65.[15] In his influential *China Illustrata* (1677), for example, the German Jesuit polymath Athanasius Kircher catalogued the corruption of Chinese society by foreign superstition. Far from original, Chinese civilization was thought to have absorbed the best and the worst of the West in the form of pagan religions as well as the promiscuous eastward movement of the Christian gospel dating back to the Syrian-Chaldeans and the legendary king and proselytizer Prester John.[16] Through their worship of false gods, the Chinese perpetuated the errors of antiquity in a modern, Christian era. In Kircher's words, "They have imported so many different fables that one can scarcely straighten them out."[17] Where elsewhere in the text he praises the remarkable political order of the monarchy, all the more impressive for its vastness and diversity of riches, here, China evinces a type of sublime disorder—all the world's idolatry gathered into one place.

In attempting to make sense of the three main religious sects of Buddhism, Taoism, and Confucianism, or "the Idolatry of the Chineses," Kircher delineates a system of comparative religion that assigns each deity or ritual an equivalent in Western antiquity. The affinities with Greek, Roman, and Egyptian mythology mean that Fo, or Buddha, is simply an Eastern version of Jupiter, while Confucius resembles Thoyt, and so on. In addition to mapping the resemblances between East and West, Kircher fixates upon what he regards as the indiscriminant "borrowing" of the Chinese: "they seem chiefly to have borrow'd the Transmigration of Souls from the Doctrine of Pythagoras, and they have added many other Fictions to it," including ideas of "our Philosophers, but also to have borrow'd a certain Shadow from the Evangelical Light." These Pythagorean "laws of metamorphosis" amount to the "ridiculous idea of the transmigration of souls not only into animals, but even into plants, like Ovid's Daphne." Western philosophy, religion, and myth have apparently all been grafted onto Eastern ideas. Kircher thus frames metamorphosis as the diffusion of ideas from West to East: "Aren't the Chinese and Japanese idols just metamorphoses of those of the Greeks and Romans?" he asks. He later reiterates this critique of heathen uniformity by saying that "all their idolatry seemeth to have made a Voyage thence into China."[18] According to Kircher, the clarity of the Christian perspective can in effect straighten out the fables of the East. Indeed, his organizational work locates China at the center of a false universalism that must be countered by the corrective of European interpretation.

Kircher's charting of the Western origins of Chinese idolatry continued to be cited in popular writings on China by the Jesuit Louis Le Comte and the Dutch emissary Johann Nieuhof, whose illustrated travels would in turn shape the chinoiserie vogues of eighteenth-century England. Following Kircher, Le Comte describes India's Buddhism as a "Poyson [that] spread its infection thro' all the Provinces, and corrupted every Town . . . [with] Idolatry, and became a monstrous receptacle for all sorts of Errors, Fables, Superstitions, Transmigration of Souls, Idolatry and Atheism."[19] Similarly, in his account, Nieuhof describes outlying regions of China's empire, such as Korea and Ninche (Nüzhen/Jurchen), by their worship of "Fe" (Fo): "[it is] very little different from that of the other *Chineses*, being great Promoters of the Doctrine of the Transmigration of Souls out of one Body into another." To elaborate upon the history of China's idolatry, he reprints sections of Kircher's text, including remarks that travelers from ancient Indostan "have Planted their Colonies in China; for they hold a multitude of Worlds, a Metempsychosis or Transmigration of Souls into Brutes, professing all the Philosophy of *Pythagoras*."[20] China, in sharing with Indostan and Japan the belief in multiple worlds of heaven and hell, the transmigration of the souls, and a system of karmic rewards and punishments, in these writings is thus considered an exemplary "receptacle" of all the world's idolatry, from West to East.

A central difficulty in the English imaginary stemmed from attempts to make China morally legible—a process that entailed positing and negating its kinship to the Occident as well as the Orient. Of the representation systems deemed common to the East, one critic noted, "'Twas the universal Taste of the Orientals to make use of corporeal Images to represent the Properties and Operations of Spirits."[21] It was the work of eighteenth-century euhemerists to demystify these false religious beliefs through establishing the historical origins of myth. Continuing the Christian vein of historical revisionism and the comparative analysis of religion, they documented the transference of error from Egypt to China and held accountable the practitioners and interpreters of ancient rites for spreading untruths in the form of fables. Euhemerists also challenged the "universality" of the Orient by asserting alternative relationships of the material to the immaterial world. Pagan gods could be explained as improperly deified historical heroes, and, more generally, mythology could be mapped onto real events, which, over the course of time, had become distorted into supernatural occurrences.[22] In his account of ancient religions, "The History of the Soul's Immortality" (1704), the deist John Toland articulated the problem of the Eastern belief in transmigration as one of misplaced passions and an overinvestment in the corporeal that could be traced to the material practices of ancient Egyptian funeral rites. Described as a "historical Method of preserving the Memory of deserving Persons" and as "perpetuating Events," the embalming of dead bodies and their burial underground reinforced the idea of "separate or immortal souls" (45). The intense desire to remember the deceased led the Egyptians further to name constellations after loved ones. Such "eternal Monuments" of ancestor worship took on supernatural powers when disseminated from Egypt to "other Parts of Africa, over all Asia, in many places of Europe, and particularly in Greece," such that vulgar people, hearing tell of people inhabiting the stars, were unable to distinguish between fable and fact (46–47). The English fascination with Egyptian embalming, an enviable technique of material preservation, will be discussed further below. Here, I wish to highlight how the preservation of the body (and soul) is tied to larger forces of cultural preservation; namely, a legacy of misinterpretation and lack of discernment that constitutes the idea of Oriental superstition across vast distances and times.

Whereas for Kircher, China had inherited the Grecian errors of mistaking metaphor for reality, and fable for fact, Toland's schema further enacts a bifurcation between East and West through a curious defense, rather than dismissal, of the teachings of Pythagoras:

> Pythagoras himself did not believe the Transmigration which has made [him] so famous to Posterity; for in the internal or secret Doctrin he meant no more than the eternal Revolution of Forms in Matter, those ceaseless Vicissitudes and Alternations, which turn every thing into all things, and all things into any thing, as Vegetables and Animals become part of us, we become part of them, and both become parts of a thousand other things in the Universe, Earth turning into Water, Water into Air, Air into Aether, and so back again in Mixture without End or Number.[23]

Toland attempts to clear Pythagoras of any falsehood or error by displacing the idea of preserving human souls onto one of preserving organic matter, and this bifurcation reveals the anxieties that attended the interconnectedness between Asia and the ancient religions.

The continuities of the new science of the earth attributed to Pythagoras provided a clear alternative to the religious beliefs in reincarnation of India in particular. On the one hand, the seventeenth-century writings on India's practices of vegetarianism—Brahmin, Bania, and Jain—by influential travel writers like François Bernier and John Ovington promoted the Eastern virtues of nonviolence, charity, and enlightened paganism.[24] In this way, Brahmins, also called Gymnosophists, were cast as hethnics in the Renaissance Neoplatonist tradition of making virtuous pagans of figures from Western classical antiquity. On the other hand, the Hindu strictures against the killing or eating of animals were more often presented as evidence of a system of despotic and superstitious laws tied to irrational fears of harming reincarnated souls. As Tristram Stuart points out in his study of the history of vegetarianism, the seventeenth-century characterization of Hinduism as a misguided version of Pythagoreanism made Indian religions at once more assimilable to Christianity and more superstitious.[25] The relationship between Pythagoras and Hinduism was especially fraught, given the accounts of his travels to India by Alexander the Great, Philostratus, Plotinus, and Porphyry, some of whom argued that it was in fact the Indians who had first transferred to Pythagoras the theory of the transmigration of souls.[26] Toland's efforts to reinterpret soul travel through the workings of the natural world were thus attempts to exempt Pythagoras from Asian influence and to establish the authority of Western science in contradistinction to the follies of Eastern religion.

The interest taken in Eastern soul theory by a range of late-seventeenth-century English writers included radical, naturalist interpretations of transmigration by Cambridge Platonist philosophers who articulated a world of universal kinship where the pervasiveness of spirit in the terrestrial world constituted the highest form of rationalism. For one, Lady Anne Conway referred to the continual "transmutations" between species along a ladder of life, "[such] that the *Species* of divers Things are changed, one into another, as Earth into Water, and Water into Air, and air into Fire or Aether," as evidence of the principle of plenitude, God's system of punishments and rewards, and the stark contrast between divine immutability and an ever-changing natural world.[27] Influenced by the Cambridge Platonists' ideas of natural theology and rational spirituality, but dismissive of the "Eastern Nations" for their groundless, un-Christian theories of resurrection, the theologian Thomas Burnet argued that it is not the soul, but "parts of matter" that circulate through the interconnected cycles of the natural world. Carcasses dissolve and evaporate into the air only to descend to earth in the form of condensation and make their way into plants, animals, and human bodies:

> Some Nations, say they, are *Anthropophagi*; they some of them feed upon others. . . . But why do they mention some Nations? . . . we all of us feed upon the Remains of each other; not indeed immediately, but after they have had some Transmutations into Herbs and Animals: in those Herbs and Animals we eat our Ancestors, or at least some minute Parts of them. . . . [I]t may very well happen, that by taking this Compass, the same Part of Matter . . . may have inhabited more Bodies than the Soul of *Pythagoras*.[28]

Through the natural cycle of consumption, Burnet argues, humans are reduced to the organic matter that they reingest. Here the relations of nature are defamiliarized and reconstituted in a cosmic food chain through a striking claim: we are all cannibals. The argument, in refusing to condemn heathenism outright, cleverly appropriates the terms of universal kinship normally implied by transmigration.

In fact, Burnet's ironic embrace of cannibalism and dismissal of the travels of Pythagoras's soul marks a continuous effort on the part of theologians and philosophers to naturalize the supernatural implications of transmigration by contesting the validity of the Eastern part of the world in relation to its ancient Greek counterpart, Pythagoras. Even contemporary scholars have until recently dismissed the presence of distinctly Eastern ideas in English print culture. In her foundational work on Oriental tales in the eighteenth century, Martha Pike Conant asserts, "[A]ll philosophical and moral ideas . . . in these early periodicals . . . are either noticeably English in character or else universal ideas, common to English and oriental thought." She cites the "doctrine of transmigration" as the one exception "which has been attributed to oriental philosophy."[29] And yet, even this example, she says, should not be considered Eastern given that its source is either ultimately unknown or often ascribed to Pythagoras. The hasty delineation of East and West, however, neglects the complex commingling of ideas in translation as well as the fraught process of cultural appropriation. In fact, Pythagoras, as suggested above, is a contested locus between East and West, rather than a pregiven representative of one or the other. It is precisely the confusion over the Pythagorean origins of transmigration that constructs the East-West relationship as one of moral pedagogy.

According to André Dacier's *Life of Pythagoras* (1707), metempsychosis was simply a pedagogical tool used in "explaining and regulating the Worship of the Gods": Pythagoras taught only "the Truth."[30] The superstitious Egyptians, the "first authors" of transmigration, initiated the idea that bad souls are punished by being "detain'd" in the bodies of brutes. Dacier redeems the exemplary teachings of Pythagoras by criticizing the generations of philosophers after the Egyptians and Persians who have taken literally "this Metempsychosis, and who have actually taught that the Soul of a Man, to expiate his Sins after his Death, pass'd into the Body of another Man, or of an Animal, or of a Plant" (*Life of Pythagoras*, 48). Dacier further adds that not only Pythagoras but Plato inventively describes how effeminate men are punished by transmigrating into women, murderers into beasts, lascivious people into swine, and so on, to illustrate the dangers of vice. In the East Indies, however, metempsychosis is still "literally taken . . . by an ignorant Generation of Men" (69, 49). Like Dacier, Bulstrode Whitelock, in his *Essay on Transmigration* (1692), claims that Pythagoras is "mistaken everywhere; but very grossly believed in Pegu, Magor, and other parts of Asia." Easterners believe in what he brands a "gross notion of transmigration," an unacceptably literal and irrational interpretation of a fundamentally scientific theory that would locate the souls of good men in the bodies of cows (*Essay*, B2). This sentiment is echoed in later commentary on the Chinese followers of "Mahomet," who, unlike the wise Pythagoras, believe in "extravagant notions."[31] In another instance, the spread of Buddhism, or the "Worship of an Idol called Foe," from India to China is cited as further evidence of "this absurd and impious Doctrine, that Souls pass from Body to Body," a deception that Pythagoras merely borrowed from the Egyptians for his own pedagogical purposes.[32]

For these writers, the potentially profane intermingling of humans and animals and the dissolution of borders presented by the theory of transmigration must thus be re-integrated into acceptable forms of explanation. Reasoning animals and reasonable Easterners—from Egypt to India to China—appear to be two major sources of anxiety for theorists of transmigration; they represent a limit against which Pythagoreanism, Western rationality, and human uniqueness must be demarcated. Such discourse may perform the Enlightenment demystification and relegation of the supernatural to a myth-addicted East, according to which, traveling souls actually function as allegories for nature's cycles, or as flights of the imagination. At the same time, the Eastern-inspired speculation over matter and motion enables a new kind of imaginative perspective on the self and hybrid possibilities that emerge when Enlightenment thinkers, in contact with Eastern philosophies and religions, attempt to incorporate alien cosmographies into new allegories of universal kinship.

The Moral Pedagogy of the Fable: Deception, Moderation, Excess

The Oriental fable, being part of the explanatory regime that attempted to make sense of the theory of transmigration and the influence of the East more generally, contained within it the conditions of pedagogy crucial to maintaining the distinctiveness between East and West and, via such distinction, positing the virtue of English moderation. Because fables are, in effect, truths in disguise, the pleasure and the cultural work of the Oriental fable is to give the English reader the keys for stripping away the ornamental surfaces of the animal and Eastern narrational forms to reveal the core values of rational thinking.

No translators of the Oriental fable understood or underscored this work more effectively than Joseph Addison and Richard Steele, whose essayistic periodical, the widely-read *Spectator* papers (published between March, 1711 and December, 1712), canvassed contemporary London life through the fictional persona of Mr. Spectator, "an observer of life" and man-about-town who would present a "sheet-full of thoughts every morning."[33] The essays offered witty and moral commentary on topics ranging from the stock market to the female temper. The characters they invented along with Mr. Spectator, in representing good-natured social archetypes, were meant to entertain and instruct audiences in polite society and the virtues of moderate living. The *Spectator* has become an emblem of eighteenth-century coffee-house culture and London's enlightened public sphere through its solicitation of reader participation, staged dialogism, and calls for rational restraint in a vigorously partisan era.[34] Its performances of civility are, at the same time, invested in an orientalizing fascination with and characterization of the East-as-ornament that participated in the imperial expansion of the nation.

The paper's Whiggish mercantile interests are evident in its promotion of an at times overzealous consumerism.[35] One has only to consider the celebration of financial cosmopolitanism in the description of the Royal Exchange in issue number 69, which designates London as the center of the world, or "a kind of *Emporium* for the whole Earth." Mr. Spectator walks among the trade representatives of nations from around the globe and, moved to tears by the making of private and public fortunes, imagines himself to be a "Citizen of the World." This is an affective experience of commercial expansion rendered through an armchair traveler who, in the space of the market, vicariously reaps the benefits of the varied commodities brought to England from the likes of India, China, Japan, Persia, France, and America: "Traffick gives us greater Variety of what is Useful, and at the same time supplies us with every thing that is Convenient and Ornamental." Addison makes explicit the imperial reach afforded by mercantile exchange in observing that "Trade, without enlarging the British Territories, has given us a kind of additional Empire" (*Spectator*, no. 69, 296).

While the metropolis is imagined as a spectatorial space of cultural synthesis—where East pays tribute to the West—the form of the essays likewise incorporates elements of foreignness for the purposes of English self-improvement. It is not only the goods of the Indies that supply convenience and ornament for England: Oriental fables present useful fictions that paradoxically moderate the appetite for the exotic. Thus, Addison and Steele develop an efficient pedagogical force in their framing of the Orient's imported novelties. The stated aim of the *Spectator* is to "enliven Morality with Wit, and to temper Wit with Morality, that ... Readers may, if possible, both Ways find their Account in the Speculation of the Day" (no. 10, 44). This relation of wit and morality both stretches and contains the imagination. As articulated across a number of essays, wit must yoke together ideas that are at once not obviously related and yet seen to be congruous: "Ideas should not lie too near one another in the Nature of things; for where the Likeness is obvious, it gives no Surprize" (no. 62, 264). In that fables constitute the "first pieces" of "true Wit," they, too, "[consist] in this Resemblance and Congruity of Ideas" (no. 183, 62). Addison writes in another instance, "the finest and that which pleases the most universally, is *Fable*, in whatsoever Shape it appears" (no. 512, 317). The theory that the fable is an instrument of novelty and surprise not only reflects the authors' self-professed antiauthoritarianism, but also their method of mixing and matching examples from diverse texts, ancient and modern, domestic and foreign. In the essays discussed below, the concept of transmigration plays an especially crucial part in the negotiation of morality and wit that frames their telling of the Orient. It is the drawing of resemblance between unlikely things, the gathering together of ancient and modern wisdoms, the manipulation of likeness and difference between species, and the idea that souls are reborn into the brutes they resemble, that allows the authors as fabulists to translate Pythagorean teachings into reflections on relations between cultures, species, and the sexes.

The popularity of Aesopian beast fables in the period 1690 to 1722 responded to a climate of moral reform and fierce partisanship, in which talking beasts could censure bad manners as well as ventriloquize Royalist or Jacobite sentiments from thinly disguised extrapolitical vantage points.[36] While earlier Tory writers such as John Ogilby and Roger L'Estrange, and, later, the Whig author Samuel Croxall, used the genre to forward partisan polemics, Addison and Steele aimed to avoid an overt political agenda as well as coercive didacticism.[37] They tempered their Whig affiliations in part by incorporating the wisdom of antiquity in epigraphic and anecdotal form, utilizing the fable's primacy as a literary form to bridge ancient with modern literary authority. Jayne Elizabeth Lewis, in her study of the eighteenth-century English fable, calls this a "classicizing sign of literary unity" that helps to maintain political order in a time of partisan feuding and the explosion of early eighteenth-century print culture.[38] Although most studies of the beast fable of this period focus on its function as political allegory, more recent work attends to the status of the animals who deliver "antiallegorical" messages about species distinctions by locating them in the broader context of developments in the empirical sciences. As Frank Palmeri has argued, speaking animals in some cases represented not humans but animals speaking on behalf of their species' brutal treatment by humans in an explicitly "autocritical" fashion.[39] Such animal self-advocacy could take place only in a climate of human-animal relations reflected in the nascent scientific classification system of Linnaeus and shaped by the modern practice of pet keeping. As a number of historians and animal studies scholars have documented, the growing experience of proximity to the domesticated dog, cat, monkey, or bird inflected the tradition of the Aesopian beast fable with heightened realism, while revising scientific and philosophical theories of interspecies boundaries.[40] What these studies of animals, literary history, and English politics tend to overlook, however, is the importance of cultural difference, and oriental exemplarity in particular, to the human-animal basis of fabulous pedagogy.

The utility of the Orient to the *Spectator* papers is demonstrated in some detail within several of the fables themselves. In number 512, the "Fable of Two Owls," Addison offers a theory of the fable that stresses the virtues of Eastern deception. First, the fable, unlike direct exhortation, allows readers to feel as though they were teaching themselves: "the moral insinuates it self imperceptibly, we are taught by surprise, and become wiser and better unawares" (no. 512, 318). Such a vision of autodidacticism invites the reader's active participation and appears to dispense with the authoritative presence of a formal instructor. In a slightly different manner, John Dryden described this effect in *Fables Ancient and Modern* (1700) as a matter of pedagogical convenience: morals, in fable form, "leap foremost into sight, without the Reader's Trouble of looking after them."[41] Of course, the clever communication strategies of these stories produce a pleasurable reading experience and unstated reliance on the narrator that can in effect counteract independent thinking. As pedagogical strategy, Addison's formulation suggests that the proper method of communication allows one to act as a parental authority without being perceived as such: readers are taken by "surprise" and "become wiser and better unawares." Masking the fundamental superiority of the learned over the ignorant, the fable form performs the populism of public-sphere discourse even as it manages rather than actually disrupts the hierarchical roles of teacher and student, parent and child.[42] Anthony Pollock has recently referred to this disjuncture between theory and praxis as the "managerial moment" of an "aesthetic model of English publicness that theoretically assuages the violence it cannot practically prevent."[43] On multiple levels, then, deception is in fact central to the fable form.

Fables, in the wrong hands, are in effect, lies. In a recent analysis of the pedagogical dynamic between addresser and addressee, the literary critic Alexander Gelley describes the fable as a trap of sorts; by varying its targets and veiling his or her intentions, the writer of the fable in fact "regulates the force of injunction." Teaching through examples rather than direct injunction or reasoned debate shifts the emphasis from diegesis to, as Gelley puts it, the "*status* of the narrative it enframes."[44] In the eighteenth-century context, Ephraim Chambers, in his *Cyclopaedia, or an Universal Dictionary of Arts and Sciences* (1728), similarly defines fable as the shape in which truth appears: "The truth is the point of morality intended to be inculcated; the fiction is the action, or words the instruction is covered under."[45] In fact, these rhetorical surfaces, or extradiegetical frames, were topics of heated debate for eighteenth-century translators of the fable. For some, narrative indirectness was both agreeable and motivational. According to the chaplain Edward Arwaker, emulating the naturally inferior "Example of Irrational Animals" is a more attainable goal than aspiring to the exemplary actions of great men (*Truth in Fiction*, viii). Advocating the use of ancient pagan fictions for Christian ends, he titled his translations of Aesop *Truth in Fiction: Or, Morality in Masquerade* (1708): because, he argues, truth is too blinding in its nakedness, it must be adorned with the lies of the Greeks and Egyptians (x). Reiterating the defense of Pythagoras, he writes, "Pythagoras borrow'd his fabulous Metempsychosis, and fancied the Transmigration of Human souls into the Bodies of Beasts, according to their different Inclinations" and the "Resemblance and Affinity in their Manners" (xi). Metempsychosis is once again justified by its utility as moral pedagogy for the ignorant masses. As Bulstrode Whitelock wrote of such "ancient Fabulous Stories" of "good Design" in his *Essay on Transmigration*, "Since there is a necessity for it, talk of these Strange Punishments, *as if* Souls did transmigrate" (*Essay*, 114; my emphasis). The injunction of the hypothetical, though, also leaves room for morals to be misinterpreted or simply undelivered. Critics of the fable such as John Toland argued that fables not only adorned but obfuscated the truth by eschewing plain, commonsensical writing. While they might aid in explaining religious mysteries to the masses, they also placed a dangerous interpretive control in the hands of priestly authority. One risk of dressing the truth in lies is losing the truth altogether.

In his theory of the fable, Addison mediates between these positions by stressing the good judgment of the editor who merely borrows from and repeatedly disavows the use of lies—and worse, superstition—that originates in the East. The most controversial implications of transmigration, the blurring of the boundaries between species or cultures, are repeatedly reduced to a question of allegorical resemblances rather than actual or biological fusions. Importantly, it is an Oriental fable excerpted from the *Turkish Tales* that Addison chooses, over the familiar works of the ancients, to illustrate (in no. 512) the universal, "oblique manner of giving Advice."[46] He further justifies this choice by adding, "To omit many [fables] which will occur to every ones Memory, there is a pretty Instance of this Nature in a *Turkish* Tale, which I do not like the worse for that little Oriental Extravagance which is mixed with it" (no. 512, 318). In other words, through its perceived excesses, or "Oriental Extravagance," the East supplies the wit that can lead the addressee to the edifying point of surprise and self-enlightenment. Since fables work by mystifying the teacher-student relationship, the Orient performs this mystification through its representation of the supernatural. In Addison's telling of the fable, a tyrannical Sultan Mahmoud has laid to waste the villages and towns of the Persian Empire through wars and destruction. A wise visier, in order to advise reform without offending his superior, pretends to understand the language of birds. When the sultan inquires into the conversation of two owls sitting in a tree, the visier takes advantage of the moment to ventriloquize his critique of the sultan's rule. Upon hearing the fable, the sultan changes his ways and "from that time forward consulted the Good of his People" (no. 512, 319). The visier, in an act of fabulous pedagogy, manipulates the power of the sovereign, on the one hand, and placates the unruly masses, on the other.

In multiple *Spectator* essays, the fable protects its teller and delivers peace in a despotic, premodern era. Traditionally, fables allegorize unequal relations of power and the threat of imminent censorship under the conditions of absolutism, and hence employ beasts that impart political advice on behalf of their human counterparts.[47] To borrow from Annabel Patterson's study of politics and the fable form, "the fable's power resides precisely in the powerlessness of those who speak its language" (*Fables of Power*, 30). Furthermore, as Ballaster points out in *Fabulous Orients*, her study of Oriental narrative, fables were thought to be endemic to the East, where tyrannical governments purportedly made direct communication impossible. Tyranny, Addison reiterates, results from the lack of "voices"; and such voices are only made possible by the division of power exemplified by England's constitutional government.[48] The ruse of the owls' voices thus offers a weak substitute for Western liberty, and the visier's fable is a clever yet limited strategy to counter the "full Tyranny" that, Addison writes, inheres in "the Princes of the Eastern Nations."

To further understand the incorporation of examples of Eastern excess into an acceptable didacticism, one can look to the concluding example of *Spectator* no. 512—a story of how Democritus, in Pliny's *Natural History*, is said to have produced a virtuous serpent by mixing the blood of certain birds. If eaten by a human, the serpent would transfer its virtue by imbuing the person with fluency in bird language. Addison calls this a "most ridiculous Piece of natural Magick" (319). Through the example of Democritus, he denounces the absurdity of talking birds and complicit humans, as well as the mixing of species that suggests the moment of transmigrational boundary crossing. Read in light of this anecdote, the Turkish visier's story of the two owls in effect functions as a corrective to Democritus. The visier's case is one of human ventriloquism, rather than crossspecies dialogism. Through the cunning manipulation of perspective, one voice appears to speak for many. After all, the sultan's visier, even in the original Turkish tale, does not actually understand the birds. His contrivance of human wile is an example of fabulous pedagogy precisely because it simultaneously posits and demystifies the animal-supernatural. Juxtaposing the example of the Turkish visier with that of Democritus thus creates an unintended effect: Eastern fable reforms Greek myth.

While the East offers instances of strategic cunning, despotism, magic, and species indistinction to be appropriated and moderated for pedagogical purposes, the "Oriental extravagance" discarded from Addison's translation of this foreign tale might well also refer to the sexual dissimulations, and narrative waywardness, of the original collection of Turkish tales, as indicated by its English subtitle, "The Malice of Woman."[49] A generic shift occurs in the tale's translation from the *Turkish Tales* to the *Spectator*. The shift takes the form of disciplining the moral excesses of the East, which manifests itself in a number of ways. In *Spectator* no. 160, for example, the self-aggrandizing "Eastern way of Thinking" is illustrated by the case of a Persian emperor who refers to himself in far-fetched metaphors such as Sun of Glory and Nutmeg of Delight. More than simply being bad style, such prolix writing reflects the folly of the "Ancients" worldwide, even as Easterners specifically are said to indulge in extreme modes of ornamentation that can be attributed to "those of the warmer climates, who had most Heat and Life in their Imaginations" (*Spectator* 160, 128). At the same time, the geographically determined character of Eastern peoples has its virtues. In *Spectator* no. 631, we read of a dervish who is kicked by a camel at the end of the day for having forgotten to wash his hands. The animal's instinct for cleanliness, attributed to the "climate of the East," situates Islamic customs of ablution in the "neighborhood of good examples" despite the "superstitious" Mahometanism that makes Easterners fanatics and imbues camels with supernatural powers (no. 631, 158). It is from this position of moderated excess that the Orient, rendered morally and racially proximate to England, also usefully mediates between examples of civilization and barbarism.[50] Not only does the story of the dervish and the camel teach good hygiene, but its moral is further confirmed by a peculiar comparison of English with African bodies. As the author of this essay writes, "We need but compare our Ideas of a Female Hottentot and an English Beauty, to be satisfied of the Truth of what hath been advanced" (no. 631, 157). According to this logic of oriental exemplarity, the lessons of the East should be considered as universally self-evident as the difference between black femininity and white femininity—between the barbaric and the civilized. Put another way, the alleged racial superiority of North over South is posited through imagining the relative virtues of the East.

As in other instances where the religious teachings of the Koran are neutralized and reframed as a matter of Western aesthetics or philosophy, the comparisons of moral geography are mapped onto discussions of the body.[51] Oriental fables, after all, theorize the proper drawing of resemblances between disparate customs, times, and places. Just as intermediaries in the forms of visiers, doctors, or camels simulate rather than perform the out-of-body experiences of Eastern supernaturalism, the author-fabulist, in the capacity of a "Citizen of the World," gathers together the beneficial excesses of Oriental ornamentation to reveal the philosophical, moral, or rhetorical truth underneath. If, on the one hand, the East and its forms of expression are disclaimed as fictitious or fabulous, they are at the same time embraced for the ability of their "wild, but natural, Simplicity" to combine wit with morality (no. 535, 410). Thus does the fable make pedagogical use of deception to rein in the transgressive implications of transmigration. Likeness between species is only acceptable if used heuristically to allegorize the differences and similarities of human character, whether English or African, male or female. As if to model the proper work of Oriental fictions, *Spectator* no. 209 presents several types of female souls and their corresponding animal and natural characteristics in varying, unflattering comparisons. Addison cites a passage from the poet Simonides on the ten species of women's souls: swine, fox, canine, earth, sea, ass, cat, mare, ape, and bee. Of these, the only positive representation is the industriously domestic bee. The ostensible moral of this fable reads, "A man cannot possess any thing that is better than a good Woman, nor any thing that is worse than a bad one" (no. 209, 320). The doctrine of transmigration humorously aligns the innate characteristics of women and animals "they most resemble in their Manner," thus rendering the likeness between species a strategy for fixing the binaries of gender.[52] According to the logic of the fable, false appearances, or literary ornamentation, reinforce the demarcation between the ignorant and the discerning readers who can appreciate moral truth in disguise. In this framework, the references to the Orient form an integral part of the pedagogical structure of the fable's deceptiveness.[53] Just as Pythagorean authority justifies the imaginative and satiric representation of the soul's movement between human and animal bodies, these *Spectator* papers posit the East as the source of idolatrous excess that can be appropriated to regulate polite society.

The Intimacies of Animal and Orient

Even as the function of the fable is to deliver morals in pleasing form, the pleasures it makes available threaten to overtake its moral force. That fables might be consumed for pleasure rather than pedagogy raises a number of interlinked anxieties. First is an anxiety about genre. The fabulist is tasked with controlling the morality of a form that by definition works through indirection, fancy, and digression. Delighting too much in an imaginary world of animal society can diminish its allegorical relevance to human society or, even worse, undermine the set hierarchy between the species. A second concern raised by the fable form is the wavering distinction between human and animal. The fable treads what the poet Alexander Pope called the "insuperable line" between reason and the passions, and human and animal, which remain "for ever sep'rate, yet for ever near!"[54] The same pleasure of being able to see oneself through another's eyes contains a fear of losing one's uniquely human, and presumably rational, status. Transmigration heightens these anxieties about autonomous selfhood through broaching taboo forms of kinship and consumption, including cannibalism, incest, adultery, and bestiality. If we are all related, we run the risk of eating or inappropriately consorting with our loved ones in the form of animals. Moreover, transmigration, like the Oriental tales that give it narrative form, enables lives and stories to continue indefinitely. In theory, if one never dies, there can be no narrative resolution, much less didactic closure in the form of a clear moral. But fabulous pedagogy is never simply moral; it also disciplines its audience, while taking pleasure in the disciplinary act. More often than not, the Oriental fable disciplines women, whose habits of excessive consumption are targeted as a core problem of early eighteenth-century commercial culture. A third anxiety raised by the fable form thus concerns gender. As readers, we are meant to take a certain delight in seeing others duped by the fable's trick of enacting and unveiling its disguises. The disciplining of the female subject's overactive imagination and materialistic attachments by mischievous figures of male authority adds an erotic charge between pedagogue and tutee, author and reader. In numerous instances, the invocation of the East as a source of fantastic transmigrations works to resolve these anxieties about the unruly intimacies of genre, species, and gender produced by the contemporary proliferation of imports and commercial culture.

Narrative ingenuity dominates *Spectator* no. 578, the retelling of de la Croix's *Persian Tale* story of King Fadlallah and his adventures in reincarnation.[55] This version, a tale of usurpation, triangulated love, and revenge, ultimately turns on a satirical representation of women's erotic attachments to their pets. A conniving "Dervis" teaches King Fadlallah how to "reanimate" or "fling his own soul" into dead or dying bodies, and thereby tricks the king into testing out his new-learned skill by transmigrating into a doe (577). The dervish promptly kills the doe and usurps the king's unoccupied body and throne, but not before the King assumes the form of a nightingale and wins his queen Zemroude's heart by singing at her window every day. He allows himself to be caged to be near her; and when her lapdog suddenly dies, he moves even closer to her in the shape of her dog. The dervish, who has been interacting with the queen in the body of the king, attempts to console her upon the death of her nightingale by flinging himself into it, making it appear to have been magically revived. At this moment, the real king seizes the chance to reoccupy his own body and swiftly kills the dervish-as-nightingale. After the king experiences this complicated series of events to win back the lady and tell the story of his suffering and animal lives, she suddenly dies of grief upon realizing her "innocent adultery" with the dervish-as-king, a man she all along thought to be her husband. At the end of the day, the king has reclaimed his human body, but the queen is dead, along with her lapdog and nightingale.

According to the author of this issue, the "Story of Fadlallah" is meant also to illustrate John Locke's philosophies of human individuality by demonstrating the premise that instead of physical substance, it is consciousness, or the preservation of memory across time and space, that constitutes one's personal identity.[56] And yet the pleasures of reading about corporeal excess—of identity switches and hypothetical sexual transgressions—are counterbalanced by the disciplining of the female perspective and the framing of the East. As if to compensate for the lack of a real moral, the essay concludes by pronouncing Zemroude's suicide an extreme "delicacy" that is "peculiar to the Oriental Ladies" (no. 578, 580). The woman's concern for her virtue proves excessive, even given Mr. Spectator's regular calls for female chastity. His project is, after all, moderating the extremes of "Oriental extravagance" to illustrate the virtues of reason. The tragedy of her indelicate suicide, however specific to Eastern custom, links female self-immolation to English ladies' love of keeping pets; indeed, female fallibility is established as a universal truth.

In no. 343, the "Story of Pugg the Monkey," the conundrum of personal identity and the expanded parameters of the self are further explored, once again through positing as innate the binaries of gender. Like the theorists of transmigration, the writer distinguishes between ancient Pythagorean wisdom and modern Eastern superstition, both of which are reimagined to assign male virtue and female vice. Here the disciplining of the female takes the explicit form of a hoax that makes use of the colonial imaginary to perform the transmigrations of a pet monkey. One of Mr. Spectator's acquaintances, the gallant Will Honeycomb, introduces transmigration as a Pythagorean notion still practiced in the "Eastern parts of the world," where it is believed that "the Soul of a Man, when he dies, immediately passes into the Body of another Man, or of some Brute, which he resembled in his Humour, or his Fortune, when he was one of *us*" (no. 343, 273). Honeycomb then tells of how one Jack Freelove woos an unappreciative lover by borrowing the Eastern notion to spin a tale of successive transmigrations. Having been repeatedly rebuffed by the lady, he leaves an envelope for her signed in the name of her pet monkey. The enclosed letter tells of the monkey's past lives, beginning as an Indian Brahmin who, after requesting to retain his memory throughout his reincarnations, experiences an elaborate series of transformations over hundreds of years. He eventually becomes the lady's former suitor, Jack Freelove, and then is reincarnated in the pet monkey's body. Upon reading this note, the lady, not knowing what to believe, experiences an uneasy confusion when meeting the gaze of her monkey.

The moment of hesitation in which the female questions her pet's identity might be considered "fantastic," in the sense articulated by the philosopher Tzvetan Todorov: "a certain hesitation: a hesitation common to reader and character, who must decide whether or not what they perceive derives from 'reality' as it exists in the common opinion."[57] The fantastic can be characterized by a "pan-determinism" that upsets the limit between physical and mental, matter and spirit, word and thing; it is a moment of inexplicable strangeness, of erotic and even perverse desire, that surfaces when species meet. Of course, here the narrator and the reader are meant to partake knowingly in the hoax that is played against a hapless woman whose wayward erotic attachments require disciplining.[58] Telling real from fake is part of the pleasure of fabulous pedagogy; the reader is encouraged to take on the role of the male spectator whose superior reason outwits easily duped English women and Easterners alike.

At the same time, the woman who indulges in the fantastic by questioning the overlapping of animal and human intuits the profound implications of interconnected lives and existences. Like the theorists of transmigration, she brings heightened awareness to the fundamental social changes resulting from the incorporation of foreign life-forms into the intimacies of the private sphere. In her recent study of animal representations in eighteenth-century literature, Laura Brown aptly describes the pet as "commodity, companion, paragon, proxy and even kin."[59] Indeed, the interchangeability of exotic pets with luxury objects such as chinaware, husbands, and even slaves in poetry, drama, novels, and visual arts attests to the widespread critiques of female consumerist excess common to the period. Particularly prevalent were satires on ladies and their attachment to lapdogs.[60] Although the ostensible moral of *Spectator* no. 343 is the disciplining of the eighteenth-century female who indiscriminately "loves Parrots, Monkeys and Lap Dogs," the tale also exposes an underlying anxiety about the status of the animal who travels and retains a cultural memory of being part of a global network of exchange (273). Through his fantastic past lives, Jack Freelove moves from the banks of the Ganges to the forest, and from being an Indian tax gatherer to an English banker on Lombard-Street. After a stint as a mite and a bee, he ends up in Ethiopia in the form of a monkey, who is then caught by a servant of an English factory and sent to Britain to be put into captivity. This is thus an allegory of enslavement by love and by colonial relations. In this respect, transmigration completes a circuit of commercial, erotic, and existential exchanges from Asia to Europe.

Transmigration articulates geographical and colonial intimacies in terms of sexual or erotic relations. Moreover, the links between human, animals, and objects are radically globalized, beyond questions of metaphorical connections or proxy relations, when cast in terms of the supernatural possibilities of reanimated lives and the transmigrational fluidity of places and identities. The trajectories of tales and lives as they make their way from the East enable the omniscient perspective of the male trickster, Jack Freelove, who trades in stories and simultaneously maps his knowledge of the globe. Yet although he adopts the perspective of world traveler, the only actual traveler here is the pet monkey. More than simply an instrument of an Englishman's prank, the monkey mediates the relations between the sexes by emphasizing at once the distance between them and their common dependence on the foreign commodity in their midst. The question of the monkey's identity and origins is raised, but not easily or succinctly answered, for it entails a story of global circulation as well as the greater conundrum of human uniqueness. Correcting the excesses of the female consumer seems an insufficient response to the scope of the problem. For this reason, the tale is framed by a yet more encompassing moral, Will Honeycomb's critique of the excesses of superstition practiced in the "Eastern parts of the world."

The traveling perspective of the animal commodity eludes male and female alike. As conveyed by the narrator, it offers an overarching yet intimate view of the routes of the East Indies trade, turning an incomprehensibly vast network of exchange into a series of entertaining, concretely bounded biographical stories. Where the colonial imaginary is only suggested in the *Spectator*, the pleasures and anxieties of borrowing from the East become the explicit theme of Thomas Gueullette's 1725 *Chinese Tales*, a French Oriental-tale sequence directly modeled on *Spectator* no. 343. The idolatrous East is subjected to criticism not only by being invoked in the cautionary moral that prefaces the tales, but also as providing a subject for religious conversion.

In Gueullette's framing tale, Fum-Hoam, a mandarin, seeks to convince

Gulchenraz, the new sultaness of China, of the doctrine of transmigration—a tenet of the "Chinese" religion—through recollecting his many lives and adventures.[61] She and her father, the recently deposed king of Georgia, had fled to China for sanctuary. There, the king, or "Sultan," of China, after falling madly in love with her, allowed her to continue practicing her Muslim religion,[62] and in fact agreed to convert to Islam himself should the mandarin Fum-Hoam fail to turn her to the Chinese form of "Mahometanism." Like Jack Freelove, Fum-Hoam appears to possess the transmigrational ability to narrate all of world history, and world religion, through his countless lives and perfectly preserved memory. He boasts: "I have appeared in all parts of the world in very different forms; have consequently been of all religions, and all sects, and by a peculiar power, have preserved to this day the remembrance of all the chief facts whereof I was an eye-witness or agent myself" (*Chinese Tales*, 33).

That a single narrator recounts his own experiences sets the *Chinese Tales* apart from other collections of Oriental tales. The appeal of the eyewitness storyteller is staged through the question linking the tales, posed by Gulchenraz to Fum-Hoam: "But what became of you afterwards?" (214). In the end, the battle of faiths between Fum-Hoam and Gulchenraz proves to be a false opposition, for the mandarin is not what he seems. After Fum-Hoam's exhaustive storytelling, the sultan of Georgia, Gulchenraz, and the sultan of China are magically transported back to Georgia. The princess awakes, having dreamed that Fum-Hoam has conceded Mahomet to be the prophet of the one true God. At that moment, Fum-Hoam discloses his real identity, that of Prince Alroamat, her long-lost brother. Kidnapped by pirates and raised by a jeweler, Alroamat learned cabalistic powers from a wise physician in the North Indies. Hearing of his father and sister's banishment, he used his new powers to disguise himself as Fum-Hoam the mandarin and traveled to China to save his sister from converting to the religion of the king of China. Attempting to seduce her with the stories of his heathen transmigrations, he tested her faith in God, and she passed. We learn that his stories were meant to ridicule transmigration and, contrary to his stated aim, to convert the sultan of China to Islam. Upon hearing Alroamat's story, the sultan of China instantly agrees to convert to a "good Mussulman," and the pregnant Gulchenraz is declared to give birth to a son who will be a cabalistic philosopher like his uncle (251). Alroamat's confession is worth quoting at length:

> For, in truth, is there any thing more contrary to good sense, than the transmigration of the soul from one body to another? . . . How can they, according to their own principles, remember in one body, what was transacted in another? But suppose

they could, upon the supposition of the soul's passing from body to body; how miserable must it needs be, to be always subject to the prevailing inclinations of the form it inhabits? For, in short, all wild beasts have a sad and cruel tincture of their own species. (*Chinese Tales*, 24)

Further citing transmigration's "ridiculous fables" and "idle stories," he objects to its trivialization of death and its rendering of cows sacred (247, 248). He religiously quotes from the "Alcoran" and sermonizes on the importance of worshipping only one God. Interestingly enough, he then returns to China still disguised as Fum-Hoam to destroy China's various idols and establish "the religion of Mahomet," a religion at once comparable to Christianity and distinct from pagan pantheism (31). Also, in this vision of Chinese religion, it is Islam that vanquishes the pagan practices of Buddhism and Hinduism, while Confucianism remains curiously absent.

Guellette's tale clearly follows the discourse of Eastern superstition established by the English theorists of transmigration. To make the case for the falsity of transmigration, Gueullette cites the "Story of Pugg the Monkey" in its entirety. He then corrects the *Spectator's* definition of metempsychosis by reviewing Whitelock's *Essay on Transmigration* for the proper interpretation of the travels of the sensitive spirit and the rational soul. While Gueullette likewise argues from a Christian standpoint against "gross" Eastern beliefs, he freely uses transmigration as the subject and mode of narrating the tales of "China" that follow. Indeed, the pleasures of transmigrational fables are taken to a satiric extreme, through an emphasis on the body and bodily violence, continuous memory, animal subjectivity, female pedagogy, and the staging of an elaborate hoax.

In her reading of *Chinese Tales,* Ballaster makes a provocative statement that China is the most self-reflexive and "fullest transmigratory space."[63] She attributes this in part to China's inaccessibility to the West, which allows the greater projection of Western imagination onto its culture. I would further argue that the anxieties of genre, species, and gender raised by the idea of transmigration are most exaggerated in the example of China because its empire represents the height of idolatry and hybridized religions of the East; as Athanasius Kircher put it in *China Illustrata*, "all their idolatry seemeth to have made a Voyage thence into China." In other words, China is exemplary of the excesses of Eastern superstition and thus fulfills the Western Christian fantasy of converting the East. In her study of the Oriental tale, Martha Pike Conant dismisses Gueullette's work for being a preposterous and inauthentic collection of "pseudo-Oriental tales." It is, she writes, "extravagant in the use of magic, fantastic in description and incident, employing European legends freely and oriental colouring very slightly, sometimes moralizing, sometimes coarse, seldom satirical, imitating the faults rather than the excellences of genuine oriental translations, these narratives are frequently entertaining, but possess little intrinsic value."[64] The ire with which Conant accuses Gueullette of inauthenticity, though, misses the point of fabulous pedagogy, which borrows from Eastern religion in order to make the Orient an object of didactic and epistemological control. Indeed the *Chinese Tales*' overindulgence in the profane is counterbalanced by an equally outsized moral, the destruction of all the idols of China and the conversion of its vast empire. Metempsychosis, as represented in the Oriental fable, works to weave together imaginatively the different parts of the East into a geography of idolatry, since the soul can be reborn in any number of Eastern locations.[65] Alroamat, passing as Fum-Hoam, is born in Persia and lives in India, Greece, Malabar, Tartary, Canada, Armenia, Abyssinia, Georgia, and China. While his transmigrations are ultimately revealed to be fabricated, these fictions seem to catalogue the East. European translators of Oriental tales commonly deemed them useful for relating truthful accounts of Asian culture: "[T]he Geography is here exactly observed, wherein the Scene of every Action is laid, whether in Tartary, Persia, or Egypt; and the Manners, Customs, and Habits of the different People of Asia, which sufficiently Characterize them, are here handsomely set forth."[66] We need to remember that transmigration, though referred to as Eastern, is not a marker of cultural authenticity but rather a hybrid idea produced by cultural encounters between different religious and philosophical systems. These tales seem to preserve the diverse customs of the East, but they do so by containing its perceived religious excesses and turning its superstitions into useful knowledge, all the while expanding the bounds of the colonial imagination. As a result, ideal British mores and manners are illustrated through their imagined proximity to and distance from the East.

The Eastern idea of transmigration enables the narrativization of intimacy and proximity on a number of related levels: interpersonal, interspecies, and international. As the fake spirits Jack Freelove and Alroamat narrate their adventures on a global scale, their efforts can be compared with the transmission of epic history in one of the *Spectator's* sources of transmigration, Ovid's *Metamorphoses*. In Book 15, "Of the Pythagorean Philosophy," the scholar Numa, having transmigrated through the ages, narrates the fall of Troy as the inevitability of historical flux: "All changing Species should my song recite: / Before I cease'd wou'd change the Day to Night. / Nations and Empires flourish, and decay, / By turns command, and in their turns obey. . . . The wages and flow of history." Preserved by transmigration, the authoritative memory of the bardic subject records a genealogy of empires that foresees the rise of Rome. Dryden's translation legitimizes the reign of Augustus through a *translatio imperii*, a transfer of history, culture, and political power, enabled by transmigration's ability to preserve personal as well as collective identities. Numa weaves together a lineage through his composite identity: "Ev'n I, who these mysterious Truths declare, / Was once Euphorbus in the Trojan War; / My name and Lineage I remember well." Furthermore, he reflects on how the cities "Mycene, Sparta, Thebes of might Fame, / Are vanish'd out of Substance into Name."[67] The preservation of the past serves the founding of future empires, including that of England. The fables of transmigration that follow the Oriental-tale tradition flout the decorum of epic or heroic history; in their comedic narrations of personal and plebian histories of travels between Asia and Europe, they reflect a new empire of mercantile exchange and consumerism. The sites of the Orient are mapped through the adventures of singular Oriental-tale personae and their fabulous transmigrations. The idea that souls circulate between bodies and places requires the imagining of universal forms of kinship, a network of interconnected lives, and the philosophical and material transfer of virtues, or vices, from one civilization to another.

Commerce, Immortality, and Object Life

The *Spectator's* organization of religious and philosophical knowledge into the form of Oriental fables makes a virtue of cultural appropriation: ideas of Eastern superstition are transformed into instructive stories through the authors' self-conscious acts of imitating, framing, and moderating the perceived excesses of the Orient. Fabulous pedagogy, in purporting to borrow and improve upon the ideas of Eastern antiquity, has an analogue in the commercial sphere. Like the discourse of transmigration, the marketing of Asian commodities such as tea, porcelain, and lacquerware, or japanwork, exploited the idea of borrowing from the ancient civilizations and technologies of the East to imagine new forms of global intimacy and proximity between unlike things, humans, animals, and objects.

One commodity in particular exemplifies the quality of preservation associated with Eastern antiquity. Japanning, the European imitation of Asian lacquerwork, was essentially the practice of protecting the surfaces of objects from erosion while adding the aesthetic value of decorative polish. In a global marketplace where goods were transported over long distances and periods of time, such Eastern patina promised a type of everlasting life: the perfectly preserved object, and thus the ideal commodity. As discussed in the preceding chapter, the popularity of lacquer panels in the 1670s and early 1680s spurred an English japanning trade that strove to emulate the superior artisanship of China and Japan. In fact, the desirability of relatively unattainable Asian manufactures propelled scientific experimentation at home; these innovations would in turn usher in an age of industry.[68] In the 1710s, George Psalmanazar, for one, had used his identity as a virtuosic impersonator of Formosa and Japan to vouch for and advertise japanwork's approximation of Eastern craftsmanship. The broader discourse on japanning marketed the virtues of the Orient's ancient yet modern techniques of preservation. In fact, japanning's professed ability to stop the forces of age and decay enacts a fantasy of immortality with curiously wide-ranging implications.

Japanning, which referred both to a technique of applying lacquer, the protective surface applied, and the finished object, offered to English consumers the sought-after qualities of durability and permanence. To cite once more from John Stalker and George Parker's popular craft manual, *A Treatise of Japaning and Varnishing* (1688):

> [A]s Painting has made an honourable provision for our Bodies, so Japanning has taught us a method, no way inferior to it, for the splendor and preservation of our Furniture and Houses. These Buildings, like our Bodies, continually tending to ruin and dissolution, are still in want of fresh supplies and reparations. . . . the Art of Japanning has made them almost impregnable against both [time and weather]. . . . True, genuine Japan, like the Salamander, lives in the flames, and stands unalterable. . . . Just so the Asbeston of the Ancients, the cloath in which they wrapped the dead bodies, lay unchanged and entire on the Funeral Pile, and preserved the body, when reduced to ashes, from being mixt with common, and undistinguisht dust.
> (*Treatise of Japanning*, preface)

The successive analogies that enumerate the benefits of this new technology render "bodies," "furniture," and "buildings" alike in need of preservative arts that can be traced back to the religious practices of Egyptian funeral rites, or the "Asbeston of the Ancients." The invocation of these sacred acts, that keep human ashes sealed off from common dust, attribute to japanning an ancient ability to preserve culture and civilizations as well as the uniqueness of human identity. In his study of eighteenth-century consumption, Grant McCracken argues that with the advent of fashionable consumer culture, commodities were no longer as valued for their "patina," or the status accorded to them by their age and ties to inherited wealth and aristocratic tradition. Fashion dictated a break with the past and the valuing of objects for their novelty.[69] In the case of japanning, however, patina conveys Eastern tradition in fashionable form, adding value precisely through arranging a marriage between ancient and modern, foreign and domestic.

Along with the promise of ancient forms of preservation and the preservation of antiquity, one of the greatest assets of japanning was its applicability to all types of surfaces. Earlier arts manuals on japanning read like trial-and-error recipe books of early modern scientific experimentation. In William Salmon's *Polygraphice: Or, The Arts of Drawing, Limning, Painting* (1672), a section on cosmetics follows one on varnishing, and the coloring of furniture and coloring of faces share a technique of application that leaves "bodies" undifferentiated. The end result is the same: the creation of lasting value through adding an extra skin. Japanning is, after all, the general "art of covering bodies."[70] Indeed, one cosmetics manual from later in the period includes an entry for "A curious Varnish for the Face" to "give the skin the finest lustre imaginable."[71] Another manual includes a section on "Curious Compositions to Varnish Prints and Paintings" that follows "A curious Varnish for the Face."[72] Even as these recipes are sundry and disorganized, they highlight the range of uses associated with Eastern technology. Even as late as the mid-eighteenth century, Robert Dossie's *Handmaid to the Arts* (1758), a work addressed to serious artisans that disparaged earlier texts for including "heaps of absurd stuff" such as alchemy, chiromancy, and cosmetics in an unsystematic fashion, describes japanning as a yet "mysterious art" of preserving surfaces (xix, xiv). Moreover, unlike the female cosmetic paint to which it is often compared, japanning escapes the critique of superficiality in that it, at least in theory, cannot be removed. In this respect, it troubles the accepted association of femininity with outward appearances and, hence, a disregard for inner virtue. As japanning is meant to illustrate, not all arts of covering bodies are necessarily duplicitous or ephemeral. Stalker and Parker in their treatise on japanning engage the critiques of female artfulness by arguing that, unlike common cosmetics, which only temporarily beautify the "Jezebels" and "Walking Pictures," their varnish never comes off.[73] Instead of chastising the immorality of face painting, Stalker and Parker fault its failure to measure up to the masculinized durability of japanning. In their words, japan is "not only strong and durable, but delightful and ornamental beyond expression" (*Treatise of Japanning*, xiv–xv). Here, suspicions of the cosmetic bases of female virtue are deferred; instead, we see a turn to a new and improved technology of the durable, impenetrable ornamental surface.

As we saw in the fabulists' appropriation of transmigration theory, imagining the travel of immaterial souls paradoxically results in excessive representations of the corporeal. The more one attempts to envision the invisible circulation of life-defining forces, the more present the body becomes, whether through descriptions of physical violence and death, sexual relations with animals, or inadvertent acts of cannibalism. Whereas transmigration erases the distances that separate species while preserving human uniqueness in the form of transferable memories, japanning ostensibly keeps identities intact in its methods of material conservation. At issue is the sanctity of the human, and the human body specifically. In the commercial realm, Oriental knowledge is central to the discourse of the virtuous surface, one that can be ornamental yet utilitarian. Antiquity can be valued as not only a collector's object, or patina tied to the past, but as a source of innovation and, indeed, scientific progress that enables a number of types of preservation. Interestingly enough, in this regard, a practice comparable to japanning is that of embalming, or "Preserving a Human Dead Body entire."

In *Nekrokedeia: or, the art of embalming* (1705), London surgeon Thomas Greenhill defends the embalmer's profession by associating it with a history of ancient Egyptian, Hebrew, and Greek funeral and burial rites, "the first and best Antiquities of the world" (vii). Unlike John Toland's euhemerist dismissal of Egyptian embalming as idolatrous ancestor worship, here the ancient practice is marketed as a virtuous effort to achieve immortality of the soul by material means; by salting or preserving the body such that it becomes "as durable as Marble," the soul is kept within, and the "long duration of these Bodies," in turn, "proves the Immortality of the Soul" (*Nekrokedeia*, 239). Following this logic, Greenhill reasons that bodies, the "covering" of souls, should be tended to with utmost care. In Greenhill's text, a worldly concern with preserving human beauty, a kind of toilette of the dead, outweighs the theological justifications for care of the corpse. Not only does he believe that the stench from rotting corpses poses a health hazard to the living, but that the putrefaction offends the aesthetic sense. Thus the act of embalming "[renders] the Body sweet and decorous, retaining still its natural Form, Feature and Shape" (119). It is described as "being deliciously perfum'd . . . with all the Aromatic and Odoriferous Spices and Gums of Arabia" (106), a description that recalls the toilette of Alexander Pope's Belinda, where "all *Arabia* [breathes] from yonder Box."[74] The surgeon's practice of rendering the "flesh firm" and "durable as marble" and the "features smooth" makes him at once mortician, cosmetician, and even poet (239). In fact, two poems praising Greenhill liken him to an elegist, who, beyond preserving the name of a loved one, both "keeps [his deceased] Friends alive" and "redeemed from the Injuries of Oblivion," as well as inspiring his living friends not to fear death.[75] Indeed, the embalmed body becomes a "living memory" that outshines other forms of representations, such as pictures or statues, with a unique "durability." In particular, the triumph of material over textual posterity is emphasized in this rather remarkable pitch, in Greenhill's text, for a materialist, or corporealist, vocabulary:

> Thus all Things intended to preserve a Name, whether Pictures, Statues, Medals, Buildings or Writings, may be comprehended under this general Sense of *Embalming*; nevertheless, experience teaches us the preservation of a Body by the *Balsamic Art* is not only the best way of reviving Mens Memories, and bringing their Merits fresh in our Minds, but also the most durable; for not only Tombs and Status have decay'd in a few Years, but also whole Towns and Cities have been ruin'd and demolish'd within the Revolution of an Age . . . whereas *Embalm'd* Bodies have been found entire after Thousands of Years. (117–18)

We might compare this passage to one on japanning that claims that not only individual pieces of furniture and appliances but also houses and entire civilizations can be immortalized:

> What can be more surprising, than to have our Chambers overlaid with Varnish more glossy and reflecting than polisht Marble? . . . The glory of one country, Japan alone, has exceeded in beauty and magnificence all the pride of the Vatican at this time. . . . Japan can please you with a more noble prospect, not only whole Towns, but Cities too are there adorned with as rich a Covering; so bright and radiant are their Buildings, that when the Sun darts forth his luster upon their Golden roofs, they enjoy a double day by the reflection of his beams.[76]

As with the language of embalming, japanning preserves "whole towns and cities." And as different as they seem, these practices share a discourse of craftsmanship and experimental science, of preserving surfaces and producing durability, that on the one hand pits the secular innovations of modernity against the sacrosanct; on the other hand, the craftsperson's goal of thwarting bodily decay and achieving a type of immortality is justified through the wedding of modern *tekne* with ancient *episteme*. It is no longer the exclusive purview of the poet to memorialize, as does Ovid's Numa, the great cities and civilizations "vanish'd out of Substance into name." Nor are impressive works of architecture or monuments in ruins the sole bearers of the history of empires. Instead, we are offered the monumentality of the mundane in the well-wrought object—one that is, in theory, timeless. Japanned or embalmed objects, like the animals of transmigrational fables, may function primarily as useful decoration; yet they also occasion an experience of the fantastic in their embodiment of the encounter between disparate systems of knowledge.

Even the designs of japanwork indicate the commercialization of Eastern idolatry as bourgeois spectacle. The chinoiserie equivalent to delighting in, denouncing, and converting transmigration and the rituals of Eastern excess can be seen in the assorted images offered by Stalker and Parker. Described as scenes from "Chinese" life, the copper prints appended to the text, and meant to serve as decorative patterns for japanwork, include carnivalesque architecture, "all sorts of Birds flying in Antick figures," "figures of Chinese men and women, in untoward gestures, and habits," and "their manner of worship, and reception of foreign Ministers and Embassadors" (40). To create an aesthetically pleasing Oriental pastiche, the reader is advised to mix and match the different motifs: "Here you may alter and correct, take out a piece from one, add a fragment to the next, and make an entire garment compleat in all its parts" (41). The description could well apply to the patchwork effect of chinoiserie in general and fabulous pedagogy in particular. Indeed, the authors incorporate elements of "Chinese" superstition and moral excess in their compositions. One template features "a pagod worship in the Indies," while others depict, strangely enough, human figures suffering various punishments. The image of a man in a pillory, set amid exotic birds, plants, buildings, and rocks, is meant to decorate a comb box; in another scene, a similarly prostrate and bound, seminude figure is the subject of "drawers for cabinets to be placed according to your fancy." These figures appear to be based on none other than Nieuhof's *Embassy to China*, the source for numerous chinoiserie works of the period.[77] In Nieuhof's 1673 text, the image of a mendicant in a pillory accompanies a discussion of the gruesome spectacles of self-torture performed by the country's beggars. The image appears in a section titled "Of several Chinese Handicraft-Trades, Comedians, Juglers, and Beggers," which describes with a great deal of ambivalence the famed architecture, technological feats, and products of the empire, and declares that the people are "very much addicted to Shews and Stage-Plays; and herein only do they exceed those of Europe" (159). Following the descriptions of the various types of Chinese beggars performing acts of excruciating pain is a list of Chinese trades, including chinaware and japanwork, or the "Gumming and Painting of Chests, Trunks, and Boxes." Nieuhof concludes, though, that "notwithstanding this abundance of Trades in *China*, a great Defect and Abuse is observ'd in most of the Commodities which are made there, and it is this, that they only appear and seem fair to the Eye, but are really for the most part very sleight" (163).

Stalker and Parker place with the image of the mendicant a scene with another Chinese man being punished, as if to merge Nieuhof's discussion of beggars

Chinese mendicants performing self-torture. Included in Johann Nieuhof, *An Embassy from the East-India Company of the United Provinces, to the Grand Tartar Cham*, 1673. Courtesy of Special Collections, Lehigh University Libraries.

with numerous other passages from his text that describe the punishments of Chinese by idolatrous priests. Nieuhof's description of one such "Spectacle" of torture, a man bored through the neck with a hot iron, led naked through the city on a bar with chains while whipped until bloody, is positioned as an example of the idolatry practiced by Buddhist priests who deal out such punishments upon those who transgress their laws. Appropriately enough, this description follows a discussion of the spread of transmigration from Indostan to China; it is meant to exemplify the consequence of the spread of idolatrous beliefs eastward. As such a corporealization of transmigration theory shows, China is portrayed as a society of spectacle—religious and commercial—particularly in its exemplification of Oriental idolatry. It is fitting, then, that Western audiences would continue the cycle of making a spectacle of Chinese bodies in pain. One of the lasting effects of Eastern superstition, it appears, is to be converted from religious spectacle into bourgeois Western curiosity—inscribed upon a cabinet and placed in a drawing room, an Eastern example of vice presented as ornament and sign of Western

Design for a pen, ink, and paper standish or a comb box. Included in John Stalker and Robert Parker, *A Treatise of Japaning and Varnishing*, plate 7, 1688. Courtesy of Archives and Special Collections, Franklin and Marshall College, Lancaster, Pa.

craftsmanship. Surfaces have stories to tell, including the routes they have traveled from afar, the bodies they conserve over time, and the mysterious science of their construction.

The processes of borrowing from the East explored in this chapter foreground the importance of cultural exchange to theories of moral self-improvement. The fable form, by definition, imparts lessons indirectly, incorporating the element of surprise into its pedagogical structure. It is through the exercise of the imagination that one comes to recognize oneself in another—a beast, a dervish, a mandarin—and hence to appreciate the force of analogy. The fables of the *Spectator* not only evoke alternative, parallel worlds but also reflect on their acts of drawing resemblances between unlike things. The need to explain, even more, to justify, the moral utility of Eastern religion generates a separate economy of meaning, one that is imbricated with the larger context of global commerce and the identity of the Englishman as world citizen. Through the channels of commodity exchange, even the most un-Christian of ideas acquires value upon entering the sphere of domestic consumption.

Whereas indiscriminate borrowing might mean accepting superstition as an end rather than a means, adopting the fables of antiquity, particularly their visions of cosmological fluidity, to tell new stories allows the correction of the errors of the past. In other words, age-old Eastern beliefs can be reinterpreted to reveal ever more useful modern, scientific truths. Pythagoras can be reclaimed as a teacher who used fables metaphorically, rather than literally. One can dismiss the superstitions that underlie Egyptian embalming while embracing its techniques to enhance the development of modern manufactures. Fabulous pedagogy operates by making an example of Eastern antiquity, whose powers of preservation can either imply cultural stagnation or civilizational progress. The texts discussed address, often playfully, the anxieties connected with the ancient idea of transmigration and its relevance to Western modernity. The possibility of a transmigrational world would suggest a radical lack of differentiation—the mixing of the dead with the living and the permeation of foreign souls and ideas throughout Western society.[78] At the same time, transmigration, like the fabulous surfaces of china and japanwork, links disparate times and technologies of the self—and different aesthetics of preservation—to produce new myths of intercontinental intimacy and immortality. This form of early modern orientalism does not vilify the idolatrous other so much as integrate the perceived excesses of foreign morals and commodities into everyday life and discipline the marvelous into the service of moral edification.

CHAPTER FOUR

Luxury, Moral Sentiment, and *The Orphan of China*

London audiences attending the opening of Arthur Murphy's *The Orphan of China* in February 1759 would have been struck by its elaborate staging, which was a subtle study in contrasts. Unlike Settle's *Conquest of China*, this heroic tragedy was an instant success. The fashionability of the chinoiserie costumes, glittering sets, and life-sized porcelain vases would appear to contradict visually the ancient virtues of self-sacrifice enacted by the Chinese characters of the play, which unfolded the plight of a family fighting to maintain its Confucian values amid yet a different Tartar conquest of China. I cite this example as I turn to another aspect of the eighteenth century's problem in the world of theatrical spectacle: how to theorize moral and material excess.

At the start of Murphy's tragedy, a leaderless China already languishes under the yoke of the tyrant Timurkan. The country's only hope is a virtuous mandarin named Zamti, his wife Mandane, and the secret they keep. Unbeknown to the world, twenty years before they had given away their only son to save the country's infant prince Zaphimri, orphaned during the war and the last of the royal line. Naming the prince Etan, they raised him as their own, and he has grown up unaware of his actual identity. Now, on the brink of Peking's absolute destruction, a captured resistance fighter and stranger named Hamet enters the city; believed to be the Chinese prince-in-exile come of age and returned to save the country, he is sentenced to death by Timurkan. To protect the nation's interests, the elderly couple Zamti and Mandane must hide the fact that this mysterious prisoner is not the real prince (all along in their midst), but their long-lost son, whom they must now sacrifice a second time. As witnessed by the audiences at London's Drury Lane Theater, the themes of parental anguish and conflicting loyalties to family and nation showcased the actors' skills in sentiment and, notably, the shedding of tears. Contemporary reviews found the play "prodigiously affecting," and the preeminent celebrity of the eighteenth-century stage, David

Garrick, was thought to have delivered one of the most expressive performances of his career in the role of Zamti.[1] As a testament to the play's successful run and its publication shortly thereafter, another reviewer noted, "Every one has, by this time, seen or read, and most have applauded it."[2]

In addition to moving audiences, these performances presented quite graphically two very different ways of thinking about the values of consumption in a rapidly developing Britain of the mid-eighteenth century. The way China was performed revealed something about the British elite's own anxieties and hopes. The very production of the play brought to the fore the opposed yet complementary feelings about "China," centering as it did on the effects of commerce upon virtue. On the one hand, there was a desire for moral reform at a time of rampant materialism, and on the other hand, an appetite for the commodities of the East evoked by the sheer vision of luxury on stage. In a sense, China represented both the heart of the problem and its solution: it was a source of unruly luxury and consumption that needed to be managed even as it modeled the Confucian ideals of practical morality that established social order. China's functioning as an example and counterexample of public virtue is a contradiction we have seen before; however, the particular problem raised by Murphy's *Orphan of China* has to do not with effeminacy, forgery, or idolatry, but with luxury. Through its staging, the play visualizes two forms of luxury crucial to mid-eighteenth-century discussions of virtue: one, an excess of sentiment; the other, the matter of commercial consumption.

There is a curious interaction of the props of theatrical chinoiserie with the overwrought performances of affect: as if to counteract the consumerist impulses engendered by the wealth displayed on stage, the play generates in tandem an overflow of emotion. It then works to channel the intense passions of its characters into moral sentiment that can serve the good of the nation; and the performance as a whole thus makes "luxury" a surfeit of feeling as well as depicting material wealth as a vehicle for virtue. The interaction between commerce and virtue examined in this chapter is central to the spectacle of affect that made such an impression on the theatergoing public.

This type of spectacle operates quite differently in its public pedagogy than the didacticism of Addison and Steele's *Spectator*, which posits universal wisdom through observing and managing from a critical distance the habits of its readers and the religious excesses of the Eastern imagination. Here, the basis of universal virtue is the visceral stimulation of sensibility, relations of sympathy, and affective identifications between strangers and kin who share a common desire for justice. The theatrical performances of suffering and misfortune featured in plays like

The Orphan of China modeled a moral community knit together by civilized acts of sympathy. At the same time that such refined feeling diverged from the vulgar, bodily desires of untrammeled consumerism, it was, of course, being performed on stage for public consumption. Theatrical expressions of excessive emotion underscored the broader social phenomenon of the mid-eighteenth-century culture of sensibility. Sentimentalism by definition makes private feelings public as it participates in the processes of exhibition and exchange that drive modern consumerism. In the context of eighteenth-century culture, the fashionability of feelings on public display indicated a widespread "commercialization of inner life"; practices of sentimentality signaled the exigencies of demonstrating an inner realm of virtue uncorrupted by commerce.³ Performing China was an especially compelling exercise in reconciling private with public interests—that is, in testing the ability of trade to improve economic *and* ethical character—given China's dual status as exemplary commodity and moral system.

Despite the apparent incompatibility between commerce and virtue, the example of China reveals a parallel importation of goods and values. *The Orphan of China* was itself presented to the British public through a common rhetoric of "importing" Chinese morality. Murphy's prologue announces the "imported boon" of Eastern virtue. Similarly, the playwright William Hatchett wrote in the preface to his own, unperformed version of the play, "China has furnish'd us long with her Manufactures; and . . . the Importation of her Poetry will serve to regale in its Turn."⁴ And in the introduction to *The Citizen of the World*, Oliver Goldsmith commented on the "small cargoe of Chinese morality" introduced in the wake of "the furniture, frippery and fireworks of China [which] have long been fashionably brought up."⁵ The contradictions at work in the representations of Chinese imports illuminate ongoing debates over the social effects of consumerism, theatrical innovation, and, more importantly, new articulations of commercialized virtue.

The idea of morality as an import was in fact highly contentious, and the ambivalence toward China conveyed by this expression came at a moment of intensified disputes over the impact of foreign imports, moral and economic, on Britain's wartime consumer society.⁶ Debates on luxury peaked in the period from 1756 to 1763, the span of the Seven Years' War, as evidenced by the outpouring of books and pamphlets on the subject.⁷ *The Orphan of China* participated in heightened Anglo-French tensions in being a Gallic import of sorts, an adaptation not only of a thirteenth-century Chinese opera but also of Voltaire's recent interpretation of the work, *L'Orphelin de la Chine* (1755). Murphy, a noted Anglo-Irish playwright and manager of the Drury Lane Theater, may have learned of the Chinese *Orphan* independently of Voltaire; but his version is certainly also a response to its French predecessor. He includes in the printed text of 1759 a letter to Voltaire that enumerates the virtues of his "English Orphan of China," the "moral improvements" he makes, as well as the assets of the English stage.[8] Along with the more explicit references to the ongoing Seven Years' War, the rhetoric of appropriating the "Orphan" highlights the role of nationalistic, cross-Channel competition in producing "China" as an exemplary original in need of refining. The associations with French culture made China an even more layered, and not-so-distant, example of the threat of luxury and foreign cultural influences upon an emerging British national identity.

Mid-century critics of luxury identified it with a contagious effeminacy that threatened to eviscerate the strength and honor of the nation in a number of key ways. An indulgence in passion—for example, a passion for material consumption—could either enrich or debilitate the social body. In one contemporary account, the corrupting power of commodities was thought to shift the human pursuit of society and the public good to a single-minded focus on oneself and one's material possessions. When men become vain, they lose a desire for the opposite sex to the point that consumption threatens the possibilities for procreation and leads to the "thinning" of the populace.[9] The opposite also appears to be the case, in that ingesting the products of the East and West Indies increases female sexual appetite; and, according to another commentator, there was no threat greater than the immanent loss of female chastity: "Thus has our Luxury chang'd our Natures in despight of our Climate, and our Girls are ripe as soon as those of the Indies."[10] While luxury is held primarily responsible for the alteration of the body's interior landscape, here it is vicarious exposure to the tropical Indies through the act of comparison that figures the female as a prematurely nubile, unchaste Indian. In the above instances, both the oversexed woman and passive man disrupt gender norms and the boundaries of decency through consumption of foreign goods.

In response to these numerous formulations of luxury's harmful contagion, the arguments on behalf of luxury advocated a healthy contagion of sorts. Calls to imitate foreign goods and designs to spur technological innovation and British manufacturing were being made by new societies for manufactures, which stressed the importance of developing "import-substituting industries" that could replace the superior craftsmanship of Asia in particular.[11] Against the charge that commerce and its byproduct of luxury isolated individuals and destroyed communities, it was argued that the sociability of commerce set virtue in motion. A commodity economy could create a division of labor, space for leisure, and thus practices of sympathy and humanitarianism exemplified by the virtuous Chinese family of *The Orphan of China*. The underlying question posed by eighteenth-century moralists and economists alike was how to benefit from outside influences and yet, amid the free flows of trade, preserve the integrity of the nation and the health of its populace. The fraught relationship between passions, interests, and the public good rises to the fore in the context of an increasingly commercialized society comprised of long-distance exchanges and heightened dependency on foreign goods and labor. In particular, the visions of Chinese luxury evoked by the world of *The Orphan of China* become a test case for the traditional opposition between the ancient ideals of the classical citizen and the modern subject of private interests. Three manifestations of this opposition I find especially noteworthy: first, the particular mode of theatrical spectacle communicated within *The Orphan of China* and in its reception; second, the theorization of spectatorship and Chinese spectacle in a related work, Adam Smith's *Theory of Moral Sentiments* (1759); and finally, China's controversial status in contemporary theories of fashion and luxury. What emerges from these interlinked articulations of China's exemplarity is a new standard of comparison for measuring the impact of luxury and its shifting place within the discourse of British nationalism, patriotism, and sentimentality.

Familial Passions, Patriotic Virtues

The dramatic structure of Murphy's *The Orphan of China* turns on the generation of sympathy for each member of a Chinese family unit: just as the parents set an example of virtue for the younger generation, their mutual displays of affect bind together the family as a moral community in microcosm. In fact, the profuse emotions shared between the parents and children create a circuit of sympathetic identifications that forms the Chinese resistance to Tartar tyranny. Even as affect can serve the interests of the nation, there is a heightened awareness that passions can, however, just as easily run amok or become dangerously unpatriotic. It is thus the work of the play to manage the transformation of private passions to public sentiment.

From the start, an ethical conflict between private and public is characterized through the mandarin Zamti and his wife Mandane, who are loving parents, on the one hand, and concerned citizens, on the other. As the principal moral figure and the embodiment of the "good man" of the eighteenth century,[12] Zamti must negotiate between his patriotic and paternal passions to enact his duty to the nation: "I was a subject ere I was a father," he reasons to a distraught Mandane (31). His resolution is, however, far from stoic. On remembering the city's takeover by Tartar forces, Zamti cries: "[F]resh stream my eyes.... Fresh bleeds my heart" (7). In act 2, he *"Bursts into tears"* in front of his friend Morat when thinking of the son he has sacrificed, and upon keeping secret the identity of his son Hamet, he cries, "Flow, flow my tears, and ease this aching breast" (19, 29). He sobs again with joy when he learns Hamet is still alive. And in response to the final tragedy of Mandane's desperate suicide, he concludes, "tears will have their way—Forgive this flood of tenderness" (86). Shortly after, he dies of grief and leaves the fate of China to his two sons.

It becomes evident that the father's resolve to act in spite of his feelings makes him heroic precisely because bodily affect is a disruptive force with potential to undermine the civic virtue of patriotism. Certainly, Zamti upholds the ideals of a classical patriot—one who, according to the French Enlightenment philosopher Montesquieu, "loves the laws of his country and who acts from love of the laws of his country."[13] The contrast between classical and modern modes of existence is described thus by the historian Joyce Appleby:

> A highly artificial construct, classical citizenship elevated the citizen above the crass, mundane, earthly and vulgar, and tested his fitness by his capacity to be virtuous. Commerce reeked of all the proscribed qualities, linking men and women together in new systems of interdependence while trading on physical needs, worldly tastes, undisciplined wants and preposterous yearnings.[14]

Overwrought passions thus replicate rather than refine the problems of commercial relations. Such a clash of values has also been described by the historian J. G. A. Pocock as the eighteenth-century encounter between republican civic virtues and the new economic mode of commercial wealth. The period was marked by a fundamental incompatibility between a worldview that prioritized the common good of a relatively closed, autonomous republic and one that placed individual interests at the center of a network of trade that expanded beyond the polis and that, through increasingly specialized divisions of labor, drew people together in relations of mutual dependence.[15] In such a context of commercial exchange, the corruption of the principle of civitas could spread through multiple channels, including that of family ties.

In embodying these conflicting values, the character Zamti appears to suffer from the modern illness of private feeling; and although his paternal yearning ostensibly undercuts his discipline and loyalty to the nation, emotional surplus in maternal, as well as paternal form, also becomes increasingly important to the working of public spirit. Zamti's tears for his son are trivial compared with the grief displayed by Mandane, whose outsized motherly love at first contradicts the interests of the nation. It is, however, the feminized channels of sentiment that reshape patriotism into a hybrid of classical and modern virtue that must ultimately accommodate private interests. In this way, virtuous female suffering works to undo the binary between the individual and common good. From the outset, Mandane reprimands Zamti in the name of a mother's individual woe:

> Think'st thou those tears,
> Those false, those cruel tears, will choak the voice
> Of a fond mother's law, now flung to madness?
> Oh! I will rend the air with lamentations,
> Root up this hair, and beat this throbbing breast,
> Turn all connubial joys to bitterness,
> To fell despair, to anguish and remorse. (30–31)

That she refers to a mother's "law" asserts the legitimacy of female passions even though they manifest as disordered "madness" if read by the standards of classical patriotism. Throughout the play, Mandane's reactions unsettle the men around her. When she bursts onto the scene to claim Hamet as her wrongfully targeted son, even the Tartar leader Timurkan recognizes the primacy of her "genuine voice of nature" in her "wild vehemence of grief."[16] As Timurkan expounds, "Where is this wild / Outrageous woman, who with frantic grief / Suspends my dread command" (47–48). Interestingly, the tyrant appears to identify with her unrefined bodily desire, one that is antithetical to the classical stoicism to which the mandarin Zamti aspires. And yet, however wild Mandane's sentiments, they represent the side of civilization rather than barbarism. Maternal anguish, at once elevated and crude, demarcates a mixed form of virtue by dethroning the loftiness of classical patriotism while exhibiting a nobility of the senses that thoroughly confounds the northern barbarian. As if to acknowledge the moral question at the heart of the play, Timurkan cries, "What art thou Virtue!" (63). Chinese and Tartar, it seems, are equally confronted by the foreignness of female sensibility.

The eighteenth-century dramatic convention of feminine distress, beginning with the genre of the she-tragedy, signaled both a virtuous transparency of character and a potential for revolutionary disruption of the polite male public sphere.[17] Theatrical performances drew from the common representation of the female body as an unstable and morally ambiguous figure of illness, a subject of pseudoscientific theories of hysteria whose symptoms, including tears, sighs, and blushes, highlighted her vulnerability to external stimuli.[18] On stage, the increasing popularity of emotive female roles marked a shift from noble male conquerors to women as the locus of a "goodness of character" based on delicacy of sensations instead of superior social status.[19] According to the eighteenth-century health code of virtuous passions, one should indulge in feeling, but at the same time avoid a "luxury of feeling" that could emasculate men and defile women. Emotionalism as practiced on and off stage became either a sign of healthy, virtuous passion or overindulgence in the sensual.[20] Theatricalized social practices like Methodist preaching used techniques of weeping and emotional display to win over a religiously minded audience calling for the reformation of consumerist tendencies.[21] Sentimental fiction of the period, too, rejected material luxury in exchange for a "luxury of grief."[22] The commercialization of sentiment implied by this expression was further reflected by the potential for sympathy to mimic the contagious tendencies of luxury; like luxury, the contagion of sympathy could in theory provide the social glue of an envisioned community of virtuous citizen-consumers. Unlike the emotional experience of an individual, sympathy was understood to be a communicative act of the imagination meant to put to rest the fear of rampant emotions worsened by commerce. By engendering proper sympathetic identifications one could internalize another's suffering and propagate relations of virtue rather than base, materialistic desires. As David Hume wrote, it was "the propensity we have to sympathize with others, and to receive by communication their inclinations and sentiments," that defined national character above all else.[23] I will address the philosophical workings of sympathy in more detail further on, but what matters here is the pivotal role of the mother in forming an affective community that, in treading the line between healthy and decadent passions, also demonstrates its revolutionary potential.

In *The Orphan of China*, the figure of the distressed mother solicits sympathy by her own example of suffering. It is the law of the mother, the feminized "voice of nature," that generates the unique, private-public bonds of familial interdependence and the transference of shared feeling between formerly estranged family members who must for the first time come together to protect self and nation. The fate of the two "sons" of China perhaps best illustrates the sympathetic transmission of individual passions across distances. In fact a contemporary review of the play especially praised a moving scene in which Hamet, the courageous stranger from afar, is imprisoned, having been mistaken for the real prince.[24] In this scene, he is visited by a distraught Etan, who has just learned that Zamti and Mandane are not his real parents, as he is the orphaned prince of China. Previous to this point, both of these young men had pledged their lives to the enigmatic figure of Zaphimri, the prince whose existence remained unknown. Inspired by

Hamet's bravery behind bars and willingness to sacrifice himself to protect the identity of the true prince, Etan is moved to tears: "Thy own example fires me," he says, and refers to himself by his new name, "[Y]es, virtuous envy rises in my soul . . . Zaphimri loves and wonders at thy virtue" (60). The moment of homosocial pedagogy imbues the prince of China with a legitimacy derived not from blood but, rather, from affect. Like their parents' emotional interchange, their exchange of gratitude, love, grief, groans, and anguish situates them in an affective community that shores itself up through a process of comparison, imitation, and sympathy. Brothers of a sort, adopted and biological son must learn their new, respective roles as prince and citizen-son while maintaining their former loyalties.

As demonstrated by the play's conclusion, the ties of sympathy can in fact reconcile contradictory social interests. Private passions enable the overthrow of tyranny and the transformation of China into a properly enlightened monarchy. It is Zamti who, mourning the death of Mandane, imparts upon the new prince Zaphimri the lesson, "The moral duties of the private man / Are grafted in thy soul" (86). Ultimately, even "China's ancient line" is eclipsed by the value of family bonds. As Zaphimri says to Hamet:

> My Ancestors!
> What is't to me a long-descended line,
> A race of worthies, legislators, heroes,—
> —Unless I bring their virtues too? (59)

His words recall a remarkable moment when Mandane pleads the case of familial ties over the royal prerogative:

> Our kings!—our kings!
> What are the scepter'd rulers of the world?—
> Form'd of one common clay, are they not all
> Doom'd with each subject, with the meanest slave,
> To drink the cup of human woe?—alike
> All levell'd by affliction?—Sacred kings!
> 'Tis human policy sets up their claim.—
> Mine is a mother's cause—mine is the cause
> Of husband, wife, and child;—those tend'rest ties!
> Superior to your right divine of kings!— (33)

The universal identifications of sympathy that stem from motherly experience not only compete with, but in this moment radically displace the divine right of kings. Ultimately, though, public and private are merged into a new virtue of compromise performed by not one, but a family of patriots. As the epilogue announces, "So many heroes,—and not one in love!"[25]

Zamti's overlapping identities of public leader and private citizen, patriot and parent are, of course, built into the play's plot device of switched infants and confounded paternal ties. Of the dual virtues of his adopted father, Zaphimri writes, "[he was a] firm patriot, whose parental care / Should raise, should guide, should animate my virtues" (86). In their position as the nation's new parental figures, Hamet and Zaphimri pay homage to Zamti and Mandane by constructing an ancestral monument to their parents and "with tears / Embalm their memories" (88). Even the idolatrous ritual of Chinese ancestor worship here assumes a sentimentalized virtue. The real monument, though, is the law of the mother now internalized and incorporated into the state. It is not a prince's place to mourn his parents: he must live for his people; and Hamet advises Zaphimri to forget his role of son and refrain from taking on "woes like mine." Zaphimri, formerly Etan, while accepting his new role, also makes a place for the past and for the grief that his mother exemplified. Taking on a feminized role, he addresses Hamet thus: "I will live, / To soften thy afflictions; to assuage / A nation's grief, when such a pair expires. / Come to my heart:—in thee another Zamti / Shall bless the realm" (87–88). Curiously, Mandane is not mentioned, but the afflictions of grief by which she lived and died both challenged the stability of the state and reshaped its mandate.[26] Ultimately, hers is an emotional excess that the male characters absorb and channel into a proper balance of private and public virtue.

Confucian Laws and the Spirit of China

As a performance of mid-century sentimental drama, Murphy's *The Orphan of China* sheds romance and the aristocratic ideal of honor for new forms of virtue associated with the rising middle-class family and its domestic ideologies of bourgeois consumerism and the reformation of manners. To be sure, in the culture at large, social and familial relationships (between master and servant or father and daughter, for example) were coming under increasing public scrutiny through literary modes of didacticism, including novels, newspapers, magazines, and conduct manuals. If the family performs a civilizing function and a calibration of social change across Britain, Chinese kinship in *The Orphan of China* is an exemplary medium through which the conflicting principles of ancient honor and modern sentiment are theatrically articulated.[27] Each character demonstrates a form of sentimentalized virtue—genuine nature, patriotism, fraternity, filial piety—that amounts to the family's collective self-sacrifice. As Zamti defiantly announces, "Lo! Here the father, mother, and the son! . . . here we stand . . . all resolv'd to die / The votaries of Honour!" (51). The result is an unconquered China. As pointed out in the epilogue, the play has not one but "so many heroes."[28] As much as the *Orphan* concerns the British virtues of modern family sentiment and the contested place of female virtue, it also evokes a specifically Chinese morality through the association of family values with Confucian law. What codes the luxury of grief as Eastern is not merely the costumes and props but also the unlikely mapping of sensibility onto much-debated ideas of Chinese national character. It is not just that the unruly passions of the "mother's law" must be contained by the patriarchal forces of the play. As the reception of the play makes clear, Chinese law in general becomes a reference point for assessing the potentials and hazards of public feeling.

The efforts on the part of contemporary writers and thinkers to locate a non-Christian system of highly developed morality outside Europe has a double effect of affirming China's distinctiveness while using its example to demonstrate the universal force of those values considered innately Western. To British and European audiences, by far the most impressive feature of China's civilization was its Confucian structure of governance and clearly defined social hierarchies. For eighteenth-century deists and advocates of natural religion, Confucius was not only an individual exemplar but also a pervasive presence whose ancient legacy structured an entire society and transcended Christian and pagan sects alike. He represented the adherence to moral law and, in Leibniz's terms, China's superior "practical philosophy" and "political morality."[29] Undoubtedly, deist virtue in the form of Confucianism inspires the patriot hero of Murphy's *The Orphan of China*. From the start, the true religion of China is positioned against the false idolatry of the Tartars and their "monstrous worship of Lama," their so-called priestcraft (*Orphan*, 65, 25). While Zamti worships a god ambiguously referred to as an "all-gracious Being" and "most High," his religiosity is an expression of both his dual loyalty to country and family and, above all, his refusal of idolatry (*Orphan*, 44). As a modern disciple of Confucius, Zamti invokes the philosopher's name throughout the play to signal that a foundational principle of Chinese history is being put to the test: "In vain Confucius / Unlock'd his radiant stores of moral truth"; "what the great Confucius / Of moral beauty taught"; "Now by the ever-burning lamps that light / Our holy shrines, by great Confucius' altar"; and "by great Confucius, / that is my Etan."[30] If one dramatic quandary is the generational transfer of the noble past to the degenerated present, then Confucius functions as an original authority that must be recuperated and preserved by the mandarin-father for the continuation of the moral species.

That the filial relations of the play are meant to illustrate as well the virtues of contemporary Chinese society can be seen in the ancillary materials published along with the text. One review of Murphy's play appended a short treatise called "The Fundamental Laws of China," which elaborates upon the practices of the "real" Chinese "by Way of Illustration." Most of these fundamental laws concern the propriety of prescribed social stations; for example, the need for children to be "real imitators of the noble actions and virtues of their fathers."[31] Murphy's root source, the Jesuit translator Jean-Baptiste Du Halde, had attached to his printing of the original Chinese opera the essay "Of Moral Philosophy among the Chinese," which identifies five principle relations of morality: father and children; prince and subjects; husband and wife; elder and younger brothers; friend and friend.[32] Likewise, Thomas Percy reprinted the Du Halde text as *The Little Orphan of the House of Chao: A Chinese Tragedy*, preceded by the essay "Rules of Conduct, by a Chinese Author," which lists maxims of virtue such as moderation and filial piety.[33] Each of these addenda thus provides a schema of Chinese family relations to interpret the play, in its various translations and adaptations, as a sociological artifact as well as to offer a practical guide to virtuous behavior for its European readers.

The problem with such clearly defined social relations is not a lack of order but, rather, the danger of overregulation by a system of laws that is by some accounts, paradoxically, presumed to be innate to Chinese character. Against the idealization of China's legal system by philosophers such as François Quesnay, the political theory of Charles de Secondat, Baron de Montesquieu defined China by its despotism.[34] In his *Spirit of the Laws* (1748), Montesquieu famously argues that Confucian rites, while emblematic of the nation's character, collapse all customs, manners, laws, and religions into an overly capacious category of virtue: "The works of Confucius, which confuse an immense detail of civil ceremonies with moral precepts, thereby putting the most trifling things on the same plane as the most essential, greatly affect the Chinese mind." He continues, "Their customs, manners, laws, and religion, being the same thing, they cannot change all these at once; and as it will happen, that either the conqueror or the conquered must change, in China it has always been the conqueror."[35] Unlike the heroic effeminacy presented by Settle's *Conquest of China*, here the source of China's resilience against repeated Tartar conquests, and its resistance to change, is also a moral and epistemological shortcoming. This theory of the "Chinese mind" is in fact referenced by Murphy's portrayal of Chinese law. When the mandarin Zamti defies the tyrant Timurkan, he defends China's quality of self-preservation with the evocative phrase, "spirit of the laws":

> Thy will
> Thy law in China!—Ill-instructed man!—
> Now learn an awful truth . . .
>   . . . the soul,
> Which gave our legislation life and vigour,
> Shall still subsist—above the tyrant's reach—
> —The spirit of the laws can never die—. (66)

When read in light of Montesquieu's theory, what initially appears to be virtuous resoluteness instead carries much more ambivalence. While Zamti's resilience in the face of conquest may be admirable, such spirit would simultaneously infer a surfeit of virtue that stems from China's fundamental confusion of categories, or inability to differentiate between private and public spheres.[36] Furthermore, Montesquieu argues that a nation's "spirit" remains unique and distinct—essentially unchangeable—given the particular confluence of its climate, laws, and government; British liberty and Chinese despotism exemplify two opposing national types in this systematic charting of the "nature of things."[37]

The contrast between China's moral excess and British liberty is highlighted in the prologue to *The Orphan of China*. The words of poet-laureate William Whitehead begin by praising the playwright for importing Confucian virtue to the world of British theater: "Enough of Greece and Rome. . . . To China's eastern realms [he soars]: And boldly bears / Confucius's morals to Britannia's ears." When it comes to the characterization of the "overzealous" patriot Zamti, however, Whitehead absolves the playwright of any immoral intentions by censuring China's misguided laws:

> On China's tenets charge the fond mistake,
> And spare his error for his virtue's sake.
> For Britain knows no right divine in kings;
> From freedom's choice that boasted right arose,
> And thro' each line from freedom's choice it flows. (prologue)

Ironically, in the play, the Chinese family refuses the mandate of absolutism. The defense of British liberty in the lines above recalls Mandane's critique of the "divine right of kings" discussed earlier. Although preserving Confucian tradition is tied to the preservation of the royal bloodline, the play also prioritizes private family bonds over the dictates of the state. The ascension of the true orphan of China to the throne, we will recall, is tempered by the presence of multiple heroes and a privileged place for the private citizen.[38] Nonetheless, the prologue's invocation of "China's tenets" to explain the possible construal of the play's absolutism or political zealotry has the effect of scapegoating the "real" China for an improper balance between personal and public interests.[39]

According to the discourse of Chinese spirit, the same proliferations of passion that comprise the characters' virtuous acts of sympathy can bind them into a community of misguided zealots. China's all-pervasive Confucianism in this play makes a natural religion of morality. The unchanging uniformity of China's moral laws so embraced by deist proponents of natural religion creates a culture consumed by morality and antiquity. Again, China becomes an example and counterexample of the virtues of private feeling. From one perspective, the copious, shared tears of the play's Chinese family communicates an antityrannical spirit in the form of sympathy, a civilizing force of change and a reconciliation of private and public interests. Excesses of sentiment can, in the play, infuse patriotism with humanistic moral authority, a desirable balance of freedom and discipline. China's blend of ancestor worship, reverence of the divine, embrace of political and religious liberty, and rejection of idolatry mixes the best and worst of monarchy, bringing together and testing out the multiple and divergent interpretations of virtue—and of Chineseness—central to emerging political articulations of national character. China's unconquered virtue can be read as either cultural resilience or stagnation. It is, though, through the performance of Chinese customs, errors, and virtues, that British moral sentiment acquires its distinctive quality of freedom. In other words, China becomes a kind of template through which the British feel their way toward rectitude at a time of upheaval of moral and material possibility.

Adam Smith's Examples of China

Through its performances of sentiment, *The Orphan of China* poses an ethical dilemma that extends beyond the mise-en-scène to questions of national and moral character: how does one decide between self-interest and the greater good, and where does this capacity for moral judgment originate? If Murphy's play presents ideal virtue as a balance of private and public passions, it is nonetheless ambivalent about whether the Chinese can provide this balance for themselves. China becomes an example and counterexample of public virtue in a number of ways. Within the play, the spirit of Confucius invoked by the father figure extols the practical morality of the Chinese as a form of communal rather than divine or state authority. It is this pervasiveness of Confucian morality that makes China a model of secular ethics in eighteenth-century deist writings and in the growing movement to unlink moral judgment from traditionally circumscribed propriety and the dictates of theism.[40] However, Montesquieu's critique, and the broader discourse of Chinese exemplarity that impinges upon the play, asserts that Confucian morals are limited by its society's lack of proper perspective; the Chinese cannot distinguish between passion and zealotry, mere idolatrous ritual and true morality. As a result, they rely solely on external laws to conduct all manner of affairs, and this comes at the expense of developing an internal capacity for moral judgment. Contemporary British theories of moral sentiment take up this question of the social forces that shape inner virtue by further exploring the complex process of importing morality into the self. According to the philosophical writings of David Hume and Adam Smith, sympathy offers the possibility of a self-regulating morality that emerges through the comparison of oneself with another; sympathy is an indirect and highly mediated process of imagining the feelings of others and internalizing this imagined experience for oneself. It is therefore structured by the distances across which it must operate. The greater the distance, the stronger the force of sympathy required.[41] A community is held together by acts of imagined relations between its members; we can know the interest of the public only if we can access the experiences of others to weigh our own sense of moral judgment. In my reading of Smith's *Theory of Moral Sentiments*, the hypothetical other is central to the act of imagining the self's determination of moral judgment. In particular, Smith's reflections on theater and spectatorship rely on examples of distances that are at once physical, cultural, and geographical; and China's remote civilization and exported commodities—its function as cultural spectacle and moral exemplar—plays a subtle but significant part in the articulation of the limits and possibilities of British moral selfhood.

As acknowledged by Smith, theater has a role to play unique to commercial society, where people are unmoored by social changes. Whether considered a reforming or corrupting influence, the stage was a locus of discussions about the modern relations of commerce and virtue. Indeed, the theater, a site of staged virtue and glittering wealth working in tandem, was a natural simulacrum of sociability and commerce, much to the disapproval of eighteenth-century moralists who insisted that the stage was a hotbed of vice. Whereas puritanical theater reformers deemed it possible and necessary to protect sympathy, goodwill, and moral values from commodification and from the showy world of performance and materialism, defenders of the stage argued for its promotion of moral virtues. The eighteenth-century Scottish philosopher Adam Ferguson, for one, describes tragedy's "continued moral from beginning to end" and the virtuous communication between the audience and performance, "where the sentiments they express raise admiration or pity, and where the very faults they commit become so many warnings to the spectator."[42] Smith's *Theory of Moral Sentiments*—first published in 1759, the same year as Murphy's *The Orphan of China*—likewise proliferates with references to the theater in its consideration of such a spectator society.[43]

For Smith, the performance of power and greatness—for example, the "heroic magnanimity" of Cato and Alexander and the misfortunes of kings—moves an audience to grief, solicits its admiration, and creates a community of "fellow-feeling" within the world of theater analogous to and in dialogue with civil society's collective consciousness. Drawing on the metaphor of the theater, Smith explains the process of enacting moral judgment in terms of spectatorship and role playing. As a spectator of human behavior, one enters into a circuit of identification with another and is able to "not only change circumstances . . . but change persons and characters."[44] Furthermore, we can thus "survey our own sentiments and motives" and "enter into" or "transport ourselves in fancy to [distant] scenes" (120). Such a scheme of self-evaluation proposes an internalization of virtue premised on a perspectival shift, an exercise of imagining oneself through another, indeed through a type of performance: "We suppose ourselves the spectators of our own behaviour. . . . This is the only looking-glass by which we can, in some measure, with the eyes of other people, scrutinize the propriety of our own conduct" (164). An ability to form ethical judgments derives from this act of self-distancing. In fact, the role of an imagined outside, the "eyes of a third person," compensates for the limited and fleeting effects of sympathy. For benevolence alone, Smith reiterates, cannot motivate actions of justice or prudence (192).

This imagined switch of identity underscores the relevance not only of theater but, obliquely, of the spectacle of cultural difference to the process of self-discovery. Crucial to the mediated thought process of moral reflection is the act of comparing oneself with another. Smith's illustrations of the internal constitution of self and civil society make use of the distant example of China in two key passages. Their evocation of China's empire links theatrical spectacle to ethical spectatorship by way of cross-cultural comparison. By way of concluding a discussion on the difficulty of adjudicating ethical dilemmas, Smith cites none other than Voltaire's adaptation of the original Chinese play:[45]

> In that beautiful tragedy of Voltaire, the Orphan of China, while we admire the magnanimity of Zamti, who is willing to sacrifice the life of his own child, in order to preserve that of the only feeble remnant of his ancient sovereigns and masters; we not only pardon, but love the maternal tenderness of Idame, who, at the risque of discovering the important secret of her husband, reclaims her infant from the cruel hands of the Tartars, into which it had been delivered. (*Theory of Moral Sentiments*, 227)

Tellingly, Smith does not adjudicate between the conflicting passions of Zamti and Idame (Mandane, in Murphy's play) but instead offers the play as exemplary of the type of dilemma that the impartial, internal "third person" spectator must decide. With a Stoic belief in providence, Smith calls on the reader to "listen with diligent and reverential attention to what he [the spectator] suggests to us" (133). The surfeit of passions exhibited by the Chinese characters generates an ethical impasse powerfully communicated through the act of theatrical spectatorship; this quandary can only be resolved by, in turn, imagining a further act of spectatorship.

In an earlier essay printed in the *Edinburgh Review*, Smith praises the play with a much greater degree of ambivalence toward the excessive passions of the Chinese:

> The original and inventive genius of that Gentleman [Voltaire] never appeared more conspicuous than in his last tragedy, the orphan of China. It is both agreeable and surprising to observe how the *atrocity*, if I may say so, of Chinese virtue, and the rudeness of Tartar barbarity, have been introduced upon the French stage, without violating those nice decorums of which that nation are such delicate and scrupulous judges.[46]

Here, the exchange between French, Chinese, and Tartar seems to create a new affective alloy in Smith, who describes his own "agreeable" feelings at how the different modes of Asiatic customs, however violent, yet produce a pleasing balance.[47] What he finds so surprising is that unappealing Eastern customs can be aesthetically and ethically improved by French theater conventions. The references to "rude" Tartar barbarity and "atrocious" Chinese virtue are absent from the passage in the *Theory of Moral Sentiments* discussed earlier. In both instances, however, Chinese manners and the consideration of the foreign example, in all its excess, allows for the theorization of an ethical impasse; the theatricalized example of China is meant to direct, even enable, a self-reflective turn inward. Key to this model is a theory of distance between self and other that must be maintained: not only can sympathy not eradicate distance, but distance enables a person to move outside oneself, gain perspective, and thus become accustomed to virtuous social relations. Smith's use of the Chinese example shows us how a theory of morality leans on and yokes together the theatrical and the foreign to promote the internalization of spectatorship and the turning of the gaze inward—in essence, the importation of morality into the self.[48]

At another key moment, Smith's theory of sympathy relies on an example of contemporary China to illustrate how the capacity for moral judgment is internalized and the line between passion and zealotry calibrated. To emphasize the temporary efficacy of feeling for others across distance, Smith introduces the famous example of the Chinese earthquake, or, more specifically, the European's ability to relate to Asian suffering. A hypothetical Chinese earthquake illustrates the shortcomings of sentiment and the necessity of ethical reason to motivate proper compassion:

> Let us suppose that the great empire of China, with all its myriads of inhabitants, was suddenly swallowed up by an earthquake, and let us consider how a man of humanity in Europe, who had no sort of connection with that part of the world, would be affected upon receiving intelligence of this dreadful calamity. (*Theory of Moral Sentiments*, 192)

The European, Smith continues, might feel momentary sympathy for the Chinese, but such thoughts quickly turn from "strong sorrow for the misfortune of that unhappy people" to "the vanity of all the labours of man" to "the effects which this disaster might produce upon the commerce of Europe, and the trade and business of the world in general" and, ultimately, to the detached state of business as usual (193).

Smith's discussion of China denies the lasting effects of unmediated sympathy. And yet, despite the tendency for individuals to aggrandize their own suffering, when pushed to a decision, they would not actually choose to sacrifice the lives of a hundred million Chinese brethren for their own small misfortune.[49] As Eric Hayot argues in his illuminating study of the "hypothetical mandarin," the trope of Chinese suffering deployed by Smith's example was foundational to nineteenth- and twentieth-century ideas of Western humanism.[50] Indeed, imagining the Western responses to Asian suffering in the wake of environmental disaster is an exercise that has in recent history proven to be far from hypothetical. According to Smith, the Western reactions of altruism or philanthropy would be based neither on benevolence nor love of one's neighbor or mankind but rather on a virtuous self-love; and love of one's own good character is shaped once again by reason and the ethical voice of the imagined spectator. The solution to sentiment's failings is not the imposition of rules of conduct but, rather, the construction of the "impartial spectator," also referred to as the "man within," "demigod within the great," "great judge and arbiter of our conduct," or "judge within." This outsider-insider functions as an internal conscience in place of God's authority, a kind of cultural superego whereby the construction of a mediated self is routed through an imagined other.

Smith invokes the hypothetical Chinese earthquake in the wake of a catastrophe experienced close to home, the great Lisbon earthquake of 1755 that in fact destroyed parts of Spain and northern Africa, generated tsunamis that reached the English coast as well as the Antilles across the Atlantic, and provoked strong religious reflections and an outpouring of sympathy for the tens of thousands of victims. China thus plays a particular role as the Eastern substitute for Lisbon. It is in imagining the response to a more remote China that one imagines the spectator within, who then chooses an ethics of caring for strangers. The force of the Chinese earthquake example is premised on what Smith calls "no sort of connection with that part of the world." Of course, as will be discussed below, it is precisely the connections to China in this period that made it such a powerful example of empire. Even in Smith's formulation, one's sympathy for imagined Chinese victims has to overcome concerns about the financial consequences of such a disaster on Europe. The combined remoteness and economic prowess of an empire in the "Far East" thus makes its imaginary destruction a potent example of the limitations to benevolence and the force of ethical reason. There are, once again, two China's invoked: an ancient China of the play and a modern China of economic consequence. In such a way, China as example and counterexample generates a set of affective responses that produces the conditions for theorizing as well as imagining the Western moral self. It is thus through a multiple mediated act of cross-cultural comparison that the reader is meant to make the leap from example to practice. In effect, thinking about China motivates the move from fleeting, outward reaction to lasting, inner conviction, and thus supports Smith's key tenet that, beyond the traditional idea of sympathy as a contagion, only a "stronger power"—an irreligious one—can ensure that virtue is properly instilled. The example of China functions in these instances as a nontheistic arbiter of the balance between virtue and vice. By reading such examples in conjunction with the metaphors of spectatorship, we can see how the internal other theorized by Smith infers a geographical and cultural other, and an exercise in imagining universal feeling is at once an exercise in imagining shared moral geography and the invisible forces of the global economy that tie

East to West. The play between the general and particular references to China's remote empire, a site of abstract theatrical exoticism and real economic impact, makes evident how central the process of the foreign example is to the project of determining the limits of sympathy and the possibilities of moral judgment.

Manufacturing the "True Chinese"

For Smith, China's distance from Europe makes it a useful example with which to formulate the type of ethical self-reflectiveness and sympathetic identifications that can potentially stave off the corrupting influences of commercial society. Although the worldly workings of commerce have no explicit place within the elevated framework of heroic tragedy or his theory of moral sentiment, China's status as a foreign commodity crucially impinges upon the imagination of moral selfhood across vast distances. Thus far, we have considered two cases of performing China and performing virtue occasioned by the adaptations of a Chinese play for the British and French stage. In each instance, a theoretical China is presented as an example and counterexample of virtuous passions.

In the first instance, the sufferings of Murphy's fictional family are staged for public consumption; within the workings of the play, conflicting values, love of family and love of country, can coexist thanks to the persistence of motherly sentiment, on the one hand, and fatherly Confucian law, on the other. As suggested by the play's framing devices and surrounding commentary about the "real" eighteenth-century China, it is the civilizing force of British dramaturgy that transforms the raw energy of Chinese customs into a theatrical model of patriotic feeling. From this perspective, China's excesses are beneficial to others while harmful to itself. Such regulation of unruly passion is also the aim of Smith's theory of sympathy; here, theatrical performance itself models the ethical process of identifying with the suffering of others across distance. It is the moral regulation of one's inner self—the performance of British virtue—that can result from the contemplation of China's performances of excess.

Two Chinas are at work in the making of Chinese spectacle, as I suggested earlier: one of sentiment and one of commerce. China supplies, metaphorically, the foreign "luxury of woe" for British consumption. The material forms of luxury invoked alongside China's moral excesses are equally controversial and equally productive of theories of national identity premised upon virtuous consumerism. It is worthwhile examining the marketing of China's cultural authenticity and disavowal of its foreign excess in contemporary discourses of luxury. Again, as example and counterexample, China was concurrently blamed and idealized for its system of producing and exporting commodities like tea and porcelain; but, above all, the British ambivalence toward imitating Chinese fashions and manufacturing casts China as a hethnic arbiter, rather than mere scapegoat of modern values.

In mid-eighteenth-century discussions of luxury and fashion, China's moral excesses, identified thus far in terms of its overflowing passions, "spirit of laws," and "atrocity of virtue" were also tied to material forms of excess. The juxtaposition of virtue and commerce is apparent even in critical reception of Murphy's play by his contemporaries. As Oliver Goldsmith wrote, the play could be faulted for its "luxury of woe."[51] In linking the excesses of wealth generally attached to China with the play's overwrought sentimentality, the phrase condenses the competing visions of virtue, moral and economic, into a single expression of luxury. So, too, does the play's framing and staging evoke two parallel visions of China that are opposed yet complementary: the "ancient China" of the play and the "real China" of commercial prowess commented on in its prologue, epilogue, and ancillary materials. Following this structure of exemplarity, the play's "Confucian morals" are, as earlier mentioned, introduced in the language of commerce—the "imported boon," the "spoils" of travel abroad—that makes China the fashionable new Greece or Rome, an idealized and yet contested object of consumption. In part, such language reflects a desire to advertise China as a type of imported morality, an antidote to modern corruption that can nonetheless make use of commercial routes for the exchange of virtue. Voltaire, writing to the duke of Richelieu about his own play using the Chinese orphan theme, comments, "My Lord, I would have presented you with a piece of fine marble; but, instead of it, can only offer you a few Chinese figures."[52] And the Jesuit Dominique Parrenin, in a letter to Du Halde, remarks: "If there prevails in *Europe* a remarkable fondness for all the manufactures imported from *China*, I am of opinion that the genius and character of the *Chinese*, their present manners, their usages and customs, contain what might equally excite a laudable curiosity."[53]

The rhetoric of importing China recognizes the impact of Chinese commodity culture upon British consumerism and, moreover, the shared economy of commerce and virtue. It also broaches the possibility that the same channels of commerce can be used to transfer morality from one culture to another. A core question posed by both theorists of sympathy and of luxury—one that is dramatized in *The Orphan of China* and exemplified by the space of the theater—is thus how to incorporate self-interest into the pursuit of the public good. In particular, the example of Chinese manufacturing generates debate over the dangers foreign luxuries enact upon British character. The mercantilists and physiocrats who believed in the advances of commerce also held that the spreading influence of luxury could stimulate rather than debilitate domestic production.[54] The question becomes how to determine the line between productive and destructive forms of luxury, and it is through a process of dissociation from and imitation of the foreign culture that luxury can be imagined as a vice that nonetheless has social benefits.

Calls to imitate China test and redefine the benefits of foreign luxury upon social health. This is, in other words, a theory of cultural appropriation that addresses the place of not only the foreign commodity in society but the role of the example in imagining a balanced relationship between the private and public spheres. Lavish productions like *The Orphan of China*, by displaying the allure of Eastern wealth on stage, provoked fervent criticisms of the ruinous influence of luxury upon the health of the nation. Typically, metaphors of disease and contagion compare the atrophy of individual bodies with that of the body politic. According to the Reverend Samuel Fawconer, "luxury is of that assimilating insinuating nature, that its infection, like a pestilence, runs thro' every order of the community, from the throne to the cottage."[55] He further envisions an external transformation of the body in the form of troubling reversals of gender. Men become "more soft, more languid, and more passive than Women," and women "are Masculine in their Desires, and Masculine in their Practices."[56] The possibility of widespread emasculation through excessive consumption of foreign imports ranging from Italian opera to French produce in turn threatens the security of the nation in a time of war; an indulgence in luxury, as the classical argument goes, takes away the strength and will to fight. Of such a depletion of martial spirit Fawconer laments, "Oh luxury! Alas! Patriotism!"[57] He makes the links between consumption and the public good explicit further on: "Luxury eradicates all those patriotic affections . . . of the social nature. . . . Our national effeminacy seems to have extinguished our national spirit."[58]

The demand for Chinese goods and European chinoiserie reflected these concerns about the ills of overconsumption that were thought to result in financial and moral ruin. In his poem *Of Taste* (1756), James Cawthorn catalogs the dangers of internalizing cultural difference not through physical ingestion of foreign goods but similarly through an infectious spread throughout society:

Of late, 'tis true, quite sick of Rome and Greece
We fetch our models from the wise Chinese;
European artists are too cool and chaste,
For Mand'rin only is the man of taste;

. . . .
Form'd on his plans, our farms and seats begin
To match the boasted villas of Pekin.
On every hill a spire-crown'd temple swells,
Hung round with serpents, and a fringe of bells;
Junks and balons along our waters sail,
With each a gilded cockboat at his tail;
. . . .
In Tartar huts our cows and horses lie,
Our hogs are fatted in an Indian style;
On ev'ry shelf a Joss divinely stares,
Nymphs laid on chintzes sprawl upon our chairs;
While o'er our cabinets Confucius nods,
Midst porcelain elephants, and China gods.[59]

The poem traces the encroaching influence of Chinese goods from the English landscape (farms, seats, hills, harbors) into the space of domestic interiority (huts, cabinets, chairs). The colonization of the private sphere is evidenced by the placement of Confucius, the bearer of wisdom and virtue, amid a hodgepodge of "Chinese" objects and practices that collapses all distinctions between Eastern identities, customs, and habits. Clearly, the philosophical investment in Eastern virtue has been popularized to the point that virtue itself becomes yet another mass-produced object to be imported and collected. This is a far remove from the mandarin Zamti and his world of contagious affect and patriotic passions. Here the impropriety of the Chinese model ultimately stems from the failed resuscitation of ancient virtue in the modern, commercialized world. Even early Jesuit accounts of China had lamented the centuries-long degeneration of classical Confucianism. Here, we witness, instead of a chaste alternative to Greece or Rome, the trivialization of antiquity, or Confucius on a shelf. This new luxury of consumption threatens to degenerate the nation in the vein of Rome's seduction by foreign commodities—what Suvir Kaul aptly refers to in his study of eighteenth-century poetry and empire as an "iconography of decline."[60] Adding to this vision of dissolution is a total commercialization of British life into a culture of Eastern imitation.

Elizabeth Kowaleski-Wallace, in her work on eighteenth-century consumption, analyzes the ways that the practice of tea drinking brought together in the space of the domestic the anxieties over imperial expansion and the regulation of female desire. The feminized ritual of the tea table, especially later in the period, placed the woman's body at the center of the controversies surrounding the civilizing and contaminating effects of foreign imports consumed in tandem—in this case, the commodities of tea, sugar, and china. In texts like Jonas Hanway's *An Essay on Tea* (1699) and Simon Mason's *The Good and Bad Effects of Tea Considered* (1701), the foreign substance was imagined to corrupt upper- and lower-class women alike through its addictive properties, which solicited unnecessary expenditures of money as well as time.[61] The depletion of the British economy as attributed to tea and porcelain consumption has also been brilliantly examined by David Porter, who focuses not only on the denigration of women and the gendering of consumption but also on the climate of economic protectionism that held China and the East India Company trade responsible for the drain on British silver bullion. In his account, it is Chinese legitimacy that has, by the late eighteenth century of Lord Macartney's embassy to China, been degraded and rendered virtually antithetical to the idealization of Confucian moral authority of a century before.[62] Certainly, mid-eighteenth-century critiques of chinoiserie and Eastern tastes made scapegoats of female consumers as well as Chinese producers; by examining further the performances of Chinese spectacle, though, we can see that China's commercial exemplarity also inspired a culture of virtuous imitation and productive luxury.

Nowhere is the process of modeling taste more apparent than in the mimetic context of the theater. For one, the theatrical sets of *The Orphan of China* put the novelty of trade itself on display. The stage directions to the play indicate that the tyrant Timurkan makes his grand entrance in the first act through an impressive set of "two large folding gates in the back-scene."[63] According to one critic, the sets live up to Timurkan's description of the "glitt'ring palace": "It would be difficult to give a complete description, on once seeing, of so many pleasant novelties. An eastern traveller would imagine himself at Pekin—and a Cockney in a new world."[64] Although an exact account of the scenery is not available, it was reportedly reused from David Garrick's production of *The Chinese Festival* in 1755.[65] For this project, Garrick commissioned the French ballet choreographer Jean-Georges Noverre and a team of designers, including the painter François Boucher and the costume designer Louis-René Boquet, to reproduce the French version of the pantomime in London. The description of the 1754 production in Paris gives us a sense of the mechanics of "Chinese" spectacle:

> [A] public square, decorated for a festival; at the back is an amphitheatre, on which sixteen Chinamen are seated. By a quick change of scene, thirty-two Chinamen appear instead of sixteen, and go through a pantomimic performance on the steps.

> As they descend, sixteen other Chinamen, mandarins and slaves, come out of their houses and take their places on the steps. . . . At the end of this round-dance the Chinamen take up their places anew on the amphitheatre, which changes into a porcelain shop. Thirty-two vases rise up, and hide from the audience the thirty-two Chinese. M. Monnet has spared nothing that could possibly assist M. Noverre's rich imagination. . . . The dresses were made from M. Boquet's designs.[66]

The Chinamen, mandarins, and slaves of the pantomime, themselves moving props, are meant to interact with the scenery, which recalls the exotic technology of Restoration spectacle—ladies in breeches, Moroccans dancing with palm trees, and flayed and dismembered male and female bodies on display. Rather than a torture chamber, harem, or imperial court, the scene has here become a porcelain shop, imported from China by way of France, a spectacle of commodities that makes interchangeable "thirty-two vases" and "thirty-two Chinese."

In yet another Tartar-conquest play of the period, the characters, plots, and staging are alike reduced to objects of trade. The ostensible subject of Michael Clancy's *Hermon, Prince of Chorea: Or, The Extravagant Zealot* (1746) is political corruption and courtly intrigue following the deaths of the emperor of China and the prince of Tartary. Its prologue details the expense of staging such an Oriental fantasy. What is striking is the conflation, in the prologue, of material excess with moral excess:

> His Play seems built on a fantastick Topick,
> And for the Scene, that's—somewhere near the Tropick.
> His Nymphs are China-Ware; *East-Indian* Queens;
> His Heroes, painted Pagods—fit for Screens,
> His Moral is wild Zeal; his Persons such,
> As no Religion have, or have too much—
> The Players round, and such, as judge of Plays,
> Pronounce the Style, refin'd, and true *Chinese,*
> But such Exotic Scenes befit a bare House,
> Or is the Theatre, an *Indian* Ware-house.
> 'Must we find Robes, that might *Confucius* fit,
> 'And the new Dress supply his Want of Wit?
> . . . .
> 'The Plot's at Court—and 'tis by all confess'd,
> 'If *Mandarins* must act, they must be dress'd,
> 'In Oriental Robes, how grand is Man!
> 'And can a Drugget please, like *Point d'Espagne?*

'As for the House—to more Expence 'twill lead her,
'The Stage must be japan'd, the Boxes, Cedar.

The Oriental characters that blend into the scenery, and indeed are eclipsed by it, exhibit either a surfeit of or complete lack of "Religion." Ornate surfaces indicate the bankrupted morality and "wild Zeal" exemplified in the play by a corrupt priest who indulges in luxury and is fittingly named "Xury." The above comparison of the theater's "House" with an "Indian Ware-house" is at once metaphorical and material, as indicated by the final reference to the cost of a "japan'd" stage, which thus bemoans the financial burden of performing "true Chinese" for a theatergoing public.

That "Oriental Robes" compensate for "Confucian wit" may signal the degeneration of Eastern morals into a proliferation of compensatory props. At the same time, the theatrical displays of conspicuous consumption not only reflect the commercialization of virtue in the broader social context; they indicate as well the commercialization of cultural difference. Fashion stays current by appropriating the customs of distant others and making a consumable object of Eastern antiquity.[67] At the same time, the changeability of fashion is both a sign of Western modernity and a threat to the stability of tradition. It is this shift between distinct systems of value that the foreign commodity, in embodying ancient customs in modern form, is meant to bridge. The phrase "true Chinese" is particularly telling, insofar as the effectiveness of the foreign exemplar lies less in its authenticity as much as in the ways it enables the idea of imitating the other while disassociating oneself from whatever negative influences might pertain to that other. The rhetoric of blaming foreign imports for draining a nation of its productive spirit makes frequent reference to the working of contagion, which, despite the bombast, implies a far from straightforward logic of transferring innate properties between individuals and cultures through the exchange of commodities. The "true Chinese" may be the model of new tastes, but the British are the ones who imitate them. In his attack on luxury, the eighteenth-century critic John Dennis captures the necessity of imitation in a competitive world market, and the challenges of managing its unruly effects: "'Tis indeed our Duty to emulate the Virtue and Knowledge of other Nations; but by imitating their Manners, which are the Objects of Sense, we come to affect their Vices" (*Essay Upon Publick Spirit,* 5). The difference between emulation and imitation depends on one's ability to control the transmission of influence, and this is a task that requires strategically citing and disavowing—making an example and counterexample of—the very idea of China's cultural authenticity.

In the epilogue to *The Orphan of China,* the actress Mrs. Yates, dressed as Mandane, addresses the challenge of appropriating China's "tastes and fashions" for British consumption while avoiding its purported vices. She remarks of her costume, "Ladies, excuse my dress—'tis true Chinese." Once again, this rhetoric of "true Chinese" is meant both to lend value to the fashion commodity and to signal the difference between the excesses of the foreign origins and the virtues of the borrower. In the case of fashion, the ability to imitate Chinese style also conveys a sense of Western progress. Fashion commentators of the period praise the quality of European copies of foreign fashions; one such claim is that stage dresses in general "are no longer the heterogeneous and absurd mixtures of foreign and ancient Modes, which formerly debased our tragedies."[68] The available comments and illustrated guides of the time demand culturally specific representations of foreign fashion or, at the very least, insist upon an imagined authenticity. Costumes for the stage and society were created from illustrated books on dress from other parts of the world and from meticulous ethnographic accounts of foreign "habits" and "modes."[69] The actress Mrs. Siddons recounts of a performance of Murphy's play the "splendid assemblages of foreign dress."[70] According to one critic, "Mrs. Yate's [dress] will, we imagine, make great improvements in the lady's dress for the year 1759; as the greatest part of the female audience seemed to envy her successful appearance, and entirely attribute it to her ornamental habit."[71] As a testament to the crossover between theater and fashion, Mrs. Garrick commissioned Boquet's costume designs for her personal wardrobe.[72] In the Dublin production of *The Orphan of China*, too, the costumes, though made in London, were touted to have been made from models imported from China, scenery painted "in the true Chinese style, by the celebrated Carver."[73]

Louis Le Comte, in his "Of the peculiar Character of the Chinese Nation, its Antiquity, Nobility, Manners, and its good and bad Qualities," gives an exhaustive account of fabrics, colors, patterns, and seasonal styles for every wearable piece of a Chinese outfit. An advocate of headdresses, he writes, "I am perswaded if Peoples should see the Model of them in *France,* they would go near to be tempted to quit that extravagant Company of Ornaments they use, to dress their Heads *a-la-mode de Chineses.*"[74] For Le Comte, the entire country of China is defined in terms of fashion. Its people, unlike the barbarians elsewhere, are "handsomly Drest," despite being out of date due to certain innate preferences for antiquity. The Chinese, after all, "dote upon Antiquity, [and] will not be cured of it in haste."[75] Jean-Baptiste Du Halde, in his *General History of China,* attributes China's unchanging fashion to its "uniformity of government," claiming that the habits have "always been the same from the Infancy of the empire to the Conquest of

Illustration of Mandane and Zamti included in Arthur Murphy, *The Orphan of China*, 1797. By permission of the Folger Shakespeare Library.

it by the Tartars."[76] Ironically, its stasis—the unchanging spirit of its laws and fashions—fuels an ever-changing trend of fashion in Europe and England. Distance adds value to its authenticity. Even social historians Neil McKendrick and John Brewer, in their analysis of eighteenth-century consumer culture, reiterate this trope of Asiatic stagnation when they compare England's fast-changing fads with the inert style of the East: "[I]n China women have scarcely any new fashions."[77] Paradoxically, China's purported lack of progress also makes it a source of Europe's developing trends.

As the travel writings illustrate, a consideration of fashion slides easily into essentializing talk of cultural difference. It becomes clear that dress is not separable from those who wear it, despite the efforts to appropriate Chinese fashion for a

Mrs. Yates as Mandane in "The Orphan of China." Painting by Tilly Kettle, ca. 1765. Reproduced by permission, © Tate, London, 2010.

British audience. If we return to the epilogue of Murphy's play, we can see that the praise for Chinese fashion is accompanied by a critique of its customs:

> First, as to beauty—Set your hearts at rest—
> They're all broad foreheads, and pigs eyes at best.
> And then they lead such strange, such formal lives!—
> —A little more at home than English wives!
> Lest the poor things should roam, and prove untrue,
> They all are crippled in the tiny shoe.

"The various Habits of the Chinese and Tartars," from Jean-Baptiste Du Halde, *The General History of China*, 1741. Courtesy of the Rare Book and Manuscript Library, University of Pennsylvania.

> Then they've no cards, no routs, ne'er take their fling,
> And pin-money is an unheard-of thing!
> Then how d'ye think they write?—You'll ne'er divine—
> From top to bottom down in one straight line.

If this quotation from the epilogue exposes, on the one hand, the disjuncture of the play with reality in general and an authentic China in particular, the idea of the "true Chinese" also works to satirize the English society lady and her ways—cards, routs, and pin money.[78] These framing truths appear to create a distinction between the "real" and the performed China, and between Eastern oppression and Western freedom.[79] At the same time, the binaries of culture mask an underlying critique of the universal female sex. In the interdependent worlds of commercial exchange and theatrical performance, the virtues and vices of self and other are mutually constructed and performed. There is thus a pedagogy of consumption in the epilogue: we *can* imitate manners without vices, the speech seems to imply. Even when it distinguishes between Chinese fashions that can be appropriated separately from the unseemly characteristics of the culture, this is part of a process of imitation—or exemplarity—rather than a simple disavowal of the other. More than simply generating racial stereotypes, the negative descriptions of Chinese women posit cultural authenticity, or the idea of the "true Chinese," as a way of controlling the contagious effects of consuming fashion.

This negotiation of race, commerce, and virtue can be illuminated by contemporary scholarship on imitation and consumer culture. Grant McCracken, for one, has argued that acts of differentiation are "the first moment of the imitative process. The negative act of disassociation is what precedes the act of imitation."[80] That disassociation is part of a larger imitative process also sheds light on the function of foreign examples when we consider luxury; perhaps they are not simply scapegoats but, rather, part of a circuit of identifications that tests the limits and possibilities of contagion. Alarmist critiques of consumption align the desires for foreign goods and manners with a threat to patriotic sentiment and moral agency; to succumb to the latest tastes and fashions is to give in to the type of uncontrollable passions that cedes British bodies, markets, and national autonomy to external forces. The idea that imitation can be a means of improvement would thus justify acts of consumption. Consumption was, in fact, also interpreted as a means of improving and converting the other. With the aim of reversing the East-West flow of commercial influence, the potter and entrepreneur Josiah Wedgwood, for one, boasted of his new porcelain ware: "Don't you think we shall have some Chinese Missionaries come here soon to learn the art of making Creamcolour?"[81] The language of imitation as improvement is further evidenced by Goldsmith, who, in his scathing review of the overzealous emotionalism of *The Orphan of China*, still lauds Voltaire and Murphy for improving upon the "calm insipidity of the Eastern original." Chinese productions, Goldsmith reasons, are by nature "phlegmatic," and hence, "as the plot has become more European, it has become more perfect. By omitting many of the circumstances of the original story . . . Mr. Murphy has given us a play, if not *truly Chinese*, at least entirely poetical."[82] Each of those instances claims a standard of excellence that self-reflexively seeks both to establish and to widen the distance between England and China, and imitation and original. Whether delivered as insult, demand for novelty, accusation of excess, judgment of quality, or patriotic one-upmanship between London and Paris, the label "true Chinese" makes of imported fashion a sign of virtuous imitation.

Moreover, in contrast with the critics of consumption, certain calls to imitate

China draw on its ancient yet modern status to forge a narrative of luxury as progress and productivity. As Maxine Berg has argued, an "economy of quality" that uses fine arts and design combined with modern manufacturing techniques emerged in eighteenth-century Britain in response to Asian luxury products; and this taste for Eastern cultural authenticity spurred British technological innovation; in fact, imitation is "part of the design aesthetic of oriental commodities" and Asian imports prepare the market for new industries.[83] For a manufacturing world desirous of emulating high-quality Chinese products, China becomes a sign of harmonious continuity between ancient custom and modern progress, a model of utility and technological advancement. The eighteenth-century Scottish philosopher Adam Ferguson had nothing but praise for China in this regard: "After a history of some thousand years employed in manufacture and commerce, the inhabitants of China are still the most laborious and industrious of any people on the surface of the earth."[84] With its admirable legal and criminal system, prioritization of education in its government structure, and its inexhaustible pool of human resources, China is idealized as a model of society and industry—indeed, the antithesis of luxury. As further articulated by economist Malachy Postlethwayt, the "indefatigable" labor of the Chinese, coupled with the emperor's veneration of agriculture, produces an exemplary canal system and technological modernity that explains in part the "plenty and prosperity which reign in China." He writes, "For this added to their other industrious arts, renders the trade carried on in the heart of the empire so great, that the traffic of all Europe can scarce be compared with it."[85] It is "the example of the Chinese" that can improve British agriculture and manufacturing; in fact, the Chinese prefer "useful" to "agreeable" things (they plant gardens for the "public good" rather than ornamental "parterres, flowers, and fine walks"). In this respect, luxury, which turns precisely on the distinction between ornament and utility, could not be further from China's character.[86]

Divorcing the example of China's empire from traditional ideas of the excesses of "Asiatic luxury" of the Persian and Ottoman Empires, and modern commerce from the idea of luxury, becomes key to the revaluation of contagious luxury by promoters of foreign trade. By virtue of its physical and cultural distance from Britain as well as the Near East, China essentially provides a screen onto which the dangers and possibilities of a new moral economy can be projected. In order to advocate on behalf of the advantages of commercial exchange, the specter of foreign contamination, as symbolized by Asiatic luxury, must be expelled. In histories of empires, effeminacy traditionally signifies a lack of military prowess, as we saw in the portrayal of the "soft Chinese" and "hard northern Tartars" and in references to the fall of Rome, whose atrophied martial spirit was thought to exhibit Asiatic tendencies dating back to the campaigns of Sulla in Asia Minor.[87] Against this Oriental legacy, the philosopher Jean-François Melon argued that luxury does not make a nation "effeminate" by weakening its armies; for a frugal army boasts no more courage than an affluent one. Moreover, he distinguishes China's "well-governed Society" from the Near East's "Eastern Luxury . . . an indolent Laziness, which enervates Courage, in a wretched Seraglio."[88]

David Hume further refutes those who charge luxury goods with contaminating the domestic sphere by redefining luxury as a potential force and social benefit that may ignite desire—a passion that animates men—but that does not inherently injure. In his essays on commerce, Hume rebukes the "severe moralists" who rail against luxury and link the "example of ancient Rome" to the corrupting force of "Asiatic luxury." He attributes the fall of Rome instead to its mismanaged government and rejects the common view that the power of ancient states lies with their large armies and abstinence from luxury. Neither do practices of luxury deprive the state of laborers to be employed in public services. Unlike the martial structure of the ancient world, by now, Hume writes, states have increased in size such that an all-pervasive militarism is a modern impossibility. Luxury is neither innocent, as portrayed by the libertines, nor corrupting, as the "severe moralists" maintain; one must "correct both . . . extremes."[89] Hume aims to strike a balance between the ancients and the moderns, the merchants and the landed gentry, and the hedonists and the ascetics. Indeed, to supplant the outdated republican virtue of the ancients with a new "sense of honour," he calls upon "other passions" like the "spirit . . . of luxury."[90] According to Hume, "To declaim against present times, and magnify the virtue of remote ancestors, is a propensity almost inherent in human nature."[91]

Significantly, Hume calls upon the spirit of luxury to enact a new form of honor in an age of bourgeois sentimentality and reform, thus reaffirming the contagious nature of Asiatic luxury but imparting it with the characteristics of health, rather than disease. It is, after all, the principle of contagion that binds together a community of moral sentiment as well as a commercial public sphere. Essays such as Postlethwayt's *Britain's Commercial Interest Explained and Improved* (1757) use the language of infectious "spirit" to demand improvement of the arts, and hence of technologies of trade and manufacture: "What an emulous spirit will not this raise throughout the kingdom among the thinking and active part of mankind?" (196). This "spirit" of combining philosophy and mechanics will "raise our commerce and navigation, as to enable us to beat the French in trade" (197). Such language recasts the idea of luxury's contagion spreading throughout a community to forge a sense of fortified, rather than atrophied, national character. In this vision of healthful contagion, commerce can unite the country's provinces, "whereby they become all united, and convey unspeakable abundance to all the cities, and render all their productions, and their manufactures so extremely cheap, that they beat all the world therein; and induce all nations to come to them."[92] Hume presents a similar paradigm of emulation in his elaboration upon the question of luxury and foreign trade: embracing the heretofore corrupting influence of foreign nations directs the consumer toward self-reliance.[93] The importance of imitating the East for the improvement or "refinement" of domestic manufactures is such that "[t]heir [England's] own steel and iron, in such laborious hands, become equal to the gold and rubies of the Indies."[94] The equivalences drawn—and the projection of home resources as future substitutes for foreign imports—posit the East as a standard of measurement to be emulated and surpassed. In an age of manufacture, ideas of virtuous action dictate the possibility of refinement or improvement of character through imitation of the other. At the same time, praising the benefits of imitation does not guarantee a fixed model or antimodel of national virtue. The transferability of national character across cultures and the demarcation of moral good from commercial good are questions that remain unresolved by defenders and opponents of luxury alike. As Hume writes, "The bounds between the virtue and the vice cannot here be exactly fixed, more than in other moral subjects."[95] And yet, by refusing to preach for or against luxury, Hume's positing of the absence of a clear line also loosens the grasp of aristocratic or republican definitions of virtue. It is this tenuous boundary between virtue and vice that must constantly be negotiated by the new moral subject articulated by Adam Smith.

The eighteenth-century discourse of luxury shares with the discussion of China's exemplarity a structure of moral ambivalence, whereby figures of foreignness perform the historical shift in cultural values. *Luxury* is a term whose proliferation in this period signals a crisis of meaning; its potential benefits and harms to society parallel the cultural exemplar's functions of imitation and warning. The positing of the extremes of this ambivalence, and the process of working out the shape and location of excess, also carves out a space for a moderate, or improved, Englishness. In mid-century debates on luxury, the likening of physical health to the health or "sickness" of the body politic extends the idea of an ingestible contaminant to the wearable, watchable, or readable objects whose inner-reaching effects can spread through acts of imagination and emulation and create entire communities both consumerist and consumptive.[96] More often than not, the external influence is maligned for its perceived degradation of social decorum; but even the act of assigning blame reveals a tenuous border between virtue and vice. Accepting "strangers and superfluities" as a bona fide virtue rather than a necessary evil demands a reconceptualization of luxury and its excesses as something other than harmful contagion.[97] Where the example of Rome's empire falls short in its embodiment of degenerative luxury, China's empire appears to successfully preserve morality and economic greatness. Made to play a dual role, China is the object of excess and an index of the line between excess and moderation. In this capacity, its example can be read as an instrument for redefining luxury as a public virtue. China becomes a moral exemplar precisely through its role as a mediator between classical virtue and commercialized virtue; through its embodiment of ancient honor, sentimental passions, and modern trade, it registers and resolves key oppositions between past and present, public and private, virtue and vice. The distance traveled by the "true Chinese" in philosophical and theatrical performances endows China with a staggered temporality—an aura of antiquity and the mark of modernity—that also reflects the contradictions of a new world of remote commercial transactions. It is not that China is solely a scapegoat of foreign luxury; rather, it functions as an arbiter between the traditionally held idea of a pernicious and degenerative Asiatic luxury of empires past and the benefits of commerce that transform luxury into a matter of healthful consumption.

The space of the theater highlights perfectly the interpenetration of two modes of exemplarity: morality and manufactures. Indeed, the theater is a locus of literary and material culture where ideas about virtue and foreignness are marketed as well as performed. Locating the "true Chinese" in the dress of the actress and in the Confucian family values of the characters creates two registers for the China portrayed by Murphy's *Orphan* play: one, the material world of surfaces and appearance; the other, the inner world of ideas and philosophy—precisely that which resists the corrupting, trivializing force of the first. Whether the view of China is positive or negative, its flipping polarities and moral exemplarity reflect the contradictions of its essentialized character. The bipartite structure of China's exemplarity can be found in the contrast and interplay between, on the one hand, the discussion in *The Orphan of China's* framing epilogue and prologue on the looks, manners, and morals of the "real" China and, on the other hand, the play's content—its staging of Confucian family values, selflessness, and sacrifice that also provide the excuse for excessive emotions. The repeated resolution of Chineseness into Englishness and ethnography into spectacle in plays about China's conquest defers the idea of a "true China" to an ever more external outside, to a space of moral and material excess that can be imaginatively moderated and disciplined into English virtue proper.

The theatrical reliance on the past and the recollection of an ever more ancient period in which to stage exoticism and spectacle draw on philosophy and ethnography to make a model of fashion and a scapegoat for the dangerous excesses of British consumerism. These plays, and their exemplification of the ambivalent reconciliation of commerce with virtue, evidence the theatrics of performing the self through performing the other. This performance of Chineseness, superficial as it may be, registers and resolves the dilemma between private and public passions through fusing a Confucius of ancient honor with the modern contagion of the sentimental family. Because China signifies an excess of material wealth, it is a powerful means of overlaying and identifying this new conceptualization of luxury with the virtues of filial relations and sentiment. In material form, luxury thus enables the growth of the British nation rather than a weakening of its defenses and patriotic resolve; similarly, the private passions of the family are made to envision a new form of civic virtue that uses to its advantage rather than deficit the excesses of the private and domestic sphere. The example of China functions in these performances and theories of luxury as an adjudicator of where to draw the line between virtue and vice. It demonstrates in these various types of spectacle a new language of virtue for a modernizing economy of ever more integrated communities both within the borders of the nation and between international sites of global trade. Through the performances of theatrical and philosophical spectatorship, the oppositions of private and public, and virtue and commerce, are reconfigured into relations of mutual dependence, thus expanding the parameters of British moral selfhood by way of China's imported morality.

EPILOGUE

Orientalism, Globalization, and the New Business of Spectacle

The moral and material excesses of Eastern empires were of particular interest to seventeenth- and eighteenth-century English reflections on the changing nature of global commerce and its increasing impact on everyday metropolitan life and the wealth of the nation. Early modern orientalism, especially as expressed in performance and spectacle in the theater, exhibited China by staging histories of heroism, violence, and conquest, creating out-of-body adventures that extended the limits of the human and depicted the novelty of Eastern wealth, customs, and religions.

Audiences learned that the grandeur of ancient civilizations like Egypt and Persia represented an accumulation of wealth that doomed them to fall under the weight of their own luxury. Unlike the cautionary example of Rome's demise, these Asiatic empires formed part of an "Oriental" lineage that continued into the eighteenth-century present and was imagined to stretch from Egypt to China, linking along a moral axis "all the peoples of Asia, all the way to China—Mahometans, pagans or idolaters."[1] The cultural work of imagining China's place within this heathen geography was one key feature of early modern orientalism; another was making a virtue of consuming Eastern spectacle through turning its idolatrous excesses into lessons of moral self-improvement. If we recall the fictional dialogue between Socrates and Confucius that opened this book, China's marvelous feats of technology were deemed a dubious "spectacle"; they appear to be original inventions but are revealed to be mere imitations of Egyptian civilization. While China's economic strength could not be denied, the legitimacy of its antiquity, and hence its moral character, could be undermined as fake. Ironically, the comparison calls into question the cultural authority of both Egypt and China, one for being an original but defunct civilization, the other for being derivative, thus registering the Western ambivalence toward Eastern models of empire, old and new. Eighteenth-century meanings of China circulated in relation to other sites of the Orient and to the routes of East-West trade. As we have seen, they also foregrounded a logic of temporal dislocation: the more modern the British Empire, the greater the fascination with ancient China, and with the conquest of China in particular.

The ideological utility of Eastern antiquity for Western empire-building has long persisted, and present-day reiterations of early modern orientalism—specifically, two from the closing decades of the twentieth century—illustrate the ongoing commercialization of Eastern antiquity in the context of neoliberal economic projects. By way of conclusion, I turn now to the revivification of the Egypt-to-China trajectory in recent performances of Asia. The profits made from promoting the cultural authenticity of the East in these cases rearticulate the relationship of virtue and commerce as one of the ideological and material effects of twentieth- and twenty-first-century globalization.

We can see the relevance of oriental exemplarity today, by looking at an eighteenth-century paradigm of cultural tourism that provides a framework for understanding the moral significance of spectacle: the treatment of the East in Samuel Johnson's *The History of Rasselas, Prince of Abyssinia* (1759) offers valuable insight into the workings both of early modern orientalism and two contemporary performances of opera—Giacomo Puccini's *Turandot* and Giuseppe Verdi's *Aida,* the former being staged in China, the latter in Egypt. In that these multinational productions involve state-sponsored tourism, they are also self-orientalizing fictions. Moreover, they draw upon the acts of spectatorship and contemplation of ancient monuments theorized in eighteenth-century literature to make consuming Eastern antiquity once again a virtue of modern life. As in the earlier historical context of chinoiserie, China's current strength in the world economy makes it a particularly powerful screen onto which to enact fantasies of cultural authenticity that are not only virtuous, but hugely profitable. The eighteenth-century framework reminds us of the exigencies of deriving moral as well as aesthetic value from the consumption of foreign luxury.

Before moving to the contemporary context, I begin with one of the foremost Oriental tales of the eighteenth century, Samuel Johnson's *History of Rasselas*, in which cultural tourism becomes an exercise in training English audiences to be critical spectators and, in effect, ethical consumers. The comparison of Egyptian and Chinese monuments is particularly instructive to the main characters of the novel, an Abyssinian prince and his royal entourage, who journey through Egypt in search of happiness and the meaning of life. Their guide, the philosopher Imlac, justifies a visit to the pyramids on the grounds that surveying the ruins of civilization enables the discovery of one's moral strengths and defects in relation to the past. More important than any physical measurements that could be taken of the pyramids is their status as a warning about the dangers of greed. As Imlac points out, "Example is always more efficacious than precept."[2] In contrasting the pyramid with the Great Wall of China, he argues that whereas the latter can at least be used to defend the empire's borders, the pyramids were built for no purpose other than an indulgence in despotic excess. By gazing upon this sublime construction, though, one can reach a transformative self-realization: "Whoever thou art, that, not content with a moderate condition, imaginest happiness in royal magnificence, and dreamest that command or riches can feed the appetite of novelty with perpetual gratifications, survey the pyramids, and confess thy folly!" (109). A didactic instrument, the monument also illustrates the mind's perception of reality. Imlac reasons, "It is no less certain, when you think on a pyramid, that your mind possess the idea of a pyramid, than that the pyramid itself is standing. What space does the idea of a pyramid occupy more than the idea of a grain of corn?" (148). As a result, the transformation of the physical pyramid into abstract, immaterial form, the "idea of a pyramid," further renders Eastern empires past yet timeless props of edifying discourse. Assigning such metaphorical value to the edifice places it within a moral rather than material economy of signification. At the same time, though, its status as a touristic commodity already structures the conditions of the thought experiment. And the idea of its cultural authenticity continues to be appropriated and marketed for the purposes of Western consumption.

A comparison of Egypt and China that turns architectural ruins into moral lessons further indicates the commercialization of cultural difference that characterized eighteenth-century writings on the Orient. As earlier discussed, the structure of ambivalence toward China's moral and economic exemplarity defies a strict binary division of East and West, vice and virtue. While early modern orientalism includes the vilification of the idolatrous other, it focuses more on the example's function of mediating between contested systems of value. Again, it is the contradiction of China's ancient yet modern empire that makes it a particularly potent example of virtue and commerce. Moreover, in the eighteenth-century context, appropriating the East's antiquity, imitating its manufactures, and integrating its commodities into everyday life was viewed as crucial to Western progress. This idealization and ambivalence can thus be distinguished from nineteenth-century Orientalist visions of Asia's historical stagnation, where, in Hegel's words, the "gorgeous edifices of Oriental empires" are fixed into an image of the backward Western other.[3] The images of marvel, luxury, and sensuality that circulated in the Oriental tale and travel writing traditions of the eighteenth-century would, through reproduction and circulation, certainly become subject to the iterative mode of what Edward Said has called Orientalism's accumulation, reconstruction, and repetition.[4] Perhaps the most ambitious and contested endeavor of Said's theory of representation is his assertion of an iterative discourse whose breadth, both temporal and spatial, spanned vastly different historical periods, precapitalist and capitalist—from Homer to Marx and beyond—and thus appeared to betray its Foucauldian basis; that is, the historical specificity of epistemic constructions. Orientalism as a critical discourse has been taken to task for inadvertently replicating the framework of the Orientalist's fantasy: assuming a complete, unified, and essentialized East, at the mercy of a Western-controlled system of misrepresentations. Such a self-other binary fails to acknowledge the heterogeneity and instability of East-West relations, not to mention that of *an* East or *a* West.[5] Nonetheless, the challenge raised by Said, perhaps even more relevant today, is how to account for both the universality and the particularity of Anglo-European cultural imperialism in different parts of the globe.

Today, the cultural work of making and remaking an Orient "all the way to China" draws together the three major strands of Said's *Orientalism*: scholarly and disciplinary expertise; ontological distinctions between Europe and its negative other; and the colonial administration and business of imperialism. However, there is now a critical urgency to understanding how the reiterative force of Orientalism draws from eighteenth-century articulations of China's moral and economic exemplarity as a mutually constitutive relationship. It is through the commercializing of cultural authenticity that the spectacles of the Orient continue to be reinvented and to shape innovations of genre in textual narratives and live performances. China's exemplarity, as it is tied to an idea of the "true Chinese," is produced under ever more mediated networks of trade. In the twenty-first century, it is once again a model of economic development and of contested morality for the West; in the current moment, made-in-China exports, while no longer symbols of luxury, continue to provoke fierce debates about national identity, foreign contamination, and the ethics of consumption.

It is true that, following the logic of colonial-discourse analysis attributed to Edward Said, the West's inherited perception and knowledge of the East contrasts with a lived reality of the East. But who benefits from the manufacturing of Orientalism, and what kind of Orientalism are we now talking about? No longer tenable as a purely "Western style for dominating, restructuring and having authority over the Orient,"[6] the transnational structure of the new Orientalism, and its protean nature, might more reflect globalization's conjunction of political and market forces working across nations through neoliberal rather than colonial or imperial conquest. The marketing of the particular in the name of the universal suggests an Orientalism that has gone global, even as it continues to remake itself across geography and history through a discourse of authenticity and the resuscitation of the eighteenth-century cultural imaginary. The new business of Orientalism disrupts the traditional West-to-East representational structure in complex ways, for no longer (or perhaps never, really) simply the object of Europe's colonial accumulation and acquisition, Asia too participates in the self-orientalizing act of translating and reiterating the image of its commodified self. In revisiting Said's investigation of the connections between history, imperialism and Orientalism, we can see that eighteenth-century Europe's interest in the contradictions of China's ancient yet modern empire is perhaps more relevant now than ever, as the legacy of eighteenth- and nineteenth-century colonial rule, the uses of history, and the old Oriental trajectory of "all the peoples of Asia," from North Africa to China, are being recast by the current forces of global capital.

Turandot in China

Certainly, the business of global tourism perpetuates the West's fascination with the ruins of past empires. And yet, West and non-West alike invest in the creation of new markets for antiquity. The adaptation of an eighteenth-century Oriental tale into modern-day spectacle vividly illustrates the convergence of the old and the new, the marketing of history in the context of globalization, and the continual reinvention of early modern orientalism. For one week, September 5–13, 1998, Puccini's opera *Turandot* was performed for the first time inside the Forbidden City, in Beijing. The libretto famously features an exquisite yet tyrannical Chinese princess named Turandot who poses three riddles to any suitor who dares ask her hand. Countless suitors fail the test and submit to being executed, until one man, the foreign prince Calaf, answers correctly and wins her heart. This performance of the opera, directed by the Chinese filmmaker Zhang Yimou in collaboration with the Indian conductor Zubin Mehta, of the Israel Philharmonic, was meant to accomplish the feat of bringing *Turandot* "home" to its roots in China—or at least to the site designated by Puccini as the opera's exotic setting in the "Imperial City" of "Peking." Publicized as an historic homecoming, it was the most expensive opera ever produced and was hailed by the media as "the last great cultural event before the new millenium."[7] If it was not Chinese to begin with, it became so for the purposes of reclaiming an eighteenth-century European fantasy of Eastern excess.

Allan Miller's documentary film *The Turandot Project* (2001) shows the production of the opera to be an ambitious and uneasy international enterprise; several of its participants nonetheless share an obsession with producing a culturally "authentic" *Turandot* that could thus be distinguished from generations of previous performances. As Zubin Mehta remarks in the film, "Usually *Turandot* is full of Chinese clichés; it looks like a big Chinese restaurant. But I think this is different, because this is really authentic. They have not invented anything that looks Chinese—this is really it."[8] At the same time, to reinvent the opera, Zhang Yimou added a host of new cultural markers: Chinese ballet dancers, elements of Beijing Opera and Ming dynasty ornamentation, and the brilliant red and yellow silks featured in the visually lavish films for which he is known.[9] His notable and costly insistence on period detail included the use of an actual imperial ancestral temple, the Tai Miao, as part of the scenery, much to objection of preservationists from China's State Cultural Relics Administration. The costumes were made by tailors from the Suzhou region, famous for its silk trade, where generations of women have retained and passed down the skills of making clothes for the nobility and the imperial family dating back five hundred years.[10] Over a span of months, more than a hundred rural families sewed by hand the nine hundred sets of costumes. In another show of life imitating art, Zhang called in hundreds of members of the People's Armed Police to play the opera's soldiers after the extras failed to perform accurately the Ming-styled choreography. With the aid of these laboring bodies, *Turandot* acquired a manufactured Chinese identity based not upon its historical precedence but, rather, upon its difference from the Italian original. As Zhang stressed, "That my *Turandot* does not have much to do with traditional Italian opera makes it more interesting. I made it more Chinese."[11]

That the opera could have nothing and everything to do with China is a central paradox of the oriental exemplarity discussed throughout this book. So, too, are the moral and material excesses of Puccini's fabricated China rooted in eighteenth-century ideas of Oriental spectacle, and in the original fable upon which the opera was based, "The Story of Prince Calaf and the Princess of China," taken from the same *Persian Tales* collection referenced in Addison and Steele's *Spectator*.[12] The framing narrative of the *Persian Tales*, we should remember, is of a nurse who tells stories to the obstinate princess of Caschmire to convince her of the virtues of men and the benefits of marriage. The story of Turandot is thus meant to be a lesson in the futility of female independence; and it concerns once again the conquest of a feminine China by a masculine Tartar. As narrated in the *Persian Tales*, the Turkic Nogais prince Calaf goes into exile when his Tartar empire is defeated by the sultan of Carizme and his family is betrayed by its allies in neighboring Circassia.[13] Eventually Calaf makes his way to China to seek the aid of the powerful King Altoun-can, and it is there that he falls in love with the man-hating "Tourandocte." Not only does Calaf solve the riddles that have eluded all previous suitors, but Tourandocte willingly consents to marry him according to her father's wishes. Omitted from later versions of the story are the circuitous journeys of Calaf's exile to China and eventual return home to reinstate his family's reign.[14]

Rather than trace the interconnections and narrative digressions that get lost in translation, I am interested in how Turandot's character—inscrutable, effeminized, brutal yet fragile—and the spectacle of Chinese imperial power become signs of Chineseness that circulate discursively and materially through performance. The text's descriptions of silks, crimsons, mandarins, canopies, musicians, and countless soldiers of the imperial court—all the narrative regalia of Oriental fiction—pair material grandeur with the tragedy and triumph of love. These are the sumptuous details that make their way into the exoticized setting of Puccini's China. In Orientalist fashion, Puccini's opera redacts the original tale by intensifying the princess's despotism, her traumatic, vengeful disposition toward men, and resistance to the love of an outsider. The Peking of her jurisdiction symbolizes effeminized despotism and xenophobia by association. From the perspective of Orientalist discourse, the fact or nonfact of *Turandot*'s actual Chinese origins, its history of translations, borrowings, and attributions, matters less than the character's allegorical significance in a climate of high-stakes cultural politics. Some accounts of the opera read Turandot's cruelty as evidence of China's age-old barbarism, and in doing so turn representation into reality. One journalist reporting on the Beijing production compared the princess's heartless executions with Beijing's current high rate of death-penalty cases, surmising that the opera would have been censored had Chinese officials understood enough Italian to realize the extent of Turandot's despotism.[15] Another common news angle emphasized the naturalness of the connection between the opera's theme of cruelty and the function of the ancestral temple, Tai Miao, as a place where barbaric sacrifices were made in the past. Such readings of the opera as political allegory and China as a transhistorical regime of brutality and unyielding isolationism constitute the classic Orientalism of Said's formulation. What they omit, however, is the complicity of East and West in the production of transnational spectacle, and the nationalist revival of traditional customs in response to world economic practices and the unevenness of globalization's homogenization of culture.[16] The intersection of national and international interests thus indicates a more capacious form of orientalism, one of multiple ideological and economic investments.

Although the ending of the opera leaves us with (yet another) conquest of China by a foreign suitor, we can see also the marriage of two worlds and a scene of cross-cultural negotiations that resonates with the recent conditions of the opera's staging and with making a spectacle and virtue of international collaboration. Its production team declared *Turandot* a feat of cross-cultural exchange between the artists and the often clashing worlds they represented—classical opera and contemporary film, the musical and the visual, as well as the West and the East in a time of the tenuous opening up of Sino-American relations and Chinese markets to international capital. China's minister of culture at the time of the production, Sun Jiazheng, praised the opera for being one of more than a thousand "exchange activities" of the year, including cultural agreements with other countries to share museum displays and orchestra performances.[17] In Zhang Yimou's words, the opera became a kind of cultural ambassador between East and West, bringing "people of different countries in a real exchange and mutual understanding—a spiritual and emotional exchange."[18] At the same time, Beijing's *Turandot* was a bid for yet bigger profits and Olympian international standing. As one commentator put it, "an image of a European soprano as Princess Turandot—backed by an Italian and Chinese chorus, conducted by . . . Zubin Mehta, and created by an international Chinese director—would be a persuasive visual argument in any future Olympic bid or Chinese tourist footage."[19] If Olympic sport is understood to promote healthy international competition and to defuse, enact, or divert global tensions, operatic spectacle promotes the promoter. The *Turandot* project made a bid and sought to create the most lavish opera production of the century; given the cost, size, and international scope, and China's successful bid for the 2008 Olympics, whose artistic director would once again be Zhang Yimou, the opera appears to have succeeded.[20]

The self-orientalizing gestures of Chinese spectacle therefore extend our understanding of Orientalism in several ways. That the Chinese media and organizers overtly acknowledged the fakeness of Puccini's Chinese fantasy only furthered the logic of reappropriation and self-orientalization: since Puccini had never set foot in China, why not right history and the spirit of a dead author's unrealized intentions? As Zhang bluntly pointed out, "There is no need to discuss questions of East and West. . . . The story has nothing to do with China. It can be told in any setting. It is a fable. Since Puccini set it in China, we won't pursue why he set it in China. We just enjoy the opera."[21] Such blatant disregard for authenticity of one kind and the marketing of another kind unsettles the tenuous premise of bringing Turandot "home," while at the same time rewriting the terms of authenticity.

The image of a driven Zhang makes apparent the need for China to prove to the world its ability to master as well as embrace the form and function of Western opera, while producing a universally appealing Chineseness for the Western market.[22] Cultural studies scholar Rey Chow, writing on the construction of exoticism in contemporary Chinese films, describes this marketing of authenticity as "a culture's belated fascination with its own datedness, it own alterity."[23] Putting aside the question of origins, as suggested by Zhang, therefore means deliberately remaking and retroactively concretizing a mythic past, in which the specter of the Chinese original comes back to assert itself in the form of a globally commodified exemplar. In effect, what was once an Orientalist fantasy becomes materialized through not only the suspension of history but also a saleable historical revisionism premised on China's right to own its own representation.

Opera Tourism, Egypt to China

To focus solely on the East-West or self-other Orientalism of *Turandot* would inadequately account for the nexus of local and global, national and transnational forces at work in marketing its ancient-yet-modern exemplarity. The commercialization of *Turandot's* cultural authenticity has a particular lineage of global production and history of opera and empire that both follows and diverges from the old imagined geography of the Orient that stretched from Egypt to China. The massive efforts on the part of the Chinese government and transnational corporations in and outside Asia to transform Puccini's exotic referent into a made-in-China cultural spectacle were headed by a Vienna-based production company, Opera on Original Site, Inc., which describes itself as "founded with the aim to market and produce high quality operatic events at the sites with which they are most closely associated."[24] The company initiated a transportable tradition of opera tourism that turns monuments into "live" sets and attempts to mobilize the spectacle of monumentality as political diversion, creating one memory and erasing another through the association of site with experienced event.[25] It is fitting that before the Beijing *Turandot*, Opera on Original Site's Michael Ecker, a veteran at marketing cultural authenticity, had successfully promoted Verdi's *Aida* in Luxor, Egypt, in 1987. Moving the opera back to Cairo, with the Great Pyramids of Giza as backdrop, was meant to recall and celebrate the opera's first performance in 1871, which then marked the opening of the Cairo Opera House and the influx of European high culture into Egypt. Of course, if we remember in a different vein, we would recall that *Aida* was an Orientalist's vision of Pharaonic grandeur told through the tragic story of an Egyptian officer who falls in love with his captive Ethiopian slave.

The opera was from the start enmeshed in the politics of imperialism and Orientalism. Produced in France and then transported "back" to Egypt, it exemplifies the age of opera tourism and a kind of "opera on original site" long before the founding of Ecker's company. Verdi was presented with the idea by the French producer du Locle, who had visited Egypt; his guide while there, the Egyptologist Auguste Mariette, had proposed and written an opera based on the victory of Ramses III over North African and Aegean invaders. In turn, Mariette's 1869 book, *Monuments of Upper Egypt*, included pictures from Ramses' temple, which would be the visual basis for the triumphal march featured in *Aida*.[26] The Egyptian commissioning and emulation of European opera and architecture was part and parcel of the khedive's refashioning of Cairo after a model, nineteenth-century Paris. His urban-planning project followed the principle of colonial exhibition—the recreation of a "real Egypt" in Paris and a "real Paris" in Cairo.[27] In fact, Mariette had arranged the Egyptian display at the Paris Universal Exhibition of 1867, and he was the one to oversee the staging and costuming of *Aida* from Paris to Cairo: in an ironic turn, the Orientalist managed the details of Egypt's self-exhibition.

According to historian Eric Hobsbawm, European imperialism was typified by two institutions, the secular university and the opera house, described as a "characteristic cathedral of bourgeois culture," that marked the globalization of the economy, the mass marketing of goods, and the increased density of communication networks and the unevenness of global development.[28] The history of *Aida* is a perfect example as well of the phenomenon of the world-as-exhibition studied by Timothy Mitchell, where the European tourist/observer, having viewed a simulation of Egypt, travels in search of the "real" Egypt, only to be disappointed in what he finds. The journey results in the tourist's return to Paris and turn to an aesthetic form such as opera for a vision of the Orient that proves to be more satisfying than the authentic experience. Like world exhibitions, operatic spectacles promoted modern capitalism, political transformation, and international trade for Europe. Whereas in the nineteenth century, the opera house was a state-sponsored instrument of imperialism, globalized opera tourism today seeks out the broken edifices of imperialism, "whether they consist of actual monuments to field marshals or the altered economies of former colonies," to borrow Caren Kaplan's phrase.[29] Current theories of tourism and modernity are premised on the West's nostalgia for a lost past, for an elusive authenticity that takes the form of the ever-displaced native. Indeed, touring has been compared with walking amid "monuments to the wreckage of Europe's greatest ambition—to rule the world."[30]

What better expression of global Orientalism, and the remains of imperialism, than Placido Domingo in the role of *Aida's* Ramadis and hundreds of Egyptian extras playing slaves and soldiers at the monumental site of the three-thousand-year-old Luxor Temple? The 1987 extravaganza organized by Opera on Original Site borrowed the physical remnants of imperialism to stage its modern touristic spectacle at this site, home to the second largest existing obelisk in Egypt. Like the use of the Tai Miao in Beijing, the ancient pyramid attains a new use-value as a modern prop of cultural authenticity, a new iteration of the phenomenon of making souvenirs and moral examples of colonial objects of desire. For the Egyptian performance, the obelisk was lit up in its place at the eastern side of the entrance, as if to recall the shadow of its missing twin on the western side, which now stands at the Place de la Concorde in Paris. (The pair that had been erected by Ramses II was separated in the 1830s when the Egyptian viceroy of that day had one obelisk hewn down and transported to France as a gift, in exchange for a large clock—an ancient piece of technology for a modern one.) The set-design crew for the 1987 *Aida* tried to construct a substitute obelisk out of parts imported from Britain, but it proved too unwieldy to be raised near its original spot; in fact, it was deemed a hazard to the surrounding buildings and was relegated to the back of the stage, leaving the original pairing unrestored.[31]

As suggested by such travels of a disembodied pyramid, the projects of Opera on Original Site are acts of absenting, rather than restoring, authenticity, or what the cultural theorist Jean Baudrillard would point to as "supplementary subterfuge" and "fictions of the real." To the journalist who reported that "The Aida phenomenon has nothing to do with . . . music, or the history of Egypt as it is today," Baudrillard might say: questioning the "reality" of the representation in an age of simulacra and simulation is beside the point.[32] The journalist's lament, however justified, fails to consider the partnership between "cultural exchange" and transnational capital, or the instrumental aestheticization of the colonial past with globalization's present. In other words, global Orientalism is no longer limited to a conflict between real and representation; it is also increasingly concerned with the compensatory project of attaining the monetary rights to representation. As the journalist reporting on *Aida* went on to remark, "Egypt does not own her, the Milanese music publishing house of Ricordi does. And they take very good and careful care of her drawing power with a vast public who never go to any other opera."[33]

Perhaps the main difference between *Aida* and *Turandot* was precisely the Chinese insistence on owning and profiting from the rights to its cultural space. Commenting on the high charge of renting the Forbidden City, Ecker complained, "We did not get one single dollar from the Chinese tourist authority for promoting this project. In Egypt, you would get millions of dollars."[34] Although it was touted as a financial coup at the time, Ecker later admitted that the profits for the Beijing *Turandot* were "disappointing," and that his company would be lucky to break even. The Chinese government benefited, however, reaping from $80 million to $100 million in tourism and, of course, paving the way for future state-sponsored spectacles like the 2008 Beijing Olympics and the 2010 Shanghai World Exposition.[35] Convinced by the promise of numbers, which were in the end delivered, the Chinese culture industry took advantage of the "cultural and spiritual exchange" to reclaim the authenticity of origins and to make some business out of Orientalism.

It is thus not only opera but also a range of other modern spectacles, including international sports, that participate in the politics and commerce of cultural authenticity. The afterlife of the Beijing *Turandot*, particularly the spread of performances throughout East Asia, attests to the ongoing reinvention of the Orient. In the ever-expanding compression of time and space, and the sportslike ambition of outdoing one's previous record of opera tourism from Luxor to Beijing, a potentially new form of Orientalism, memory making, and traveling culture can be discerned—a kind of *spectacle translatio* that links the remains of imperialisms, an obelisk, a pyramid, a Ming dynasty temple, and even a soccer stadium.[36] For, though a far cry from popular culture, opera has nonetheless become tied to the spaces, vendors, and cultural packaging that make up globally mediated sporting events such as the Olympics and the soccer World Cup. As a testament to the synergy between opera and sport, in 2003 from May 8 to 11 South Korea staged its own *Turandot* in none other than the 2002 World Cup stadium. It was marketed as "the world's largest outdoor opera to be staged to celebrate the First Anniversary of the 2002 FIFA World Cup Korea-Japan." In fact, in an attempt to outdo Beijing by emulating Beijing, the Korean set was twice as big as that of the Forbidden City and spanned the entire length of the stadium. A replica of the Ming temple was built, along with four life-sized pagodas, double the number of Beijing's. As if following in the footsteps of Opera on Original Site, the Seoul Arts Center and CnAKorea production team followed up on *Turandot* by staging *Aida* in another outdoor sporting venue, the Olympic Stadium.[37] International sports and opera, perhaps new institutions of global spectacle, simulate, dramatize, and civilize geopolitical tensions in virtual battle, making apparent the relevance of nationalism and the unevenness of modernity's progress amid the forces and euphoric triumphalism of globalization.[38] Across an array of venues, spectacle provides a testing ground for technologies that, deterritorialized to begin with, can then be deployed in multiple sites, from opera house to sports stadium. And yet, cases like the Opera on Original Site enterprise point to the possibility that globalization relies on the cultural vocabulary of empire and a chinoiserie collage of past exoticisms, now brought together in a new, undifferentiated form.

The consideration of the ongoing reinvention of Orientalism through these instances of modern media spectacle underlines the complexities and ambiguities of its logic of expansion and deterritorialization. These maps of commerce and virtue incorporate eighteenth-century history into the machinery of cultural production. It may be the case that the language of globalization and capitalist investment is cultural exchange—one way of attempting to cover over the traumatic histories of colonialism and imperialism. But while the past might be the stumbling block for international accord and global capital alike, its transformation into the material of spectacle leads us to reflect on key trajectories and complexities of orientalisms past and present: the Chinese nationalist iterations of an eighteenth-century Persian tale; the theft of one monument and the replication of another; the trade in culture; and those bodies that perform the labors of global spectacle and the materiality of representation. Today's performances of China remain sites of the struggle over the relevance of ancient history to modern progress. In eighteenth-century religious, scientific, and mercantile context, China, a model for Europe, may not have been formally colonized, but it was an integral part of the colonial circuits of exchange that produced the complex and mediated orderings of culture, race, and nation upon which the British Empire was founded. The strong ambivalence exhibited by Europeans toward Asiatic empires, and China in particular, reveals the cross-cultural comparisons through which new forms of virtue were negotiated. China was and continues to be constructed and consumed as part of a broader Orient in literary and artistic performances, and such instances of spectacle and cultural performance are worth examining not merely for their Orientalist misrepresentations of China but rather for their mutual constructions of East and West.

Throughout this book, the object of inquiry has been neither England nor China alone, but rather the transcultural production of knowledge. Located at one extreme of an ever-more-specific, ever-more-homogenized East, China epitomized the excesses and possibilities of a commercial empire on a par with the greatness of ancient Rome, except that it was far from defunct. In its capacity as a competing example of civilization, a consummate performance, and a spectacle of contradiction, "China" revealed the processes of desiring as well as disavowing multiple objects and others in the search for modern virtue. The particular logic of eighteenth-century European expressions of oriental exemplarity emerged in conjunction with the first major wave of imported Chinese products and virtues. This cultural construction served as a material and ideological premise of the early British imperial enterprise, and the orientalized nexus of commerce and virtue has persisted into the current day by continuing to structure not only Western attitudes toward the East but also the self-orientalizing efforts of the other.

NOTES

Introduction. China as Exemplar

1. I use the term *English*, not *British*, to refer either to events or literature written in England before the 1707 Act of Union or to linguistic, cultural, or political traditions that pertain primarily to the geography of England rather than that of Scotland, Wales, or Ireland.

2. "Olympics Opening Ceremony," television program. Beijing: NBC Television, Aug. 8, 2008.

3. Richard Williams, "Patriot Games: China Makes Its Point with Greatest Show," *Guardian*, August 9, 2008, www.guardian.co.uk/sport/2008/aug/09/olympics2008.opening ceremony.

4. The event would be surpassed by the National Day Parade on Oct. 1, 2009, and the Shanghai World Exposition, 2010.

5. Fénelon, *Dialogues des Morts*, in *Œuvres*, 299; my translation. Thanks to David Agruss for help with interpreting this phrase. Modeled after Fontenelle and Lucian, the dialogues between ancient and modern historical figures were conceived by Fénelon in the 1690s and then published in batches in and after 1700. Written to educate the ten-year-old duc de Bourgogne in princely etiquette and the qualities of a good ruler, they consist of fifty-one dialogues between ancients, twenty-seven between moderns, and one between an ancient and a modern. See Davis, *Fénelon*, 64–73.

6. Ibid., 299. The French reads: "Selon ces relateurs, le peuple de la terre le plus vain, le plus superstitieux, le plus intéressé, le plus injuste, le plus menteur, ce'st le Chinois."

7. Defoe, *Tour Through the Whole Island of Britain*, 65.

8. See Chambers's entry on porcelain in *Cyclopaedia*, 2: 842. See also Liu, "Robinson Crusoe's Earthenware Pot," 728–57.

9. Temple, *Of Heroic Virtue*, in *The Works of Sir William Temple*, 3: 328.

10. Waller, *Of Tea, Commended by her Majesty* (1663), in *Works of Edmund Waller*, 131–32.

11. Defoe, *Tour Through the Whole Island of Britain*, 65.

12. Berg, "Asian Luxuries and the Making of the European Consumer Revolution," in *Luxury in the Eighteenth Century*, 241. See also Berg, *Luxury and Pleasure in Eighteenth-century Britain*.

13. Pomeranz, *The Great Divergence*; Frank, *Reorient*; Wong, *China Transformed*; Chaudhuri, *Asia before Europe*; Arrighi, *Adam Smith in Beijing*. See also the revisionist work of Goldstone, "Efflorescences and Economic Growth in World History," 323–89, and *Why Europe?*

14. Frank, *Reorient*, 149; Sugihara, "East Asian Path of Economic Development," 79, 89–90, quoted in Arrighi, *Adam Smith in Beijing*, 33, 331. See also Arrighi's discussion of Chinese exemplarity in *Adam Smith in Beijing*, 69, 336.

15. Ovington, *Essay Upon the Nature and Qualities of Tea*, 2, 36.

16. Brown, "Thing Theory," 5, 4.

17. Goldsmith, *Citizen of the World*, 24.

18. Mandeville, *The Fable of the Bees and Other Writings*, ed. Hundert, 96.

19. According to Pocock, "The appropriate material foundation . . . was land: real property cognizable as stable enough to link successive generations in social relationships belonging to, or founded in, the order of nature . . . fortified by immemorial customs." See Pocock, *The Machiavellian Moment*, 458–60.

20. Ibid., 451, 445.

21. Pocock, *Virtue, Commerce, and History*, 122.

22. Wycherley, *The Country Wife*, 70.

23. Rowe, *The Biter*, 13.

24. See Collier, *Short View of Immorality and Profaneness*.

25. Publications from the historical period of the mid-seventeenth century alone include Peter Heylyn, *Cosmographie* (1657); Martino Martini [Martin Martinius], *Novus Atlas Sinensis* (1655) and *Bellum Tartaricum* [*De Bello Tartarico*], *or the Conquest of the Great and Most Renowned Empire of China, by the Invasion of the Tartars* (1654); Alvarez Semedo, *The History of that Great and Renowned Monarchy of China* (1655); Johann Adam Schall, *Historica relatio de ortu* (1665); Athanasius Kircher, *China Illustrata* (1667); Johann Nieuhof [John Nieuhoff], *An Embassy from the East-India Company . . . to the Grand Tartar Cham* (1669); Olfert Dapper, *Atlas Chinensis* (1671); Juan de Palafox y Mendoza, *The History of the Conquest of China by the Tartars* (1671); John Ogilby, *Asia* (1673); Gabriel de Magalhães, *Nouvelle relation de la Chine* (1679); Domingo Fernandez Navarette, *An Account of the Empire of China* (1676).

26. Orr, *Empire on the English Stage*.

27. Choudhury, *Interculturalism and Resistance in the London Theater*.

28. Le Comte, *Memoirs and Observations*, 148.

29. Du Halde, *General History of China*, 141.

30. For an excellent discussion of visual representations of Chinese ritual, see Clark, "Chinese Idols and Religious Art," 235–50. See also Standaert, *Interweaving of Rituals*.

31. Le Comte, *Memoirs and Observations*, 139.

32. Agnew, *Worlds Apart*. This follows the work of Hirschman, *Passions and the Interests*.

33. Phelan, introduction to *The Ends of Performance*, 3.

34. Schechner, *Performance Studies*, 30.

35. Dryden, *The Life of Plutarch*, 92.

36. Agamben, *Homo Sacer*, 22. For Agamben, the discourse of Western civilization

and the emergence of the city inaccurately presumes a precedent, the state of nature, that actually proves to be a principle internal to political formation: the outside within. This discussion of sovereignty and the overdetermined signification of the example shares with debates over early modern exemplarity an examination of how boundaries are established between categories of sacred and secular, ancient and modern, religious and political. At the threshold of modern conceptions of freedom, the example constitutes a state of being other to oneself—of being "shown beside"—and thus illuminates the process of defining what Agamben *(Homo Sacer,* 22) calls the "belonging and commonality of individuals."

37. Gelley, introduction to *Unruly Examples,* 14, 2.
38. Hayot, introduction to *The Hypothetical Mandarin,* 3–35.
39. Johnson, *Dictionary of the English Language,* vol. 1.
40. In this section I draw from Timothy Hampton, *Writing from History,* 198.
41. Rigolot, "The Renaissance Crisis of Exemplarity," 557–63. On the disruption of stability and confusion of values opened up by humanist uses of the exemplar as a rhetorical tool, see Cornilliat, "Exemplarities," 613–24.
42. See Jensen, *Manufacturing Confucianism.*
43. Israel, *Enlightenment Contested,* 652–54; Mungello, *Curious Land,* 357, 92. Archbishop James Ussher, in his *Annals of the Old and New Testament* (1650–54), dated the world's creation at 4004 BC, according to his reading of the bible. The issue of China's chronology was raised with the Latin publication of the Jesuit Martino Martini's *The First Ten Divisions of Chinese History* (1658). See Mungello, *Great Encounter of China and the West,* 87.
44. As noted earlier, the French Jesuit Louis Le Comte wrote in 1697: "China for two thousand years had the knowledge of the true God, and [has] practis'd the most pure Morality, while Europe and almost all the World wallow'd in Error and Corruption." Like Voltaire later, he emphasized the sheer fact of China's longevity over its disputed number of years: "The *Chineses* are so Ancient in the World, that it fares with them as to their Original, as with great Rivers whose source can scarce be discovered. . . . [F]ive or Six hundred years, more or less, does not produce any notable diminution in its Antiquity": Le Comte, *Memoirs and Observations,* 121. See Voltaire, *Philosophical Dictionary,* 1:166–70.
45. Kant, *Observations on the Feeling of the Beautiful and Sublime,* 109, 110.
46. Ibid., 110. Kant here cites and revises the comments of David Hume's essay "Of National Characters."
47. Gelley, introduction to *Unruly Examples.*
48. Lloyd, "Race under Representation," 249–72. Other studies of Kant and race include Armstrong, "'Effects of Blackness,'" 213–36; Judy, "Kant and the Negro"; Eze, introduction to *Race and the Enlightenment.*
49. Spivak, *Critique of Postcolonial Reason,* 9. It should be noted that Kant's anthropology shows the attempt to derive a moral science that is not reducible to pragmatic or material or empirical concerns, even as postcolonial scholars have attempted to read the anthropological use of example as constitutive of his aesthetic and ethical system.
50. Aravamudan, *Tropicopolitans,* 16.
51. Ibid., 4.
52. Spivak, *Critique of Postcolonial Reason,* 1.

53. See, for example, Kaul, *Eighteenth-century British Literature and Postcolonial Studies*.

54. Carey and Festa, *Postcolonial Enlightenment*, 3.

55. See Archer's discussion of early modern sites of colonialism in *Old Worlds*. See also Wheeler, *Complexion of Race*. For an excellent study of eighteenth-century Orientalism that adapts the East-West binary structure of Said's Orientalism by figuring in the importance of gender, see Lowe, *Critical Terrains*.

56. I find particularly instructive the past scholarship on colonial discourse, race, empire, and eighteenth-century globality by Srinivas Aravamudan, Laura Brown, Peter Hulme, Betty Joseph, Suvir Kaul, Felicity Nussbaum, Bridget Orr, and Charlotte Sussman.

57. Recent work in East Asian and Asian American studies, for example, has productively analyzed both the relevance and limitations of Orientalism and postcoloniality, in part by addressing the critical juncture of East Asian development and globalization. See Shih, *Visuality and Identity*, and Krishnan, *Reading the Global*. Concurrently, historians of East Asia have approached the question of Chinese empire in the Ming-Qing period of the mid-seventeenth century through a comparative lens that questions European rubrics and the historical periodizations of modern and early modern. See especially Struve, introduction to *The Qing Formation in World-Historical Time*; Hostetler, *Qing Colonial Enterprise*; Waley-Cohen, "New Qing History," 193–206.

58. See Ballaster, *Fabulous Orients*; Batchelor, "Concealing the Bounds," 79–92; Yu Liu, *Seeds of a Different Eden*; Markley, *The Far East and the English Imagination*; Min, "China between the Ancients and the Moderns," 115–30; Porter, *Ideographia*; Starr, "Defoe and China," 435–54; Watt, "Thomas Percy, China, and the Gothic," 95–110; Zuroski, "Disenchanting China," 254–71.

59. For an excellent collection of work on the China-Europe relationship published by Chinese scholars between the 1930s and 1950s, see Hsia, *Vision of China*.

60. For the purposes of this study, *Orientalism* (capitalized) refers to the nineteenth-century phenomenon theorized by Edward Said; *orientalism* (lowercased) is used to signify the particular, fluid logic at work in the early eighteenth century.

61. See Yang, "Asia Out of Place," 235–53.

62. See Andrea's discussion of "proto-orientalist fluidity" in "Persia, Tartaria, and Pamphilia," 26; and Barbour, *Before Orientalism*.

63. Maclean, *Looking East*, 20, 98.

Chapter 1. Heroic Effeminacy and the Conquest of China

1. According to John Genest, the play was far from flawless: "Downes says that Jevon acted a Chinese Prince who kills himself that he may not be taken prisoner by the Tartars—Jevon, instead of falling on the point of his sword, laid it in the scabbard at length on the ground, and fell upon it saying 'now I am dead.'" See Genest, *Some Account of the English Stage*.

2. See note 25 in my introduction.

3. The Chinese nationalist narrative of Sinicization used to explain the success of Manchu rule has recently been challenged and revised by historians of the Qing dynasty who

explore the factors of Manchu identity and ethnicity. Scholars who form part of this "new Qing history" include Pamela Crossley *(A Translucent Mirror)*, Mark C. Elliott *(The Manchu Way)*, and Laura Hostetler *(Qing Colonial Enterprise)*. For a helpful overview of the debates around Sinicization, see Waley-Cohen, "The New Qing History," 193–206.

4. Spinoza, *A treatise partly theological, and partly political* (London, 1689), 81.

5. Whereas England's own dependency on and shortage of silver continued to be a serious national concern from the civil war period on, China by the middle of the seventeenth century, the "silver century," held the majority of the world's entire production. See Flynn and Giráldez, "China and the Spanish Empire," 314; Flynn, *World Silver*, 42, 50; Davis, *Rise of the Atlantic Economies*, 98. For more recent studies of a China-centered global economy and the role of world silver flows, see Kenneth Pomeranz, *Great Divergence;* Frank, *Reorient*.

6. See Spurr, *England in the 1670s*.

7. Armitage, "The Cromwellian Protectorate and Languages of Empire," 533. See also Armitage, *Ideological Origins of the English Empire*.

8. See, for example, Erskine-Hill, *The Augustan Idea in English Literature;* Weinbrot, *Augustus Caesar in "Augustan" England;* Ayres, *Classical Culture and the Idea of Rome*.

9. Furber, *Rival Empires of Trade*.

10. Temple, *Of Heroic Virtue*, in *The Works of Sir William Temple*, 3: 328.

11. According to Peter Heylyn, Chingis (Genghis) Khan changed the name of Scythians to Tartars in 1162: *Cosmographie*, 861. Modern-day scholars continue to differ on the etymology and usage of *Tartar*, which during the seventeenth and eighteenth centuries was broadly used and could refer to Mongol or Manchu. One possible origin for the term is the Chinese word *dada*, meaning northern nomads, adapted by Europeans after the Mongol invasions of the 1200s. The name was changed from Tatar to Tartar through associations with the Latin word for Hades, *Tartarus*, made by medieval writers such as Matthew Paris and Chaucer. See Elliot, "Limits of Tartary," 625–26. According to C. W. Connell, *Tartar* refers to the thirteenth-century Mongols and their invasion of China. In the medieval period, for example, the term is shrouded within a biblical discourse that conflates all Orientalized, Muslim invaders as agents of the anti-Christ. See Connell, "Western Views of the Origin of the 'Tartars,'" 115–37. See also Daniel, *Islam and the West*, 80; Mote, *Imperial China*, 409.

12. Gibbon, *Decline and Fall of the Roman Empire*, 3: 71.

13. Nieuhof, *An Embassy from the East India Company*, 282.

14. Palafox y Mendoza, *History of the Conquest of China*, 561, 79, 82.

15. d'Orléans, *History of the Two Tartar Conquerors of China* (London, 1854), 12, 17.

16. As pointed out by Howard Erskine-Hill, seventeenth-century receptions of Augustus and the Roman Empire were split largely between republicans, such as James Harrington, who argued that the Roman republic had been betrayed by the Julian house, and monarchists following Jean Bodin and Robert Filmer, who argued that Augustan rule had transformed the republic into a virtuous monarchy: *The Augustan Idea in English Literature*, 199, 205, 221. According to Philip Ayres, the most praised element of Rome (not Augustus, per se) was its balanced constitution, praised especially by Whigs in drawing comparisons between republican Rome and the 1688 settlement. The aristocratic critics of luxury were

landed Tories resentful of the commercial class who cast themselves as oligarchic, senatorial authorities who advocated civic virtue: *Classical Culture and the Idea of Rome*, 18.

17. See Sekora, *Luxury*, 37.

18. Bhabha, *Location of Culture*, 123, quoted in Krishnaswamy, *Effeminism*, 294, 304. See also Sinha, *Colonial Masculinity*.

19. See, for example, Connell's theory that masculinity is formed throughout history repeatedly at the colonial frontier, beginning with the "ethics of conquest" during the sixteenth-century Spanish invasions of the Americas: Connell, *Masculinities*, 247.

20. For the meanings of effeminacy in relation to *virtu* and *imperium* in the Roman context, see chapter 4 of Williams, *Roman Homosexuality*.

21. As noted by Rana Kabbani, the "lascivious sensuality and inherent violence" of nineteenth-century Orientalism can be traced back to the popularization of the *Arabian Nights* in the eighteenth century: *Europe's Myths of Orient*, 6, 25–26, 40.

22. For an excellent and comprehensive study of Restoration theater and empire to which I am indebted, see Orr, *Empire on the English Stage*.

23. Puritan minister Thomas Beard includes a section entitled "Of effeminate persons, Sodomites, and other such like Monsters" in his *The theatre of Gods judgements* (1642), 281.

24. Nussbaum offers a very helpful summary of the meanings of effeminacy in *Limits of the Human*, 17, 72.

25. On news of China, see Van Kley's highly informative article "News from China," 561–82.

26. Judith Halberstam's study *Female Masculinity* helpfully underscores the importance of understanding masculinity as performance of gender that is not necessarily tied to the male body.

27. De Pauw, *Battle Cries and Lullabies*, 52.

28. For the identification of Amazons with Persians and the threats posed by the Persian Empire upon Greece, see Blundell, *Women in Ancient Greece*, 61–62.

29. Of course, there were plays that dealt with Amazons in a protofeminist vein, especially after 1688, reflecting the rule of Queen Anne; see Orr, *Empire on the English Stage*, 188. Orr discusses John Weston's *The Amazon Queen* and Edward Howard's *Six Days Adventure of the New Utopia*, as well as *The Women's Conquest*, in which Amazons occupy a tenuous position of rule set in border zones of Scythia or utopic islands, where their rule is overturned. There was a turn to national heroes like Boadicea later in the 1690s to establish the links and differences between Romans and Britons in plays like George Powell's *Bonduca: Or, the British Heroine* (1696) and Charles Hopkins's *Boadicea* (1697). See Orr, *Empire on the English Stage*, 254.

30. Hall, *Things of Darkness*; Loomba, "Great Indian Vanishing Trick," 173. The female utopias of Greek Amazonia and India actually complicate a binary of "female East vs. patriarchal West" by associating lustful males with effeminacy, as argued by Stone in "Indian and Amazon," 100.

31. Schwarz, *Tough Love*, 22.

32. Among these distinguished women are popular cross-dressing heroines, like Huang Chonggu, and heroic widows known for committing suicide. See Fong, "Signifying Bodies," 117.

33. For an account of Settle's sources, see Downes, *Roscius Anglicanus*, and Baker, *The Companion to the Play-House*. The actual historical figure was Qin Liangyu, who, with her husband and brothers, also military commanders, founded and led the "White Stick Troop." Leading up to and during the Qing occupation of Beijing in 1644, Qin Liangyu fought on behalf of the Ming imperial army, earning a royal title by the southern Ming regime and maintaining control over her region of Shizhu until her death. See Peterson's *Notable Women of China*; see also Hummel, *Eminent Chinese of the Ch'ing Period*, 168–69. I use the pinyin spelling of Chinese names unless otherwise noted.

34. d'Orléans, *History of Two Tartar Conquerors*, 11. Magalhães describes an "Amazone" of "Suchuen" who fights "Cham hien Chum," citing the work of Couplet and Martini; see Magalhães, *Nouvelle relation de la Chine* (1679), 67.

35. This follows the report by Michael Boym in 1652. See Lach, *Asia in the Making of Europe*, 3: 1666, 1668.

36. See Martini, *Bellum Tartaricum* [*De bello tartarico*], 262. All citations are taken from the English edition included at the end of Semedo's *History of that Great and Renowned Monarchy of China* (1655).

37. For the relevance to seventeenth-century theater of Penthesilea, the mythical Amazon queen who fought on behalf of the Trojans, see Shepherd, *Amazons and Warrior Women*.

38. See Martini, *Bellum Tartaricum*, 295–96.

39. I will include parenthetically Martini's Latinized spellings as well as alternate spellings to the current-day pinyin format of mainland China, where relevant, for the sake of recognizability. Abahai later renamed the government Qing to invoke the earlier Jin dynasty. For studies of the Manchu banner system and relations of tribute to the Ming, see Elliott, *The Manchu Way*, and Crossley, *The Manchus*.

40. See Hummel, *Eminent Chinese*, under the entry for Abahai. A confluence of factors enabled the eventual Manchu victory over both the Ming regime and Chinese usurpers such as the notorious rebel Li Zicheng (Li Tzu-ch'eng). In April 1644, having risen against the financially dissolute Ming government, the rebel-usurper (and by some accounts, populist hero) Li Zicheng established a temporary six-week rule in Beijing, the Shun Interregnum, only to be in turn overthrown by the Manchus with the aid of Ming forces under the commander Wu Sangui (Wu San-kuei). Martini includes an extended account of two "bandits," Licungzus and Changhienchungus. These names all reappear nearly exactly in Settle's play, which begins with a historically based plot of vengeance by "Amavanga" against Zhang Xianzhong (Chang Hsien-chung, or Changhienchungus) to defend her family honor (*Conquest of China*, 1.1.7).

41. New historical studies of the Ming/Qing transition that take into account Manchu texts have, as mentioned above, revised the narrative of Manchu acculturation to Chinese ways. Among these studies, see Perdue's comparative examination of global agrarian crises in western Europe and China that contributed to rebellions and fiscal crises in both regions of the world: *China Marches West*, 110. See also Waley-Cohen, *Culture of War in China*.

42. The Tartars' benevolent imperialism is exhibited first by Thienzungus and further by his successor and son, Zungteus. Regarding the former, Martini notes that "though he

lived not long yet he served for a good example for his Son to conquer *China* more by Civility and Humanitie, than by force of Armes" (*Bellum Tartaricum*, 264). In fact, Martini is mistaken in referring to the two men as separate rulers, Tienzungus and Zungteus, for the names instead refer to the two reign titles of Abahai taken at different moments (Tianzong and Chongde). The English ecclesiastic Peter Heylyn, in his genealogy of the Qing court, also refers to Thienzungus's "son" Zungteus, who in 1636 is "secretly brought up amongst the Chinese and is called into China by Usangueius," taking over Peking and then the rest of the kingdom. See Heylyn, *Cosmographie*, 400.

43. Martini, *Bellum Tartaricum*, 298.

44. Ibid., 293–95, 298. Adrien Greslon, in *Histoire de la Chine, sous la Domination des Tartares* (1671), describes one "Prince Amavan," whose courage as uncle and tutor helped raise the young emperor to the position of "Maistre de toute la Chine." In the advertisement to Greslon's text, we read, "La Chine est un Empire qui a plus d'entude, plus d'habitans & plus de richesses que tous les Royaumes de l'Europe. . . . Dans un Empire si puissant & d'une estendue si vaste, il ne se peut faire que les evenemens ne soient remarquables. Mais on ne craint point d'asseurer, que tout ce qu'on a veu, jusques a cette heure, touchant la Chine, n'est pas comparable a cette Histoire."

45. See Martini, *Bellum Tartaricum*, 278. Thanks to Peter Perdue and Mark Elliott for their translation advice about the Manchu word.

46. See, for example, Dapper, *Atlas Chinensis*. As Van Kley points out, while Jesuits such as Adam Schall von Bell and Gabriel de Magalhães write first-hand accounts of their experiences in China, Palafox y Mendoza not only borrows freely from other sources but, like the Domincan Domingo Fernández Navarette, takes an ideologically opposite stance with respect to the Jesuits; Van Kley, "An Alternative Muse," 22. While Settle's play is in fact based on history to a surprising degree, the license it takes has led to its dismissal as a fake: "To what extent Settle's play is Chinese may be judged from the names of the characters: Orunda, Alcinda, Amavanga, Quitazo, and Lycungus. Like all the heroic plays, whether Roman, Egyptian, Spanish, or Mexican in setting, *The Conquest of China* suffers from a total lack of either the historic or the geographical sense": Allen, *Tides in English Taste*, 22.

47. As Donald Lach points out, in contrast to Martini and Palafox y Mendoza, Magalhães, Navarette, and Bouvet offer bloodless accounts of the conquest: *Asia in the Making of Europe*, 3: 1674–75.

48. As made more explicit in Nieuhof's *Embassy from the East India Company to the Grand Tartar Cham* (1669), Zungteus "exchanged the rough and savage behaviour of his own Country, for the more civil and gentle behaviour of the Chineses" to reign with "mildness, moderation, and stability" and rather than with force of arms (300, 308). The year of this publication, 1669, also saw the start of Emperor Kangxi's reign; the new emperor, like his predecessor Shunzhi, extended favors toward the Jesuits that had been revoked in the five-year period (1664–69) between reigns. That Jesuit accounts of the conquest of China make legitimate heroes of the Tartars also reflects their situation of preferment, however tenuous, under the newly installed Qing regime. Numerous Jesuits at court, including the German astronomer Adam Schall von Bell, provided scientific counsel to the emperor and supplied firsthand accounts of their experiences for European readers. Schall acted as interpreter, in fact, for the Dutch embassy visit by Nieuhof in 1656. Nieuhof also incorporates the observations of Martino Martini, who in *Bellum Tartaricum* repeatedly moralizes

the mercy shown by the Tartars toward the Chinese and Christians alike. In his *History of the Two Tartar Conquerors,* d'Orléans similarly chronicles Adam Schall's efforts to convert the young emperor, "Xunchi" (Shunzhi), and interweaves Christian morals alongside critiques contrasting the "characteristic effeminacy of the Chinese" with "that constancy which we admire in the ancient Romans" (11, 12).

49. David Quint has outlined the difference between epic winners and losers according to the generic conventions of epic and romance. Romance, characterized as the loser's deviation from the epic plot and its goal of conquest, is associated with "the East, woman, nature, irrationality, and chaos, [which] consequently also embody a potential, indeed inevitable, collapse of narrative . . . and in the circuitous wanderings of romance." See Quint, *Epic and Empire,* 120.

50. This is much as the great, unknown outsider Almanzor, the lost son of the duke of Arcos and a Spaniard who fights on behalf of the Moors, is introduced in Dryden's seminal *Conquest of Granada* (1672). By comparison, the Chinese woman warrior Amavanga is introduced by Settle minus the epic similes and poetic eloquence but with arguably greater action.

51. Settle, *Conquest of China,* 1.1.7. On Chanquincungus, see note 40, above.

52. There is a rich body of scholarship on the ambiguity of the Restoration tragic hero, including the works of Loftis, *The Politics of Drama in Augustan England,* Staves, *Players' Scepters,* and Brown, *English Dramatic Form.* In his early work on Dryden's heroic plays, Derek Hughes argues for a depth of character, in particular a complex, flawed self-delusion of heroes like Almanzor, who in his striving for ideals is nonetheless far from exemplary. I am interested in shifting the discussion away from the exemplary hero to the exemplary cultures that inform spectacle; see Hughes, *Dryden's Heroic Plays.*

53. Dugaw, *Warrior Women and Popular Balladry,* 152.

54. Out of 375 plays produced between 1660–1700, 89 have one or more transvestite roles for actresses, 14 required women to don breeches to play roles originally written for men, and at least 3 plays were acted entirely by women taking on both male and female roles. See Franceschina, *Homosexualities in the English Theatre,* 119; Wilson, *All the King's Ladies,* 73. According to Howe, one-fourth of these Restoration plays used breeches roles. There was a great deal of competition between, for example, Killigrew and the Duke's Company for actresses and scenery: *First English Actresses,* 56–61.

55. Milhous, "Multimedia Spectacular on the Restoration Stage," 101. Howe, *First English Actresses,* 42. See also Hunt, "Restoration Acting," 448. The eroticized female body was not only a key component of Restoration spectacle, but also of developments in dramatic form and the shift from masculine conventions of heroic romance to the bourgeois ideology of the eighteenth century: Lowenthal, *Performing Identities;* Marsden, *Fatal Desire.* Canfield argues for a sudden shift from aristocratic to bourgeois ideology with the Glorious Revolution that differs from previous accounts of drama scholars like Susan Staves, Laura Brown, and Jean Marsden. See Canfield, *Heroes and States,* 145.

56. Although the first edition of the play was printed in 1676, it was acted first in 1673 or 1674: Brown, *Elkanah Settle,* 84. Lee reached the height of her success in the mid-1670s playing lead tragic roles, including three out of four of Settle's melodramas and, in addition to the cross-dressed Amavanga, swashbucklers in Thomas Durfey's *Madam*

Fickle (1676) and Settle's *Love and Revenge* (1674). As a vehicle for displaying the novelty of the woman actor, the epilogue was itself an innovation of Restoration theater, which controversially blurred the line between women's roles on and off stage. Epilogues as well as prologues were written especially for women, and they were personalized according to the particular actress and her private/public stage identity. During the period from 1660 to 1710, at last one hundred epilogues were spoken by named actresses, and twenty-six out of eighty actresses before 1689 delivered one or more prologues and epilogues. See Howe, *First English Actresses*, 94–95. See also Lowenthal, "Sticks and Rags," 222. Restoration critics like Jeremy Collier denounced the indecency of the familiarity assumed between actor and audience and the extension of the play's world of sexual passing into the space of live interaction with the audience. For Collier, women stepping out of a role to address the audience directly would be one step away from prostitution. See Collier, *Short View of Immortality and Profaneness*.

57. Waith, *Ideas of Greatness*, 223.

58. In fact, Van Kley, Orr, and Ros Ballaster read the comments as directed toward Amavanga, while Jeannie Dalporto, in her study of Settle's play, reads the stage directions as suggesting that Zungteus addresses solely Quitazo. Dalporto argues that the marriage between Tartar man and Chinese woman, on the one hand, and the political alliance of Tartar and Chinese male leaders, on the other, allegorizes the politics of England's Exclusion Crisis, thus reassuring Royalists and Protestants of the stability of monarchy. See Ballaster, *Fabulous Orients*, 202; Van Kley, "An Alternative Muse," 37; Orr, *Empire on the English Stage*, 107; Dalporto, "Succession Crisis," 142.

59. Bouvet, in *Portrait Historique de L'empereur de La Chine*, offers extreme praise for "Cang-hii" and "Amavang," such that Chinese are blamed for destroying themselves (60–61). On the balance between Tartar and Chinese, he writes of "des Tartars, par ce qu'ils disposent à la guerre; & à cultiver les Sciences, dont les Chinois sont presque tout leur merite" (14). In Martini's *Bellum Tartaricum*, Zungteus performs a gentle conquest of China: he exhibits "Humanity, and obliging courtesie" and an admirable recognition that "To the end he might conquer that Empire . . . as well by Love as by Arms" (266, 267). The representation of benevolence also reflects Jesuit efforts to convert China: this favorable assessment of Manchu strategy is juxtaposed with a Jesuit agenda of effective conversion apparent in the digression, "Love and humanity do work more upon mens hearts, in conquering and conserving Kingdomes, than Arms" (267).

60. Langbaine, *An Account of the English Dramatic Poets* (1691), 440. Langbaine includes as Settle's sources "Palafox Y Mendoza, John Gonzales de Mendoza, Lewis de Guzman, & etc." He curiously omits Martini, who is considered to be the authority of the period and who is often cited in subsequent accounts of China's conquest by the Tartars, including those of Johann Nieuhof and Peter Heylyn. The titles of the latter two works referred to by Langbaine are Juan Gonzales de Mendoza, *Historia de las cosas más notables, ritos y costumbres del gran reyno de la China* (trans. 1588); and Luis de Guzman, *Relacion de la entrada de algunos padres de la campagnia de Iesus en la China* (1605).

61. Hayot, *Hypothetical Mandarin*, 14. See also Hopkins, "Marlowe's Asia and the Feminization of Conquest," 115–30.

62. For studies of female virtue and suicide in chastity cultures in the Ming and early Qing period, see Ropp, Zamperini, and Zurndorfer, eds., *Passionate Women*.

63. Dryden, preface to *Aureng-Zebe*.

64. See Loftis, *Politics of Drama in Augustan England*, and Spurr, *England in the 1670s*.

65. Crowley, *Description of the Academy of the Athenian virtuosi*, 18.

66. Orr, *Empire and the English Stage*, 11, 61–62, 76.

67. See Orr's analysis, ibid, 3. She also rightly objects to the practice of "read[ing] through the exoticism of the Restoration heroic drama, to locate a local political meaning allegorized."

68. Markley, *The Far East and the English Imagination*.

69. Settle begins writing pope-burning pageants for the Whig party in 1679, followed by politicized plays like *Fatal Love* (1680) and *The Female Prelate* (1680) and pamphlets such as *The Character of Popish Successor* (1681). He changes his party alliance around 1683 with the rise of Tory power and is appointed City Poet in 1691, after which he returns to writing drama and opera, along with pageants and drolls for the Bartholomew's Fair. See Brown, *Elkanah Settle*.

70. Henry Morley, *Memoirs of Bartholomew Fair* (1874), quoted in Rogers, "Pope, Settle, and the Fall of Troy," 452.

71. Milhous, "Multimedia Spectacular on the Restoration Stage," 41.

72. This play, unlike the other two, achieved enough commercial success to be published with several "Sculptures," or engravings, of its elaborate set. Settle's spectacles of conflagration—including, later, *The Virgin Prophetess, or the Fate of Troy* (1701); *The Siege of Troy* (1707), and his *Elegy on the late Fire and Ruins of London* (1667)—even earned him a place in Alexander Pope's *Dunciad* as a representative of degenerate Grub Street culture. See Rogers, "Pope, Settle, and the Fall of Troy."

73. It should be noted that by the time he wrote *Aureng-Zebe*, Dryden already expressed dissatisfaction with the rhymed heroic. See Hume, "Dryden on Creation," 301. For details of the Dryden-Settle debates, see Doyle, ed., *Elkanah Settle's The Empress of Morocco*; Novak, *The Empress of Morocco and Its Critics: Settle, Dryden, Shadwell, Crowne, Duffet*; Settle, *Notes and observations on the Empress of Morocco*; Dryden, *Notes and observations on The empress of Morocco*.

74. Dryden, *Of Heroic Plays*, in *John Dryden (Three Plays)*, 7, 8–9, 10. In his preface to *The Rival Ladies* (1664), Dryden writes that rhyme "Bounds and Circumscribes the fancy": *Works of John Dryden*, 8:101.

75. In *Of Heroic Plays*, Dryden further writes of the freedom of the imagination such that the poet is "not tied to a bare representation of what is true, or exceeding probable": preface to *Conquest of Granada by the Spaniards* (1672). Cowley echoes this sentiment in *Description of the Academy of the Athenian virtuosi*, 22.

76. Quoted in Doyle, *Elkanah Settle's The Empress of Morocco*, xxi.

77. Toledo, *Politics and Reform in Spain and Viceregal Mexico*. According to Min-sun Chen, Palafox received letters via the Philippines from Macao most likely in 1648 or early 1649, shortly before he left Mexico for Spain. The English translation of his history appeared in 1671, with a second edition in 1676 and a third in 1670. See Chen, *Mythistory*

in Sino Western Contacts, 161. Palafox wanted European Christians to take the initiative to attack Ottoman Turks as the Tartars had attacked China: ibid., 167.

78. See Cummins, *Jesuit and Friar,* 409–10.

79. d'Orléans, *History of the Two Conquerors,* iv.

80. Palafox, *History of the Tartars,* 27, 37. From hereon I cite from the 1679 edition of the text. The suicide of the Empress Zhou and thirteen court ministers, along with the Chongzhen emperor's murder of the Princess Kunyi and wounding of two other women of the court, did occur, as did his own suicide, on April 25, 1644 (he strangled himself with his sash); but the existence of a suicide note and its purported contents has been a subject of continuing debate. See chapter 3 of Wakeman and Wakeman, *Telling Chinese History,* 67–70.

81. Van Kley, "An Alternative Muse," 37. See also Dalporto's reading of this episode, note 58.

82. Dryden, "Notes and Observations on *The Empress of Morocco,*" quoted in Doyle, *Elkanah Settle's Empress of Morocco,* 258. Although little documentation exists for the production of *The Conquest of China,* one of Settle's earlier plays, *Cambyses, King of Persia,* has been described as follows: "Theatrical effect is obtained by a duel, scenes with horrible stabbings, the appearance of a dead body, the head of which 'floats in a pail of blood,' 'bloody' clouds as portents, a masque in which spirits descend and ascend, and a woman's hand appears holding a bloody dagger, and finally, by the appearance of the ghosts of the murdered Cambyses and his brother Smerdis": Brown, *Elkanah Settle,* 82.

83. For a comparison of Restoration theater and civic pageantry in Lord Mayor's Day shows of the period, see Montaño, "Quest for Consensus," 31–51.

84. Temple, *Of Heroic Virtue,* 328.

85. See Orr, *Empire and the English Stage,* 61.

86. Canfield, *Heroes and States,* 24.

87. Orr argues that British themes and oceanic empire were too difficult to fit with traditional models of empire and "too ideologically fraught with republican valences" to compose plays. Although "trade was remarkably resistant to heroic celebration," plays set in the Ottoman Empire and India and China were produced during key disputes over England's naval campaigns and trade voyages to sites like Morocco and China: *Empire and the English Stage,* 258, 98.

88. Evelyn, *Navigation and Commerce,* 15.

89. Ibid., 53–54.

90. Semedo, preface to *History of that Renowned Monarchy.*

91. Le Comte, *Memoirs and Observations,* 320. Also quoted in Appleton, *A Cycle of Cathay,* 48.

92. For more on this theological controversy, see Mungello, *Curious Land,* 330–40.

93. The first French mission to China of 1685 consisted of six royal mathematicians, including Le Comte, and was headed by Jean de Fontaney. For further background on the mission, see Mungello, *Curious Land.* And for the work of these Jesuit scientists in the Qing court, see Elman, *On Their Own Terms.*

94. Le Comte, *Memoirs and Observations,* 24; emphasis added.

95. See Armistead, "Dryden's 'King Arthur,'" 53–72, and Merriman, *Flower of Kings*.

96. According to the *Oxford English Dictionary*, Banyans (or Banians) could refer to Gujarati or Hindu traders or to Hindus of Western India more generally. *Gentée* is most likely a variant of *Gentoo*, meaning Hindus, as well as being tied to the idea of gentiles, or heathens.

97. Ferguson, *A sober enquiry*, 21, 232.

98. Werner Sollors refers to the past usages of the term *ethnic* as the "pagan memory" of religious otherness, which is retained in current American usage and infers a "contrast between heathens and chosen people": *Beyond Ethnicity*, 25.

99. For a specific study of the links between ethnicity and nationalism in the British context, see Kidd, *British Identities*, and Yadav, *Before the Empire of English*. The relevance of ethnicity to empire with respect to the Qing dynasty has been explored by a number of historians, including Elliot, *The Manchu Way*, and Hostetler, *Qing Colonial Enterprise* (see note 3, above).

100. For detailed background on *Confucius Sinarum Philosophus*, see chapter 8 of Mungello, *Curious Land*.

101. The strategic idealization of Confucius initiated by Matteo Ricci was meant to delegitimize Buddhist and Taoist worldviews and promote Confucian virtues of *ren* (humanity), *li* (rituals and prosperity), *yi* (duty), and *zhi* (wisdom) in concert with Western learning. See Gernet, *China and the Christian Impact*, 55.

102. Israel, *Enlightenment Contested*, 649–55.

103. Ibid., 661.

104. Ibid., 641.

105. Temple, *Essay Upon the Ancient and Modern Learning*, 455, 460. All citations from this essay and *Of Heroic Virtue* are taken from the Clark Memorial Library 1964 edition.

106. Min, "China between the Ancients and the Moderns," 127.

107. Of course, the exemplification of rulers whose virtues contradict those of conquest or rule by force, and the example of Roman virtù, is not unique to Temple; see, for example, Erskine-Hill's discussion of Jean Bodin, Renaissance political theorist and author of *Six Livres de la République*, in *The Augustan Idea in English Literature*, 131.

108. For his armchair account of China's empire, Temple draws on travel writings by Paulus Venetus, Martino Martini, and Athanasius Kircher, but emphasizes that no one has traveled the extent of the country. The encyclopedic description of each of the four remote monarchies creates a mutually enforced standard of world civilization: the formulaic inventory of founding myths, history of invasions, architectural and scientific feats, and topographical features. Temple also links the distant parts of the globe through the language of heroic drama: "The next hero that came upon the stage was Cyrus"; "the stage of all these empires . . . is but a limited compass"; "the famous scene of the four great monarchies"; "peace and riches improving and adorning the several scenes of the world." Temple, *Of Heroic Virtue*, 320, 321, 322, 405.

109. Tooley, "Bodin and the Medieval Theory of Climate," 77.

110. In an earlier essay, without mention of China, Temple discusses the effect of climate upon governmental constitution: "The Nature of Man seems to be the same in all

times and places, but varyed like their statures, complexions, and features: by the force and influence of the several Climates where they are born and bred." *Essay Upon the Original and Nature of Government*, 45.

111. Lach, *Asia in the Making of Europe*, 3:1574–75.

112. The medieval theory of *translatio studii* held that in world history power transferred across four empires: one diffusion was from a second Renaissance in the Turks' conquest of Greece and Greek migrations to the Germans, Italians, and French. See Stierle, "Translatio Studii and Renaissance." For a useful study of Temple's use of cyclical history and climate theory, see also Macpherson, "Sir William Temple, Political Scientist?" 39–43.

113. See Marburg, *Sir William Temple: A Seventeenth Century "Libertine,"* 56–58.

114. Temple followed the lead of Jean Bodin, who also extolled the ideal ruler as one not the "conqueror by the sword . . . but the lawful or royal monarch" who followed the laws of primogeniture and nature and property (*Six Livres de la République*, quoted in Erskine-Hill, *The Augustan Idea in English Literature*, 131).

Chapter 2. Sincerity and Authenticity

1. A related imposture that preceded Psalmanazar's was a French woman named Couronné who claimed to be a Chinese princess and converted heathen. See Le Comte, *Memoirs and Observations*, 129–35. Fake Asiatic visitors and authorial personae rendered in printed form, largely through epistolary fictions, ranged from Giovanni Marana's Turkish spy, in *Letters Writ by a Turkish Spy* (London, 1687–94) and Montesquieu's Usbek and Rica in the *Persian Letters* (1721) to Oliver Goldsmith's Chinese philosopher Lien Chi Altangi in *The Citizen of the World* (1762).

2. A second, revised edition of the text was issued in English the following year in 1705; translations into French (1705) and German (1716) quickly followed. Unless otherwise noted, I cite from the 1704 edition and refer to it as the *Description of Formosa*.

3. *True and Faithful Account*, 32–33; quoted in Bond, *Queen Anne's American Kings*, 136. Psalmanazar describes the "addition of a letter or two" to the name, once he arrived in England. There are various spellings of the name in the eighteenth century, in particular the twice-doubled *a*, which was dropped over time. See Psalmanazar, *Memoirs of ****. Commonly known by the Name of George Psalmanazar*, 169.

4. Notable eighteenth-century literary forgers of lost relics of antiquity included Charles Bertram, James Macpherson, and Thomas Chatterton. According to Psalmanazar's *Memoirs*, he received 10 guineas for the first edition and 12 guineas for the second edition of the *Description of Formosa*. *Memoirs*, 220.

5. Piozzi, *Anecdotes of the late Samuel Johnson*, 173–75. Psalmanazar's Grub Street writings included articles for Samuel Palmer, *The General History of Printing* (1732); Emanuel Bowen, *A Complete System of Geography* (2 vols., 1744), to which he contributed entries on thirty countries including China and Japan and a confessional piece on Formosa; and *An Universal History from the Earliest Account of Time* (8 vols., 1736–50) and its twenty-volume octavo second edition (1747–54). To this he contributed writings on ancient history, including entries on the Jews, Scythians, and Ancient Greece. In addition, Psalmanazar drafted

a chapter for the continuation of Samuel Richardson's wildly successful epistolary novel, *Pamela*, in 1741 (roundly rejected by Richardson). The manuscript, "Pamela in Her Charities," is reprinted in Foley, *Great Formosan Impostor*, appendix B, 107–17.

6. For an excellent overview of European knowledge of Tokugawa Japan's policy of *sakoku*, see Lach, *Asia in the Making of Europe*, vol. 3. Although it happened long after Psalmanazar's claims of the Japanese colonization of Formosa, it should be noted that Taiwan was ceded to Japan from 1895 to 1945, following the Sino-Japanese War.

7. Ibid., 3: 1907.

8. For more thorough treatments of the entirety of his life and works, I defer to the number of full-length studies of Psalmanazar, in particular Foley's *Great Formosan Imposter*, Keevak's *Pretended Asian*, and Swiderski's *False Formosan*.

9. Notable studies of Psalmanazar's literary and ethnographic forgery and the related culture of eighteenth-century forgery include Stewart, *Crimes of Writing*, Liu, *Tokens of Exchange*, Needham, *Exemplars*, Adams, *Travelers and Travel Liars*, Lynch, *Deception and Detection*, Day, "Psalmanazar's 'Formosa,'" During, "Rousseau's Patrimony," and Mason, "Ethnographic Portraiture in the Eighteenth Century," 58–76.

10. Viswanathan, *Outside the Fold*, 43.

11. Agamben, *Homo Sacer*, 22. See the discussion of Agamben in my introduction.

12. Johnson, *Dictionary of the English Language*, vol. 1.

13. *Gentleman's Magazine* (London: Nov.–Jan. 1764). A 1764 review of his *Memoirs* also remarks, "[there is] no doubt of the genuineness of this performance"; quoted in Foley, *Great Formosan Impostor*, 73.

14. Evidence of the canonization of Psalmanazar as an example of eighteenth-century culture can be seen in the online edition of *The Norton Anthology of English Literature*, which opens its overview of "Travel, Trade, and the Expansion of Empire" with the story of Psalmanazar's fraud: www.wwnorton.com/college/english/nael/18century/topic_4/welcome.htm; accessed December 18, 2009.

15. Dryden, *Life of Plutarch*. See my introduction.

16. See Miller, *Popery and Politics in England*, and Haydon, *Anti-Catholicism in Eighteenth-century England*.

17. Preface to *Conversions and Persecutions of Eve Cohan*.

18. For a critique of the "Trade of Religion" with respect to corrupt clergymen, written from a deist position, see Toland, *Christianity Not Mysterious*, in Browne, *History of British Deism*, 203.

19. Hallywell, "Discourse of sincerity," in *The excellency of moral vertue*, 168.

20. Sheppard, *Sincerity and hypocrisy*, 5.

21. Hallywell, "Discourse of sincerity," 156, 162.

22. Psalmanazar, *Memoirs*, 130.

23. *History of the Works of the Learned* (April 1704), 244–45. Also in 1704, correspondence between John Locke and Anthony Collins around Psalmanazar shows an interest in his status of being a "Convert from paganism": Locke mss. c.7, f39 in the Bodleian Library, Oxford, quoted in Foley, *Great Formosan Impostor*, 23. The combination of the status of convert and native is invoked in references to Psalmanazar throughout his life. For example, John Hawkins wrote of "George Psalmanazar, a Frenchman, but who pretended

to be a native of the island of Formosa, and a convert from paganism to Christianity." *Life of Samuel Johnson Ll.D.*, 483.

24. Trilling, *Sincerity and Authenticity*, 2.

25. I borrow these terms from Shapin, *Social History of Truth*, xxvi.

26. Viswanathan, *Outside the Fold*, 16.

27. Questier, *Conversion, Politics, and Religion*, 18.

28. Psalmanazar, *Enquiry into Objections*, 60.

29. Japan and China were "classified as a single province in 1605" by the Jesuits, and Macao was an early base for missions to Japan, China, and Indochina. The early Christian missions to Japan produced an abundance of reports on Japan in the sixteenth century; hence, European readers' familiarity with the country at the beginning of the seventeenth century. Nonetheless, there was no new information about Japan between 1646 and 1669 as a result of the closed-door policy. See Lach, *Asia in the Making of Europe*, 3: 168, 174, 1829, 1886, 1689.

30. Psalmanazar, *Description of Formosa*, 20. In addition, the text throughout repeatedly refers to Jesuit "impostors" who "forge lies," and enact "impostures" and "artifice." Against the reported Jesuit successes in Asia, Anglican apologists attacked the motivations of the missionaries, the validity of Roman Catholic doctrines, and the validity of the conversions themselves. According to one source, Jesuits "tell the world of whole bodies of men, whole Nations and Countries and Sovereign Princes becoming Converts, when they know the contrary to be the real truth." See *The Missionarie's Arts Discovered*, 64. See also Vigne, *Sure and Honest Means*, 82–83; and *Epistle from a late Roman Catholick*, 16.

31. According to Psalmanazar, his father, a Japanese royal, employed de Rode to teach him Latin; see *Description of Formosa*, 4–5. In fact, Alexandre de Rhodes was a seventeenth-century Jesuit missionary stationed in Cochin-China and Vietnam who took a Chinese convert named Cheng Wei-hsin to Rome in the 1660s. This is another instance where Psalmanazar borrows details from Chinese history for his description of Japan. See later in this chapter for further details on de Rhodes.

32. Some of these details were based on ethnographic descriptions of Formosa and Japan by travel writers like Bernhardus Varenius, François Caron, Olfert Dapper, Arnoldus Montanus, Martino Martini, and Georgius Candidius, whose *A Short Account of the Island of Formosa* (1646) was the basis for most European writings on Formosa. But, as Michael Keevak has pointed out, Psalmanazar had not read Candidius before composing most of his *Description of Formosa*, which consists of fabricated details. Furthermore, the various historical sources themselves contained highly improbable and inconsistent information. See Keevak, *The Pretended Asian*, 21.

33. Foley, *Great Formosan Impostor*, 22.

34. By multiple accounts, as early as 1706 Psalmanazar was commonly known to be a fraud: Ibid., 38.

35. Psalmanazar, *Description of Formosa*, 72, 37. The text makes repeated mention of the "absurdities" of these doctrines (17, 20, 27, 30, 37, 130).

36. Ibid., 172.

37. According to his *Memoirs*, Psalmanazar developed an "uncommon genius for languages," beginning in his native France. He describes having received a classical educa-

tion at a Franciscan monastery and a Jesuit college. He studied Thomist and Dominican philosophy and later attended several French universities as a student of theology. By the time he decided to pose as an Asiatic heathen, his invented language was, he claimed, such a mixture of European languages that it could not be easily identified. (He cited as evidence of his linguistic showmanship the confusion of the Royal Society member Dr. Mead, who guessed his Formosan to be actually Dutch or German.) He claimed to have acquired the skill of writing in "Formosan," an even lesser-known language than Japanese, under the tutelage of his fellow impostor, the Reverend William Innes. Eventually, Psalmanazar changed his identity from Irish to Japanese because of Japan's relative obscurity. See *Memoirs*, 73.

38. See Keevak, *Pretended Asian*, 97.

39. Liu, "The Question of Meaning-Value in the Political Economy of the Sign," in Liu, *Tokens of Exchange*, 19.

40. Psalmanazar, *Description of Formosa*, 10.

41. According to the Englishman Edward Cresset upon returning from a visit to Holland, "some Thousands of Indians had of late beene converted, by means of a Dutch Minister conversing amongst them!" In a letter to Amsterdam, the consistory of Formosa reported that the Dutch Reformed missionary, the Reverend Robertus Junius, had baptized more than fifty-four hundred Formosans; the numbers grew to "the Conversion of five thousand nine hundred East Indians in the Isle Formosa, neere China, to the Profession of the true God, in Jesus Christ" in another account. And "seventeene thousand of those Indians were turn'd from their Paganism so farre," indicating the successful spread of the gospel in foreign parts and the achievement of an entire population of converts. See the Rev. William Campbell's *Account of missionary success in the island of Formosa*, 23. Although there was a lack of Protestant missionism in other parts of Asia, Formosa was a site of early Dutch proselytizing and development of a native church in the 1640s, beginning with the arrival in 1627 of Georgius Candidius, who was joined by Junius two years later. According to Donald Lach, by the 1690s, "Certainly by comparison to the English, the Dutch had won enough missionary successes in the seventeenth century to stir the envy and admiration of those across the channel who were then just beginning to think seriously about foreign missions": Lach, *Asia in the Making of Europe*, 3: 284. The late seventeenth century was a time of increased conversions in China as well, doubling from 105,000 in 1663 to 200,000 in 1695. See Brockey, *Journey to the East*, 141.

42. Campbell, *Account of missionary success*, 144–45. Native recitations included the Law of God, Articles of Belief, the Lord's Prayer, morning and evening prayers, and prayers before and after meals. Ibid., 98.

43. Ibid., 36.

44. Williams, *Keywords*, 215.

45. Psalmanazar makes repeated mention of his "passing" in *Memoirs*, 134, 176.

46. Gwinnet and Thomas, *Pylades and Corinna*, 65.

47. Shapin and Schaffer, *Leviathan and the Air-Pump*, 55–79.

48. Shapin, *Social History of Truth*, 126.

49. Boyle, *Christian Virtuoso*, 37. It should be noted that Boyle, in the capacity of an East India Company director, also proposed the propagation of the gospel in the East In-

dies after the example of Dutch missionary work in Batavia as early as 1677. See Lach, *Asia in the Making of Europe*, 3: 288.

50. Royal Society Journal Book 11, April 26, 1704; May 2, 1705; June 28, 1704. Foley very helpfully collects correspondence about Psalmanazar and reviews of his work, including other letters between Psalmanazar and Samuel Reynolds and details of his exchanges with critics such as the Jesuit Jean de Fontaney and the Huguenot pastor Isaac d'Amalvi, whose suspicions were published in *Eclaircissements Necessaires* early on. See Foley, *Great Formosan Impostor*, 86–106.

51. McKeon, *Origins of the English Novel*, 21.

52. Psalmanazar, *Memoirs*, 6.

53. Psalmanazar, *Description of Formosa*, 2nd preface. It should also be noted that, although European missionaries had been at work in Japan since the late sixteenth century, translations of Jesuit records reached England only in the 1720s and 1730s, and these accounts were themselves riddled with inconsistencies.

54. Newman, "Some Queries," April 24, 1705, Letter Book 14, 97. The minutes of a June 20, 1705 meeting state: "[S]ome Letters were Read from Mr. Newman to Mr. Griffith, & Answers from Mr. Griffith to Mr. Newman, concerning Formosa; Mr. Griffith (who has been at Formosa, and tarried long there,) does in these his Letters contradict the Account lately given of it by Mr. George Psalmaanasaar. Mr. Grifffyth, Mr. Newman, & Mr. Chamberlayne were Order'd the Thanks of the Society." See Index of Papers, 703. It should be noted that "Tayouan" did, in fact, refer to a small island off the southwestern coast of Formosa in the 1600s; it was the original site of a Dutch fortification that would become Fort Zeelandia.

55. Newman, "Second Letter of Queries," May 29, 1705.

56. While they contained some details about regional practices, a rejection of Psalmanazar's account of child sacrifice, and general skepticism toward "romantic" facts, Griffiths's responses nonetheless reflected his ignorance of a number of matters such as language, internal geography, and foreign trade. He had visited Formosa in 1672 and traveled between there, Amoy, and finally Bantam over a five-year period; but more often than not, he was unable to refute with certainty Psalmanazar's claims. Moreover, he confirmed some of Psalmanazar's Formosan behaviors, such as heavy smoking.

57. Psalmanazar attempted to dismiss the damaging testimony of Isaac d'Amalvi, minister of the French church at Sluys where he was converted, by accusing him of personal bias. See d'Amalvi, *Eclercissements necessaires*. Psalmanazar also blames the French translator often for some of d'Amalvi's objections and cites the language barrier, the translation from Latin to English to French, as being a "false Translation" (*Enquiry into the Objections*, 68). In response to d'Amalvi's book, he includes an "Answer to a Book Entitled *Eclercissements*" at the end of his *Enquiry*.

58. Psalmanazar, *Dialogue Between a Japonese and a Formosan*, 27.

59. Psalmanazar, *Enquiry*, 20.

60. It is Candidius who writes that the Chinese call Formosa Paceande, which later becomes Psalmanazar's Pakando. This corresponds with the third-century AD Malayan word for south Formosa, Pekan. See Goddard, *Formosa: A Study in Chinese History*, xvi.

61. See Jacques Derrida's definition of supplementarity, borrowed from Levi-Strauss's

figure of the *bricoleur*: [T]he sign which replaces the center, which supplements it, taking the center's place in its absence—this sign is added, occurs as a surplus, as a *supplement*. The movement of signification adds something, which results in the fact that there is always more, but this addition is a floating one because it comes to perform a vicarious function, to supplement a lack on the part of the signified (91). Derrida, "Structure, Sign, and Play," 88.

62. Psalmanazar, *Enquiry*, 44.

63. Psalmanazar, *Description of Formosa*, 222.

64. Michael Keevak offers an informative study of the question of Psalmanazar's whiteness by comparing available engravings of Formosans, whose primary physical differences, he argues, had more to do with clothing than skin color. See chapter 2 of Keevak's *Pretended Asian*.

65. Journal Book 11, August 11, 1703.

66. Psalmanazar, *Description of Formosa*, 223.

67. Wheeler, introduction to *Complexion of Race*.

68. For two additional, useful overviews of the climate theories of Montesquieu, Buffon, and other Enlightenment philosophers, see Popkin, "Philosophical Basis of Eighteenth-Century Racism," 3: 245–62, and Eze, *Race and the Enlightenment*.

69. In addition to his Feb. 2, 1703 debate with Fontenay at the Royal Society, he describes a dinner on Feb. 9 with Hans Sloane, Lord Pembroke, Spanhemius, the king of Prussia's envoy, and Fontaney. Also, he meets with Fontaney and "several Noblemen" at the Temple Coffee House in Devereux Court. See preface to the *Description of Formosa*, x, xi.

70. See Shapiro, introduction to *A Culture of Fact*.

71. Locke, *Essay concerning Human Understanding*, 656.

72. Shapin interprets Locke as leaving out the factor of trust and making the error of being too systematic a skeptic; Locke's "problem of Siamese skepticism" in turn demonstrates the interrelation of "thing-knowledge" and "people knowledge": *Social History of Truth*, 291.

73. Robert Boyle further presents the scenario that the East Indian accuses the Englishman of lying about the cold, which is meant to illustrate that natural phenomena can seem incredible, and therefore merit analysis. See Shapin's account of Boyle's experiments with extreme cold and the levity of icebergs in seawater in *Social History of Truth*, 253–66.

74. Among the public responses to the presence of the "Indian Kings" were imaginative accounts by Joseph Addison in two issues of the *Spectator*, April 27, 1711 (no. 50) and May 4, 1711 (no. 56). Excellent studies of the Indian Kings in London include Bond, *Queen Anne's American Kings*; Roach, *Cities of the Dead*, chap. 4; and Brown, *Fables of Modernity*, chap. 5.

75. See Brown, *Fables of Modernity*, 187.

76. *True and Faithful Account*, 32–33; quoted in Bond, *Queen Anne's American Kings*, 136.

77. Foss, "European Sojourn of Philippe Couplet and Michael Shen Fuzong," 124.

78. De Rhodes was known primarily for his missionary work in Vietnam and Cochin-China. See Rouleau, *The first Chinese priest of the Society of Jesus*, 3–50.

79. See Foley, *Great Formosan Impostor*, 34, n. 44.

80. I am indebted to the research of Theodore Foss in particular for details of the life of Shen Fuzong. Shen was the son of prominent Christians in China. He left China via Macao in 1681 with the Jesuit Philippe Couplet. They arrived in Holland in 1683 and traveled throughout the continent making court appearances to promote the Jesuit mission and to aid with scholarship on China. While in Paris, Shen helped Couplet with his *Clavis Sinica* and possibly Gabriel de Magalhães with his *Nouvelle Relation de la Chine* (1690) between Spring 1686 and November 1687. In Rome, they made an ambitious request to Pope Innocent XI for approval of the use of Chinese language in the liturgy; their petition marked the heightening controversy over the Jesuit accommodation of native rites and customs, and in particular whether the practice of Confucianism by Chinese Christians constituted idolatry. Although Couplet's request was eventually denied by Rome, he did succeed in challenging its authority over the Chinese mission by gaining the support of Catholic France. Foss attributes the initiation of the French mission to China in 1685 to the impact of Shen Fuzong's Paris visit. See Foss, "European Sojourn," 123, 129–30, 135. For information on Shen's time in England, including his cataloguing of Chinese books at Oxford's library and correspondence with the antiquarian and Orientalist Thomas Hyde, see Wood, *Anthony Wood's Life & Times*, vol. 3, 236–37. Another informative study of Shen Fuzong that draws on Foss's work is Timmermans, "Michael Shen Fuzong's Journey to the West," 173–203. Thanks to Mark Stephen Mir for directing me to this source.

81. Kneller's life-size work was hung in the Presence Chamber of James II. For studies of this painting, described as one of Kneller's finest, see Barnett, "The Chinese Convert," and Stewart, *Sir Godfrey Kneller*. The king received the papal nuncio at court in July 1687. Timmermans suggests that his commissioning of Shen's portrait was an attempt to align himself with Louis XIV at a moment when he was also attempting to appoint a Roman Catholic president to Magdalen College. Shen was thus "an obvious symbol of the exiled king's ambitions to reconcile his lost kingdom within a Roman Catholic *imperium*": "Michael Shen Fuzong's Journey to the West," 192–93.

82. "Chinese Convert" appears to be a misnomer in that Shen was born of Christian parents and was thus not technically converted by Couplet; however, the term *convert* could be used to refer to the offspring of converts as well. See Timmermans, "Michael Shen Fuzong's Journey to the West," 189.

83. Fr. De La Chaize, confessor to Louis XIV, called Shen "an object of great royal attention, clothed in green silk and deep blue brocade adorned with Chinese dragons and eating with chopsticks." Quoted in Mungello, *Curious Land*, 255.

84. Another exemplary Chinese Christian behind the scenes was Candida Xu, a devout Catholic of Songjiang who donated to Couplet embroideries for churches in Europe. See Brockey, *Journey to the East*, 140.

85. For overviews of chinoiserie in eighteenth-century England, see Honour, *Chinoiserie: The Vision of Cathay*; Impey, *Chinoiserie*; Jacobson, *Chinoiserie*.

86. See, for example, Liu, *Seeds of a Different Eden*, 13, 14.

87. Porter, *Ideographia*, 135–37.

88. Chambers, *Cyclopaedia*, 1: 367.

89. This distinction has not been well understood. Keevak, for example, mistakes the

product for "chinaware." See *Pretended Asian*, 9. In an effort to build upon yet differentiate Formosa from China, Psalmanazar, in his *Description of Formosa*, claimed that the Formosans were superior makers of porcelain compared with the Chinese: "very curious in making Dishes, which they call *Porcellane*, and the *English China-Ware*; and 'tis very well known, that in this Art they excel the *Chinese* and all the oriental People" (292). By opting to use the Italian name for porcelain, *porcellana*, named for the polished cowrie shells it resembled, Psalmanazar highlights the constructedness of the idea of "China," a place-name subject to multiple translations and Western fictions of origins.

90. This definition of japanning is taken from *The Oxford English Dictionary*. For further analysis of the discourse of japanning, see Yang, "Asia Out of Place," 235–53.

91. Stalker and Parker, *A Treatise of Japaning and Varnishing* (London, 1688), xiv–xv.

92. Chinese "specimens" (gunpowder, sesame, and washballs of soap) were brought back, tabulated, and examined among a host of other curiosities. Royal Society Journal Book 11, March 1, 1703/4.

93. Royal Society Journal Book 11, Feb. 2, 1703/4.

Chapter 3. Transmigration, Fabulous Pedagogy, and the Morals of the Orient

1. According to Galland, "Sous le nom des Orientaux, je ne comprens pas seulement les Arabes & les Persans; mais encoure les Turcs & les Tartares, & presque tous les peuples de l'Asie jusques à la Chine, Mahometans & Païens ou Idolatres": preface to *Les Paroles Remarquables*.

2. To cite from the first English translation of the Koran in 1649, "Good reader, the great Arabian impostor, now at last, after a thousand years, is, by way of France, arrived in England, and his Alcoran . . . hath learned to speak English": Ross, *The Alcoran of Mahomet*, in Chew, *Crescent and Rose*, 449. This French translation of the Koran was made by Le Sieur du Ryer in 1649. An English version of this translation came out in the same year, accompanied by a biography of Mahomet and commentary on the potential dangers and benefits of reading it. George Sale's influential version was not published until 1734. See Chew, *Crescent and Rose*, 448–51; also Smith, *Islam in English Literature*, 106, 502.

3. Although the original Arabic manuscript was written in Egypt or Syria during the thirteenth century, only half of the published *Nuits* actually come from the original manuscript. See Haddawy, introduction to *The Arabian Nights*, ix–xxxi; and Mahdi, *The Thousand and One Nights*, 33, 11, 29.

4. Oriental tales, after all, offered fantasies of consumerism and magical out-of-body experiences of the type that could transform a street urchin like Aladdin, with the aid of an ordinary-looking lamp, into a ruler of the kingdom of China, the outermost edge of the moral geography of the Orient and the exemplification of its commercial and moral excesses. The story of Aladdin is actually obtained separately, orally and in writing, from a Christian Maronite named Hanna of Damascus. In fact, Galland writes the thousand and first night in order to create a unified work that is then attributed to the intentions of a single Arabic author, and later canonized as a coherent work of Oriental literature. See Mahdi, *The Thousand and One Nights*, 32. Also, see Mack, introduction to *Arabian Nights'*

Entertainments. In Galland's redactions of the *Arabian Nights*, China appears in numerous tales as a magical setting of jewels and porcelain, east of east. The overland and overseas trade networks that linked China to numerous other empires and tributary states thus also positioned it as part of a wide-ranging and imagined moral-economic geography. See, for example, studies of the history of Eurasia on the early Silk Routes as well as the later maritime and tributary trades of the Qing empire that determined the wide-ranging and shifting coordinates of China and the Orient: Wood, *The Silk Road*; Perdue, *China Marches West*; Struve, *The Qing Formation in World-Historical Time*. See also work on European entrance into the Asian trading world by Chaudhuri, *Trading World of Asia*, and Furber, *Rival Empires of Trade*.

5. By Egyptian accounts, metempsychosis entailed a system of punishments whereby animals contained the souls of the wicked for thousands of years before returning to mortal form. See Long, *Study of the Doctrine of Metempsychosis in Greece*. Different versions are attributed to Pythagoras by accounts of Herodotus, Porphyry, Dicaearchus, and Philolaus. Later theories of metempsychosis by Empedocles were also attached to dietary restrictions on eating animals. See Kahn, *Pythgaoras and the Pythagoreans*, Sorabji, *Animal Minds and Human Morals*, and Riedweg, *Pythagoras*.

6. For Walter Benjamin, "Oriental" narrators like Sheherazade exemplify the art of epic storytelling. Benjamin is interested in the decline of the epic, the disintegration of the storyteller's memory, and the development of the novel as based on a singular hero rather than a multitude of epic events. Srinivas Aravamudan has argued for the Oriental foundations of the Western novel by scrutinizing the teleological emphasis on the rise of realism by Western literary scholars of the novel: see "In the Wake of the Novel," 5–31.

7. Two translations of an edited compilation of these tales, *The Persian and the Turkish Tales, Compleat*, by Ambrose Philips and William King, were also published in 1714.

8. The *Spectator* was published daily, except for Sundays, from March 1, 1711, to December 1712 (nos. 1–555). After this, the papers were issued three times a week, without Steele's participation, from June to December, 1714 (nos. 556–635). In addition to Addison and Steele, regular contributors included John Hughes, Eustace Budgell, and Thomas Tickell. The issues examined in this chapter are largely authored by Addison, although the names of the authors of some of the issues are unknown. For scholarship on Oriental tales, see Caracciolo, *The Arabian Nights in English Literature*. Most recently, the work on the Oriental tale has recognized the global reach of its influence. See Makdisi and Nussbaum, *The Arabian Nights in Historical Context*.

9. Brown, *Fables of Modernity*.

10. Ballaster, introduction to *Fabulous Orients*.

11. The unavailability of the resin of the *Rhus vernicifera* in Europe and North America forced Europeans to use other tree deposits such as gum-lac, seed-lac, and shell-lac. See Huth, *Lacquer of the West*; Appleton, *A Cycle of Cathay*.

12. Temple, *Of Heroic Virtue*, in *Works of Sir William Temple*, 382. One of the most graphic literary accounts of idolatry in China is in Defoe's *Farther Adventures of Robinson Crusoe*. See Markley, " 'So inexhaustible a treasure of gold': Defoe, Credit, and the Romance of the South Seas," in *The Far East and the English Imagination*, and Starr, "Defoe and

China," 435–54. The translation of the *Morals of Confucius* (1692) also laments that rational Confucianism has given way to idol worship in China.

13. Repeated pronouncements against the rituals of ancestor worship by the Roman Catholic Church would culminate in the papal bull *Ex quo singulari*, issued by Pope Benedict XIV in 1742. See *100 Roman Documents Concerning the Chinese Rites Controversy*, 21.

14. See Porter's discussion of the Jesuit denouncement of Buddhist "superstition" in *Ideographia*, chapter 2. See also Pocock, "Gibbon and the Idol Fo," 15–34.

15. Accounts of Buddhism did, however, differentiate between the belief in reincarnation as successive punishments for external actions and belief in rebirths, which proceed according to degrees of enlightenment: Lach, *Asia in the Making of Europe*, 3:1654–56.

16. For an excellent study of Kircher's interest in the history of Nestorian-Christians in China, see Billings, "Untranslation Theory," 89–114.

17. Kircher, *China Illustrata*, 127.

18. Ibid., 217, 134, 397.

19. Le Comte, *Memoirs and Observations*, 323.

20. Kircher in turn references the earlier Jesuits Martino Martini and Nicolas Trigault. See Nieuhof, *Embassy*, 260, 262, 395.

21. Ramsay, *Travels of Cyprus*, 70.

22. For a discussion of euhemerism, see the very informative account in Manuel, *The Eighteenth Century Confronts the Gods*, 85–128.

23. Toland, "The History of the Soul's Immortality," in *Letters to Serena*, 57.

24. Bernier, *Travels*; Ovington, *Voyage to Surat*.

25. Stuart, *Bloodless Revolution*, 53.

26. Ibid., 41–48.

27. Even the most distasteful and taboo aspects of corporeality are employed to illustrate the "Order of Things" that connects and levels all living creatures. See Conway, *The Principle of the Most Ancient and Modern Philosophy*, 182, 232. Influenced by Jewish mysticism and the ancient teachings of Origen, Cambridge Platonists like Henry More and Joseph Glanvill adapted Origen's ancient theological teachings on the soul's preexistence into a spiritual philosophy of the soul's eternal travels outside the human body, between heaven and earth. They drew from the "pagan" writings of Plato, Socrates, Plotinus, and Pythagoras. Borrowing from this range of ancient and "Oriental" belief systems, their Anglican brand of Platonism espouses the worldly presence of spirit as an eternal truth on which nature is patterned. Later generations of theosophists, with interests in Buddhism and Brahmanism, considered the Cambridge Platonists "Mystic Guides." See, for example, Pope, *Mysticism*, preface.

28. Burnet refuses to speculate on the fate of the soul after the body's death, arguing that it can be known only by God. Originally written in Latin, Burnet's *De statu mortuorum* was published in English posthumously as the *Treatise Concerning the State of Departed Souls* (London, 1739, 2nd ed.), 110.

29. Conant, *The Oriental Tale in England*, 118.

30. Dacier, *Life of Pythagoras*, 36.

31. Stackhouse, introduction to Gueullette, *Chinese Tales*, 2nd ed. (1740).

32. Gueullette, *Chinese Tales* (1725), 1: viii, xv.

33. Among the society that Mr. Spectator keeps is Sir Roger de Coverly, Sir Andrew Freeport, Captain Sentry, and Will Honeycomb; see no. 3: Bond, introduction to *Spectator*, xviii, xx.

34. Habermas, *Structural Transformation of the Public Sphere*.

35. See Mackie, introduction to *Commerce of Everyday Life*, 2–3. I am indebted to Mackie's groundbreaking study of women and consumption in *Market à la Mode*.

36. The efflorescence of the fable form between 1692 and 1722 is marked by the collections of Aesopic fables by Tory Sir Roger L'Estrange and Whig Samuel Croxall. See Daniel, "Political and Philosophical Uses of the Fable," 153.

37. See Lewis, *The English Fable*, 63. Other notable fables were La Fontaine's translations of Aesop and Phaedrus, published between 1668 and 1694. English partisan fables included Dryden's *The Hind and the Panther* (1687) and *The Cock and the Fox* (1700). Addison's Whiggism can be contrasted with Ogilby and L'Estrange's Tory and Jacobite sympathies. Addison cites L'Estrange frequently and appropriates his fables for nonpolemical purposes; for example, in *Spectator* nos. 23 and 25. For Addison's Whig politics, see Bloom and Bloom, *Joseph Addison's Sociable Animal*. For Addison's place in the changing social economy, see also Pocock, *Virtue, Commerce, and History*, 235.

38. Lewis, *The English Fable*, 49–50.

39. Palmeri, *Humans and Other Animals in Eighteenth-Century British Culture*, 84. For a study of the impact of natural history and empirical science on the culture of fables, see also Robbins, *Elephant Slaves and Pampered Parrots*. For key studies of the fable in eighteenth-century literature, see Lewis, *The English Fable*; Loveridge, *History of Augustan Fable*; Blackham, *Fable as Literature*; Noel, *Theories of the Fable*.

40. Other influential studies of the changing attitudes toward animals in the seventeenth and long eighteenth centuries include Thomas, *Man and the Natural World*; Serpell, *In the Company of Animals*; Plumb, "The Acceptance of Modernity"; Ritvo, *The Animal Estate*; Fudge, *Perceiving Animals*; Brown, *Fables of Modernity*, and *Homeless Dogs*; and Palmeri, *Humans and Other Animals*.

41. Preface to *Fables Ancient and Modern*. *Spectator* nos. 343 and 578 are prefaced by Ovidian epigraphs, and no. 211 quotes a passage from Ovid's "Of the Pythagorean Philosophy."

42. Ballaster, *Fabulous Orients*, 119.

43. Pollock, *Gender and the Fictions of the Public Sphere*, 11, 12.

44. Gelley, *Unruly Examples*, 152, 161.

45. Quoted in Feldman and Richardson, *Rise of Modern Mythology*, 82.

46. For instance, see the animal fables cited in nos. 23, 25, 124, which draw from Roger L'Estrange's *Fables*. These are discussed in far less detail than the Turkish tale is here. The influence of Eastern fables can also be seen in the translations of the Indian philosopher Bidpai's fables, as the *Fables of Pilpay*, beginning in 1699. See Ballaster's discussion of Indian fables in *Fabulous Orients*.

47. For a discussion of slavery and liberty in the life of Aesop, see Patterson, *Fables of Power*, 15.

48. In no. 287, for example, Addison defends the three-branch system of English gov-

ernment and the "Civil part of [the] Constitution" against the feared "despotical government in a single person" (19). The moment of fable's triumph recalls its deployment, in *Spectator* no. 183, to quell a riotous public and prevent mutiny in ancient Greece, "when perhaps they would have torn to Pieces any Man who had Preached the same Doctrine to them in an open and direct manner" (212).

49. The preface to de la Croix's *Turkish Tales* claims that the Turks, being naturally predisposed against the "Fair Sex," call the work "The Malice of Women" derisively. It is claimed to be an authentic Turkish text, authored by one Chec Zady [or Zade] to instruct and divert his pupil, the Sultan Amurath II. In its original form in the *Turkish Tales*, "The Fable of the Two Owls" is told by the bitter young sultanness Canzada as part of a storytelling battle between the sexes to win the favor of her husband, the sultan, over his son, the falsely accused prince; see the preface to *Turkish Tales*.

50. The language of cultural proximity is also used to describe the moral of the "Story of Alnaschar," a fable about a man who learns a lesson about greed through a series of magical punishments. The genre of the Arabian fable is inherently moral, and the reader should imagine himself as a "near Relation to the *Persian* Glass-Man" (*Spectator* no. 535, 410).

51. On the "neutralization" of Judaism, Islam, and paganism in Anglican discourse of the period, see Champion, *Pillars of Priestcraft Shaken*, 114. Interestingly enough, as a rationalist and Socinian, Locke is accused of being "Moslem" because of the association of Socinians and Unitarians with Islam: ibid., 106. For instances where Addison neutralizes Eastern practices through the figure of a virtuous physician, see *Spectator* no. 195, where Addison recalls the "Story of the Grecian King and the Physician Douban," and no. 94, "Adventures of the Egyptian Sultan," another fable taken from the *Turkish Tales*. This story is introduced as an illustration of two theories of the subjective experience of time—Locke's theory of dreams and Malebranche's theory of the succession of ideas. Addison leaves it up to the reader to determine the viability of these accounts. As he concludes, "I shall leave my Reader to compare these Eastern fables with the Notions of those two great Philosophers whom I have quoted" (no. 94, 401). In drawing the resemblance, he implicitly interprets Eastern religion as a matter of misguided perspective. For an illuminating discussion of the *Turkish Tales* source of no. 94, see Ballaster, *Fabulous Orients*, 114–30.

52. The following paper, no. 211, then performs the public response of husbands and wives who write in to confirm the represented gender types. For example, one Martha Tempest writes in complaining that her husband, taken with the idea that "the Souls of some Women are made of Sea Water," addresses her volatile, sealike tempers with corresponding watery language such as "be Calm" and "do not bluster" (no. 211, 325–27).

53. While it is true that fabulous pedagogy operates through the Orient's ornamentalism, I disagree that the Orient is merely topical, or what has been called "the *image* of the unknown or unfamiliar as instilled through allusions and word choice." See Kay, *Short Fiction in* The Spectator, 8: 82.

54. Pope, *Essay on Man*, 15, line 206.

55. In the original tale, the king gives up his throne and becomes a merchant, left with his memory of Zemroude, and with a marvelous story of his past life with which to console others in distress. His triumph over adversity showcases male fidelity and undying love,

in keeping with the premise of the *Persian Tales*, in which a nurse tells story after story of virtuous men in an attempt to convince a man-hating princess to marry: de la Croix, "The Story of Prince Fadlallah, Son of Bin-Ortoc, King of Mousel," in *Persian and Turkish Tales*.

56. The author of the issue draws on Locke's philosophies of person identity, memory, and the challenge of locating identity: "[I]t is Consciousness alone, and not an Identity of Substance, which makes . . . personal Identity or Sameness" (no. 578, 575). See Locke, *Essay Concerning Human Understanding*. In chapter 27, "Of Identity and Diversity," Locke is particularly interested in the idea that the consciousness of one's actions can hold a person accountable to herself and the world around her; it is this accountability that determines her identity. While Locke disagrees with theories of transmigration that hold that bad souls are demoted to the bodies of beasts, he does allow for the movement of souls across bodies. At the same time, there is a limit to the exchangeability of identities, and that limit is the body.

57. Todorov, *The Fantastic*, 41.

58. For a consideration of talking animals in satire and beast fable with regard to the readerly pleasure involved with identifying and transposing animal and human, see Perry, "Unpicking the Seam," 19–36.

59. Brown, *Homeless Dogs*, 68.

60. Notable studies of lap dogs include Tague, "Dead Pets," 289–306; Brown's *Homeless Dogs*, and Braunshneider, "Lady and Lapdog," 31–48. Both Brown and Braunschneider refer to the interchangeability of monkey, lapdog, and china in literature of the eighteenth century. The cataloguing of commodities that objectifies the human has also been treated by Crehan, "The Rape of the Lock and Economy," 45–68. Aravamudan writes on pets and slaves in *Tropicopolitans*, and Tobin on the treatment of African slaves like animal pets in *Picturing Imperial Power*. I would further emphasize that the common eighteenth-century trio of monkey, lapdog, and china is not culturally unmarked but, rather, united by the commodities' associations with the East India trade. Not only are they Eastern imports but, as my discussion of transmigration highlights, they embody the circulations of Oriental exemplarity. See related discussion of the genre of circulating commodity and the "it-narrative" in Blackwell, *Secret Life of Things*.

61. The name Fum-Hoam appears in Heylyn's *Cosmographie in Four Bookes* as a special type of Chinese bird resembling a phoenix. This name also appears as the character of a Chinese official in Goldsmith's *Citizen of the World*. In Chinese, the *feng-huang* is a legendary, magnificent bird symbolizing luck: *feng* signifies the male, and *huang*, the female phoenix.

62. Later in the eighteenth century the legend of Hsiang-fei appears. Hsiang-fei, a beautiful Muslim princess, is captured by the Chinese emperor, Chao-hui, upon his conquest of the Eastern Turkestan capital of Yarkand in 1758. She is taken to Peking, where he builds her a Muslim quarter southwest of the Winter Palace. See Hummel, *Eminent Chinese of the Ch'ing Period*, 74. Thanks to Ho-chin Yang for this reference.

63. Ballaster, *Fabulous Orients*, 35.

64. Conant, *Oriental Tale in England*, 36.

65. "The Story of Aladdin," the supplementary *Tale*, takes place in China, the East of

the Arab world. In fact, it is in a "subterranean abode in the midst of China" that the magic lamp is first found. See Mack, *Arabian Nights' Entertainments*, 659.

66. Preface to *Persian Tales*, vol. 1.

67. Dryden, *Fables Ancient and Modern*, 527. On Dryden's translation of Ovid and further articulations of vegetarianism in the seventeenth century, including writings praising Indian religious customs toward animals, see Corse, "Dryden's 'Vegetarian' Philosopher," 1–28.

68. Dutch lacquerware experimentations begin in the 1610s and peak in the 1690s. See Jarry, *Chinoiserie*, 132, 138. For East-West manufactures, see Berg, "Asian Luxuries," 228–44. See also my discussion of japanning: Yang, "Asia Out of Place," 235–53.

69. McCracken, *Culture and Consumption*. See also Mackie's discussion of patina in *Market à la Mode*, 13.

70. Dossie, *Handmaid to the Arts*, 479.

71. Buc'hoz, *The toilet of Flora*, 233.

72. *New London Toilet*, xv, xiii.

73. In the eighteenth century, face painting and dark skin colors were thought to prevent the readability of facial features (namely, the all-revealing blush of modesty) by displaying an unapproachable stoicism. Gwilliam studies the racial and sexual politics of face painting in the West Indian context in "Cosmetic Poetics," 144–59. See also Chico, "Arts of Beauty," 1–23.

74. Pope, *The Rape of the Lock*, 8.

75. J. Oldmixon, "To His Ingenious Friend Thomas Greenhill," and B.B., "To his Friend the Author," in preface to Greenhill, *Nekrokedeia*.

76. Stalker and Parker, xiv–xv.

77. Porter, *Ideographia*; Lach, *Asia in the Making of Europe*.

78. The universal kinship normally implied by transmigration leads to unacceptable interconnections and the equally untenable ends of vegetarianism/cannibalism, as insightfully argued by Shell, "Family Pet," 129.

Chapter 4. Luxury, Moral Sentiment, *and* The Orphan of China

1. In a letter to Voltaire appended to the text of *The Orphan of China*, Murphy describes Garrick's performance as "exquisite powers . . . capable of adding Pathos and Harmony even to our great SHAKESPEAR" (96). See also the praise for Garrick as Zamti in *An Account of the New Tragedy of the Orphan of China*. As quoted in Price, *Theatre in the Age of Garrick*, Garrick was "inimitable in Zamti; in nothing he had ever performed was he greater, except in King Lear" (159).

2. Review. "Art. 24 *The Orphan of China*," 575. Note that the play was also reviewed and summarized in *The Universal Magazine* and *The London Magazine* issues of May 1759. Like Settle's *Conquest of China*, Murphy's play drastically simplifies the detailed ethnohistory of China's northern border wars; but this conquest play reaches further back in history to adapt an actual thirteenth-century Yuan dynasty play about the Mongol, rather than Manchu, invasions. *The Orphan of Zhao (Zhaoshi Guer*, or *Chao-Shih Ku-Erh)* is the

rare example of a work of Chinese literature that was translated and circulated widely in eighteenth-century Europe. A translation by the Jesuit Joseph de Brémare appears first in Jean-Baptiste Du Halde's *Description de la Chine* [*General History of China*], an authoritative source on China that underwent a spate of rival translations into English in book form and magazine installments between 1738 and 1742. Although adapted for the stage by William Hatchett in 1741 as *The Chinese Orphan: An Historical Tragedy*, the first performed version of the play was Voltaire's *L'Orphelin de la Chine*, which debuted in Paris in 1755. See Fan, *Dr. Johnson and Chinese Culture*. English translations of the original Yuan dynasty opera include Wong, *The Orphan of China*, and *Six Yüan Plays*, trans. Liu Jung-en. Liu Wu-chi transliterates the play as "Chao-Shih Ku-Er" in his article "The Original Orphan of China," 193–212. See also two translation histories of this play by Chen, "The Chinese Orphan," and Hsia, "*Orphan of the House Zhao,*" 383–97.

3. Ann Douglas, quoted in Agnew, *Worlds Apart*, 187. For studies of eighteenth-century identity and sensibility, see also the work of Barker-Benfield, *Culture of Sensibility*, and Wahrman, *Making of the Modern Self*.

4. Hatchett, *The Chinese Orphan*, vi.

5. Goldsmith, *Citizen of the World*, 24.

6. As studied by Berry, luxury is the "fault-line" of the century: *Idea of Luxury*, 139.

7. Sekora, *Luxury*, 66.

8. Murphy, *Orphan of China*, 89.

9. Brown, *Estimate of the Manners and Principles of the Times*, 170–71.

10. Dennis, *Essay Upon Publick Spirit*, 15. See also Hume, "Of National Characters," for this idea of the women who "ripen" earlier in the tropics: Hume, *Political Essays*, 90.

11. Berg and Eger, *Luxury in the Eighteenth Century*. See also Berg, *Luxury and Pleasure*. For accounts of the British protectionism against foreign imports from France and China in the 1750s, see also Berg and Clifford, *Consumers and Luxury*, 77.

12. According to Montesquieu, the "good man" upholds "the supremacy of the moral law, the principle of justice, rather than mere contract." See Wittuck, *The "Good Man,"* 192, 195.

13. Montesquieu, *Spirit of the Laws*, xli–xlii.

14. Appleby, "Consumption in Early Modern Social Thought," 167.

15. Pocock, *Machiavellian Moment*, 492–93.

16. Murphy, *Orphan of China*, 49. The name Timurkan appears to add *khan*, the honorific, to the Turkic name of the fourteenth-century military leader Temür, popularly referred to as Tamerlane in Western literature of the Medieval and Renaissance periods. Here, Timurkan is meant to stand for the Mongol Kublai Khan, founder of the Yuan dynasty in 1271.

17. For a discussion of this genre of victimized heroines, see Brown, chapter 3 of *Ends of Empire*.

18. For a discussion of female hysteria and sensibility, see Barker-Benfield, *Culture of Sensibility*; Brown, *Fables of Modernity*, 113–15, 179–80; Ellis, *Politics of Sensibility*.

19. McKeon, *Origins of the English Novel*, 156. Indeed, it has been argued that women's appearances on stage brought about the generic shift from heroic tragedy to the later she-tragedy, from the age of honor to that of virtue. A coterie of leading tragic actress-stars who excelled in representing emotions developed the new role of the suffering heroine. See, for

example, Milhous, "Multimedia Spectacular"; Straub, *Sexual Suspects;* Howe, *First English Actresses,* 111; Lowenthal, *Performing Identities.*

20. Barker-Benfield, *Culture of Sensibility,* 141, 151.

21. Ibid., 268.

22. Joyce Tomkins notes the proliferation of phrases like "luxury of tears" and "luxurious woe" in works of the mid to late eighteenth century: *Popular Novel in England,* 103 n. 1.

23. Hume, *Treatise of Human Nature,* 316.

24. See, for example, reviews in the *London Magazine,* 267; and *Account of the New Tragedy.*

25. Epilogue, *Orphan of China.* From hereon, I cite parenthetically from the 1759 text.

26. My reading of Mandane's female passion posits female influence as of less direct effect than masculine virtue, and yet more than simply the "tragic consequences of female interferences in state affairs" at work in other plays of the period. See Freeman's discussion of female passions, tragedy, and patriotism in *Character's Theater,* 143.

27. On the sentimental family as civilizing agent, see Barker-Benfield, *Culture of Sensibility,* 217.

28. Given the star power of Garrick-as-Zamti, the orphan does not take center stage, despite Murphy's intention of increasing the moral agency of Voltaire's orphan (and the Yuan orphan) by beginning the play twenty years after its original starting point. This is also evidenced by Garrick's initial indecision over which male role to play as lead. For the difficulties in Garrick's collaboration with Murphy, see Murphy, *Life of David Garrick.*

29. See Reichwein, *China and Europe,* 80.

30. Murphy, *Orphan of China,* 6, 27, 48, 71.

31. *An Account of the New Tragedy of the Orphan of China,* 16.

32. Du Halde, *General History of China.*

33. Percy, *Miscellaneous Pieces Relating to the Chinese.*

34. The physiocrat François Quesnay's idealization of enlightened Chinese despotism is reprinted in Maverick, *China: Model for Europe.*

35. Montesquieu, *Spirit of Laws,* 41, 295–96.

36. For those like Montesquieu, the Orient characterizes a despotic form of government, where there is no division between public and private. While Montesquieu supports his antiabsolutist stance by exaggerating the accounts of China's despotism that he derives from travel documents, Voltaire supports absolute monarchy and in fact idealizes China's monarchy. See Krause, "Despotism in the *Spirit of Laws,*" 231–72. See also Ching and Oxtoby, *Moral Enlightenment.*

37. Montesquieu, *Spirit of the Laws,* xliii.

38. Whitehead's *The Roman Father* is an adaptation of Corneille's *Horace* (1635) and *Creusa,* a rewriting of Euripedes' *Ion.* See Wood, "William Whitehead," 334–41. See also references in Porter, *Ideographia,* 167–68.

39. The patriotism of the above lines participates in a climate of anti-French agitation that advocates Protestant rule above all else, even the laws of kingly hereditary succession. See Linda Colley on the rise of patriotic societies in the 1750s as the "authentic voice of the bourgeois patriot" and the mutual dependence of the commercial and landed classes aligned as Britons against French Catholicism in a period of wars: *Britons: Forging the Na-*

tion, 1707–1837, 97. More specifically, Whitehead's patriotism lies in the dedication to the earl of Bute and the play's political ties to Henry Fox. His previous *Verses to the People of England* of 1758 also participates in anti-Gallic passion. That China is a degraded alternative to the classicism of Greek and Rome is in line with Whitehead's preference for classics in his poetry and in plays such as *The Roman Father* and *Creusa, Queen of Athens*. See also the work of Suvir Kaul for invocations of liberty that set Britain apart from Rome: *Poems of Nation, Anthems of Empire*.

40. The void of moral authority is then filled by, for example, utilitarianism or a discourse of individual rights; see MacIntyre, *After Virtue*, 198.

41. As Hume puts it in *A Treatise of Human Nature*, "sympathy . . . is much fainter than our concern for ourselves, and sympathy with persons remote from us much fainter than that with persons near and contiguous" (603).

42. Ferguson, *The Morality of Stage-Plays Seriously Considered*, 7.

43. Like Jean-Christophe Agnew and David Marshall, Force comments on the use of theatrical metaphors to establish social relations as one of spectator and spectacle: Agnew, *Worlds Apart*; Marshall, *Figure of Theater*; Force, *Self-interest before Adam Smith*.

44. Smith, *The Theory of Moral Sentiments* (2000), 466.

45. The section on Voltaire was likely added as early as 1760 or 1761; whereas the earthquake example appears for the first time in the 1790 edition.

46. My emphasis. Smith, *Letter to the Edinburgh Review*.

47. Thanks to Sanjay Krishnan for suggesting this point to me.

48. The metaphor of spectatorship takes the form of an outsider's perspective on English society most explicitly in the proliferation of "foreign observer fiction" of the period. In Goldsmith's *Citizen of the World*, Giovanni Marana's *Turkish Spy*, and Montesquieu's *Persian Letters*, to name a few important instances, cultural difference as articulated by various Oriental visitors becomes a mirror of the strengths and weaknesses of Western society. The effectiveness of the foreign exemplar (Chinese characters of the stage) or commentator (the visitor to England who writes letters home to China) lies less in his authenticity as much as in the shared acknowledgment of his constructedness. This text's enactment of distance—that is, the staging of foreignness—becomes the basis of a spectator's or reader's continued interest, even as it is made clear that foreignness (and the alterity it embodies) mediates the proper circulation and moral affirmation of sympathy.

49. Susan Neiman goes as far as to argue that the Lisbon earthquake marks a shift in Western thought that distinguishes the concept of natural evil from moral evil: *Evil in Modern Thought*. See Voltaire's "Poem Upon the Destruction of Lisbon"; also see his *Candide* for the attack on the idea put forth by Pope and Leibniz that "whatever is, is right": Ingram, "'The trembling Earth is God's Herald.'"

50. Hayot, *The Hypothetical Mandarin*.

51. Goldsmith criticizes the play's overemphasis of virtue (the playwright "has perhaps, too frequently, mentioned the word *virtue*"): "Review of the Orphan of China," 456, 434–35.

52. Voltaire, preface, *The Orphan of China*, 175.

53. Quoted in Percy, *Miscellaneous Pieces Relating to the Chinese*, vol. 1, 41.

54. There is a new meaning of luxury in the eighteenth century that is less about ex-

cessive display and more about the workings of commerce. See Berg and Eger, *Luxury in the Eighteenth Century*, 9.

55. Fawconer, *Essay on Modern Luxury*, 5.
56. Ibid., 15.
57. Ibid., 24.
58. Ibid., 44–45.
59. *Works of the English Poets* 14, 246.
60. Kaul, *Poems of Nation, Anthems of Empire*, 90.
61. Kowaleski-Wallace, *Consuming Subjects*, 1–37.
62. Porter, *Ideographia*, 195–98.
63. Murphy, *Orphan of China*, 1.2.431. For a discussion of the spectacular effect of this type of scene-changing, see Price, *Theatre in the Age of Garrick*, 70.
64. *Account of the New Tragedy*, 11–12.
65. The participation of French choreographers, designers, and dancers for this pantomime ignited riots by patriotic theatergoers for days. See Fitzgerald, *Life of David Garrick*, 162, 184. For more information on the French-English tensions and riots around the performances of the *Chinese Festival* in London, see Hedgcock, *Cosmopolitan Actor*. Murphy's *The Orphan of China* was itself delayed due to extensive revisions and squabbling internal to the theater world: Dunbar, *Dramatic Career of Arthur Murphy*. See Fitzgerald, *Life of Garrick*, 162, 184. See also Watts's discussion of Garrick's *The Harlequin's Invasion* as an instance of anti-Gallicism. *Cultural Work of Empire*, 7–8.
66. Hedgcock, *Cosmopolitan Actor*, 128.
67. To borrow from the philosopher Roland Barthes, "In that absolute, dogmatic, vengeful present tense in which Fashion speaks, the rhetorical system possesses reasons which seem to reconnect it to a more manageable, more distant time": Barthes, *The Fashion System*, 273.
68. Jefferys, *A Collection of the Dresses*, xiii.
69. See Price, *Theatre in the Age of Garrick*, 57. Jefferys's collection includes descriptions and engraved plates of dresses from dozens of nations and ten plates of Chinese fashion taken mostly from Du Halde. See Price, *Theatre in the Age of Garrick*, 38–47. Also included in vol. 2 of Jefferys's book is the "Habits of the English Stage."
70. Boaden, *Memoirs of Mrs. Siddons*, 69.
71. *Account of the New Tragedy*, 12.
72. Fitzgerald, *Life of David Garrick*, 388.
73. Robert Hitchcock, *An Historical View of the Irish Stage* (1788); quoted in Dunbar, *Dramatic Career of Arthur Murphy*, 69.
74. Le Comte, *Memoirs and Observations*, 128.
75. Ibid., 137.
76. Du Halde, *General History of China*, 141.
77. McKendrick, Brewer, and Plumb, *Birth of Consumer Society*, 36.
78. Mrs. Yates goes on to mention that only in cheating and greed do the Chinese resemble the Europeans—a conciliatory point often made by influential travel writers like Louis Le Comte, who also records China's "countenance, Air, Language, Disposition, Civilities, Manners and Behavior." In fact, Mrs. Yates's comments echo Le Comte's discus-

sion of differences in Chinese physiognomy, perspective, foot binding, and fashion; but he concludes in more explicit language with the absolute difference between the women of China and those of France: "the Mind, Countenance, and Behaviour of the *Chinese* women have no Affinity with those of the *Europeans*": Le Comte, *Memoirs and Observations*, 126. It is typical of these travel narratives to include extensive descriptions of dress, both women's and men's. See also works of Du Halde, *Description of China*; Palafox y Mendoza, *History of the Conquest of China*; and Kircher, *China Illustrata*.

79. The lengthiest tenet of "The Fundamental Laws" uses physiognomy to register absolute difference between Chinese and foreigners. It adopts a curious analysis of China's self-imposed insularity: "That if any foreigner be found . . . he is easily known to the world; for the Chinese have always been used to crush the noses of their children as soon as born, which render the greatest part of the Chinese *flat-nosed*, therefore any foreigner must be known by this distinction." In *An Account of the New Tragedy*, 15.

80. McCracken, *Culture and Consumption*, 100. Scholars in the past two decades, following the work of John Brewer and Neil McKendrick, have revised trickle-down theories of emulation and conspicuous consumption in a number of ways. See Campbell, *Romantic Ethic*, and Hunt, *Governance of the Consuming Passions*, 68.

81. Josiah Wedgwood, *Letter*, 1767; quoted in Berg, *Luxury and Pleasure*, 81.

82. My emphasis. Goldsmith, "Review of the Orphan of China," 434–35.

83. Berg, *Luxury and Pleasure*, 242. Elsewhere Berg notes the establishment of the Society of Arts in 1754 to create an English style in manufactures based on a principle of imitation. See Berg and Clifford, *Consumers and Luxury*, 77. Berg's study of patents issued between 1625 and 1825 is very useful for making the case for how crucial imitation is for the British economy: *Consumers and Luxury*. See also Woodruff D. Smith's discussion of the calico craze spread by Parisian salons dictating tastes and the problem of English spinners and weavers who had inferior printing technologies to Chinese silks and Indian cotton: *Consumption and the Making of Respectability*, 54, 57. The eighteenth-century writer Robert Dossie comments on the spread of luxury from East to West and the need to develop manufactures to supplant trade of imports in a climate of competition with France; imitation is crucial for the economy. Dossie, *Handmaid to the Arts*.

84. Ferguson, *Essay on the History of Civil Society*, 332.

85. Postlethwayt, *Britain's Commercial Interest*, 213, 219.

86. Ibid., 214. Hume takes a more measured approach when he writes, "[A] nation may lose of its foreign trade, and yet continue a great and powerful people. . . . China is represented as one of the most flourishing empires in the world; though it has very little commerce beyond its own territories": Hume, "Of Commerce," 155.

87. Livy and an earlier generation of writers, including Sallust and Cicero, document the dangers of Rome's conquests of Asia and avaricious plundering; see Berry, *Idea of Luxury*, and Dalby, *Empire of Pleasures*.

88. Melon, *Political Essay Upon Commerce*, 174, 176.

89. Hume, "Of Luxury," 161, 158. What he designates "innocent luxury" turns into "vicious luxury," the "source of many ills," only when abused by "excessive" human behaviors, 163, 164.

90. Hume, "Of Commerce," 155.

91. Hume, "Of Luxury," 162.

92. Postlethwayt, *Britain's Commercial Interest*, 219. Ferguson, in *Essay on the History of Civil Society*, 54, also writes about communication: "[T]he benefits arising from liberty . . . are not the fruits of a virtue, and a goodness, which operate in the breast of one man, but the communication of virtue itself to many; and such a distribution of functions in civil society, as gives to numbers the exercises and occupations which pertain to their nature."

93. Indeed, as Adam Smith concurs, in the trade wars with France, imitation proves to be a "source of wonder" in developing substitute import products: Smith, "Of the Nature of that Imitation," in *Essays on Philosophical Subjects*, 198–99, 224. See de Marchi, "Adam Smith's accommodation of 'altogether endless' desires," 18–36. Dossie, *Handmaid to the Arts*, 95, comments on the spread of luxury from East to West and the need to develop manufactures to supplant trade of imports.

94. Hume, "Of Commerce," 155.

95. Hume, "Of Luxury," 157.

96. Fawconer, *Essay on Modern Luxury*, 55.

97. I borrow the phrase "strangers and superfluities" from Mandeville, *The Fable of the Bees and Other Writings*, 96.

Epilogue. Orientalism, Globalization, and the New Business of Spectacle

1. Galland, *Les Paroles Remarquables*.

2. Johnson, *History of Rasselas*, 105.

3. Hegel, *Philosophy of History*, 163–66.

4. Said, *Orientalism*, 123.

5. See Ahmad, "Between Orientalism and Historicism"; Behdad, *Belated Travelers*; King, *Orientalism and Religion*; MacKenzie, *Orientalism*.

6. Said, *Orientalism*, 3.

7. "Puccini Prises [sic] Open Forbidden City," *South China Morning Post*, May 21, 1998, 20; *Academic Universe*. Lexis-Nexis, Cornell University, Olin Library, Mar. 6, 2003; "'Turandot' Vows Mother of All Opera Sets," *Korea Herald*, Mar. 13, 2003, accessed May 1, 2003; Lisa Minder, "Multinational Production of 'Turandot' Has Stormy Beginning in China," *Deutsche Press-Agentur*, Sept. 3, 1998; *Academic Universe*, Lexis-Nexis, Mar. 6, 2003. All references to *Academic Universe* and Lexis-Nexis were accessed at Cornell University's Olin Library.

8. Miller, *The Turandot Project*.

9. Other noteworthy interpretive changes included featuring a young Chinese acrobatic dancer in the role of Turandot's executioner; also, Zhang insisted that the slave Liu kill herself more authentically, with, instead of a dagger, a hairpin she wrests from Turandot's head. See Miller, *Turandot Project*.

10. Anne Naham and Alexandra A. Seno, "Dress Code: Ming," *Asiaweek*, July 17, 1998; www.lexis-nexis.com/. Also see Renee Schoof, "Puccini's Lavish Chinese Opera Dazzles in Beijing's Forbidden City," *Associated Press*, Sept. 4, 1998; www.lexis-nexis.com/.

11. Alexandra A. Seno and Anne Naham, "A Princess Returns," *Asiaweek*, July 17, 1998; www.lexis-nexis.com/.

12. See de la Croix, *The Persian and the Turkish Tales*. We can see the influence of *Persian Tales* and in particular the reproduction of Turandoucte's riddles in Joseph Addison's "The Persian Emperor's Riddle," *Freeholder*, no. 17, Feb. 17, 1716. The tale reached Puccini's attention in the 1920s through multiple translations—from the Italian playwright Carlo Gozzi's 1762 tragicomedy to Schiller's 1802 German interpretation of Gozzi and finally to the direct translation of this version back into Italian in 1863. See Black, "Carlo Gozzi's 'Turandot,'" 55–56.

13. The sultan of "Carizme" refers to the Khwarazmids (1096–1230), whose empire before being defeated by the Mongols covered part of Iran and neighboring Central Asia.

14. "The Story of Prince Calaf and the Princess of China" contains an embedded tale, the "Story of Prince Fadlallah, Son of Bin-Ortoc, King of Mousel," where Calaf and his family are given shelter by a man who comforts them with his own story of misfortune—a parallel tale of exile, wandering, and love for a princess. However, the stranger's case involves being tricked into transmigrating out of his own body into a series of animals before he wins back his identity, only to tragically lose his wife; he spends the rest of his days mourning her death. This storyteller is none other than Fadlallah, whose tale of transmigrations and male fidelity, "Fadlallah and Zemroude," was discussed in my chapter 3 as *Spectator* no. 578. Yet another subplot enhances the visual spectacle evoked in the tale: Tourandocte's slave Adelmule, a captive princess herself, commits suicide out of her unrequited love for Calaf. The funeral pomp to honor the slave's memory precedes the wedding of Tourandocte and Calaf and paves the way for China's support of Calaf's exiled family in regaining their throne. See *The Persian and the Turkish Tales*. Puccini's adaptation of this story from the *Persian Tales* is rich with thematic links that could be further explored; for example, see Ballaster's insightful reading of Turandot's riddles in *Fabulous Orients*, 193–202. My interest, however, is less in the details of literary adaptation than in the cultures of performance and the productions of spectacle enabled by the tale.

15. Loren Jenkins, "The 'Pornographic' Chinese Opera," *Salon Newsreal*, June 26, 1998; www.salon.com/news/1998/06/26newsb.html; accessed Apr. 4, 2003. The Ministry of Culture had promoted the *Peony Pavilion*, directed by Chen Shizheng, to be performed at New York City's Lincoln Center as part of a "cultural exchange" between China and the United States. At the last minute, the Shanghai Bureau of Culture prevented it from traveling due to the opera's purported pornography and feudal superstition. This example of cultural censorship was cited in US media coverage of President Bill Clinton's historic nine-day visit to China, during which he and President Jiang Zemin met, in June 1998. The censorship case added to pessimism over the genuine cooperativeness of China at this time. A caption next to the pictures of Jiang and Clinton read, "In China, despite currents of change, the deep despotism of the centuries is never far below the calm surface waters." See also John Pomfret and Steven Mufson, "Clinton Makes the Most of Opportunity in China," *Washington Post*, July 5, 1998; www.washingtonpost.com/wp-srv/inatl/longterm/china/stories/clinton070598.htm (Apr. 4, 2003).

16. Liu Kang argues that the academic critiques of Zhang's Orientalism and his Fifth Generation revival of the folkloric overlook "the mechanism of a global cultural market by which both the new cinema and academic film criticism are commodified as profitable cultural products." Chinese ethnic theme parks and touristic marketing of ruins "serve

the double purpose of reinforcing nationalist sentiments and transforming local space into a global site for tourism." Kang, "Is There an Alternative to (Capitalist) Globalization?" 164–88. For an analysis of the folkloric in Japan, see Ivy, *Discourses of the Vanishing*. For a useful overview of mediatized sports and theories of globalization, see Hargreaves, "Globalisation Theory, Global Sport, and Nations and Nationalism," 25–43. See also Maguire, *Global Sport*.

17. "China had 1,300 exchange activities with about 20,000 people involved in 1998. China also signed cultural agreements with Central Africa and Yemen, new executive plans with over 20 countries, and a memorandum of understanding with Canada.... Last February, over 500 relics from museums in 17 provinces were put on display in the U.S., with United Nations Secretary-General Kofi Annan attending the opening ceremony of China's largest display abroad." This statement was reported in "China Active in Cultural Exchanges in 1998," *Xinhua News Agency*, 6 January 1999. *Academic Universe*, Lexis-Nexis (Mar. 6, 2003).

18. Renee Schoof, "Zubin Mehta, Zhang Yimou to Stage Turandot in Imperial Palace," *Associated Press*, 8 July 1998, *Academic Universe*, Lexi-Nexis. For one thing, an international *Turandot* would bandage China's damaged "cultural reputation" over the government's much-criticized refusal to allow another opera, *The Peony Pavilion*, from traveling to New York's Lincoln Center three months earlier. Kevin Platt, "How Chinese Remade 'Turandot,' the Italian Opera on China," *Christian Science Monitor*, Sept. 14, 1998, *Academic Universe*. Lexis-Nexis (Mar. 6, 2003). See also Susan H. Greenberg and Leslie Pappas, "Forbidden Arias," *Newsweek*, Sept. 14, 1998, Atlantic ed. *Academic Universe*. Lexis-Nexis (Mar. 6, 2003). See "Puccini Prises Open Forbidden City," *South China Morning Post*, May 21, 1998: 20; www.lexis-nexis.com/.

19. "Puccini Prises [sic] Open Forbidden City."

20. Despite China's censorship of his films in the 1980s and 1990s—among them, *Ju Dou*, *Raise the Red Lantern*, and *To Live*—Zhang has now had a run of state-sponsored or state-friendly spectacles that have moved beyond the movie theater into the arena of opera and sports. Both the film *Hero* (2002) and the opera *The First Emperor* (2006), commissioned by the New York City Metropolitan Opera, glorify the violent unification of China into the Qin Dynasty in 221 BC by the first emperor, Qin Shi Huangdi. For an excellent study of Zhang Yimou's earlier filmmaking, his controversial use of Orientalism, and relationship to the Chinese government, see Chow's chapter "The Force of Surfaces," in *Primitive Passions*. Writing against Western critics of Zhang Yimou's Orientalism, Chow reinterprets the seemingly clichéd representation of the Orient as a subversive and deliberately confrontational gesture. She is interested in the "parodying [of] orientalism's politic of visuality" and the "affect of exhibitionism," rather than the Western spectator's "voyeurism" (169–71).

21. Ong Sor Fern, "Life! Cover Story Riddles If You Want to Marry Her," *Straits Times*, Singapore, Sept. 9, 1998; www.lexis-nexis.com/.

22. See Miller, *Turandot Project*.

23. Chow, *Primitive Passions*, 145. See also Shih's incisive discussion of Orientalism and Sinophone artists working in and through the Asian diaspora in *Visuality and Identity*.

24. Opera on Original Site, Inc., official Web site, www.opera-on-site.com/home_e

.html, accessed May 15, 2003. The unprecedented $15 million budget produced eight consecutive, globally televised performances by three sets of international leading divas and soloists. The thirty-three thousand available tickets ranged in price from $150 to $2,000. Elites from around the world traveled to the imperial palace grounds, which were configured to seat an audience of forty-two hundred. An outdoor sound system was engineered by the Vienna State Opera.

25. Such was the strategy later adopted by the Egyptian government in deciding to transfer *Aida* out of Luxor after a militant attack in 1997 that killed some sixty tourists in front of the Queen Hatshepsut Temple, where the opera had most recently been staged. "Middle East Aida Comes Home," *BBC News Online*, Oct. 13, 1998; www.lexis-nexis.com/. See also Douglas Jehl, "70 Die in Attack at Egypt Temple," *New York Times on the Web*, Nov. 18, 1997; www.lexis-nexis.com/; accessed May 19, 2003.

26. For the further history of the Italian and Egyptian geopolitics involved with the production and ideology of *Aida*, see Budden, *Operas of Verdi*, and Brener, *Opera Offstage*.

27. As the Khedive stated, "My country is no longer in Africa. I have made it part of Europe." Quoted in Tambling, *Opera and the Culture of Fascism*, 77. See the work of Abu-Lughod, *Cairo*, and Mitchell, *Colonizing Egypt*.

28. Opera, from the start a state-sponsored art form, also stages the renewal of violence and the rise of the crowd: in *Turandot* and *Aida*, we see the spectacular suffering of Asiatic women at the mercy of the masculine will. It is worth noting that the works of Puccini and Verdi span periods of economic depression and losses of national glory that stimulate the type of nationalist mythmaking that would some decades later accompany the rise of fascism in Italy. Opera, and *Aida* in particular, entered Egypt at a moment that preceded the transition from French to British colonial rule in 1882. On the introduction of the term *imperialism* in the 1870s, see Hobsbawm, *Age of Empire*, 51.

29. Kaplan, *Questions of Travel*, 63.

30. Horne, *Great Museum*, as quoted in Kaplan, *Questions of Travel*, 63. See MacCannell, *The Tourist*; Smith, *Hosts and Guests*; and Chow, *Primitive Passions*.

31. For the 1998 World Cup festivities, the missing obelisk, transplanted from the Luxor Temple to the Place de la Concorde in Paris, was transformed into a "towering replica of the World Cup, topped by video screens"—an original, a sign of civilization removed from its original site, is transformed into a modern sign of global inclusiveness. While its twin obelisk was featured in an opera on site amid the commodified ruins of civilization, it performs the sportsmanship of the future, globalization's dream of civilization, dressed up in media technology. Once again, Eastern antiquity is imported by the cosmopolitan West: Jon Henley, "All Eyes Rivetted on Paris for Fete du Foot," *Indian Express*, June 10, 1998; www.expressindia.com/ie/daily/19980610/16150754.html.

32. Rehab Saad, "Verdi's Aida Moved Back to the Pyramids," *Al-Ahram Weekly On-line*, 375 (1998); http://weekly.ahram.org.eg/1998/375/egy7.htm. See also Baudrillard, *Simulacra and Simulation*, 13.

33. Saad, "Verdi's Aida Moved Back to the Pyramids."

34. Teresa Poole, "Financial Curtains for Puccini in Peking as Asian Crisis Bites," *Independent*, Sept. 18, 1998; www.lexis-nexis.com/.

35. The Italian Culture Ministry invested $1.5 million for costumes, orchestra, and cho-

rus. The China Performing Arts Agency was responsible for 10 percent of the budget in return for 45 percent of gross ticket sales. Opera on Original Site put in $11 million, which it attempted to earn back through sale of media rights, sponsorship, and donations, and 55 percent of ticket sales. Apart from the China Performing Arts Agency, all media music rights were presold to CLT UFA International, owned by German media conglomerate Bertelsmann, for a fee of approximately $2.5 million. These figures are cited in Poole, "Financial Curtains."

36. A future project for Opera on Original Site, Bizet's *Carmen,* in Sevilla, Spain, would actually incorporate tourism into the performance itself by scheduling each act at a different historic site in Sevilla, with intermissions an hour-plus long to allow the audience to promenade to the next act/site. As the website advertisement notes, "For those who do not wish to walk and for the handicapped, picturesque horse-drawn carriages and buses will be available. These changes of location are an integral part of the evening and will add a new dimension to the enjoyment of an evening out." Promenades will of course include local food, artisan items, and entertainment along the way—meant to emulate the traditional Spanish *paseo* and parade: *Carmen in Sevilla: Newsletter,* www.carmen-in-sevilla.com/C_E/newsletter_e.htm; accessed May 15, 2003.

37. *Turandot* official Web site, www.turandot.co.kr/sub_en_01_01.html; accessed May 1, 2003. See also Warren Lee, "'Turandot' Scores Big at World Cup Stadium," *Korea Herald,* May 10, 2003; "'Turandot' Vows Mother of All Opera Sets," *Korea Herald,* Mar. 13, 2003; "Spectacular Year Ahead for Local Opera Fans," *Korea Herald,* Apr. 5, 2003; and Choe Yong-shik, "'Turandot' Opera Set to Shatter Korean Ticket Price Record in May," *Korea Herald,* Feb. 12, 2003; www.lexis-nexis.com/. At 6 billion won, this was the most expensive Korean opera production ever. This use of opera, and *Turandot* in particular, as a mark of Westernization can also be seen in the case of Turkey's efforts to join the European Union. As argued in one journalistic article, "Turkey will be fully European when we have an opera going public. . . . *Turandot* in my mind with its rich cast and setting should travel to Europe and if possible to all 15 EU member countries, to display how Turkey become part of the European culture, musically and artistically": Yuksel Soylemez, "Opera Notebook: A Chinese Princess Passed through Ankara," *Turkish Daily News,* Jan. 9, 2003; www.lexis-nexis.com/.

38. In reality, of course, the difficulty of gaining admission into the international football federation due to economic and political barriers has led to critics' designation of a World Cup State. See Miller, *Globalization and Sport,* 12–13, 24–27. See also Alan Tomlinson, "Theorizing Spectacle: Beyond Debord," in Sugden and Tomlinson, *Power Games,* 44–60.

Abu-Lughod, Janet. *Cairo: 1001 Years of the City Victorious*. Princeton, N.J.: Princeton University Press, 1971.
An Account of the New Tragedy of the Orphan of China, and Its Representation . . . to Which Are Subjoined, by Way of Illustration, the Fundamental Laws of China. London [1759].
Adams, Percy G. *Travelers and Travel Liars, 1660–1800*. Berkeley: University of California Press, 1962.
Addison, Joseph. "The Persian Emperor's Riddle." *Freeholder*, no. 17, Feb. 17, 1716.
Addison and Steele: Selections from the Tatler *and the* Spectator. 2nd. ed. Ed. Robert J. Allen. New York: Holt, Rinehart & Winston, 1970.
Agamben, Giorgio. *Homo Sacer: Sovereign Power and Bare Life*. Trans. Daniel Heller-Roazen. Stanford, Calif.: Stanford University Press, 1998.
Agnew, Jean-Christophe. *Worlds Apart: The Market and the Theater in Anglo-American Thought, 1550–1750*. Cambridge: Cambridge University Press, 1986.
Ahmad, Aijaz. "Between Orientalism and Historicism." *Studies in History* 7, no. 1 (1991): 135–63.
Alexandre, Noel. *Conformité des cérémonies chinoises avec l'idolatrie grècque et romaine*. Cologne, 1700.
Ali, Muhsin Jassim. "The Arabian Nights in Eighteenth-Century English Criticism." *Muslim World* 67 (1977): 24–25.
Allen, B. Sprague. *Tides in English Taste, 1619–1800: A Background for the Study of Literature*. Vol. 2. Cambridge, Mass.: Harvard University Press, 1937.
Alvarez y Toledo, Cayetana. *Politics and Reform in Spain and Viceregal Mexico: The Life and Thought of Juan de Palafox, 1600–1659*. Oxford: Clarendon Press, 2004.
Andrea, Bernadette. "Persia, Tartaria, and Pamphilia: Ideas of Asia in Mary Wroth's *The Countess of Montgomery's Urania, Part II*." In *The English Renaissance, Orientalism, and the Idea of Asia*, ed. Debra Johanyak and Walter S. H. Lim, 23–50. New York: Palgrave MacMillan, 2009.
Appleby, Joyce. "Consumption in Early Modern Social Thought." In *Consumption and the World of Goods*, ed. John Brewer and Roy Porter, 162–76. London: Routledge, 1993.
Appleton, William W. *A Cycle of Cathay: The Chinese Vogue in England during the Seventeenth and Eighteenth Centuries*. New York: Columbia University Press, 1951.

Aravamudan, Srinivas. "In the Wake of the Novel: The Oriental Tale as National Allegory." *Novel: A Forum on Fiction* 33, no. 1 (1999): 5–31.

———. *Tropicopolitans: Colonialism and Agency, 1688–1804.* Durham, N.C.: Duke University Press, 1999.

Archer, John. *Old Worlds: Egypt, Southwest Asia, India, and Russia in Early Modern English Writing.* Stanford, Calif.: Stanford University Press, 2001.

Armistead, J. M. "Dryden's 'King Arthur' and the Literary Tradition: A Way of Seeing." *Studies in Philology* 85, no. 1 (1988): 53–72.

Armitage, David. "The Cromwellian Protectorate and the Languages of Empire." *Historical Journal* 35, no. 3 (1992): 531–55.

———. *The Ideological Origins of the English Empire.* Cambridge: Cambridge University Press, 2000.

Armstrong, Meg. "'The Effects of Blackness': Gender, Race, and the Sublime in Aesthetic Theories of Burke and Kant." *Journal of Aesthetics and Art Criticism* 54, no. 3 (1996): 213–36.

Arrighi, Giovanni. *Adam Smith in Beijing: Lineages of the Twenty-First Century.* London: Verso, 2008.

Arwaker, Edmund. *Truth in Fiction: Or, Morality in Masquerade.* London, 1708.

Assman, Jan. *Moses the Egyptian: The Memory of Egypt in Western Monotheism.* Cambridge, Mass.: Harvard University Press, 1997.

Ayres, Philip. *Classical Culture and the Idea of Rome in Eighteenth-Century England.* Cambridge: Cambridge University Press, 1997.

Backscheider, Paula R., ed. *Restoration and Eighteenth-Century Dramatists.* Second series, vol. 84. Detroit: Gale, 1989.

Baker, David Erskine. *The Companion to the Play-House, or an Historical Account of All the Dramatic Writers.* London, 1764.

La Balance Chinoise, ou Lettres d'un Chinois Lettré Sur L'education, Contenant un Parallel de celle de la Chine avec celle de l'Europe. Amsterdam and Leipzig [1763].

Ballaster, Ros. *Fabulous Orients: Fictions of the East in England, 1662–1785.* Oxford: Oxford University Press, 2005.

The Baptized Turk, or a Narrative of the Happy Conversion of Signior Rigep Dandulo. [London] 1658.

Barbour, Richard. *Before Orientalism: London's Theatre of the East, 1576–1626.* Cambridge: Cambridge University Press, 2003.

Barker-Benfield, G. J. *The Culture of Sensibility: Sex and Society in Eighteenth-Century Britain.* Chicago: University of Chicago Press, 1992.

Barnett, Cherry. "The Chinese Convert." *History Today* 52, no. 7 (2002): 5.

Barthes, Roland. *The Fashion System.* Trans. Matthew Ward and Richard Howard. Berkeley: University of California Press, 1983.

———. *Mythologies.* Trans. Annette Lavers. Frogmore, St. Albans, U.K.: Paladin, 1973.

Batchelor, Robert. "Concealing the Bounds: Imagining the British Nation through China." In *The Global Eighteenth Century*, ed. Felicity A. Nussbaum, 79–92. Baltimore: Johns Hopkins University Press, 2003.

Baudrillard, Jean. *Simulacra and Simulation*. Trans. Sheila Faria Glaser. Ann Arbor: University of Michigan Press, 1994.
Baxter, Richard. *Of the Nature of Spirits, Especially Man's Soul*. London, 1682.
Beard, Thomas. *The theatre of Gods judgements wherein is represented the admirable justice of God against all notorious sinners*. London, 1642.
Behdad, Ali. *Belated Travelers: Orientalism in the Age of Colonial Dissolution*. Durham, N.C.: Duke University Press, 1994.
Behn, Aphra. *Oroonoko, or, the Royal Slave*. 1688. New York: W. W. Norton, 1973.
Benjamin, Walter. *Illuminations*. Trans. Harry Zohn, ed. Hannah Arendt. New York: Schocken, 1968.
Berg, Maxine. *Luxury and Pleasure in Eighteenth-century Britain*. Oxford: Oxford University Press, 2005.
Berg, Maxine, and Helen Clifford, eds. *Consumers and Luxury: Consumer Culture in Europe, 1650–1850*. Manchester: Manchester University Press, 1999.
Berg, Maxine, and Elizabeth Eger, eds. *Luxury in the Eighteenth Century: Debates, Desires, and Delectable Goods*. New York: Palgrave, 2003.
Bernier, François. *Travels in the Mogul Empire, A.D. 1656–1668*. 1670. Rev. ed., Vincent A. Smith. London: Humphrey Milford, 1916.
Berry, Christopher. *The Idea of Luxury: A Conceptual and Historical Investigation*. Cambridge: Cambridge University Press, 1994.
Bevis, Richard W. *English Drama: Restoration and Eighteenth Century, 1660–1789*. Ed. David Carroll and Michael Wheeler. Longman Literature in English Series. London: Longman, 1988.
Bhabha, Homi. *The Location of Culture*. London: Routledge, 1994.
Billings, Timothy. "Untranslation Theory: The Nestorian Stele and the Jesuit Illustration of China." In *Sinographies: Writing China*, ed. Eric Hayot, Haun Saussy, and Steven Yao, 89–114. Minneapolis: University of Minnesota Press, 2007.
Black, Jeremy *Eighteenth-Century Britain, 1688–1783*. Palgrave History of Britain. New York: Palgrave, 2001.
Black, John. "Carlo Gozzi's 'Turandot' and Its Transformation into Puccini's Libretto." In *Turandot*, by Giacomo Puccini, ed. Nicholas John. Opera Guide Ser. 27. London: John Calder, 1984.
Blackham, H. J. *The Fable as Literature*. London: Athlone Press, 1985.
Blackwell, Mark, ed. *The Secret Life of Things: Animals, Objects, and It-Narratives in Eighteenth-Century England*. Lewisburg, Pa.: Bucknell University Press, 2007.
Bloom, Edward A., and Lillian D. Bloom. *Joseph Addison's Sociable Animal: In the Market Place, on the Hustings, in the Pulpit*. Providence, R.I.: Brown University Press, 1971.
Blundell, Susan. *Women in Ancient Greece*. Cambridge, Mass.: Harvard University Press, 1995.
Boaden, James. *Memoirs of Mrs. Siddons. Interspersed with Anecdotes of Authors and Actors*. Philadelphia: H. C. Carey & I. Lea, 1827.
Bond, Donald F., ed. *The Spectator*. In 5 vols. Vols. 1–5. Oxford: Clarendon Press, 1965.
Bond, Richmond P. *Queen Anne's American Kings*. Oxford: Clarendon Press, 1952.
Borges, Jorge Luis. *Siete Noches*. Mexico: Fondo de Cultura Económica, 1980.
Bouvet, Joachim. *Portrait Historique de L'empereur de La Chine*. Paris, 1697.

Boyle, Robert. *The Christian Virtuoso*. London, 1690.

Braudel, Fernand. *The Wheels of Commerce*. Trans. Sian Reynolds. Vol. 2, *Civilization and Capitalism, Fifteenth-Eighteenth Century*. New York: Harper & Row, 1986.

Braunshneider, Theresa. "The Lady and the Lapdog: Mixed Ethnicity in Constantinople, Fashionable Pets in Britain." In *Humans and Other Animals in Eighteenth-Century British Culture: Representation, Hybridity, Ethics*, ed. Frank Palmeri, 31–48. Burlington, Vt.: Ashgate; 2006.

Brener, Milton. *Opera Offstage: Passion and Politics behind the Great Operas*. New York: Walker, 1996.

Brewer, John, and Roy Porter, eds. *Consumption and the World of Goods*. London: Routledge, 1993.

Brockey, Liam Matthew. *Journey to the East: The Jesuit Mission to China, 1579–1724*. Cambridge, Mass.: Belknap Press of Harvard University Press, 2007.

Brown, Bill. "Thing Theory," *Critical Inquiry* 28, no. 1 (2001): 1–22.

Brown, Frank Clyde. *Elkanah Settle: His Life and Works*. Chicago: University of Chicago Press, 1910.

Brown, John. *Estimate of the Manners and Principles of the Times*. London, 1757.

Brown, Laura. *Ends of Empire: Women and Ideology in Early Eighteenth-Century English Literature*. Ithaca, N.Y.: Cornell University Press, 1993.

———. *English Dramatic Form, 1660–1760: An Essay in Generic History*. Ithaca, N.Y.: Cornell University Press, 1993.

———. *Fables of Modernity: Literature and Culture in the English Eighteenth Century*. Ithaca, N.Y.: Cornell University Press, 2001.

———. *Homeless Dogs and Melancholy Apes: Humans and Other Animals in the Modern Literary Imagination*. Ithaca, N.Y.: Cornell University Press, 2010.

Buc'hoz, Pierre-Joseph. *The toilet of Flora; or, a collection of the most simple and approved methods of preparing baths, essences, pomatums*. London, 1772.

Budden, Julian. *The Operas of Verdi*. Vol. 3, *From Don Carlos to Falstaff*. 1973. Rev. ed. Oxford: Clarendon Press, 1992.

Burnet, Thomas. *A Treatise Concerning the State of Departed Souls, before, and at, and after the Resurrection*. 2nd ed. [London] 1739.

Butler, Judith. *Bodies That Matter: On the Discursive Limits of "Sex."* New York: Routledge, 1993.

Butler, Judith, Ernesto Laclau, and Slavoj Žižek, *Contingency, Hegemony, Universality: Contemporary Dialogues on the Left*. London: Verso, 2000.

Campagnac, E. T. *The Cambridge Platonists*. Oxford: Clarendon Press, 1901.

Campbell, Colin. *The Romantic Ethic and the Spirit of Modern Consumerism*. Oxford: Blackwell, 1987.

Campbell, William. *An account of missionary success in the island of Formosa: published in London in 1650*. London: Trübner, 1889.

———, ed. *The Articles of Christian Instruction in Favorlang-Formosan Dutch and English from Vertrecht's Manuscript of 1650 with Psalmanazar's Dialogue between a Japanese and a Formosan and Happart's Favorlang Vocabulary*. London: Kegan, Paul, Trench, Trüber, 1896.

———. *Missionary Success in the Island of Formosa.* Vol. 1, 1650. Reprinted with copious appendices, London, 1889.

Canfield, J. Douglas. *Heroes and States: On the Ideology of Restoration Tragedy.* Lexington: University Press of Kentucky, 2000.

Caracciolo, Peter L., ed. *The Arabian Nights in English Literature: Studies in the Reception of the Thousand and One Nights into British Culture.* Houndmills, Basingstoke, U.K.: St. Martin's Press, 1988.

Carey, Daniel, and Lynn Festa, eds. *The Postcolonial Enlightenment: Eighteenth-century Colonialism and Postcolonial Theory.* Oxford: Oxford University Press, 2009.

Cass, Victoria. *Dangerous Women: Warriors, Grannies, and Geishas of the Ming.* New York: Rowman & Littlefield, 1999.

Cassirer, Ernst. *The Platonic Renaissance in England.* Trans. James P. Pettegrove. New York: Gordian Press, 1970.

Cawthorn, James. "Of Taste. An Essay." In *The Works of the English Poets, from Chaucer to Cowper,* 14. London, 1810.

Chambers, Ephraim. *Cyclopaedia.* London, 1728.

Champion, J. A. I. *Pillars of Priestcraft Shaken: The Church of England and Its Enemies, 1660–1730.* Cambridge: Cambridge University Press, 1992.

Chardin, Sir John. *Travels into Persia and the East Indies.* [London] 1686.

Chaudhuri, K. N. *Asia before Europe: Economy and Civilisation of the Indian Ocean from the Rise of Islam to 1750.* Cambridge: Cambridge University Press, 1990.

———. *The Trading World of Asia and the English East India Company, 1660–1760.* Cambridge: Cambridge University Press, 1978.

Chen, Min-sun. *Mythistory in SinoWestern Contacts: Jesuit Missionaries and the Pillars of Chinese Catholic Religion.* Thunder Bay, Ontario: Lakehead University Printing Service, 2003.

Chen, Shouyi. "The Chinese Orphan: A Yuan Play. Its Influence on European Drama of the Eighteenth Century." In *The Vision of China in the English Literature of the Seventeenth and Eighteenth Centuries,* ed. Adrian Hsia, 359–82. Hong Kong: Chinese University Press, 1998.

Chew, Samuel C. *The Crescent and the Rose: Islam and England during the Renaissance.* New York: Oxford University Press, 1937.

Chico, Tita. "The Arts of Beauty: Women's Cosmetics and Pope's Ekphrasis." *Eighteenth-Century Life* 26, no. 1 (2002): 1–23.

Ching, Julia, and Willard G. Oxtoby. *Moral Enlightenment: Leibniz and Wolff on China.* Monumenta Serica Monograph Ser. 26. Nettetal: Steyler, 1992.

Choudhury, Mita. *Interculturalism and Resistance in the London Theater, 1660–1800: Identity, Performance, Empire.* Lewisburg, Pa.: Bucknell University Press, 2000.

Chow, Rey. *Primitive Passions: Visuality, Sexuality, Ethnography, and Contemporary Chinese Cinema.* Ed. John Belton. Film and Culture Series. New York: Columbia University Press, 1995.

Clancy, Michael. *Hermon, Prince of Chorea: Or, The Extravagant Zealot.* London, 1746.

Clark, Catherine E. "Chinese Idols and Religious Art: Questioning Difference in *Cérémo-*

nies et Coutumes Religieuses." In *Bernard Picart and the First Global Vision of Religion*, ed. Lynn Hunt, Margaret Jacob, and Wijnand Mijnhardt. Los Angeles: Getty, 2010.

Clark, T. Blake. *Oriental England: A Study of Oriental Influences in Eighteenth Century England as Reflected in the Drama.* Shanghai: Kelly & Walsh, 1939.

Clunas, Craig. *Chinese Export Art and Design.* London: Victoria and Albert Museum, 1987.

Cohen, J. M. *Myths of Plato.* London: Centaur Press, 1960.

Colley, Linda. *Britons: Forging the Nation, 1707–1837.* New Haven: Yale University Press, 2005.

Collier, Jeremy. *Short View of the Immorality and Profaneness of the English Stage.* London, 1698.

Conant, Martha Pike. *The Oriental Tale in England.* New York: Columbia University Press, 1908.

A Confession of Faith of James Salgado, a Spaniard, and Sometimes a Priest in the Church of Rome: With an Account of His Life and Sufferings by the Romish Party, since He Forsook the Romish Religion. London, 1681.

[Confucius]. *The Morals of Confucius, a Chinese Philosopher.* Trans. and abridged from R. F. Incorcetta and Couplet. London, 1691.

Connell, C. W. "Western Views of the Origin of the 'Tartars': An Example of the Influence of Myth in the Second Half of the Thirteenth Century." *Journal of Medieval and Renaissance Studies* 3 (1978): 115–37.

Connell, R. W. *Masculinities.* Berkeley: University of California Press, 1995.

The Conversions and Persecutions of Eve Cohan, Now Called Elizabeth Verboon, a Person of Quality of the Jewish Religion. London, 1680.

Conway, Lady Anne. *The Principle of the Most Ancient and Modern Philosophy*, ed. Peter Loptson. The Hague: Martinus Nijhoff, 1982.

Cornilliat, François. "Exemplarities: A Response to Timothy Hampton and Karlheinz Stierle." *Journal of the History of Ideas* 59, no. 4 (1998): 613–24.

Corse, Taylor. "Dryden's 'Vegetarian' Philosopher: Pythagoras." *Eighteenth-Century Life* 34, no. 1 (2010): 1–28.

Cowley, Abraham. *A Description of the Academy of the Athenian virtuosi with a discourse held there in vindication of Mr. Dryden's Conquest of Granada.* London, 1673.

Crehan, Stewart, "The Rape of the Lock and the Economy of 'Trivial Things.'" *Eighteenth-Century Studies* 31, no. 1 (1997): 45–68.

Crossley, Pamela Kaye. *The Manchus.* Oxford: Blackwell, 2002.

———. *A Translucent Mirror: History and Identity in Qing Imperial Ideology.* Berkeley: University of California Press, 1999.

Cudworth, Ralph. *A True Intellectual System of the Universe.* London, 1678.

Cummins, J. S. *Jesuit and Friar in the Spanish Expansion to the East.* London: Variorum, 1986.

Dacier, André. *Life of Pythagoras.* Trans. Nicholas Rowe. London, 1707.

Dalby, Andrew. *Empire of Pleasures: Luxury and Indulgence in the Roman World.* New York: Routledge, 2000.

Dalporto, Jeannie. "The Succession Crisis and Elkanah Settle's *The Conquest of China by the Tartars.*" *Eighteenth Century: Theory and Interpretation* 45, no. 2 (2004): 131–46.

d'Amalvi, Isaac. *Eclercissements Necessaires*. The Hague, 1706.
Daniel, Norman. *Islam and the West: The Making of an Image*. Edinburgh: Edinburgh University Press, 1958.
Daniel, Stephen H. "Political and Philosophical Uses of Fables in Eighteenth-Century England." *The Eighteenth Century* 32, no. 2 (1982).
Dapper, Olfert. *Atlas Chinensis: being a second part of a relation of remarkable passages in two embassies from the East-India Company*. London, 1671.
Davis, James Herbert, Jr. *Fénelon*. Boston: Twayne, 1979.
Davis, Ralph. *The Rise of the Atlantic Economies*. London: Weidenfeld & Nicolson, 1973.
Day, Robert Adams. "Psalmanazar's 'Formosa' and the British Reader (including Samuel Johnson)." In *Exoticism in the Enlightenment*, ed. G. S. Rousseau and Roy Porter. Manchester: Manchester University Press, 1989.
Defoe, Daniel. *The Farther Adventures of Robinson Crusoe, Being the Second and Last Part of His Life*. London: W. Taylor, 1719.
———. *The Life, Adventures, and Pyracies, of the Famous Captain Singleton*. Ed. Shiv K. Kumar. Oxford: Oxford University Press, 1990.
[———]. *A System of Magic; or, a History of the Black Art*. London, 1727.
———. *A Tour Through the Whole Island of Great Britain*. Abr. and ed. P. N. Furbank, W. R. Owens, and A. J. Coulson. New Haven: Yale University Press, 1991.
de la Croix, François Pétis. *The Persian and the Turkish Tales, Compleat*. Trans. Dr. King. London, 1714.
———. *Turkish tales; Consisting of several Extraordinary Adventures: With the History of the Sultaness of Persia, and the Visiers*. London: Jacob Tonson, 1708.
De Marchi, Neil. "Adam Smith's Accommodation of 'altogether endless' Desires." In *Consumers and Luxury: Consumer Culture in Europe, 1650–1850*, ed. Maxine Berg and Helen Clifford. Manchester: Manchester University Press, 1999.
Dennis, John. *An Essay Upon Publick Spirit . . . Upon the Manners and Luxury of the Times*. London, 1711.
De Pauw, Linda Grant. *Battle Cries and Lullabies: Women in War from Prehistory to the Present*. Norman: University of Oklahoma, 1998.
Derrida, Jacques. "Structure, Sign, and Play in the Discourse of the Human Sciences." In *Critical Theory since 1965*, ed. Hazard Adams and Leroy Searle, 83–94. Reprint, Tallahassee: Florida State University Press, 1986.
A Description of the Academy of the Athenian virtuosi with a discourse held there in vindication of Mr. Dryden's Conquest of Granada. London, 1673.
Dirlik, Arif. "Chinese History and the Question of Orientalism." *History and Theory* 35, no. 4 (Dec. 1996).
Dossie, Robert. *The Handmaid to the Arts*. London, 1764.
Downes, John. *Roscius Anglicanus*. Ed. Judith Milhous and Robert D. Hume. London: Society for Theatre Research, 1987.
Doyle, Anne T., ed. *Elkanah Settle's the Empress of Morocco and the Controversy Surrounding It: A Critical Edition*. New York: Garland, 1987.
Dryden, John. *Aureng-Zebe*. Ed. Frederick M. Link. Lincoln: University of Nebraska Press, 1971.

———. *Fables Ancient and Modern*. 1700.

———. *John Dryden (Three Plays)*. Ed. George Saintsbury. Mermaid Dramabook. New York: Hill & Wang, 1957.

———. *The Life of Plutarch*. London, 1683.

———. *Notes and observations on The empress of Morocco, or, Some few errata's to be printed instead of the sculptures with the second edition of that play*. London, 1674.

———. *Of Dramatic Poesy, and Other Critical Essays*. Ed. George Watson. London: J. M. Dent, 1962.

———. *The Works of John Dryden*. Vol. 8, ed. John H. Smith, Dougald MacMillan, and Vinton A. Dearing. Berkeley and Los Angeles: University of California Press, 1965.

Dugaw, Diane. *Warrior Women and Popular Balladry, 1650–1850*. Cambridge: Cambridge University Press, 1989.

Du Halde, Jean-Baptiste. *The General History of China*. London, 1741.

———. *The General History of China, Containing a Geographical, Historical, Chronological, Political and Physical Description of the Empire of China*. London, 1736.

Dunbar, Howard Hunter. *The Dramatic Career of Arthur Murphy*. New York: MLA of America, 1946.

During, Simon. "Rousseau's Patrimony: Primitivism, Romance, and Becoming Other." In *Colonial Discourse / Postcolonial Theory*, ed. Peter Hulme, Francis Barker, and Margaret Iversen, 47–71. Manchester: Manchester University Press, 1994.

Elliott, Mark. "The Limits of Tartary." *Journal of Asian Studies* 59, no. 3 (2000): 625–26.

———. *The Manchu Way: The Eight Banners and Ethnic Identity in Late Imperial China*. Stanford, Calif.: Stanford University Press, 2001.

Ellis, Markman. *The Politics of Sensibility: Race, Gender, and Commerce in the Sentimental Novel*. New York: Cambridge University Press, 1996.

Elman, Benjamin. *On Their Own Terms: Science in China, 1500–1900*. Cambridge, Mass.: Harvard University Press, 2005.

An Epistle from a Late Roman Catholick to the Very Reverend Dr. Edward Stillingfleet. London, 1679.

Erskine-Hill, Howard. *The Augustan Idea in English Literature*. London: Edward Arnold, 1983.

Evelyn, John. *Navigation and Commerce, Their Original and Progress*. London, 1674.

Eze, Emmanuel Chukwudi, ed. Introduction to *Race and the Enlightenment: A Reader*, 1–9. Malden, Mass.: Blackwell, 1997.

Fabian, Johannes. *Time and the Other: How Anthropology Makes Its Object*. New York: Columbia University Press, 1983.

Fan, Tsen-Chung. *Dr. Johnson and Chinese Culture*. China Society Occasional Papers, ed. W. Perceval Yetts. Vol. 6. London: China Society, 1945.

Fawconer, Samuel. *An Essay on Modern Luxury: Or, An Attempt to Delineate its Nature, Causes, and Effects*. London, 1765.

Feldman, Burton, and Robert D. Richardson, eds. *The Rise of Modern Mythology, 1680–1860*. Bloomington: Indiana University Press, 1975.

Fénelon, François de Salignac de la Mothe-. *Oeuvres*. Ed. Jacques Le Brun. Paris: Gallimard, 1983.

Ferguson, Adam. *An Essay on the History of Civil Society.* Edinburgh, 1767.
———. *The Morality of Stage-Plays Seriously Considered.* Edinburgh, 1757.
Ferguson, Robert. *A sober enquiry into the nature, measure and principle of moral virtue.* London, 1673.
Fitzgerald, Percy. *The Life of David Garrick.* London: Simpkin, Marshall, Hamilton, Kent & Co., 1899.
Flynn, Dennis O. *World Silver and Monetary History in the Sixteenth and Seventeenth Centuries.* Aldershot, Hants., U.K.: Variorum, 1996.
Flynn, Dennis O., and Arturo Giráldez. "China and the Spanish Empire." *Revista de Historia Económica* 14, no. 2 (1996): 309–38.
Foley, Frederic J. *The Great Formosan Impostor.* Vol. 1, Sources and Studies for the History of the Far East. St. Louis, Mo.: Jesuit Historical Institute, 1968.
Fong, Grace. "Signifying Bodies: The Cultural Significance of Suicide Writings by Women in Ming-Qing China." In *Passionate Women: Female Suicide in Late Imperial China*, ed. Paul S. Ropp, Paola Zamperini, and Harriet T. Zurndorfer, 104–42. Leiden: Brill, 2001.
Force, Pierre. *Self-interest before Adam Smith: A Genealogy of Economic Science.* Cambridge: Cambridge University Press, 2003.
Forman-Barzilai, Fonna. *Adam Smith and the Circles of Sympathy: Cosmopolitanism and Moral Theory.* Cambridge: Cambridge University Press, 2010.
Forster, Thomas Ignatius Maria. *An Apology for the Doctrine of Pythagoras as Compatible with That of Jesus Christ: Being a Defense of the New Sect of Christians.* Boulogne sur Mer: C. Aigre, 1858.
Foss, Theodore Nicholas. "The European Sojourn of Philippe Couplet and Michael Shen Fuzong, 1683–1692." In *Philippe Couplet, S.J., 1623–1693: The Man Who Brought China to Europe*, ed. Jerome Heyndrick, 121–40. Nettetal: Steyler-Verlag, 1990.
Foucault, Michel. "What Is an Author?" In *Language, Counter-Memory, Practice*, ed. Donald F. Bouchard, 113–38. Ithaca, N.Y.: Cornell University Press, 1977.
Franceschina, John Charles. *Homosexualities in the English Theatre: From Lyly to Wilde.* Westport, Conn.: Greenwood Press, 1997.
Frank, Andre Gunder. *ReOrient: Global Economy in the Asian Age.* Berkeley and Los Angeles: University of California Press, 1998.
Freeman, Lisa. *Character's Theater: Genre and Identity on the Eighteenth-Century English Stage.* Philadelphia: University of Pennsylvania Press, 2002.
Fudge, Erica. *Perceiving Animals: Humans and Beasts in Early Modern English Culture.* Champaign: University of Illinois Press, 2002.
Furber, Holden. *Rival Empires of Trade in the Orient, 1600–1800.* Minneapolis: University of Minnesota Press, 1976.
Galland, Antoine. *Les Mille Et Une Nuits, Contes Arabes.* Ed. Jean Gaulmier. Paris, 1965, 1:21–22. Quoted in Muhsin Mahdi, *The Thousand and One Nights.* Leiden: E. J. Brill, 1995, 21.
———. *Les Paroles Remarquables, les Bons Mots, et les Maximes des Orientaux. Traduction de leurs Ouvrages en Arabe, en Persan & en Turc, avec des Remarques.* Paris, 1694.
Gelley, Alexander, ed. *Unruly Examples: On the Rhetoric of Exemplarity.* Stanford, Calif.: Stanford University Press, 1995.

Genest, John. *Some Account of the English Stage, from the Restoration in 1660 to 1830.* Bath: H. E. Carrington, 1832.
Gentleman's Magazine. London. Issues for Nov.–Jan. 1764, and Feb. 1766, 78–81.
Gernet, Jacques. *China and the Christian Impact: A Conflict of Cultures.* Trans. Janet Lloyd. Cambridge: Cambridge University Press, 1990.
Gibbon, Edward. *The History of the Decline and Fall of the Roman Empire.* Vol. 3, ed. J. B. Bury. New York: Heritage Press, 1946.
Gibson, William, ed. *Religion and Society in England and Wales: Documents in Early Modern Social History.* London: Leicester University Press, 1998.
Ginsburg, Elaine, ed. *Passing and the Fictions of Identity.* Durham, N.C.: Duke University Press, 1996.
Glanvill, Joseph. *Lux Orientalis, or an Enquiry into the Opinion of the Eastern Sages Concerning the Praexistence of the Souls.* [London] 1682.
Goddard, W. G. *Formosa: A Study in Chinese History.* London: Macmillan, 1966.
Goldsmith, Oliver. *Citizen of the World, or Letters from a Chinese Philosopher Residing in London to His Friends in the East.* 1762. Reprint, London: Folio Society, 1969.
———. "Review of the Orphan of China, a Tragedy, by Arthur Murphy." *Critical Review* 7, no. 9 (May 1759): 434–35.
Goldstone, Jack. "Efflorescences and Economic Growth in World History: Rethinking the 'Rise of the West' and the Industrial Revolution." *Journal of World History* 13, no. 2 (2002): 323–89.
———. *Why Europe? The Rise of the West in World History, 1500–1850.* New York: McGraw-Hill, 2008.
Goodman, Grant K. *Japan: The Dutch Experience.* London: Athlone Press, 1986.
Greenhill, Thomas. *Nekrokedeia: or, the art of embalming.* London, 1705.
Greslon, Adrien. *Historie de la Chine, sous la Domination des Tartares.* Paris, 1671.
Gueullette, Thomas-Simon. *Chinese Tales, Or, the Wonderful Adventures of the Mandarin Fum-Hoam.* London, 1725; 2nd ed., trans. Rev. T. Stackhouse. London, 1740.
Guffey, George, Maximillian E. Novak, and Robert Vosper, eds. *The Empress of Morocco and Its Critics: Settle, Dryden, Shadwell, Crowne, Duffet.* Los Angeles: William Andrews Clark Memorial Library, University of California, 1968.
Gwilliam, Tassie. "Cosmetic Poetics: Coloring Faces in the Eighteenth Century." In *Body and Text in the Eighteenth Century*, ed. Veronica Kelly and Dorothea von Mücke, 144–59. Stanford, Calif.: Stanford University Press, 1994.
Gwinnett, Richard, Esq., and Mrs. Elizabeth Thomas. *Pylades and Corinna: Or, Memoirs of the Lives, Amours, and Writings of Richard Gwinnett Esq. And Mrs. Elizabeth Thomas.* London, 1731.
Habermas, Jürgen. *The Structural Transformation of the Public Sphere.* Trans. Thomas Burger and Frederick Lawrence. Cambridge, Mass.: MIT Press, 1989.
Haddawy, Husain. *The Arabian Nights.* Trans. Husain Haddawy. New York: W. W. Norton, 1990.
Halberstam, Judith. *Female Masculinity.* Durham, N.C.: Duke University Press, 1998.
Hall, Kim. *Things of Darkness: Economies of Race and Gender in Early Modern England.* Ithaca, N.Y.: Cornell University Press, 1995.

Hallywell, Henry. *The excellency of moral vertue*. London, 1692.
Hampton, Timothy. *Writing from History: The Rhetoric of Exemplarity in Renaissance Literature*. Ithaca, N.Y.: Cornell University Press, 1990.
Hanway, Jonas. *An Essay on Tea*. In *A Journal of Eight Days Journey from Portsmouth to Kingston upon Thames*. London, 1756.
Hargreaves, John. "Globalisation Theory, Global Sport, and Nations and Nationalism." In *Power Games: A Critical Sociology of Sport*, ed. John Sugden and Alan Tomlinson, 25–43. London: Routledge, 2002.
Harrison, Peter. "Animal Souls, Metempsychosis, and Theodicy in Seventeenth-Century English Thought." *Journal of the History of Philosophy* 31, no. 4 (1993): 519–44.
Hatchett, William. *The Chinese Orphan: An Historical Tragedy*. London, 1741.
Hawkins, John. *The Life of Samuel Johnson Ll.D*. Dublin, 1787.
Haydon, Colin. *Anti-Catholicism in Eighteenth-Century England, C.1714–80: A Political and Social Study*. Manchester: Manchester University Press, 1993.
Hayot, Eric. *The Hypothetical Mandarin: Sympathy, Modernity, and Chinese Pain*. Oxford: Oxford University Press, 2009.
Hedgcock, Frank A. *A Cosmopolitan Actor: David Garrick and His French Friends*. London: Stanley Paul, 1912.
Hegel, G. W. F. *The Philosophy of History*. New York: P. F. Collier, 1902.
Heylyn, Peter. *Cosmographie in Four Bookes*. [London] 1652.
Hirschman, Albert O. *The Passions and the Interests: Political Arguments for Capitalism before its Triumph*. Princeton, N.J.: Princeton University Press, 1977.
The History of the Works of the Learned. Apr. 1704, 244–52.
The History of the Works of the Learned. Sept. 1706, 515–20.
Hobsbawm, Eric. *The Age of Empire, 1875–1914*. New York: Vintage, 1989.
Holwell, J. Z. *A Review of the Original Principles, Religious and Moral, of the Ancient Bramins . . . With a Dissertation on the Metempsychosis, commonly, though erroneously, called the Pythagorean Doctrine*. London, 1779.
Honour, Hugh. *Chinoiserie: The Vision of Cathay*. London: John Murray, 1961.
Hopkins, Lisa. "Marlowe's Asia and the Feminization of Conquest." In *The English Renaissance, Orientalism, and the Idea of Asia*, ed. Debra Johanyak and Walter S. H. Lim. New York: Palgrave MacMillan, 2009.
Hoppit, Julian. *A Land of Liberty? England, 1689–1727*. New Oxford History of England. Oxford: Clarendon Press, 2000.
Horne, Donald. *The Great Museum: The Re-Presentation of History*. London: Pluto Press, 1984.
Hostetler, Laura. *Qing Colonial Enterprise: Ethnography and Cartography in Early Modern China*. Chicago: University of Chicago Press, 2001.
Howe, Elizabeth. *The First English Actresses: Women and Drama, 1660–1700*. Cambridge: Cambridge University Press, 1992.
Hsia, Adrian, ed. *The Vision of China in the English Literature of the Seventeenth and Eighteenth Centuries*. Hong Kong: Chinese University Press, 1998.
Hughes, Derek. *Dryden's Heroic Plays*. Lincoln: University of Nebraska Press, 1981.
Hume, David. "Of Commerce" and "Of Luxury." In *Essays and Treatises on Several Subjects*. London, 1758.

———. "Of National Characters." In *Political Essays*, ed. Knud Haakonssen, 78–92. Cambridge: Cambridge University Press, 1994.

———. *A Treatise of Human Nature*. Ed. L. A. Selby-Bigge. Oxford: Clarendon Press, 1888.

Hume, Robert D. *The Development of English Drama in the Late Seventeenth Century*. Oxford: Clarendon Press, 1976.

———. "Dryden on Creation: 'Imagination' in the Later Criticism." *Review of English Studies* 21 (1970): 295–314.

Hummel, Arthur W., ed. *Eminent Chinese of the Ch'ing Period*. Taipei: Ch'eng-wen Publishing, 1967.

Hunt, Alan. *Governance of the Consuming Passions: A History of Sumptuary Law*. New York: St. Martin's Press, 1996.

Hunt, Hugh. "Restoration Acting." In *Restoration and Eighteenth-Century Comedy*, ed. Scott McMillin, 178–92. New York: W. W. Norton, 1973.

Huth, Hans. *Lacquer of the West*. Chicago: University of Chicago Press, 1971.

Hyma, Albert. *A History of the Dutch in the Far East*. Ann Arbor, Mich.: George Wahr, 1953.

Impey, Oliver. *Chinoiserie: The Impact of Oriental Styles on Western Art and Decoration*. New York: Scribner, 1977.

Ingram, Robert G. "'The trembling Earth is God's Herald': Earthquakes, Religion, and Public Life in Britain during the 1750s." In *The Lisbon Earthquake of 1755: Representations and Reactions*, ed. Theodore E. D. Braun and John B. Radner, 97–115. Oxford, U.K.: Voltaire Foundation, 2005.

Israel, Jonathan I. *Enlightenment Contested: Philosophy, Modernity, and the Emancipation of Man, 1670–1752*. Oxford: Oxford University Press, 2006.

———. *Radical Enlightenment: Philosophy and the Making of Modernity, 1650–1750*. Oxford: Oxford University Press, 2001.

Ivy, Marilyn. *Discourses of the Vanishing: Modernity, Phantasm, Japan*. Chicago: University of Chicago, 1995.

Jacobson, Dawn. *Chinoiserie*. London: Phaidon, 1993.

Jarry, Madeleine. *Chinoiserie: Chinese Influence on European Decorative Art, Seventeenth and Eighteenth Centuries*. Trans. Gail Mangold-Vine. New York: Vendome, 1981.

Jefferys, Thomas. *A Collection of the Dresses of Different Nations, Antient and Modern*. Vol. 1. London, 1757.

Jensen, Lionel. *Manufacturing Confucianism: Chinese Traditions and Universal Civilization*. Durham, N.C.: Duke University Press, 1997.

Johanyak, Debra, and Walter S. H. Lim, eds. *The English Renaissance, Orientalism, and the Idea of Asia*. New York: Palgrave MacMillan, 2009.

Johnson, Samuel. *A Dictionary of the English Language*. London, 1755.

———. *The History of Rasselas, Prince of Abyssinia*. 1759. Reprint, edited and introduced by D. J. Enright, London: Penguin Books, 1985.

———. *The Rambler*. The British Essayists, with prefaces, historical and biographical, ed. Alexander Chalmers. Vol. 16. London, 1823.

———. *Samuel Johnson: Selected Poetry and Prose*. Ed. Frank Brady and W. K. Wimsatt. Berkeley and Los Angeles: University of California Press, 1977.

Jourdain, Margaret, and R. Soame Jenyns. *Chinese Export Art in the Eighteenth Century.* London: Country Life, 1950.
Judy, Ronald. "Kant and the Negro." *Surfaces* 1, no. 8 (1991).
Kabbani, Rana. *Europe's Myths of Orient.* Bloomington: Indiana University Press, 1986.
Kaempfer, Engelbert. *The History of Japan, Together with a Description of the Kingdom of Siam, 1690–92.* Trans. J. G. Scheuchzer. Vol. 1. Glasgow: J. MacLehose & Sons, 1906.
Kahn, C. *Pythagoras and the Pythagoreans.* Indianapolis: Hackett, 2001.
Kant, Immanuel. *Observations on the Feeling of the Beautiful and Sublime.* Ed. John T. Goldthwait. Berkeley and Los Angeles: University of California Press, 2004.
Kaplen, Caren, *Questions of Travel: Postmodern Discourses of Displacement.* Durham, N.C.: Duke University Press, 1996.
Kaul, Suvir. *Eighteenth-century British Literature and Postcolonial Studies.* Edinburgh: Edinburgh University Press, 2009.
———. *Poems of Nation, Anthems of Empire: English Verse in the Long Eighteenth Century.* Charlottesville: University Press of Virginia, 2000.
Kay, Donald. *Short Fiction in The Spectator.* Studies in the Humanities, vol. 8. University: University of Alabama Press, 1975.
Keevak, Michael. *The Pretended Asian: George Psalmanazar's Eighteenth-Century Formosan Hoax.* Detroit: Wayne State University Press, 2004.
Kidd, Colin. *British Identities before Nationalism: Ethnicity and Nationhood in the Atlantic World, 1600–1800.* Port Chester, N.Y.: Cambridge University Press, 1999.
King, Richard. *Orientalism and Religion: Post-Colonial Theory and the "Mystic East."* London: Routledge, 1999.
Kircher, Athanasius. *China Illustrata.* Trans. Charles D. Van Tuyl from the 1677 original Latin edition. Muskogee, Okla.: Indian University Press, Bacone College, 1987.
Kowaleski-Wallace, Elizabeth. *Consuming Subjects: Women, Shopping, and Business in the Eighteenth Century.* New York: Columbia University Press, 1997.
Krause, Sharon. "Despotism in the Spirit of Laws." In *Montesquieu's Science of Politics: Essays on* The Spirit of Laws, ed. David W. Carrithers, 231–72. Lanham, Md.: Rowman & Littlefield, 2001.
Krishnan, Sanjay. *Reading the Global: Troubling Perspectives on the British Empire in Asia.* New York: Columbia University Press, 2007.
Krishnaswamy, Revathi, *Effeminism: The Economy of Colonial Desire.* Ann Arbor: University of Michigan Press, 1999.
Lach, Donald F., ed. *The Preface to Leibniz'* Novissima Sinica: *Commentary, Translation, Text.* Honolulu: University of Hawaii Press, 1957.
Lach, Donald F., and Edwin J. Van Kley, eds. *Asia in the Making of Europe.* Vols. 1–3. Chicago: University of Chicago, 1993.
Langbaine, Gerard. *An Account of the English Dramatic Poets.* London, 1691.
Le Comte, Louis. *Memoirs and Observations . . . Made in a Late Journey through the Empire of China.* London, 1697.
Leibniz, Gottfried W. Preface to Novissima Sinica, 1697. Quoted in Adolf Reichwein, *China and Europe: Intellectual and Artistic Contacts in the Eighteenth Century* (Taipei: Ch'eng-wen Publishing, 1967), 80.

Levine, Joseph M. *The Battle of the Books: History and Literature in the Augustan Age.* Ithaca, N.Y.: Cornell University Press, 1991.

———. *Between the Ancients and the Moderns: Baroque Culture in Restoration England.* New Haven: Yale University Press, 1999.

Lewis, Jayne Elizabeth. *The English Fable: Aesop and Literary Culture, 1651–1740.* Cambridge Studies in Eighteenth-Century Literature and Thought, ed. Howard Erskine-Hill and John Richetti, vol. 28. Cambridge: Cambridge University Press, 1996.

Liu, Kang. "Is There an Alternative to (Capitalist) Globalization? The Debate about Modernity in China." In *The Cultures of Globalization,* ed. Fredric Jameson and Masao Miyoshi, 164–88. Durham, N.C.: Duke University Press, 1998.

Liu, Lydia. "Robinson Crusoe's Earthenware Pot." *Critical Inquiry* 25, no. 4 (1999): 728–57.

———, ed. *Tokens of Exchange: The Problem of Translation in Global Circulations.* Durham, N.C.: Duke University Press, 1999.

Liu, Wu-chi. "The Original Orphan of China." *Comparative Literature* 5, no. 3 (1953): 193–212.

Liu, Yu. *Seeds of a Different Eden: Chinese Gardening Ideas and a New English Aesthetic Ideal.* Columbia: University of South Carolina, 2008.

Lloyd, David. "Race under Representation." In *Culture/Contexture: Explorations in Anthropology and Literary Studies,* ed. E. Valentine Daniel and Jeffrey M. Peck, 249–72. Berkeley and Los Angeles: University of California Press, 1998.

Lobo, Father Jerome. *A Voyage to Abyssinia.* Trans. Samuel Johnson. [London] 1735.

Locke, John. *An Essay Concerning Human Understanding.* 1700. 4th ed., ed. Peter H. Nidditch, Reprint, Oxford: Clarendon Press, 1975.

Loftis, John. *The Politics of Drama in Augustan England.* Oxford: Clarendon Press, 1963.

The London Magazine: Or, Gentleman's Monthly Intelligencer (May 1759): 267.

Long, Herbert Strainge. "A Study of the Doctrine of Metempsychosis in Greece: From Pythagoras to Plato." Dissertation, Princeton University, 1948.

Loomba, Ania. "The Great Indian Vanishing Trick—Colonialism, Property, and the Family in *A Midsummer Night's Dream.*" In *A Feminist Companion to Shakespeare,* ed. Dympna Callaghan, 163–87. Oxford: Blackwell, 2000.

Lovejoy, Arthur O. *The Great Chain of Being: A Study of the History of an Idea.* Cambridge, Mass.: Harvard University Press, 1976.

Loveridge, Mark. *A History of Augustan Fable.* Cambridge: Cambridge University Press, 1998.

Lowe, Lisa. *Critical Terrains: French and British Orientalisms.* Ithaca, N.Y.: Cornell University Press, 1994.

Lowenthal, Cynthia. *Performing Identities on the Restoration Stage.* Carbondale: Southern Illinois University Press, 2003.

———. "Sticks and Rags, Bodies and Brocade: Essentializing Discourses and the Late Restoration Playhouse." In *Broken Boundaries: Women and Feminism in Restoration Drama,* ed. Katherine M. Quinsey, 219–34. Lexington: University Press of Kentucky, 1996.

Lynch, Jack. *Deception and Detection in Eighteenth-Century Britain.* Aldershot, U.K.: Ashgate, 2008.

MacCannell, Dean. *The Tourist: A New Theory of the Leisure Class*. New York: Shocken, 1976.

MacIntyre, Alasdair. *After Virtue: A Study in Moral Theory*. Notre Dame, Ind.: University of Notre Dame Press, 1984.

Mack, Robert L., ed. *Arabian Nights' Entertainments*. Oxford: Oxford University Press, 1995.

MacKenzie, John. *Orientalism: History, Theory, and the Arts*. Manchester University Press, 1995.

Mackie, Erin, ed. *The Commerce of Everyday Life: Selections from The Tatler and The Spectator*. New York: Bedford, 1998.

———. *Market à La Mode: Fashion, Commodity, and Gender in the* Tatler *and the* Spectator. Baltimore: Johns Hopkins University Press, 1997.

Maclean, Gerald. *Looking East: English Writing and the Ottoman Empire before 1800*. Houndmills, Basingstoke, U.K.: Palgrave Macmillian, 2007.

Macpherson, C. B. "Sir William Temple, Political Scientist?" *Canadian Journal of Economics and Political Science* 9, no. 1 (1943): 39–43.

Magalhães, Gabriel de. *Nouvelle relation de la Chine*. Paris, 1688.

Maguire, Joseph. *Global Sport: Identities, Societies, Civilizations*. Cambridge, U.K.: Polity Press, 1999.

Mahdi, Muhsin. *The Thousand and One Nights*. Leiden: E. J. Brill, 1995.

Makdisi, Saree, and Felicity Nussbaum, eds. *The Arabian Nights in Historical Context: Between East and West*. Oxford: Oxford University Press, 2008.

Mandeville, Bernard. *The Fable of the Bees: Or, Private Vices, Publick Benefits*. Ed. F. B. Kaye. Oxford: Clarendon Press, 1924.

———. *The Fable of the Bees and Other Writings*. Abridged and ed. E. J. Hundert. Indianapolis: Hackett Publishing, 1997.

Manuel, Frank E. *The Eighteenth Century Confronts the Gods*. Cambridge, Mass.: Harvard University Press, 1959.

Marana, Giovanni Paolo. *Letters Writ by a Turkish Spy*. Ed. Arthur J. Weitzman. New York: Columbia University Press, 1970.

Marburg, Clara. *Sir William Temple: A Seventeenth Century "Libertine."* Oxford: Oxford University Press, 1932.

Markley, Robert. *The Far East and the English Imagination, 1600–1730*. Cambridge: Cambridge University Press, 2006.

Marsden, Jean I. *Fatal Desire: Women, Sexuality, and the English Stage, 1660–1720*. Ithaca, N.Y.: Cornell University Press, 2006.

Marshall, David. *The Figure of Theater: Shaftesbury, Defoe, Adam Smith, and George Eliot*. New York: Columbia University Press, 1986.

Martini, Martino [Martinius, Martin]. *Bellum Tartaricum, or the Conquest of the Great and Most Renowned Empire of China, by the Invasion of the Tartars*. London, 1654.

Mason, Peter. "Ethnographic Portraiture in the Eighteenth Century: George Psalmanaazaar's Drawings." *Eighteenth-Century Life* 23, no. 3 (1999): 58–76.

Maverick, Lewis A. *China: Model for Europe*. San Antonio: Paul Anderson, 1946.

McCracken, Grant. *Culture and Consumption: New Approaches to the Symbolic Character of Consumer Goods and Activities*. Bloomington: Indiana University Press, 1988.

McKendrick, Neil, John Brewer, and J. H. Plumb. *Birth of a Consumer Society: The Commercialization of Eighteenth-Century England*. Bloomington: Indiana University Press, 1982.

McKeon, Michael. *The Origins of the English Novel, 1600–1740*. Baltimore: Johns Hopkins University Press, 1987.

Melon, Jean-François. *A Political Essay Upon Commerce*. Trans. David Bindon. Dublin, 1738.

Merriman, James Douglas. *The Flower of Kings: A Study of the Arthurian Legend in England between 1485 and 1835*. Lawrence: University Press of Kansas, 1973.

Milhous, Judith. "The Multimedia Spectacular on the Restoration Stage." In *British Theatre and Other Arts, 1660–1800*, ed. Shirley Strum Kenney, 41–66. Washington D.C.: Folger Shakespeare Library, Associated University Press, 1993.

Miller, Allan. *The Turandot Project*. VHS. Alternate Current, Four Oaks Foundation, EuroArts Entertainment, 2000.

Miller, John. *Popery and Politics in England, 1660–1688*. Cambridge: Cambridge University Press, 1993.

Miller, Toby, Geoffrey Lawrence, Jim McKay, and David Rowe. *Globalization and Sport: Playing the World*. London: SAGE, 2001.

Milton, Anthony. "A Qualified Intolerance: The Limits and Ambiguities of Early Stuart Anti-Catholicism." In *Catholicism and Anti-Catholicism in Early Modern English Texts*, ed. Arthur F. Marotti, 85–115. Basingstoke, U.K.: Macmillan, 1999.

Min, Eun Kyung. "China between the Ancients and the Moderns." *Eighteenth Century: Theory and Interpretation* 45, no. 2 (2004): 115–30.

———. "The Rise and Fall of Chinese Empires on the English Stage, 1660–1760." *Journal of Eighteenth-Century Literature*, Korea Society for Eighteenth-Century English Literature 3, no. 1 (2006).

The Missionarie's Arts Discovered: Or, an Account of Their Ways of Insinuation, Their Artifices and Several Methods of Which They Serve Themselves in Making Converts. London, 1688.

Mitchell, Timothy. *Colonizing Egypt*. Berkeley and Los Angeles: University of California Press, 1991.

Montaño, John Patrick. "The Quest for Consensus: The Lord Mayor's Day Shows in the 1670s." In *Culture and Society in the Stuart Restoration: Literature, Drama, History*, ed. Gerald Maclean, 31–51. Cambridge: Cambridge University Press, 1995.

Montesquieu, Charles-Louis de Secondat. *Persian Letters*. 1722. Reprint, trans. C. J. Betts, London: Penguin Books, 1993.

———. *The Spirit of Laws*. Ed. David Wallace Carrithers. Berkeley: University of California Press, 1977.

More, Henry. *Philosophical Poems*. London, 1647.

Morton, Timothy. *Shelley and the Revolution in Taste: The Body and the Natural World*. Cambridge: Cambridge University Press, 1994.

Mote, F.W. *Imperial China: 900–1800*. Cambridge, Mass.: Harvard University Press, 1999.

Mungello, David E. *Curious Land: Jesuit Accommodation and the Origins of Sinology*. Honolulu: University of Hawaii Press, 1989.

———. *Great Encounter of China and the West, 1500–1800.* Lanham, Md.: Rowman & Littlefield, 1999.

Murphy, Arthur. *The Life of David Garrick, Esq.* London, 1801.

———. *The Orphan of China, a Tragedy, as It Is Performed at the Theatre-Royal in Drury Lane.* London, 1759.

———. *The Orphan of China.* In *The Modern British Drama, in Five Volumes.* Vol. 2. London, 1811.

Navarette, Domingo Fernández. *An Account of the Empire of China, Historical, Political, Moral and Religious.* In *A Collection of Voyages and Travels.* Vol. 1. London, 1704.

Needham, Rodney. *Exemplars.* Berkeley and Los Angeles: University of California Press, 1985.

Neiman, Susan. *Evil in Modern Thought: An Alternative History of Philosophy,* Princeton, N.J.: Princeton University Press, 2002.

The New London Toilet. London, 1778.

Newman, Henry. Index of Papers no. 703. Archive of the Royal Society, London.

———. "Second Letter of Queries on the Same Subject." Letter Book 14. Archive of the Royal Society, London.

———. "Some Queries Sent by Mr. H. Newman to Mr. Sam Griffiths Concerning Mr. Psalmanaazars Hist. Of Formosa." Letter Book. Archive of the Royal Society, London.

Nieuhof, Johann. *An Embassy from the East-India Company . . . to the Grand Tartar Cham.* London, 1669.

Noel, Thomas. *Theories of the Fable in the Eighteenth Century.* New York: Columbia University Press, 1975.

Novak, Maximillian E. *The Empress of Morocco and Its Critics: Settle, Dryden, Shadwell, Crowne, Duffet.* Los Angeles: William Andrews Clark Memorial Library, 1968.

Nussbaum, Felicity. *The Limits of the Human: Fictions of Anomaly, Race and Gender in the Long Eighteenth Century.* Cambridge: Cambridge University Press, 2003.

———, ed. *The Global Eighteenth Century.* Baltimore: Johns Hopkins University Press, 2003.

100 Roman Documents Concerning the Chinese Rites Controversy (1645–1941). Trans. Donald F. St. Sure, S.J. Ed. Ray R. Noll. San Francisco: University of San Francisco, Ricci Institute for Chinese-Western Cultural History, 1992.

Orléans, Pierre-Joseph d'. *History of the Two Tartar Conquerors of China.* London: Hakluyt Society, 1854.

The Orphan of China. Trans. Alan Wong. London: Mitre Press, 1973.

Orr, Bridget. *Empire on the English Stage, 1660–1714.* New York: Cambridge University Press, 2001.

Ovington, John. *An Essay Upon the Nature and Qualities of Tea.* London, 1699.

———. *A Voyage to Surat in the Year 1689.* London, 1696.

Palafox y Mendoza, Juan de. *History of the Conquest of China.* New Delhi: Deep & Deep, 1978.

———. *The History of the Conquest of China by the Tartars.* London, 1671.

———. *The History of the Tartars: Being an Account of Their Religion, Manners, and Customs, and Their Wars with, and Overthrow of the Chineses.* London, 1679.

Palmeri, Frank, ed. *Humans and Other Animals in Eighteenth-Century British Culture: Representation, Hybridity, Ethics*. Burlington, Vt.: Ashgate, 2006.
Patterson, Annabel M. *Fables of Power: Aesopian Writing and Political Theory*. Durham, N.C.: Duke University Press, 1991.
Percy, Thomas. *Miscellaneous Pieces Relating to the Chinese*, Vol. 1. London, 1762.
Perdue, Peter C. *China Marches West: The Qing Conquest of Central Eurasia*. Cambridge, Mass.: Harvard University Press, 2005.
Perry, Kathryn. "Unpicking the Seam: Talking Animals and Reader Pleasure in Early Modern Satire." In *Renaissance Beasts: Of Animals, Humans, and Other Wonderful Creatures*, ed. Erica Fudge, 19–36. Urbana: University of Illinois Press, 2004.
Peterson, Barbara Bennett, ed. *Notable Women of China: Shang Dynasty to the Early Twentieth Century*. Armonk, N.Y.: M.E. Sharpe, 2000.
Phelan, Peggy. *The Ends of Performance*, ed. Peggy Phelan and Jill Lane. New York: New York University Press, 1998.
Piozzi, Hester Lynch. *Anecdotes of the Late Samuel Johnson During the Last Twenty Years of His Life*. London, 1786.
Plumb, J. H. "The Acceptance of Modernity." In *The Birth of a Consumer Society: The Commercialization of Eighteenth-Century England*, ed. Neil McKendrick, John Brewer, and J. H. Plumb. Bloomington: Indiana University Press, 1982.
Pocock, J. G. A. "Gibbon and the Idol Fo: Chinese and Christian History in the Enlightenment." In *Sceptics, Millenarians and Jews*, ed. David S. Katz and Jonathan I. Israel, 15–34. Leiden: E.J. Brill, 1990.
———. *The Machiavellian Moment: Florentine Political Thought and the Atlantic Republican Tradition*. Princeton, N.J. and Oxford: Princeton University Press, 1975.
———. *Virtue, Commerce, and History: Essays on Political Thought and History, Chiefly in the Eighteenth Century*. Cambridge: Cambridge University Press, 1985.
Pollock, Anthony. *Gender and the Fictions of the Public Sphere, 1690–1755*. New York: Routledge, 2009.
Pomeranz, Kenneth. *The Great Divergence: China, Europe, and the Making of the Modern World Economy*. Princeton, N.J.: Princeton University Press, 2000.
Pope, Alexander. *An Essay on Man*. Dublin, 1733.
———. *The Rape of the Lock. An Heroi-comical Poem*. 2nd ed. London, 1714.
Pope, Mary. *Mysticism*. London, 1908.
Porter, David. *Ideographia: The Chinese Cipher in Early Modern Europe*. Stanford, Calif.: Stanford University Press, 2001.
Postlethwayt, *Britain's Commercial Interest Explained and Improved*. London, 1757.
Pratt, Mary Louise. *Imperial Eyes: Travel Writing and Transculturation*. London: Routledge, 1992.
Price, Cecil. *Theatre in the Age of Garrick*. Totowa, N.J.: Rowman & Littlefield, 1973.
Prideaux, Humphrey. *The True Nature of Imposture Fully Displayed in the Life of Mahomet*, 1697. Quoted in Byron Porter Smith, *Islam in English Literature*, eds. S. B. Bushrui and Anahid Melikian (Delmar, N.Y.: Caravan Books, 1977), 36.
Psalmanaazaar, George. *An Historical and Geographical Description of Formosa, An Island subject to the Emperor of Japan*. London, 1704.

———. *An Historical and Geographical Description of Formosa, An Island subject to the Emperor of Japan.* 2nd. ed. London, 1705.

[———]. *Memoirs of ****. Commonly known by the Name of George Psalmanazar; A Reputed Native of Formosa.* London, 1764.

[Psalmanaazaar, George]. *A Dialogue Between a Japonese and a Formosan, About some Points of the Religion of the Time.* London, 1707.

———. *An Enquiry into the Objections against George Psalmanaazaar of Formosa.* London, 1710.

Puccini, Giacomo. *Turandot.* Ed. Nicholas John, Opera Guide Ser. 27. New York: Riverrun, 1984.

Questier, Michael C. *Conversion, Politics, and Religion in England, 1580–1621.* New York: Cambridge University Press, 1996.

Quint, David. *Epic and Empire: Politics and Generic Form from Virgil to Milton.* Princeton, N.J.: Princeton University Press, 1993.

Ramsay, Andrew. *The Travels of Cyrus.* London, 1728. Quoted in Burton Feldman and Robert D. Richardson, *The Rise of Modern Mythology, 1680–1860,* 70.

Reasons of the Conversion of Mr. John Sidway from the Romish to the Protestant Religion. London, 1681.

Reichwein, Adolf. *China and Europe: Intellectual and Artistic Contacts in the Eighteenth Century.* Taipei: Ch'eng-wen Publishing, 1967.

Review. "An Account of the new Tragedy, entitled, *The Orphan of China.*" *The London Magazine: Or, Gentleman's Monthly Intelligencer* (May, 1759): 264–70.

Review. "Art. 24. *The Orphan of China,* a Tragedy." *The Monthly Review* 20, no. 24 (June 1759): 575–76.

Review. "A Summary Account of the New Tragedy of the *Orphan of China.*" *The Universal Magazine* (May, 1759): 245–56.

Review of *Memoirs of ****, commonly known by the Name of* George Psalmanazar; a reputed Native of Formosa. *Monthly Review* 31 (Nov.–Dec. 1764): 364 85, 441–54.

Richardson, Alan, ed. *Three Oriental Tales.* Boston: Houghton Mifflin, 2002.

Riedweg, Christoph. *Pythagoras: His Life, Teaching, and Influence.* Ithaca, N.Y.: Cornell University Press, 2005.

Rigolot, François. "The Renaissance Crisis of Exemplarity." *Journal of the History of Ideas* 59, no. 4 (1998): 557–63.

Ritvo, Harriet. *The Animal Estate: The English and Other Creatures in the Victorian Age.* Cambridge, Mass.: Harvard University Press, 1987.

Roach, Joseph. *Cities of the Dead: Circum-Atlantic Performance.* New York: Columbia University Press, 1996.

Robbins, Louise. *Elephant Slaves and Pampered Parrots: Exotic Animals in Eighteenth-century Paris.* Baltimore: Johns Hopkins University Press, 2002.

Rogers, G. A. J., ed. *The Cambridge Platonists in Philosophical Context.* Dordrecht, Netherlands: Kluwer Academic, 1997.

Rogers, Pat. "Pope, Settle, and the Fall of Troy," *Studies in English Literature, 1500–1900* 15, no. 3 (1975): 447–58.

Ropp, Paul S., Paola Zamperini, and Harriet T. Zurndorfer, eds. *Passionate Women: Female Suicide in Late Imperial China*. Leiden: Brill, 2001.

Rose, Craig. *England in the 1690s: Revolution, Religion, and War*. History of Early Modern England. Oxford: Blackwell, 1999.

Ross, Alexander. *The Alcoran of Mahomet*, 1649. Quoted in Samuel C. Chew, *The Crescent and the Rose: Islam and England during the Renaissance* (New York: Oxford University Press, 1937), 449.

Rouleau, Francis A. *The First Chinese Priest of the Society of Jesus, Emmanuel de Siqueira, 1633–1673*, 3–50. In *Archivum Historicum Societatis Jesu*, 27. Rome: Institutum Historicum S.I., 1959.

Rousseau, G. S., and Roy Porter, eds. *Exoticism in the Enlightenment*. Manchester: Manchester University Press, 1989.

Rowe, Nicholas. *The Biter*. London, 1705.

Royal Society Journal Book 11. Archive of the Royal Society, London, 1704–5.

Rycaut, Sir Paul. *The Present State of the Ottoman Empire*. [London] 1668.

Said, Edward. *Culture and Imperialism*. New York: Vintage, 1994.

———. *Orientalism*. New York: Vintage, 1979.

Schechner, Richard. *Performance Studies: An Introduction*. London: Routledge, 2002.

Schwarz, Kathryn. *Tough Love: Amazon Encounters in the English Renaissance*. Durham, N.C.: Duke University Press, 2000.

Sekora, John. *Luxury: The Concept in Western Thought, Eden to Smollett*. Baltimore: John Hopkins University Press, 1977.

Semedo, Alvarez. *The History of that Great and Renowned Monarchy of China*. London, 1655.

Serpell, James. *In the Company of Animals: A Study of Human-Animal Relationships*. Cambridge: Cambridge University Press, 1986.

Settle, Elkanah. *The Conquest of China, By the Tartars. A Tragedy*. London, 1676.

———. *The Empress of Morocco. A tragedy*. London, 1673.

———. *Notes and observations on the Empress of Morocco revised with some few errata's to be printed instead of the postscript, with the next edition of the Conquest of Granada*. London, 1674.

Shapin, Steven. *A Social History of Truth: Civility and Science in Seventeenth-Century England*. Chicago: University of Chicago Press, 1994.

Shapin, Steven, and Simon Schaffer, *Leviathan and the Air-Pump: Hobbes, Boyle, and the Experimental Life*. Princeton: Princeton University Press, 1985.

Shapiro, Barbara J. *A Culture of Fact: England 1550–1720*. Ithaca, N.Y.: Cornell University Press, 2000.

Shell, Alison. "Multiple Conversion and the Menippean Self: The Case of Richard Carpenter." In *Catholicism and Anti-Catholicism in Early Modern English Texts*, ed. Arthur F. Marotti, 154–97. Basingstoke, Hants., U.K.: Macmillan, 1999.

Shell, Marc. "The Family Pet." *Representations* 15 (1986): 121–53.

Shepherd, Simon. *Amazons and Warrior Women: Varieties of Feminism in Seventeenth-Century Drama*. New York: St. Martin's Press, 1981.

Sheppard, William. *Sincerity and hypocrisy*. Oxford, 1658.
Shih, Shu-mei. *Visuality and Identity: Sinophone Articulations across the Pacific*. Berkeley and Los Angeles: University of California Press, 2007.
The Sincere Popish Convert, or, a Brief Account of the Reasons Which Induced a Person Who Was Some Years since Seduced to the Romish Church to Relinquish Her Communion, and Return into the Bosom of the Church of England. London, 1681.
Sinha, Mrinalini. *Colonial Masculinity: The "Manly Englishman" and the "Effeminate Bengali" in the Late Nineteenth Century*. Manchester: Manchester University Press, 1995.
Six Yüan Plays. Trans. Liu Jung-en. Baltimore: Penguin, 1972.
Smith, Adam. *Essays on Philosophical Subjects*. London, 1795.
———. *Letter to the Edinburgh Review*. In *Essays on Philosophical Subjects*, ed. W. P. D. Wightmann and J. C. Bryce. Oxford: Clarendon Press, 1980.
———. *The Theory of Moral Sentiments*. Ed. Knud Haakonssen. Cambridge: Cambridge University Press, 2007.
———. *The Theory of Moral Sentiments*. Ed. D. D. Raphael and A. L. Macfie. Oxford: Clarendon Press, 1976.
Smith, Byron Porter. *Islam in English Literature*. Ed. S. B. Bushrui and Anahid Melikian. Delmar, N.Y.: Caravan Books, 1977.
Smith, Valene L., ed. *Hosts and Guests: The Anthropology of Tourism*. Philadelphia: University of Pennsylvania Press, 1989.
Smith, Woodruff D. *Consumption and the Making of Respectability, 1600–1800*. New York: Routledge, 2002.
Smollett, Tobias. *The History and Adventures of an Atom*. Ed. O. M. Brack Jr. Athens: University of Georgia Press, 1989.
Sollors, Werner. *Beyond Ethnicity: Consent and Descent in American Culture*. New York: Oxford University Press, 1986.
Sorabji, Richard. *Animal Minds and Human Morals*. Ithaca, N.Y.: Cornell University Press, 1993
Spence, Jonathan D. *The Chan's Great Continent: China in Western Minds*. New York: W. W. Norton, 1998.
Spinoza, Benedictus de. *A treatise partly theological, and partly political*. London, 1689.
Spivak, Gayatri Chakravorty. *A Critique of Postcolonial Reason: Toward a History of the Vanishing Present*. Cambridge, Mass.: Harvard University Press, 1999.
Sprague, B. Allen. *Tides in English Taste, 1619–1800: A Background for the Study of Literature*, vol. 2. Cambridge, Mass.: Harvard University Press, 1937.
Spurr, John. *England in the 1670s: "This Masquerading Age."* Malden, Mass.: Blackwell, 2000.
Stalker, John, and George Parker, *A Treatise of Japaning and Varnishing*. London, 1688.
Standaert, Nicolas. *The Interweaving of Rituals: Funerals in the Cultural Exchange Between China and Europe*. Seattle: University of Washington Press, 2008.
Starr, G. A. "Defoe and China." *Eighteenth-Century Studies* 43, no. 4 (2010): 435–54.
———. *Defoe and Spiritual Autobiography*. Princeton, N.J.: Princeton University Press, 1965.

Staves, Susan. *Players' Scepters: Fictions of Authority in the Restoration.* Lincoln: University of Nebraska Press, 1979.

Stewart, J. Douglas. *Sir Godfrey Kneller and the English Baroque Portrait.* Oxford: Clarendon Press, 1983.

Stewart, Susan. *Crimes of Writing: Problems in the Containment of Representation.* Durham, N.C.: Duke University Press, 1994.

Stierle, Karlheinz. "Translatio Studii and Renaissance: From Vertical to Horizontal Translation." In *The Translatability of Cultures: Figurations of the Space Between,* ed. Sanford Budick and Wolfgang Iser, 55–67. Stanford, Calif.: Stanford, University Press, 1996.

Stone, James W. "Indian and Amazon: The Oriental Feminine in *A Midsummer Night's Dream.*" In *The English Renaissance, Orientalism, and the Idea of Asia,* ed. Debra Johanyak and Walter S. H. Lim. New York: Palgrave MacMillan, 2009.

Straub, Kristina. *Sexual Suspects: Eighteenth-Century Players and Sexual Ideology.* Princeton, N.J.: Princeton University Press, 1992.

Struve, Lynn, ed. *The Qing Formation in World-Historical Time.* Cambridge, Mass.: Harvard University Press, 2004.

Stuart, Tristram. *The Bloodless Revolution: A Cultural History of Vegetarianism from 1600 to Modern Times.* New York: W. W. Norton, 2007.

Sugden, John, and Alan Tomlinson, eds. *Power Games: A Critical Sociology of Sport.* London: Routledge, 2002.

Sugihara, Kaoru. "The East Asian Path of Economic Development: A Long-Term Perspective." In *The Resurgence of East Asia: 500, 150, and 50 Year Perspectives,* ed. G. Arrighi, T. Hamashita, and M. Seldon, 78–123. London: Routledge, 2003.

Sussman, Charlotte. *Consuming Anxieties: Consumer Protest, Gender, and British Slavery, 1713–1833.* Stanford, Calif.: Stanford University Press, 2000.

Swiderski, Richard. *The False Formosan: George Psalmanazar and the Eighteenth-Century Experiment of Identity.* San Francisco: Mellen Research University Press, 1991.

Swift, Jonathan. "A Modest Proposal." In *The Norton Reader,* 942–49. New York: W. W. Norton, 1996.

———. *Gulliver's Travels.* Ed. Louis A. Landa. Boston: Houghton Mifflin, 1960.

Tague, Ingrid H. "Dead Pets: Satire and Sentiment in British Elegies and Epitaphs for Animals." *Eighteenth-Century Studies* 41, no. 3 (2008): 289–306.

Tambling, Jeremy. *Opera and the Culture of Fascism.* Oxford: Clarendon Press, 1996.

Tavernier, J. B. *Les Six Voyages.* [London] 1676.

Temple, Sir William. *An Essay Upon the Original and Nature of Government, Written in the Year 1672. Miscellanea.* London, 1672. Augustan Reprint Society, William Andrews Clark Memorial Library: UCLA, 1964, no. 109. Introduction by Robert C. Steensma.

———. *The Works of Sir William Temple,* vol. 3. London: S. Hamilton, Weybridge, 1814.

Thomas, Keith. *Man and the Natural World: A History of the Modern Sensibility.* New York: Pantheon, 1983.

Timmermans, Glenn. "Michael Shen Fuzong's Journey to the West: A Chinese Christian Painted at the Court of James II." In *Culture, Art, Religion: Wu Li,(1632–1718) and His Inner Journey,* 173–203, Macao: Macau Ricci Institute, 2006.

Tobin, Beth Fowkes. *Picturing Imperial Power: Colonial Subjects in Eighteenth-Century British Painting.* Durham, N.C.: Duke University Press, 1999.

Todorov, Tzvetan. *The Fantastic: A Structural Approach to a Literary Genre.* Trans. Richard Howard. Ithaca, N.Y.: Cornell University Press, 1975.

Toland, John. *Christianity Not Mysterious.* 1696. In *History of British Deism*, ed. Peter Browne. London: Routledge/Thoemmes Press, 1995.

———. *Letters to Serena.* 1704. Reprint, Stuttgart-Bad Cannstatt, Germany: Friedrich Frommann Verlag [Günther Holzboog], 1964.

Tomkins, Joyce. *The Popular Novel in England, 1770–1800.* Westport, Conn.: Greenwood Press, 1961.

Tooley, Marion J. "Bodin and the Medieval Theory of Climate." *Speculum* 28, no. 1 (1953): 64–83.

Trenchard, John. *The Natural History of Superstition.* [London] 1709. Quoted in Burton Feldman and Robert D. Richardson, *The Rise of Modern Mythology, 1680–1860.* Bloomington: Indiana University Press, 1975, 36.

Trilling, Lionel. *Sincerity and Authenticity.* Cambridge, Mass.: Harvard University Press, 1972.

A True and Faithful Account of the Last Distemper and Death of Tom Whigg, Esq. Part One. [London] 1719, 32–33. Quoted in Richmond P. Bond, *Queen Anne's American Kings*, Oxford: Clarendon Press, 1952, 137.

Van Kley, Edwin J. "An Alternative Muse: The Manchu Conquest of China in the Literature of Seventeenth-Century Northern Europe." *European Studies Review* 6 (1976): 21–43.

———. "News from China: Seventeenth-Century European Notices of the Manchu Conquest." *Journal of Modern History* 45, no. 5 (Dec. 1973): 561–82.

Vigne. *Sure and Honest Means for the Conversion of All Hereticks.* London, 1688.

Viswanathan, Gauri. *Outside the Fold: Conversion, Modernity, and Belief.* Princeton, N.J.: Princeton University Press, 1998.

Voltaire, François-Marie Arouet. *The Orphan of China.* In *The Works of Voltaire: The Dramatic Works of Voltaire*, Vol. 15. Trans. William F. Fleming. Paris, London, New York, Chicago: E.R. Dumont, 1901.

———. *Philosophical Dictionary.* Trans. and ed. Peter Gay. New York: Basic Books, 1962.

———. "Poem Upon the Destruction of Lisbon." *The Works of M. de Voltaire*, Vol. 20. Trans. T. Smollett. Dublin, 1772–73.

Wahrman, Dror. *The Making of the Modern Self: Identity and Culture in Eighteenth-Century England.* New Haven: Yale University Press, 2004.

Waith, Eugene M. *Ideas of Greatness: Heroic Drama in England.* New York: Barnes & Noble, 1971.

Wakeman, Frederic E., and Lea H. Wakeman, eds. *Telling Chinese History: A Selection of Essays.* Berkeley and Los Angeles: University of California Press, 2009.

Waley-Cohen, Joanna. *The Culture of War in China: Empire and the Military under the Qing Dynasty.* London: I. B. Tauris, 2006.

———. "The New Qing History." *Radical History Review* 88 (2004): 193–206.

Waller, Edmund. *The Works of Edmund Waller, Esq.* Dublin, 1768.

Walsh, John, Colin Haydon, and Stephen Taylor, eds. *The Church of England C.1689–C.1833: From Toleration to Tractarianism*. Cambridge: Cambridge University Press, 1993.

Watt, Ian. *The Rise of the Novel: Studies in Defoe, Richardson, and Fielding*. Berkeley and Los Angeles: University of California Press, 1957.

Watt, James. "Thomas Percy, China, and the Gothic." *The Eighteenth Century: Theory and Interpretation* 48 (2007): 95–110.

Watts, Carol. *The Cultural Work of Empire: The Seven Years' War and the Imagining of the Shandean State*. Toronto: University of Toronto Press, 2007.

Weinbrot, Howard D. *Augustus Caesar in "Augustan" England: The Decline of a Classical Norm*. Princeton, N.J.: Princeton University Press, 1978.

Wheeler, Roxann. *The Complexion of Race: Categories of Difference in Eighteenth-Century British Culture*. Philadelphia: University of Pennsylvania, 2000.

Whitelock, Bulstrode. *An Essay of Transmigration, in Defense of Pythagoras; or, a Discourse of Natural Philosophy*. London, 1692.

Wild, Antony. *The East India Company, Trade, and Conquest from 1600*. London: HarperCollins, 1999.

Williams, Craig Arthur. *Roman Homosexuality: Ideologies of Masculinity in Classical Antiquity*. New York: Oxford University Press, 1999.

Williams, Raymond. *Keywords: A Vocabulary of Culture and Society*. Rev. ed., New York: Oxford University Press, 1983.

Wilson, John Harold. *All the King's Ladies: Actresses of the Restoration*. Chicago: University of Chicago Press, 1974.

Wittuck, Charles. *The "Good Man" of the Eighteenth Century*. London: George Allen, 1901.

Wong, R. Bin. *China Transformed: Historical Change and the Limits of European Experience*. Ithaca, N.Y.: Cornell University Press, 1997.

Wood, Anthony. *The Life and Times of Anthony Wood, antiquary, of Oxford, 1632–1695, described by Himself*, ed. Andrew Clark, vol. 3. Oxford: Oxford Historical Society, Clarendon Press, 1894.

Wood, Frances. *The Silk Road: Two Thousand Years in the Heart of Asia*. Berkeley and Los Angeles: University of California Press, 2002.

Wood, Martin J. "William Whitehead." *Restoration and Eighteenth-Century Dramatists*, second series, vol. 84, ed. Paula R. Backscheider. Detroit: Gale, 1989.

The Works of the English Poets, from Chaucer to Cowper, 14. London, 1810.

Wycherley, William. *The Country Wife*. London, 1675.

Yadav, Alok. *Before the Empire of English: Literature, Provinciality, and Nationalism in Eighteenth-Century Britain*. New York: Palgrave Macmillan, 2004.

Yang, Chi-ming. "Asia Out of Place: The Aesthetics of Incorruptibility in Behn's *Oroonoko*." *Eighteenth-Century Studies* 42, no. 1 (2008): 235–53.

Young, Edward. *Conjectures on Original Composition*. London, 1759.

Zuroski, Eugenia. "Disenchanting China: Orientalism and the Aesthetics of Reason in the English Novel." *Novel: A Forum on Fiction* 38, nos. 2–3 (2005): 254–71.

INDEX

Abahai (Hung Taiji), 41, 45. *See also* Chongde (Zungteus)
Addison, Joseph, 189, 217n74, 220n8, 222n37, 222–23n48, 223n51; and "Fable of Two Owls," 128–30; and fables, 125–26, 127; and Murphy, 149; and Oriental tales, 29–30, 116; purpose and method of, 124–25; and Simonides, 131; and theory of fable, 128
"Adventures of the Egyptian Sultan," 223n51
Aesopian beast fable, 126–27, 128
Agamben, Giorgio, 16, 80
allegory, 19, 53, 54, 74, 190; and fables, 124, 126, 129, 131, 132; and Oriental tales, 116; and "Story of Pugg the Monkey," 135; transmigration, 128, 135
Amavanga, 32, 41, 42, 45, 54, 74, 207n50, 208n58
Amazons, 38–44, 61, 62, 75, 204n29; ambiguity of, 29, 39; as border figures, 27; and female effeminacy, 37; and geography, 39; and heroic virtue, 28; and Martini, 60; and masculinity, 37; as mediating, 74; and Palafox y Mendoza, 57–58, 59, 60; and Psalmanazar, 76; and Settle, 32, 33, 45, 48
animal-human distinctions, 115, 116, 124, 126, 132. *See also* pets
antiquity, and modernity, of China, 2, 9, 68, 117, 166, 168, 179, 184; and Confucius, 27, 61; and exemplarity, 17, 34, 54, 182, 186; and Restoration stage, 11, 54; and self-preservation, 28, 33
Arabian Nights, The, 29, 116, 118, 219n3, 219–20n4
Arabian Nights Entertainments, 114–15
aristocracy, 9, 28, 53, 54, 55; and commerce, 62; and virtue, 18–19, 181

Aristotelianism, 115
Aristotle, 20
Arwaker, Edward, *Truth in Fiction*, 128
authenticity, 108, 173; and chinoiserie, 109; and Murphy, 177; and Psalmanazar, 83, 85, 87, 92, 99, 102, 109, 110
authenticity, cultural, 185; and *Aida*, 192, 194; and Chineseness, 171, 173–74; and commerce, 187; and foreign commentator, 15; and imitation, 173; and innovation, 179; and Johnson, 186; marketing of, 30–31, 167; and modern spectacles, 195; and Murphy, 178; and profit, 185; and theater, 54; and transmigration, 138; and *Turandot*, 192

Balance Chinoise, 7, 8, 14
barbarians/barbarism, 18, 20, 27, 35, 71, 73, 75, 154, 190
Bayle, Pierre, 66
Beijing Olympics, 1–2, 3, 13, 191, 195
Benjamin, Walter, 115–16
Bernier, François, 121
Bible, 20, 65, 66, 68, 70
Bodin, Jean, 69–70, 212n114
body, 131, 137, 142–43, 150, 181; female, 37, 46, 52, 58, 60, 154–55, 171, 207n55. *See also* women
Boquet, Louis-René, 171
Boucher, François, 171
Bouvet, Joachim, 20, 66, 208n59
Boyle, Robert, 93, 215–16n49, 217n73
Buddhism, 20, 114, 118–19, 123–24, 137, 145, 211n101, 221n15
Burnet, Thomas, 122

Cambridge Platonists, 122, 221n27
Candidius, George, *A Short Account*, 95
cannibalism, 76, 87, 112, 122, 132, 142
Catherine of Braganza, 5
Cawthorn, James, *Of Taste*, 169–78
Chambers, Ephraim, *Cyclopaedia*, 18, 127
Charles II, 5
Cheng Wei-hsin (Emmanuel de Siqueira), 105, 214n31
china, 3–4, 5, 29, 110, 147. See also porcelain
Chinese Festival, The, 171–72
Chinese Rites Controversy, 19, 66
chinoiserie, 108–9, 119, 148, 149, 171, 185, 196; and japanning, 110, 118, 144; and Oriental fables, 118; and orientalism, 25; and Psalmanazar, 110, 111
Chongde (Zungteus), 41, 42, 48–50, 205n40, 205n42
Chongzhen (Ch'ung-chen), 56–57, 58
Christianity, 20, 29, 64–65, 69, 119, 121, 137; and chronology, 70; and Confucius, 19, 20, 27, 66, 118, 158; and Psalmanazar, 86; and Temple, 68, 72; universalism of, 60, 65. See also converts/conversion
Church of England / Anglicanism, 82, 84, 85, 87, 104, 112
civilization, 18, 35, 36, 73, 75, 117, 154
Clancy, Michael, *Hermon*, 172–73
Clement XI, 118
climate theory, 70, 71, 130
Collins, Anthony, 20, 66
colonialism, 24–25, 62, 92, 104, 193, 194; circuits of exchange of, 196; and Psalmanazar, 80, 90, 113; and race, 22–23; and racism, 21; and "Story of Pugg the Monkey," 133, 135; and tropicopolitan, 22
commerce, 1, 5, 26, 33, 75, 155, 184, 187; and aristocracy, 62; and Cawthorn, 170; and Chinese effeminacy, 74; and Confucius, 27; and conversion, 81, 108, 111; and crisis of heroism, 38; and effeminacy, 29, 64; and family, 153; and Indian Kings visit, 105; of inner life, 150; and japanning, 142; and Johnson, 186; and landowners, 62; and luxury, 180, 181, 228–29n54; and missionaries, 80–81; and Murphy, 30, 149, 150, 153, 168; and porcelain and lacquer, 117; and protectionism, 171; and Psalmanazar, 76, 78, 79, 80, 82, 103, 104, 109; and public good, 151, 152; and republicanism, 153; in Restoration period, 62; and Smith, 162, 165, 167; sociability of, 151–52; and *Spectator*, 125; and "Story of Pugg the Monkey," 135; and territorial conquest, 74; and theater, 162; and transmigration, 139; and *Turandot*, 192; and valor, 74; and virtue, 7–10, 25, 30, 100, 108; and women, 132. See also trade
commodity/commodities, 5, 10, 14–15, 109, 146, 149, 167, 186; converts as, 103–11; and cultural appropriation, 139; and economy, 151–52; and japanning, 140; and Oriental fable, 117; ranking of, 6–7; and *Spectator*, 125; and "Story of Pugg the Monkey," 134, 135
Compton, Henry, 77, 84
Conant, Martha Pike, 123
Confucianism, 10, 114, 218n80; degeneration of classical, 170; and governance, 4; and Gueullette, 137; and idolatry, 29; and Islam, 118; and Kircher, 119; and morality, 171; and Murphy, 148, 149, 167, 168, 182; and Psalmanazar, 87; and Roman Catholicism, 118; and Whitehead, 160
Confucius, 61–62, 65–74, 75, 184; *Analects of Confucius*, 66; and Cawthorn, 170; and Chinese governance, 25; and Christianity, 19, 20, 27, 66, 158; and commercialism, 27, 170; cult of, 19; *Doctrine of the Mean*, 66; and effeminacy, 51; and exemplarity, 19; and family values, 158, 159; in Fénelon, 2, 9; *Four Books*, 66; and gender ambiguity, 29; *The Great Learning*, 66; and heroic virtue, 28; and Jesus Christ, 66; and Kircher, 119; and Matteo Ricci, 211n101; as mediator, 74; as model hethnic, 27; Montesquieu on, 159; *The Morals of Confucius*, 65–66, 67; and Murphy, 158–62; native genius of, 71; as philosopher-king, 28, 66; and Psalmanazar, 76; and Temple, 68, 69, 71, 118; and theater, 183; as virtuous pagan, 27
Confucius Sinarum Philosophus, 19, 66
conqueror, conquered, 33, 62, 71, 73
consumerism, 1, 3–4, 9, 30, 117, 167, 183, 185; and commodity culture, 168; and Murphy, 150, 157; and Oriental tales, 219n4; and *Spectator*, 125; and "Story of Pugg the Monkey," 135; and theater, 10; and transmigration, 139; and women, 134
consumption, 37, 132, 146, 168, 171, 185, 186;

and Cawthorn, 169–78; and Confucianism, 170; and conversion, 178; emasculation through, 169; as harmful vs. healthy, 151; and metempsychosis, 115; and morality, 8, 178; and Murphy, 149, 178; and public good, 169; virtue as object of, 7
converts/conversion, 91, 111–14; and alterity, 106; before-and-after dichotomy of, 103; and Chinese, 105–8, 112; and civilization and barbarism, 80; as commodities, 81, 103–11; concept of, 84; and consumption, 178; and cultural liminality, 108; and disputation, 84; and duplicity, 82–83; and Dutch Protestant missions, 91; as epistemology, 79; and exemplarity, 81; experimental nature of, 79; fantasy of, 137; by force vs. assimilation, 112; Formosan, 91; genuine, 106; and Gueullette, 136; Indian, 91; and Indian Kings visit, 104; and language, 90; and local customs, 106; and moral authority, 85–86; as performance, 29, 75; and Psalmanazar, 29, 77–78, 79, 82, 85–86, 87, 90, 94, 98, 99, 103, 112, 113; and sincerity, 83, 87, 111; and truth, 79–80; and virtue, 81. *See also* Christianity
Conway, Anne, 122
cosmetics, 141, 142, 225n73
Couplet, Philippe, 66, 105, 218n80
Croxall, Samuel, 126

Dacier, André, *Life of Pythagoras*, 123
Davenant, William, *Siege of Rhodes*, 53
Defoe, Daniel, 3–4, 5
deism, 20, 67, 99, 100, 101, 158, 161, 162
de la Croix, François Pétis: *Persian Tales*, 116, 132, 189; *Turkish Tales*, 116, 128, 130, 223n49
Dennis, John, 173
de Rhodes, Alexandre, 105, 214n31, 217n78
de Rode, Alexander, 85, 105, 214n31
despotism, 30, 33, 60, 121, 159, 160, 186, 190; and effeminacy, 37, 51, 67, 190; and English court politics, 53; and enlightenment, 18, 61; and fables, 129, 130; and Restoration tragedy, 53
Domingo, Placido, 194
Dominicans, 66
Dorgon (Amavangus), 41–42
d'Orléans, Pierre-Joseph, 56; *History*, 35, 40
Dossie, Robert, *Handmaid to the Arts*, 141

Dryden, John, 16, 30, 52, 55, 61, 82, 209n73, 209n75; *Aureng-Zebe*, 53; *Fables Ancient and Modern*, 127; translation of Ovid by, 139
Du Halde, Jean-Baptiste, 12, 13, 159, 168; *The General History of China*, 72, 174–75, 177
du Locle, Camille, 193
Dutch East India Company, 5
Dutch missions and trade, 11, 84, 91, 96–97, 215n41

East India Company, 5, 11, 15, 171
East Indies, 25, 34, 64, 93, 123; trade with, 1, 5, 11, 53, 62, 63, 104, 135
Ecker, Michael, 192, 195
effeminacy, 36, 37, 39, 54, 64, 75, 190; as alternative to heroic virtue, 38; boundaries with masculinity, 35; and civilization, 36, 71; and commerce, 29, 64; and Confucianism, 67; and Confucius, 62; and cultural degeneracy, 36, 57; and despotism, 37, 51, 67, 190; and fall and preservation of China, 61; and fall of empire, 28–29; female, 37, 40–41, 45; and female body, 46; and heroism, 29, 68; as justifying conquest, 42–43; and luxury, 151, 179–80; in Martini, 40–41, 56, 60; as mediating idiom, 74; and moral virtue, 68; and Murphy, 149; in Palafox y Mendoza, 56, 57–58, 60; and Settle, 32, 33, 44, 45, 47, 49, 50, 159; and Temple, 71, 72
Egypt, 115, 119, 123, 184, 185–86, 192–95; and embalming, 120, 121, 142, 147; funeral and burial rites of, 140, 142
emasculation, 37, 50, 51, 52, 155, 169
embalming, 120, 121, 142–43, 147
empire/imperialism, 23, 38, 64, 117, 139, 193, 194, 196; ambiguity of female-gendered, 71; conflicting attitudes about, 33, 75, 179; and Confucius, 62; economic vs. territorial, 34; and effeminacy, 28–29, 36, 37; and gender, 36; of Great Britain, 5, 6, 185, 196, 197; and preservation of cultural memory, 117; in Restoration tragedy, 53; and *Spectator*, 125; and Temple, 71, 72; and theater, 11
enamelwork, 109–10
England, 11, 25, 34, 62–63, 73, 146, 181; as corrupt, 69; and East and West Indies, 34; and East Indies trade, 63; and empire building, 33–34; and Empire of Learning, 64–65; and

England *(continued)*
  political stability, 33; Restoration, 34, 37, 38, 62; turbulent political climate of, 50. *See also* Great Britain
Enlightenment, 19, 20, 21, 22, 66, 67, 124
eroticism, 37, 132, 135, 207n55
ethnic/ethnicity, 27, 33, 65
ethnography, 56, 82, 85
euhemerism, 120, 142
Europe, 4, 21, 33, 59, 60, 68, 158; and Asian other, 94; and Empire of Learning, 65; scrutiny of manners of, 13–14
Evelyn, John, 63
example, 16–19, 21, 200–201n36; and fables, 127; and Johnson, 186; and Psalmanazar, 82
exemplarity, 16–17, 19, 25, 54, 81, 182, 185, 192; ambivalences of, 28; and antiquity, 18; and Confucius, 19, 62, 66, 67; of Eastern empires, 9; and Englishness in Chinese dress, 17; and example and counterexample, 30, 61, 149, 161, 166, 167–68, 173; and imitation, 18, 61; and inclusive exclusions, 16, 21; and Kant, 21; and luxury, 181; modern performance of Oriental, 30–31; and morality, 26; and morality and manufactures, 182; and Murphy, 162, 168, 178; Oriental religious, 114; and Palafox y Mendoza, 59, 60; and particular and universal, 16; and performance, 16; and Psalmanazar, 78, 80, 83, 113; and race and orientalism, 25, 26; and Temple, 69, 71; and Turandot, 189

"Fable of Two Owls," 127, 128–30, 223n49
fables, 146, 147; Addison's theory of, 125–26, 127, 128; and morality, 131–32; and *Spectator*, 125–39; and Toland, 128; and truth, 120, 127–28, 131
facts, 82, 99–103
"Fadlallah and Zemroude," 223–24n55
fashion, 10, 12, 13, 152, 168, 174–75, 183, 229n67; as changeable, 107–8, 173; and Du Halde, 12, 177; and Le Comte, 12, 174; and Murphy, 174, 178; and Palafox y Mendoza, 59. *See also* chinoiserie
Fawconer, Samuel, 169
femininity, 37, 38, 39, 42, 59, 62, 130, 141. *See also* women

Fénelon, François, 199n5; *Dialogues des Morts*, 2–3
Ferguson, Adam, 163, 179
Fontaney, Jean de, 95
Formosa, 29, 78–79, 91, 92, 110, 111; and Jesuits, 84–85; and native expertise, 82; pagan rituals of, 87; and revealed religion, 103; and Royal Society, 94; and virtue, 90, 113. *See also* Psalmanazar, George
Foucquet, Jean-François, 20, 66
France, 11, 64, 104, 150, 151
Fulin (Shunzhi, Xunchi), 41
Fundamental Laws of China, The, 159, 230n79
Fu Xi (Fo-hi), 20

Galland, Antoine, 114, 184, 219n4
Garrick, David, 148–49, 171–72, 225n1, 227n28
Garrick, Mrs., 174
gender, 29, 36, 43, 75, 132, 133, 151, 169; and Settle, 28, 32, 33. *See also* femininity; masculinity; women
geography, 39, 69–70, 94, 101, 131
Gibbon, Edward, *The History*, 34–35
globalism, 24, 81, 193; and economy, 5, 6, 24, 53, 81
globalization, 7, 185, 187; and economy, 30; and empire, 196; and marketing of history, 188; and Puccini, 190; and trade, 34; and transmigration, 135
Goldsmith, Oliver, 7, 168, 178, 228n51; *The Citizen of the World*, 14, 150, 224n61, 228n48
Great Britain, 5, 6, 150, 151, 160, 185, 197; and colonial circuits of exchange, 196; and France, 104, 150. *See also* England
Greece, 2, 3, 27, 61, 66, 75, 119, 168; and Confucianism, 114, 170; funeral and burial rites of, 142; ideals of, 63, 64; literary explorations of, 34; and metempsychosis, 115; and morality, 65; and Persia, 36; and Tartars, 35; and Temple, 68–69, 71, 73; and virtue, 9
Greenhill, Thomas, *Nekrokedeia*, 142–43
Griffiths, Sam, 95, 216n56
Guardian, 116
Gueullette, Thomas-Simon, 30, 116, 135–38

Hanway, Jonas, *An Essay on Tea*, 171
Harrington, James, 9

Hatchett, William, 150
heathen/heathenism, 27, 65, 78, 80, 86, 116, 122. *See also* hethnic/hethnicity
Hegel, G. W. F., 186
Herdtrich, Christian, 66
hermaphroditism, 46, 49, 54
heroic drama, 54, 55, 57, 62
heroism / heroic virtue, 28, 36, 46, 54, 56, 62, 63–64, 68; Chinese lack of, 34, 35; and Chinese resilience, 38; and Confucius, 62, 118; and effeminacy, 29, 37, 38; in Martini, 40, 41–42; and Palafox y Mendoza, 57, 59; and Restoration, 46, 53, 62; and Settle, 32–33, 44, 48, 49, 50, 51, 159; and Temple, 62, 68–69, 70, 71, 72. *See also* virtue
hethnic/hethnicity, 27–28, 30, 65, 75, 115, 121
Hinduism, 20, 29, 115, 121–22, 137
Hua Mu Lan, 39–40
Hume, David, 155, 162, 180, 181, 228n41, 230n86, 230n89

idolatry, 61, 69, 117, 120, 144, 149, 184, 218n80; and Buddhism, 118; and early modern orientalism, 186; and Egyptians, 142; and Gueullette, 135–36, 137, 138; and Kant, 21; and Kircher, 119, 137; and local customs, 106; and Murphy, 157, 158, 161, 162; and Oriental tale, 114, 115; and *Spectator*, 131; and Stalker and Parker, 145; and transmigration, 29, 147. *See also* pagans/paganism; superstition
imitation, 7, 25, 31, 60, 76, 156, 168, 230n83; of classical virtue, 18–19; and commerce, 170; and conversion, 80, 91; and cultural translation, 30; of decorative techniques, 118; and Dennis, 173; and effeminate sensuality, 37; of Egyptian civilization, 184; and exemplarity, 18, 61; and Hume, 181; and innovation, 28; and luxury, 169; and manufacturing, 5, 151, 181, 186; and Murphy, 171, 174, 178; and Oriental tales, 15, 117, 139; and Psalmanazar, 80, 92, 108, 109, 110, 111, 113; and technological innovation, 179
India, 5, 21, 36, 64, 70, 114, 119, 121; and Buddhism, 118, 123–24; colonization of, 24–25; and metempsychosis, 115; and Restoration tragedy, 53; and Temple, 68
Indian Kings, 104–5, 106, 109, 111, 112

Innes, Alexander, 77, 86, 104, 214–15n37
Intorcetta, Prospero, 66
Islam, 17, 20, 26, 114–15, 118, 130, 136–37, 219n2

James II, 105, 218n81
Japan, 5, 21, 76, 96, 103, 119, 120; lacquerwork of, 109–10; and Psalmanazar, 77, 78, 81, 84–85, 97, 104, 109, 110
japanwork/japanning, 29, 110, 117, 139–46, 147; and chinoiserie, 110, 118, 144; and identity, 140, 142; and idolatry, 144; and preservation, 110, 139, 140
Jesuits, 4, 25, 28, 41, 42, 64, 206n48, 208n59; and Chinese culture, 108; and Chinese political stability, 50; and chronology, 19–20, 201n43; and Confucianism, 66, 71, 118, 170; and converts, 105; and Fénelon, 3; and idolatry, 29; and Japan and China, 214n29; and Palafox y Mendoza, 56; and Psalmanazar, 75–76, 77, 84–85, 87, 95, 99, 214n30; and Shen Fuzong, 107; and translation, 19; and Voltaire, 67
Jews, 34, 111, 142
Johnson, Samuel, 18, 78, 80; *The History of Rasselas*, 185–86

Kangxi (K'ang-hsi), 41
Kant, Immanuel, 21–22, 201n49
kinship, 120, 122, 124, 132, 139, 157, 225n78
Kircher, Athanasius, 66, 70, 120, 121, 211n108; *China Illustrata*, 118–19, 137
Kneller, Sir Godfrey, 218n81; "The Chinese Convert," 105–6, 107, 108
knowledge, 67, 81, 94, 96, 109, 111, 116, 196; and Locke, 101, 102; and mercantile expansion, 100–101; and Psalmanazar, 29, 79, 82, 99, 100, 112; and Royal Society, 93, 94; and Temple of, 70, 71, 72, 73

lacquer/lacquerwork, 5, 109–10, 117
Langbaine, Gerald, 208n60
Langlois, Nicolas, 107–8
Le Comte, Louis, 13–14, 61, 119, 174, 201n44, 229–30n78; *Nouveaux mémoires sur l'état présent de la Chine*, 11–12, 64
Lee, Mary, 47, 207–8n56
Leibniz, Gottfried Wilhelm, 20, 66, 158

L'Estrange, Roger, 126, 222n46
Li Zicheng (Li Tzu-ch'eng), 60, 205n40
Locke, John, 133, 217n72, 223n51, 224n56; *Essay Concerning Human Understanding*, 101, 102
Longobardi, Niccolo, 66
Louis XIV, 64, 107
luxury, 7, 9, 57, 167, 173, 183, 184; ancient critiques of, 36; Asiatic, 36, 180, 182; and commerce, 180, 181, 228–29n54; and contagion, 151–52, 169, 179, 180–81; debates on, 150; and effeminacy, 151, 179–80; of grief, 155, 158; and health of body politic, 181–82; and morality, 30, 36, 169, 181, 182; and Murphy, 149, 152, 158, 168, 169

Macartney, Lord, 171
Machiavelli, Niccolò, 9
Mahometans, 114, 115
Manchus, 34, 41, 42, 73, 78; conquest by, 28, 33, 40, 44, 205n40. *See also* Qing dynasty
Mandeville, Bernard, 10; *The Fable of the Bees*, 7–8
Marana, Giovanni, *Letters Writ by a Turkish Spy*, 14, 228n48
Mariette, Auguste, *Monuments of Upper Egypt*, 193
Martini, Martino, 60, 205n40, 205–6n42, 208n59; *De bello tartarico*, 40–42, 56, 58
masculinity, 33, 38, 42, 57–59, 67; and Amazons, 37; and Confucius, 62; female, 45, 48, 50; and heroism, 35, 68; and Settle, 45, 48–49, 50, 52. *See also* gender
Mason, Simon, *The Good and Bad Effects of Tea Considered*, 171
Mehta, Zubin, 188, 189
Melon, Jean-François, 180
Mille et une nuits, Les, 114
Miller, Allan, *The Turandot Project*, 188–89
Ming dynasty, 28, 40, 41, 42, 56, 63, 75, 205n40; and Confucianism, 118; fall of, 32, 33, 34, 38, 60, 73; and Qing dynasty, 43; and Settle, 32, 51; and Temple, 71
missionaries, 4, 80–81, 84, 85, 87, 90, 104, 105
Mongols, 33, 34
Montesquieu, Charles de Secondat, Baron de, 30, 153, 162, 227n36; *Persian Letters*, 14, 228n48; *Spirit of the Laws*, 159, 160
moral certainty, 79, 82, 86, 94, 97, 103, 112

morality, 3, 7, 33, 114, 146, 181, 187; and Aesopian beast fables, 126; and China, 52, 54, 67, 68; and Chinese empire, 182; Chinese empire of, 63–64; and Chinese legibility, 120; and Chinese secular ethics, 66; and Clancy, 172; and classical antiquity, 65; and Confucianism, 171; and consumption, 8, 150, 178; and effeminacy, 36; and example, 18; and exemplarity, 22, 26; and fables, 127, 131–32; and geography, 69–70, 131; independent from church authority, 20; and Johnson, 186; and Kant, 21; and Murphy, 148, 149, 150, 152, 154, 158, 161, 162, 168, 174; and Palafox y Mendoza, 60; and Psalmanazar, 79, 92; on Restoration stage, 46; and Settle, 44; and Smith, 162, 163, 164, 165–67; and *Spectator*, 125, 126, 130, 131; and Temple, 69, 73; and theater, 11, 162–63; and transmigration in Oriental fables, 126; and women, 155. *See also* virtue
Morals of Confucius, 19
moral virtue, 27, 65, 68, 71, 92, 112, 163. *See also* virtue
Murphy, Arthur: and commerce, 30, 149, 150, 153, 168; and Confucianism, 148, 149, 167, 168, 182; and Confucius, 158–62; *The Orphan of China*, 11, 28, 30, 148–64, 168, 169, 170, 171, 174, 175–78, 182, 225–26n2; and passions, 152, 153–56, 158, 161, 162, 167, 170; and virtue, 148, 149, 150, 152, 154, 157–58, 159, 160, 161–62, 167

native, as term, 91–92
Newman, Henry, 95, 98
Nieuhof, Johann, 35, 70, 119–20; *Embassy to China*, 144–45
Ninche (Nüzhen/Jurchen), 120
Noverre, Jean-Georges, 171
Nurhaci (Tianming), 41

Ogilby, John, 126
Opera on Original Site, Inc., 192, 194, 196
Oriental fables, 116, 117, 118, 119, 124, 126, 139
Orientalism, 23, 24, 25, 26, 36, 187, 190–91, 202n60; and chinoiserie, 109; global, 188, 194, 196; and *Turandot*, 195
orientalism, early modern, 25, 31, 56, 147, 184, 186; and chinoiserie, 25, 108; and effeminacy, 37, 44, 54; and idolatrous other, 186; and Ori-

entalism, 26, 109, 202n60; and transmigration, 147; and violence, 60–61
Oriental tales, 15, 29–30, 114, 115–16, 186–87, 188, 219–20n4
Ottoman Empire, 17, 26, 179
Ovid, *Metamorphoses*, 138–39, 143
Ovington, John, 6, 121

pagans/paganism, 20, 64, 75, 87, 118–19, 120, 137; and Confucius, 158; virtuous, 26, 27, 121. See also idolatry
Palafox y Mendoza, Juan de, 35, 206n46, 209–10n77; *Historia de la Conquista de la China por el Tártaro*, 44, 56–60
Parrenin, Dominique, 168
passions, 37, 155, 180, 182, 183, 227n26; and Murphy, 152, 153–56, 158, 161, 162, 167, 170; and Smith, 164, 165, 167
Pattenden, Edward, 109
Percy, Thomas, *The Little Orphan of the House of Chao*, 159
performance, of China, 11–16
Persia, 21, 36, 53, 123, 179, 184
pets, 133, 134–35, 224n60
Picart, Bernard, "A Chinese funeral procession," 14
Plato, 20, 66, 68, 123
Pocock, J. G. A., 9, 153
Pope, Alexander, 132, 142
porcelain, 3–4, 110, 117, 139, 219–20n4; consumption of, 171; and preservation, 4; and Psalmanazar, 218–19n89; thinginess of, 6; vogue for, 5; and Wedgwood, 178. See also china
Portugal, 5, 11
postcolonialism, 22–23
Postlethwayt, Malachy, 179, 231n92; *Britain's Commercial Interest Explained and Improved*, 180–81
Prester John, 119
private vs. public spheres, 1, 14–15, 150, 152, 160–62, 169, 182
Protestantism, 77, 82, 98, 104
Psalmanazar, George, 29, 75–113, 213–14n23, 216n56, 216n57, 217n69, 218–19n89; background of, 77; and chinoiserie, 82, 109, 111; complexion of, 97–98; credibility of, 92, 96; and cultural alterity, 111; and de Rhodes, 105;

and Alexander de Rode, 97; *A Description of Formosa*, 76, 77, 81, 84, 85–87, 90, 94–95, 98, 99; *A Dialogue Between a Japonese and a Formosan*, 81, 99–102, 112; and disputation, 84; double for, 87, 100; *An Enquiry*, 81–82, 96–97, 98, 103; fakery of, 111; and Formosa, 77, 80, 81, 83, 93, 96–98, 99, 112, 113; and heathen vs. Christian, 112; impostures of, 77; and Indian Kings, 104–5; inner character of, 112; and japanning, 110, 140; and Jesuits, 214n30; lack of cultural adornment of, 111–12; and language, 87–90, 92–93, 94, 97, 113, 214–15n37; *Memoirs of ****,* 77, 89, 109, 112; name of, 111; as native, 113; native authority of, 96, 98, 102; and publishing, 77–78; and religious factionalism, 84; religious fraud of, 109; and Royal Society, 94; and Salmanazar and Shalmaneser, 111; self-marketing by, 82; self-promotion of, 99; self-reflexivity of, 86; sincerity of, 82–94, 111; and Siqueira, 105; transparency of, 111–12; travels of, 77; and White Formosan Work, 109–10
Puccini, Giacomo, 232n12, 232n14; *Turandot*, 28, 31, 185, 188–92, 195, 234n28
Pythagoras, 119, 120, 123, 124, 128, 147, 220n5, 221n27; and Hinduism, 121–22; and transmigration, 115
Pythagoreanism, 29, 126, 133–34, 138

Qing dynasty, 25, 33, 41, 42, 43, 45, 63, 78. See also Manchus
Qin Liangyu, 61, 205n33
Quesnay, François, 159

race, 21–23, 25, 36, 98, 130. See also colonialism; hethnic/hethnicity
rationalism, 86, 115, 122, 124, 125
reason, 94, 99, 100, 132, 133, 166
reincarnation, 29, 30, 132–33, 221n15
Ren Xiong, 43
Ricci, Matteo, 19, 66
Roman Catholicism, 77, 82, 84, 85, 86, 87, 98, 118
Rome, 18, 34, 61, 75, 119, 168, 196, 203n16; and Amazons, 38–39; atrophied martial spirit of, 180; and Confucianism, 170; decadence of, 35; and effeminacy, 29; exemplarity of, 18; fall of, 180, 184; ideals of, 63, 64; imperialism

Rome *(continued)*
  of, 33; and luxury, 182; sensuality of, 36; and Tartars, 35–36; and Temple, 68–69, 71, 73; and virtue, 9
Rougemont, François, 66
Rowe, Nicholas, *The Biter*, 10, 11
Royal Society, 68, 76, 93, 94, 95–96, 97–98, 103, 111

Said, Edward, 23, 25, 26, 36, 187, 190
Saint-Évremond, Charles de, 68
Salmon, William, *Polygraphice*, 141
science, 68, 93, 116, 122; and Psalmanazar, 78, 79, 82, 99, 104, 113
Scythia/Scythians, 34, 39, 57, 59, 72, 73, 111, 203n11
Semedo, Alvarez, 61; *History of the Great and Renowned Monarchy of China*, 64
sentiment, 149, 152–53, 154, 155, 166, 167. *See also* Smith, Adam
sentimentality, 1, 30, 152, 180, 182; and border figures, 27; and Murphy, 150, 157–58, 168; and theater, 183
Settle, Elkanah, 41, 207n50, 208n58, 209n69; *Cambyses, King of Persia*, 54–55, 210n82; *The Conquest of China*, 11, 28, 30, 32, 37–38, 40, 44–52, 54, 55–56, 60–61, 148, 159, 225–26n2; and Dryden, 55; and effeminacy, 32, 33, 44, 45, 47, 49, 50, 159; *Empress of Morocco*, 55; and heroism/heroic virtue, 32–33, 44, 48, 49, 50, 51, 159; and historical truth, 51; and history, 206n46; and Martini, 56; names in, 42; sources of, 42
Shanghai World Exposition, 195
Shen Fuzong (Fu-Tsung; Michael Alphonsus), 105–8, 218n80, 218nn82–83
Shen Yunying, 43
Shimabara Massacre, 84
Siam, 101
Siddons, Mrs., 174
silver, 6, 63, 171, 203n5
sincerity, 108; Christian writings on, 83; of convert, 82–84, 87, 111; and fact, 96, 99; and gentility, 92; and language, 87–88, 90; and Psalmanazar, 84–85, 87–88, 90, 92, 93, 96, 99, 102, 103, 112; and truth, 93
Smith, Adam, 181, 231n93; *Theory of Moral Sentiments*, 30, 162–67

Socrates, 2, 9, 18, 20, 27, 65, 184
Spain, 56, 85
spectacle, 7, 29, 54, 55, 75, 195; of affect, 149; and Beijing Olympics, 1–2, 3; construction of, 10, 167; and fraud and duplicity, 15; of monumentality, 192; in Murphy, 152; in Palafox y Mendoza, 56; of Restoration stage, 61; and Settle, 55, 56; and Smith, 152; and virtue and vice, 1; as warning, 4
Spectator, 29, 116, 149, 189, 217n74, 220n8; commentary of, 124–25; and cultural appropriation, 139; dervish and camel story in, 130; fables of, 128–30, 131, 139, 146; and Ovid, 138. *See also* Addison, Joseph
spectatorship, 12–13, 152, 162, 163, 164, 165, 166, 228n48
Spinoza, Baruch, 33, 34, 35, 66
Spinozists, 19
Stalker, John, and Robert Parker, 141, 144–46; *A Treatise of Japaning and Varnishing*, 140, 146
Steele, Richard, 29–30, 116, 124, 125, 149, 189, 220n8
"Story of Fadlallah," 132–33
"Story of Prince Calaf and the Princess of China, The," 189, 232n14
"Story of Pugg the Monkey," 133–35, 136, 138
"Story of the Grecian King and the Physician Douban, The," 223n51
Stuarts, 34, 53, 54
Sun Jiazheng, 191
superstition, 29, 30, 139, 146–47; and Addison, 128; and China, 137; and Confucianism, 118; in Fénelon, 3; and Gueullette, 137; and Kircher, 118; and Stalker and Parker, 144, 145; and "Story of Pugg the Monkey," 133; and transmigration, 116. *See also* idolatry; pagans/paganism
Swift, Jonathan, *A Modest Proposal*, 76
sympathy, 15, 17, 152, 162, 163, 165–67, 228n41; and Murphy, 149, 150, 152, 155, 156–57, 161

Tai Miao, 189, 190, 194
Taoism, 29, 114, 115, 119, 211n101
Tartars, 42–43, 75, 111, 189, 203n11, 205–6n42; as barbarians, 35, 63, 71; and Chinese preservation of customs and manners, 33; conquest by, 28, 148; and effeminacy, 179–80; English attitudes toward, 34–35; and heroism/heroic

virtue, 63–64; and Jesuit accounts, 41, 50, 206n48; martial character of, 34, 35, 50; in Martini, 40–41; and masculinity, 35, 45; and Murphy, 148, 152, 153, 158; and Palafox y Mendoza, 56, 57–60; and Settle, 32, 44, 45, 47, 48, 49, 50, 159; as Sinicized, 38, 43, 62; and Temple, 69, 71, 72–73. *See also* Manchus

Tatler, 116

tea, 4, 5, 6, 10, 25, 80–81, 139, 170–71

Temple, Sir William, 4, 62, 67–68, 70, 118, 211n108, 212n114; *Essay Upon the Ancient and Modern Learning*, 68; *Of Heroic Virtue*, 68–69, 70–73

theaters, 1, 10–11, 38, 76, 174, 182, 184; modeling of taste in, 171; and morality, 162–63; in Murphy, 152; and performance, 15; reopening of, 53; and Restoration, 46, 53, 54, 55, 61, 62, 67, 74; and Smith, 162, 163–64, 165; and sociability, 162

Thomas, Elizabeth, 92

Tiancong (Thienzungus), 41

Toland, John, 30, 122, 128, 142; "The History of the Soul's Immortality," 120, 121

Toleration Act, 82

tourism, 31, 188, 192, 193–94

trade, 1, 6, 21, 25, 34, 62, 171, 181; with East Indies, 5, 53, 63, 104, 135. *See also* commerce

translatio imperii, 30, 34, 75, 139

translation, 38–39, 42, 88–90

translatio studii, 70, 212n112

transmigration, 29, 30, 115, 141–42, 220n5, 224n56; and Addison, 128; and Arwaker, 128; and autonomous selfhood, 132; and border figures, 27; and Buddhism, 118; and Cambridge Platonists, 122; and Dacier, 123; and death, 132; and feminine vice and masculine virtue, 116; and global perspective, 117; and Gueullette, 136–37, 138; and Hinduism, 122; as idolatry, 29; and japanning, 144; and kinship, 225n78; and Kircher, 119; as metempsychosis, 115, 120; and nature's cycles, 122, 124; and Nieuhof, 120; and Oriental fable, 124; and Ovid, 138–39; and Plato, 123; and preservation, 117, 120, 121, 133, 136, 138–39, 147; and Pythagoras, 122, 124; and reason, 124; relevance of, 147; and sexuality, 135; and *Spectator*, 116; and Stalker and Parker, 145; and "Story of Pugg the Monkey," 133–35; and

Toland, 120, 121, 122; and universal kinship, 122; and Whitelock, 123; and women and animals, 131

transvestism, 46–47, 50, 51–52

travel literature, 4, 11, 22, 38, 100, 175, 186–87, 200n25; and Psalmanazar, 76, 94, 95, 214n32

truth: and Addison, 128; and Boyle, 93; as contrary to reason, 100; and conversion, 79–80, 81; and fables, 127–28, 131; and moral certainty, 79, 82; and Oriental fable, 117, 124; and Psalmanazar, 78, 79, 82, 84, 85–86, 90, 93, 94, 100, 103, 109, 112, 113; social history of, 113; supplementary vs. authentic, 113; and testimony, 93

universalism, 18, 19, 120, 130; and Addison, 128; and Amazons, 33; Enlightenment, 22; and Kircher, 119; and Palafox y Mendoza, 60; and racism, 21; and *Spectator*, 149; of Western values, 158

Verdi, Giuseppe, *Aida*, 185, 192–95, 234n28

violence, 37, 56, 60–61, 67, 137

virtue, 1, 6, 22, 28, 105, 125, 183, 186; aristocratic, 18–19, 181; classical, 9, 154, 182; and commerce, 7–10, 14–15, 25, 30, 33, 100, 108, 149, 150, 182; and Confucius, 67, 71; and conversion, 80, 81; and Formosa, 91, 113; and luxury, 30, 182; as mass-produced object, 170; and Murphy, 148, 149, 150, 152, 154, 157–58, 159, 160, 161–62, 167; and Oriental fable, 124; and paganism, 26, 27, 65; performance of, 25, 78; and Psalmanazar, 78, 79, 80, 82, 87, 90, 92, 112; and Smith, 163, 164, 166; and sympathy, 155; and Temple, 70–71. *See also* heroism / heroic virtue; morality; moral virtue

Voltaire, 20, 30, 67, 178, 201n44; *L'Orphelin de la Chine*, 150–51, 163–64, 168

Vossius, Isaac, 68

Waller, Edmund, 5

Wedgwood, Josiah, 178

Whitehead, William, 160

Whitelock, Bulstrode, *Essay on Transmigration*, 123, 128, 137

Wolff, Christian, 66

women, 37, 207–8n56; and Addison, 131; as artful, 141; and body, 52, 154–55, 171, 207n55;

women (continued)
and chinoiserie, 171; and commerce, 132; and consumerist excess, 134; and cross-dressing, 47, 51–52; disciplining of, 132, 133, 134, 135; and distress, 154–55; European, 59; and fables, 132; and Gueullette, 137; and luxury, 151, 169; and morality, 155; and motherhood, 154, 156; and Murphy, 154, 157, 158, 177, 178; in Palafox y Mendoza, 57–60; passions of, 154; and regulation of desire, 170; on Restoration stage, 46–47, 51–52; in Settle, 52; and sexuality and consumption, 151; and "Story of Fadlallah," 133; and "Story of Pugg the Monkey," 133, 134, 135; Tartar vs. Chinese, 57–60; and tea, 170–71; and virtue, 158; as warriors, 39, 46, 49, 51, 61. *See also* Amazons; body; gender

Wotton, William, *Reflections*, 68

Wycherley, William, *The Country Wife*, 10, 11

Yates, Mary Ann, 174, 176, 229–30n78

Zhang Xianzhong (Chang Hsien-ch'ung), 60

Zhang Yimou, 31, 188, 189, 191, 192, 232–33n16, 233n20

Zhaoshi Guer, 30, 225n2

Zungteus. *See* Chongde